MAX WEBER AND THE JEWISH QUESTION

MAX WEBER
AND
THE JEWISH QUESTION

A Study of the Social Outlook of His Sociology

Gary A. Abraham

UNIVERSITY OF ILLINOIS PRESS
Urbana and Chicago

Publication of this book was supported by
grants from St. Bonaventure University and
the Social Science History Association.

This book is printed on acid-free paper.

Library of Congress Cataloging-in-Publication Data

Abraham, Gary A., 1952–
    Max Weber and the Jewish question : a study of the social outlook
of his sociology / Gary A. Abraham.
        p. cm.
    Revision of the author's thesis (Ph.D.—University of Pittsburgh,
1987).
    Includes bibliographical references and index.
    ISBN 0-252-01841-9 (alk. paper)
    1. Weber, Max, 1864–1920. 2. Sociology—Germany—History—19th
century. 3. Jews—Germany—History—19th century. 4. Germany—Race
relations—History—19th century. I. Title.
HM22.G3W441393   1992
301'.01—dc20   91–13548
                                                                            CIP

It is always well to divorce an artist from his work, and to take *him* less seriously than *it*. He is, after all, only a condition of the work, the soil from which it grows, perhaps only the manure on that soil. Thus he is, in most cases, something that must be forgotten if one wants to enter into the full enjoyment of the work.

—Friedrich Nietzsche, "Third Essay: What Do Ascetic Ideals Mean?" from *The Genealogy of Morals* (1887)

Max Weber's entire sociological corpus rests on a conception of universal history that is only partially explicit. This conception is closely linked to his political convictions.

—Wolfgang J. Mommsen, *Max Weber and German Politics*

What is new in our present crisis is that our opponents, as unlikely as it may seem, reckon in fact with bringing about our destruction in the foreseeable future. And it is by no means only the outspoken anti-Semites who cherish this hare-brained idea, but it must be openly stated that this idea is now widely shared in the liberal sector of German society and by many whom we consider our personal friends. It is not regarded as arrogant or even as objectionable on humanitarian grounds, but rather people condone and defend it with a veneer of humanitarianism, that in this way this interminable misfortune of "our poor Jews" would finally be brought to an end. It is only sympathy and concern for the Jews which gives rise to the wish that they might disappear as Jews.

—Hermann Cohen in 1907, quoted in Ismar Schorsch, *Jewish Reactions to German Anti-Semitism,* 1870–1914

Integrity . . . compels us to state that for the many who today tarry for new prophets and saviors, the situation is the same as resounds in the beautiful Edomite watchman's song of the period of exile that has been included among Isaiah's oracles: "He calleth to me out of Seir, Watchman, what of the night? The watchman said, The morning cometh, and also the night: if ye will inquire, inquire ye: return, come." The people to whom this was said has inquired and tarried for more than two millenia, and we are shaken when we realize its fate. From this we want to draw the lesson that nothing is gained by yearning and tarrying alone, and we shall act differently.

—Max Weber, "Science as a Vocation" (1917)

Contents

Preface

This book is a selective study of the social and intellectual background of a handful of scholarly texts written by Max Weber (1864–1920), the German comparative and historical sociologist and one of the principal founders of modern academic sociology. My principles for selection are outlined in the first chapter. I have found that important parts of Weber's sociology, if not the whole, are informed by a social agenda for minorities, an agenda itself informed by a specific model of modern society common among liberals in Weber's social class. In order to identify the class-based social outlook that informs Weber's work on Judaica, I have found it necessary to survey the contexts for his scholarly treatment of Catholics and Poles as well as Jews. As far as Weber's writings on Judaica go, I have not focused on *Ancient Judaism,* as might seem logical, but rather on *The Protestant Ethic and the Spirit of Capitalism* and on the *Religionssoziologie* in *Economy and Society,* because the former does not go far beyond simply asserting Weber's thesis that the Jews are a "pariah people," a thesis more fully developed in the latter two works. Apart from Weber's texts themselves, I have relied on a number of Weber's letters and nonscholarly writings reprinted in the second, revised edition of Wolfgang Mommsen's *Max Weber and German Politics,* recently translated into English, and on Marianne Weber's biography of her husband, *Ein Lebensbild,* also translated into English, in an edition that is superior to the current German one. Consequently, there is very little if any new information in the pages that follow. Marianne Weber's biography is designed to preserve a certain *persona* she and, by the influence of her biography, many others have read into Weber's life and works. Great caution is therefore called for in using Ms. Weber's nevertheless valuable work as a source. I have avoided placing the distinctive features of Weber's personal development at the center of my presentation, as is often done in studies superficially similar to my own,[1] and where such

---

1. I am thinking particularly of the very different books by Portis, *Max Weber*

items have come up I have been at pains to show how ordinary and unheroic Weber's positions actually are. My central effort has been, rather, to bring to bear on Weber's writings much of the excellent research and conclusions in the areas of German intellectual and social history having to do with the nature of academic life in the Imperial period and in German-Jewish history, above all the various publications of the Leo Baeck Institute, especially its *Yearbook*. Once Weber's relevant writings are placed within these contexts, a key to reading his work emerges: nationalism is a stronger element in Weber's outlook than liberalism inasmuch as he shared the common majority-liberal assumption that the proper "solution" to "the Jewish question" was the radical effacement of Jewish identity, the assimilation of the Jews into German society without remainder. His epigonism, his contempt for the "political immaturity" of the German classes, and much else commonly seen as distinctive of his outlook were really not new; these were values Weber adopted from his father's generation of liberals. These values went together with a strictly conditional tolerance of the Jews from the days of Humboldt. Weber's "heroism" (if this term really applies to him) lies in representing these old liberal values under conditions to which they no longer readily applied.

In the following I often make a point of Max Weber's philosemitism, in order to contrast it with the overtly brutal discourse of anti-Semites. This point, however, ought to be sharply distinguished from Guenther Roth's use of Weber's philosemitism to disarm the criticisms of Richard Rubenstein in an exchange I take up in the introductory chapter and which is typical of one aspect of the debate about Weber's social outlook that has gone on since Weber's death. Contrary to Roth, Weber's philosemitism exists on a continuum with anti-Semitism, notwithstanding the fact that the former normally lacks anti-Semitism's often murderous consequences. Weber's position on the Jewish question is an important example of the "seemingly innocent chauvinistic universals" that mark our time, as Irving Louis

---

and Political Commitment, and Scaff, *Fleeing the Iron Cage,* each excellent in its own way. My misgivings about Scaff's point of view are laid out in "Within the Weber Circle," in *Theory, Culture, and Society,* in press. The uncritical acceptance of Weber's story about his context is a general problem in the reception and continuing commentary on and use of Weber's sociology in the social sciences. For recent work, see Sam Whimster, "Heidelberg Man: A Review of Recent Literature on Max Weber," *Theory, Culture and Society* 6 (1989): 451–69. This book is also intended to show that we need to get outside Weber, and outside the progressive German mandarins generally, to do any acceptable contextualizing of his discourse.

Horowitz has recently noted.[2] Notwithstanding the gradualism of his or her position, the philosemite can be a proponent of forced assimilation. Indeed, I am convinced that assimilationism is more fundamental to modern secular culture than is anti-Semitism.[3] Horowitz's suspicion that at the bottom of the philosemite's attitude toward the Jew lies an uncanny fascination with the "secret" of Jewish survival applies to Max Weber in particular. Only this can explain the clear lapses in rationality of some of his most pointed *sociological* statements about the Jews, reviewed in chapter 8. This brings the continuum with anti-Semitism into sharper relief: "Thus, in the past, killing Jews was a last resort, finding out their 'secrets' to success, the first recourse."[4]

I feel constrained to put these matters concerning the definition of terms here, and to make explicit their painful implications now, because these things are deliberately kept in the background of the pages to follow, perhaps even kept between the lines. Much else has been left out that has come to be expected of a study of Weber's thought, not least of which is the place of his thought in the *discipline* of sociology, where Weber enjoys the status of a "founder." But Weber's sociology—and sociology as such—does not belong to any one discipline. Modern social thought is a broad and deep practice indeed, and Weber has been received prominently within it. I do not address sociologists only, though I happen to hold a terminal degree in that discipline. I do, however, have a special interest in social theory, and in the status of Weber's thought as theory, but here especially, perhaps, one cannot limit the audience to a discipline.

Although the problem I have set for myself requires me to dwell on negative aspects of Weber's scholarship, I should make it clear here that Weber's work can continue to inspire us in worthwhile ways. Weber's explication of historical causality, his demystification of *Verstehen* and *Erleben,* and his strong support for the maxim of objectivity are all among his enduring contributions to our understanding of history and society. Weber's Protestant ethic thesis, central to all his sociology, has also stimulated much valuable original research and continues to do so. These do

---

2. "Philo-Semitism and Anti-Semitism: Jewish Conspiracies and Totalitarian Sentiments," *Midstream* 36, no. 4 (May 1990): 17–22, at 19a, top.

3. So also Horowitz (ibid., 18–19): ". . . this linkage of philo-Semitism with secular humanism or just plain secularism, is part of the history of the modern age. . . . Hence we begin to see how philo-Semitism no less than anti-Semitism, shares an inability to confront Jews as equals."

4. Ibid., 19b, bottom.

not exhaust the valuable aspects of Weber's work. There is an important difference, however, between stimulating aspects of an author's work that possess enduring value and the value and significance of that author's *system of thought*. It is the latter I am after in this book.

A note is in order here on one of my literary policies. To avoid appearing tedious, I have not put the phrase "the Jewish question" in quotes throughout. However, it should be noted that the assertion that such a question is meaningful presupposes that the integration and normalization of Jewish existence within society is problematic. The phrase, in other words, by itself bears the load of certain value judgments, judgments which most Jews in Germany during Weber's lifetime, for example, would have rejected.

This book, based on my 1987 doctoral disseration in the Department of Sociology at the University of Pittsburgh, has been substantially revised and expanded. Faculty research grants from Duquesne University in 1987 and St. Bonaventure University in 1989 aided in the writing and revision stages, respectively. Portions of the study have appeared in slightly different form in the *International Journal of Politics, Culture, and Society* and *New German Critique*. I am grateful for the comments of a number of people who have read all or part of the manuscript in various stages of progress, among them Albert Rabil, Jr.; Steven Seidman; Ernest Kilker; Frank Lechner; Daniel Tate; Jacob Katz; and my dissertation committee—Alexander Orbach, Zdenek Suda, John Markoff, Fritz Ringer, and the chair, Roland Robertson. Thanks go to John Modell and Stanley Engerman, who administered the Social Science History Association's annual President's Book Award for 1988. I thank also Richard Martin, executive editor at the University of Illinois Press, for his kind forbearance. The patience of my children, Emily and Lisa Rose (who have had to give up much time with Dad) and my wife, Wendy (who let me out nights), is the greatest, however; they provided important conditions under which this book could be written. I am especially indebted to continuing conversations with Professor Ringer, although he continues to have basic misgivings about my interpretation of Weber's methodological arguments, in chapter 4 below, and he has set me the task of proving that the parts of Weber's work on which I focus are not aberrations. I have also benefited from a series of exchanges with Bruce Lincoln, who pushed me to clarify the concept of race in Weber's work and Weber's relationship to Marxism and to German liberal Protestantism. Regardless of whether I heeded their advice, I owe thanks to all of these people for the encouragement to bring this project to fruition.

Max Weber and the Jewish Question

1

Introduction

Max Weber's life and work have become for many a symbol of stubborn, even heroic progressivism in the face of the most sophisticated understanding of modern trends, an understanding that would otherwise lead to near complete pessimism about the prospects for the future. These sentiments (largely born of a personal identification with the symbol) are usually tightly packed inside a claim that Weber's approach to the understanding of society is fundamentally liberal. Such a claim requires that we specify the kind of liberalism to which Weber was committed, and ultimately that we undertake an historical analysis of the context for his writings.

The most influential voices for the view that Max Weber was a heroic liberal in an illiberal age, however, do not proceed in this way. Just the opposite. The kind of liberalism to which Weber is supposedly committed is often defined ahistorically. Hans Gerth's claim that Weber was a "classical liberal," for example, requires that we see Weber "as the debunker of illusionist habits of thought and as a social realist without ideologies."[1] The impression Gerth wants to convey is that Weber progressively sloughed off whatever ideological blinders he may have possessed as a young man: "He was a nationalist when young, but ended as a left-wing liberal."[2] Weber, that is, progressively transcended the historical context of German liberalism, which was nationalist. But even in his youth, according to those who believe in the liberal Max Weber, "Weber's ability to empathize with, and to interpret, the meaning of human action . . . was unlimited."[3] The author of this statement wants us to believe that empathy was an abiding feature of Weber's outlook on the world, one that informed all his later sociology.

---

1. Gerth, "Max Weber's Political Morality," 29–30, 33.
2. Ibid., 35.
3. Honigscheim, *On Max Weber*, 27.

Such characterizations are part of an image of Weber built up by Weber himself during his lifetime through his personal influence on many of those in his circle. This influence was most powerful over those who attended the Sunday gatherings that took place at Weber's home in Heidelberg on a regular basis. Dirk Käsler has said that "the decisive link between Max Weber's scientific publications and their influence and acceptance is represented by the scholarly discussion circles which were an important element of the social reality of both German intellectual life and university life at that time. The interpretive models which are still influential today, especially that of an uncritical attribution [to Weber] of heroic qualities, have their origins here."[4] To this Gerd Schroeter has added: "Most of those who wrote about him later in glowing terms had gotten to know Weber in this context, rather than through his publications."[5] This applies to more critical and historically informed treatments as well, for example Fritz Ringer's influential *The Decline of the German Mandarins*.[6] Ringer has acknowledged that "my own understanding of the German mandarin tradition was aided by the work of the leading modernists among German university professors of the late nineteenth and early twentieth centuries," and in *Mandarins* Max Weber's modernism and liberalism figure as a model for the best thought that could be achieved among the German intellectuals of his time.[7]

The image of Weber as a tolerant and empathetic liberal was given perhaps its biggest boost by Marianne Weber's posthumous biography of her husband. Among many similar expressions that help structure her account are claims that Weber "was able to empathize with each individual's point of view," that Weber's "empathetic contemplation of the destinies of struggling human beings modified his own attitude toward the actions of individuals," and that "as a matter of principle Weber approached all those manifestations of the human spirit [found in the religious and ethical outlooks of world history] not *sine ira et studio* [without anger and par-

---

4. Dirk Käsler, *Einfürung in das Studium Max Webers* (Munich: Beck, 1979), 22, quoted in Schroeter, "Weber and Weimar," 159.

5. Ibid.

6. Ringer, *The Decline of the German Mandarins* (hereafter cited as *Mandarins*), 158–59: "His [Weber's] tone was that of heroic pessimist, the man who faces facts; but it was also characteristic of him that he would not tolerate the obscurantist illusion of a total escape from modernity." Unlike Gerth's treatment, this leaves room for a distinction between Weber's rhetorical "tone" and a more independent evaluation of his thought.

7. Ringer, "The German Mandarins Reconsidered."

tiality], but with *equal love,* albeit with the disinterested love of a contemplative person who has declined to possess one of these substances himself."[8] These principles, according to Ms. Weber, suggest that Max Weber was committed to an ethics of tolerance that transcended his politics: "Intellectual freedom was to him the greatest good, and under no circumstances was he prepared to consider even interests of political power as more important and attainable for the individual."[9]

Nazism and the Holocaust have given a new turn to the image of Weber as a classical liberal. Building on the image-making of Ms. Weber and Max Weber's friends, the postwar reading of Weber as a liberal supposes that his failure was that he was not effective enough in promoting his idealistic scheme for freedom and rationality in a modern economic and political order. In other words, his political and economic outlook was exemplary, but he died too soon. A recent expression of this view comes in Thomas Willey's important book on the neo-Kantian movement: "it offends both common sense and logic to suppose that a society sufficiently imbued with the personalist spirit of Kantian ethics [supposedly embodied in Weber's life and work] would not have been able to detect and defeat the threat of a racist dictatorship, however untoward the economic situation."[10] Had Weber succeeded in implementing his political ideals, according to Willey, the German people might have withstood the lure of Nazism.[11]

---

8. Marianne Weber, *Max Weber: A Biography,* 80, 347, 387, and passim (hereafter cited as Marianne Weber, *Biography).* The question of how far Ms. Weber's biography is "a hagiographic portrait which has created a legend" was raised by Sharlin ("Retrospective: Max Weber," 110–15). Wolfgang Mommsen has complained that Ms. Weber's biography is exceedingly selective and biased, even to the point of suppressing those features of Max Weber's sentiments that she, at the time of her writing, feared would be viewed negatively: "Marianne Weber repeatedly removed the characteristic sharpness from Weber's letters and other statements" (Mommsen, *Max Weber and German Politics,* 100n.41; hereafter cited as *German Politics).* Mommsen has in many places restored these statements, according to the originals in the Weber archives in Munich and a number of other archives, *Nachlass* sources, and original publications in which Weber's statements appeared; see the 1973 preface to the 2d German edition of Mommsen's book (ibid., xii-vi.)

9. Marianne Weber, *Biography,* 120. Ms. Weber also called Max "a hero from the Teutonic woods who had come to life again and whom an unmartial epoch had provided with a pen rather than a spear" (p. 206).

10. Willey, *Back to Kant,* 38.

11. Hints for this kind of interpretation can already be found in Ms. Weber's *Biography,* 253. Roth notes how Ms. Weber introduced a tragic component to

This sort of reading has led Weber's critics to equally extreme views. For example, in 1964 Herbert Marcuse claimed that Weber's thought and politics led to fascism. This only led to a yet more vociferous version of the liberal reading: Benjamin Nelson responded to Marcuse by claiming that Weber's universalism, embodied especially in his idea of "universal history" as a multidimensional series of processes of change, is designed to promote social inclusion.[12] Critics of Weber's nationalism have ever since been dismissed for willfully ignoring the universalistic aspects of his social thought.

This book takes a different point of view. It seems to me to be willful obfuscation to deny that any part of the production of the social sciences is free of the context-bound, historically determined motivations for doing social science, and the effects of such contextually embedded motives on the social science that is produced. Ideology informs social science, and social science promotes one or another ideology. This general principle is broadly assented to by all those who have seriously studied Max Weber's life and works. Thus Ringer, in elaborating on the themes of *Mandarins,* says that he, too, wants "to show at least roughly how the mandarins' self-understanding also implied a certain perspective on the rest of society."[13] But a kind of exceptionalism has nevertheless prevailed among those who want to portray Max Weber as an archliberal in his time. For example, Ernest Kilker has advanced the view that, notwithstanding the nationalist aspects of his thought, there are "universal" motives of a sort that inform Weber's work and that surely save it from any condemnation as a product of illiberalism.[14] However, this position is rarely coupled with any serious attempt to define what "universalism" is, either in Weber's time or our own. It is justified, rather, by reference to "[e]vidence from Weber's own work which

---

Weber the hero by concluding her biography with the image of Germany "the defeated country losing one its greatest minds, the university losing a scholar who was just at the point of bringing long labors to fruition" (Roth, "Marianne Weber and Her Circle," 66a).

12. This important exchange took place at the Fourteenth German Sociological Congress, held in Heidelberg in 1965 to commemorate the centenary of Weber's birth, reprinted in Stammer, *Max Weber and Sociology Today.* However, every one of the sections of the Congress led to the same type of controversy, along similar polar lines (topics were "value-freedom" and objectivity, power-politics, industrialization and capitalism, religion, bureaucracy and organizational rationality, methodology, and sociology of "pariahs").

13. Ringer, "Differences and Cross-National Similarities among Mandarins," 148.

14. See Kilker, "A Critique of the Mommsen Thesis."

incorporates and yet transcends in its logic, evidence and reasoning the problems of the immediate historical moment."[15]

The same criticism applies to Mark Warren's recent attempt to show that Weber is a "pluralist liberal."[16] Weber never used the term *pluralism,* which has numerous meanings, often unrelated to one another, so it is incumbent on anyone who makes such a claim to specify clearly what is meant by the term. Warren means by pluralism the existence of a number of independent sources of political power. His understanding of pluralism is procedural and is compatible with elitism, as he concedes. But he is unable to show that Weber's thought reflects any basic respect for plural centers of social life, for social pluralism in the sense of a principled tolerance for the growth of ethnic, religious, or other minorities, a view that is certainly associated with what we mean nowadays by liberalism.[17] Warren in fact ignores this question altogether. His interpretation is based, as is Kilker's and others', on an overly internalist reading of Weber. There are regular side-glances at the political and social contexts for parts of Weber's work, but they are for the most part determined by Weber's testimony that certain events are important.[18] This hardly counts as an independent or critical view of what Weber's work originally meant in his own time.

---

15. Ibid., 430f. I do not deny that it is possible that Weber was able to go beyond the perceptions of his class and context. I only think that the question of what such constraints were needs to be more seriously considered than I think Kilker and others have done.

16. Warren, "Max Weber's Liberalism," 31–50, where Kilker's views as expressed in an earlier article are referred to. Similarly, compare Ringer's earlier identification of a "pluralist class politics" in Weber's thought (*Mandarins,* 159). The important question is whether "class" pluralism is consistent with an anti-pluralist social agenda, or whether the two may even be connected in Weber's thought. This is a problem in basic social theory, not just political or (as it is sometimes referred to) methodological theory.

17. Cf. Warren, "Max Weber's Liberalism," 36a: "for Weber political actions have a distinctive relation to *personality:* politics is the social medium through which individuals can develop and manifest themselves as free, autonomous, and responsible agents." Kilker ("A Critique of the Mommsen Thesis") makes this same point prominent in his interpretation, indeed even more so, by placing it in the context of a theory (which he takes from Weber) of the role of this sort of individualism in the comparative development of civilizations. Neither Warren or Kilker, in my view, pay enough attention to the ideology of *Bildung* and the way it was received by Weber and his peers, which is the source of the individualist rhetoric they take over from Weber.

18. This also applies to the prodigious efforts of Gunther Roth, whose work I

Even the more historically minded interpreters of Weber as a liberal often commit a form of essentialism, an attempt to identify Weber with what they consider his best thought that seems always to withstand counterevidence, which they perceive as so many aberrations in Weber's work. My skepticism about this perspective comes from the fact that demonstrating that such aberrations exist in Weber's thought is too often easier than demonstrating Weber's universalism. To the extent that such aberrations actually made a lot of sense in the context of the time and the work, they begin to take on the appearance of a normal feature of Weber's scholarly perspective, thus standing the "exceptional liberal" interpretation on its head. This would be even more true if an interconnecting theme linking many of the aberrations existed.

At any rate, the discussion about the contexts of theory and research in the social sciences and their histories needs to take into account one more aberration in the case of Max Weber, namely his position on "the Jewish question" in Germany. This is important because Weber's position on the Jewish question is reflected in his sociology, not just in his sociology of the Jews and Judaism; this position in many ways reverberates throughout Weber's construction of a universal history, his life's work.

In contrast to the interpretations of Weber as a liberal, I assume that, in light of the handful of generations between Weber and ourselves, the original meaning of Max Weber's work is historical, and so to use the terms *liberal, universal, pluralist,* or any others in characterizing that work requires we find what sentiments and actions such terms correspond to among the intellectual community in Wilhelmine Germany. It also requires that we block out, at least in a rough way, the meaning we now attach to such terms, and that we be sensitive to the possibility that this is quite different from Max Weber's liberalism.

My findings are that this part of Weber's work is intimately connected to a general outlook on the prospects for society in the modern age, and that this outlook informs many other parts of his sociology. Indeed, I would

---

cannot do justice to here. Like Kilker, Roth wants to find some form of universalism in Weber's social outlook. For example, in an important review, Roth claims that "the uniqueness of Western civilization lies for Weber in a substantively rational notion of citizenship and human rights," citing Weber's 1894 Freiburg address and his wartime writings in support of this (*Contemporary Sociology,* 404). Also like Kilker, Roth fails to describe what "substantively rational" means; it is a common Weberianism. The Freiburg address is examined in chapter 3, where these questions are addressed at greater length.

go further to say that, probably without his full awareness, Weber constructed a system of sociology and universal history that consistently expresses his social sentiments and aspirations, and especially his aspirations for the social unification of the Second Reich and for the future of the German nation. Weber generalized these sentiments and aspirations to all modern societies while at the same time using this selective comparison of societies to describe the German predicament. I shall show that Weber's views on Judaism and the history of the Jews are both pejorative and anything but an aberration, that these views grow naturally out of his total approach to history and current events, and that they express intolerance for the normalization of a separate but integrated Jewish community in society. In other words, both his wider discourse and his particular statements on Judaica reflect an underlying social outlook or image of the ideal society that informs Weber's scholarly work as a whole and that was readily understandable among his contemporaries.

This may seem to be a harsh judgment on Weber's scholarly and extrascholarly approach to Judaism and Jews, especially in light of our knowledge of actions Weber took to help get some Jews appointed to university posts who were being unfairly discriminated against at the time.[19] There is a philosemitic element of Weber's attitude to the Jewish question, and this comes through in his scholarship as well. Notwithstanding the pejorative tone of his portrait of the Jews as a pariah people, Weber's sociology of the Jews expresses a sympathetic understanding of what he thought it meant to be a Jew. However, despite the fact that Weber often expressed tolerance of Jews, his scholarly and extrascholarly utterances on Judaism and the Jews, when taken as a whole and placed in their appropriate contexts, suggest that he was, like many other liberal nationalist Germans, less than happy with the prospect of the continued existence of the Jewish group. His real sentiments, as far as he expressed them directly or indirectly in his scholarly work or in his political statements, were rooted in an unwillingness to allow Jews to be Jews over the long term. Weber's thesis on the Jews implies a radically assimilationist position. Weber felt that the Jewish group and Judaism would (or ought to) gradually disappear within the social admixture of peoples who adopted a common national identity. When put in the

---

19. Cf. for example Marianne Weber, *Biography*, 243, 358; Hans Liebeschütz's judgment, that Weber's elegy for Georg Jellinek (reprinted in ibid., 474–78) is "an impressive document for the freedom of mind with which Weber assessed the position of an assimilated Jew in German society" ("Max Weber's Historical Interpretation of Judaism," 47n.15).

context of the widespread discussion of the Jewish question in Germany, Weber's liberal tolerance appears to be conditional, his liberalism appears to be compromised by his cultural nationalism and to be antipluralist. His clearest statements on the Jews and their religion, which we find in his sociology, reflect a subtle and troubling combination of sympathetic intent and moral preachment toward Jews who were much more made after an image than they were after Weber's flesh-and-blood fellow countrymen.

II

Max Weber's sociology of the Jews is guided by a special thesis he developed, that the Jews have been a *pariah people* since the Babylonian Exile, and that this situation has been the result of their religion. Weber developed his concept of the Jews as a pariah people in his sociology of religion and in many other parts of his general sociology. Within Weber's scholarly work the Jews and Judaism are integrated into a broad theoretical framework, which he associated with the idea of a universal history.

In *Economy and Society,* a compendium of general sociology, Weber says that a pariah people is characterized by "political and social disprivilege and a far-reaching distinctiveness in economic functioning."[20] But more important than this is the manner in which a people's religious promise promotes their pariah status. The religion of pariah peoples is based on a status legend of a disprivileged group, the belief that one's own are a "chosen people." The social or group aspect of suffering is exalted in order to compensate for revenge against those responsible for the people's misfortune. Revenge is impossible in the face of political powerlessness. This leads to *ressentiment* in Nietzsche's sense, the secret craving felt by a disadvantaged group for what they outwardly abhor, the values of the majority from which they are excluded. For a pariah people, a divine promise defers revenge to a future "end of days," but on the condition that the group maintains religious solidarity. In the comparative analysis that develops his conception

---

20. This and the following briefly summarizes Weber, *Economy and Society,* 492–500, a section headed "Pariah People and *Ressentiment:* Judaism versus Hinduism." This is part of a book-length chapter on "The Sociology of Religion." Compare the even lengthier discussion of this theme in the introductory essay to Weber, *Gesammelte Aufsätze zur Religionssoziologie* (hereafter cited as *Religionssoziologie),* translated as "Religious Rejections of the World and Their Directions," in *From Max Weber,* ed. Gerth and Mills, 269–86. I will return to these passages and their wider background in chapter 8.

of pariah peoples, Weber says:

> [Pariah] Hindu castes and Judaism show the same characteristic effects of a pariah religion: the more depressed the position in which the members of the pariah people found themselves, the more closely did the religion cause them to cling to one another and to their pariah position and the more powerful became the salvation hopes which were connected with the divinely ordained fulfillment of their religious obligations.[21]

In other words, the Jewish people are like an Indian low caste, because their religion teaches them that they will be rewarded for accepting social disprivilege and suffering. However, the Jews are distinctive, indeed unique, insofar as they seek to overturn the existing order and come out on top, a characteristic expression of *ressentiment*. In other words, the Jews' historic pariah status, Weber contended, was valorized by Judaism, and as long as the religion of the Jews conditioned their outlook on life, their pariahdom would be "self-willed" and not determined by external enmities.

The strong nature of this claim is not usually appreciated by Weber's readers.[22] Weber's thesis holds that Jews derive positive religious status from segregating themselves from Gentiles, and that they do this on account of certain hostile beliefs their religion teaches them. The thesis does not allow that pressures from the Jews' sociopolitical environment, rather than Judaism, determine the incidence of types of segregation. Weber's monograph on ancient Judaism defined Jewry as a people that maintains its cultural autonomy by virtue of ritual segregation from its host society, regardless if this is formally intended by religious law.[23] But he nevertheless argued in all his discussions of Judaism that it is the *unintended consequences* of just those beliefs he found embodied in Judaism (not religious law by itself) that accounts for Jewish "self-segregation."

Although some parts of Weber's sociology of the Jews have been reviewed favorably by historians and sociologists of Judaica, Weber's pariah-people

---

21. Weber, *Economy and Society*, 493.

22. For example, Gerth's and Mills's formulation of the Weber thesis: "Although functionally indispensable, for reasons of ethnic and religious background, such strata are socially segregated and reduced to a pariah status" (*From Max Weber*, 66). Compare Weber as quoted below in note 38.

23. Weber, *Ancient Judaism*, 3–5. This is a translation of one in a series of monographs on world religions included in Weber, *Religionssoziologie*.

thesis has been nearly universally rejected by them.[24] A review of the literature addressing Weber's thesis calls into question not only the empirical basis for the thesis, but it also raises important questions about the logical structure of his causal explanation, as well as the politics which inform the thesis and are encoded within it. I want to concentrate first on the empirical criticisms of the Weber thesis on the Jews.[25]

In 1924 the Polish sociologist Itzhak Schiper denied there was any link among a "plebeian" religion, a "pariah" nation, and "pariah capitalism," as Weber's thesis holds, and Schiper charged that "the 'facts' which Weber cites to explain the assumed causal links between Jewish religion and the economic activity of the Jews are not always correct." He further faults Weber for "consider[ing] Jewish economic history on certain *a priori* assumptions," and for "disregard[ing] the nearly two-thousand-year-old span of development of the Jewish people during the medieval Diaspora and during the wanderings in modern times."[26]

In the following year the distinguished scholar of modern Jewish studies (*Wissenschaft des Judentums*) Julius Guttman published a lengthy review of Weber's work on ancient Judaism which, while far more sympathetic than Schiper's, also faulted Weber for at times overreaching the ascertainable facts in order to support his central hypothesis, that the Jews became a pariah people in postexilic times because of a set of religiously determined inward compulsions. Guttman judged the hypothesis itself to lack any value.[27] Guttman nevertheless gave Weber high marks for employing the

---

24. An important exception to this statement is the work of Jacob Katz. Although Katz has cited Weber's discussions in support of his own use of the pariah-people concept, Katz's concept is integrated into a very different (and more sociological) thesis than is Weber's. A review of the books and articles in which Katz has developed his own pariah-people thesis, and a comparison to the Weber thesis, is included in the appendix.

25. The following is by no means a comprehensive review of the critical literature on Weber's pariah-people thesis. However, the issues dealt with below are representative of those that have come up in this literature, which is repetitive to large degree. A fairly comprehensive bibliography can be found in Schlucter, *Max Webers Studie über das antike Judentum*, 327–30.

26. Schiper, "Max Weber on the Sociological Basis of the Jewish Religion," 259–60. Schiper concluded that "the only valuable concept left to us by Weber was his analysis of the covenant and the Israel confederacy 'in the name of Yahweh.'"

27. Guttman, "Max Webers Soziologie des antiken Judentums," 321–22 (hereafter cited as "Webers antike Judentum"). Guttman went on to point out that Weber's study of ancient Judaism was only a "first analysis" of his chosen problem,

ideal-type method in an unusually objective manner, free of prejudices, rather than allowing it to degenerate into a dogmatically political or economic point of view as it had for his forerunner, Werner Sombart, who looked only for sociological aspects of historical Jewry that could be judged to be precursors of modern capitalism. This tempered Guttman's feeling that Weber's thesis was too one-sided to be altogether legitimate. In contrast to Sombart, "Weber proposes to undertake a multifaceted sociological investigation of Jewry. The fundamental problem is for him, too, the origins of post-exilic Jewry, or as he puts it, in terms that are not very pleasing to Jewish ears: the development of the Jews into a pariah-people."[28]

In 1937 and again in 1952 Salo Baron protested that Weber's analogy with the Pariah caste of India is forced, for in the case of the Jews, not only did ritual distance occur in a situation free from castes and for quite different religious reasons—these differences were noted by Weber, but evidently did not effect his standpoint—but the crucial difference is to be found in the independence of Jewish religion, which has "its own values and countervalues." The Pariah caste, in contrast, occurs within a common religious culture. Jews were not pariahs but rather members of an ongoing and well-integrated religious group who, far from acknowledging a basic inferiority to other groups, cherished the intrinsic value of their communities.[29]

Arnaldo Momigliano, pointing to a number of confusions regarding the dating for the origins of pariahdom that are internal to the Weber thesis, has concluded that Weber had in mind medieval Jewry, and that there is no possible basis for attributing pariah status to the Jews before then. However, insofar as Weber's thesis seeks to explain the Jews' relation to the medieval powers they lived under by reference to their own attitude toward these powers, Weber is wrong. Traditional Judaism, insofar as it is based on Talmudic reasoning, presupposes self-government, even in the face of loss of territorial independence. Momigliano considers this to be an empirical refutation of Weber's thesis: "Believing Jews never gave up their sovereign rights and never admitted to being without political institutions

---

and that an investigation of postexilic Judaism itself that was to have followed was never completed; Weber's presentation thus "remains a torso."

28. Ibid., 292, bottom. The recent literature is nearly unanimous in its embarrassment over the pejorative tone of the pariah-people thesis. See e.g., Joseph Maier, in Stammer, *Max Weber and Sociology Today*, 193f.

29. Baron, *A Social and Economic History of the Jews*, 1:23–25, 297n.1. This elaborates similar criticisms made in the first edition, in 1937.

of their own. This excludes that subjective acceptance of an inferior, non-political status which seems to be essential to Weber's definition of the Jews as pariahs."[30]

More serious criticisms of Weber's use of biblical texts, which were his main primary source for ancient Judaism, have been made by Jay Holstein. Holstein has pointed to several outright mistakes in the use of textual evidence (as did Julius Guttman)[31] and a series of cases of "Weber's manipulative use of text as pretext" for hypotheses that cannot be confirmed apart from a circular exegesis of the text in light of the hypotheses themselves.[32] Holstein argues convincingly that, despite a number of disagreements on matters of detail, Weber did little more than elaborate a number of theories of Julius Wellhausen.[33]

The criticism that Weber's analogy between Indian outcastes and the situation of the Jews cannot be sustained has been repeated by numerous commentators.[34] But in fact Weber said that such an analogy was not the

---

30. Momigliano, "A Note on Max Weber's Definition of Judaism as a Pariah-Religion," 316–17 (hereafter cited as "Note on Weber's Definition"). Momigliano also cites Jewish proselytism against Weber: "The ritual separation, presupposing sovereign rights, is no indication of statelessness or of guest status. It is not equivalent to segregation and ghetto life. It may not be reasonable, but it is not intrinsically hostile to ordinary human relations. It goes together with proselytism" (p. 317, bottom). Momigliano's critique is probably the best succinct *precis* of the Weber thesis.

31. These are listed in Holstein, "Max Weber and Biblical Scholarship," 170. See also Guttman, "Webers antike Judentum," 294ff.

32. These are listed in Holstein, "Weber and Biblical Scholarship," 170–73.

33. Ibid., 164: "Weber did for Wellhausen what the latter did for Graf." Many others have noted the close connection of Weber's constructions to those of the Wellhausen school. Eugene Fleischmann has charged that his reliance on Wellhausen indicates a failure on Weber's part to free himself from the religious concerns of that school: "In large part he [Weber] adopts its presuppositions, particularly those of Protestant Bible-criticism, whose religious-ideological consciousness and anti-Jewish tendencies have often been cited" ("Max Weber, die Juden, und das Ressentiment," 266–67, hereafter cited as "Weber und das Ressentiment"). On this see also Schmueli, "The Pariah-People and Its 'Charismatic Leadership,' " 185. A number of other empirical criticisms made in the literature on Weber's thesis are listed in Raphael, "Max Weber and Ancient Judaism," 59–61.

34. Cf. Schmueli, "The Pariah-People," 194; Joseph Maier's comments on Weber's monograph on ancient Judaism at the 1964 German Sociological Congress, in Stammer, *Max Weber and Sociology Today,* 193; Momigliano, "Note on Weber's Definition," 317. Schmueli's study is by far the lengthiest critique of the Weber thesis, but there is some question whether he is directly challenging the empirical

basis for his pariah-people concept. A look at the reasons he gave for discounting this analogy, however, makes it even more difficult to sustain the Weber thesis. In his chapter on "The Sociology of Religion" in *Economy and Society,* Weber took up the question of the Indian analogy directly: "The sense in which the Jews are a 'pariah' people has as little to do with the particular situation of the pariah caste in India as, for example, the concept of 'Kadi-justice' has to do with the actual legal principles whereby the *kadi* [in Islamic law] renders legal decisions."[35] In *The Religion of India,* where Weber discusses the situation of the Indian pariah castes at length, he makes it even more clear that his use of the concept of pariah people does not take its point of departure from the Indian case.

Frequently, the representatives of a guest industry are excluded from intermarriage and commensalism [i.e., eating at a common

---

basis of Weber's thesis. Many (if not most) of Schmueli's criticisms are variations on the claim that Weber neglected the nationalistic element in Judaism in order to stress the personal religiosity of the individual Jew. Thus where Weber asserted that there was little connection between ancient prophecy and the "class interests" of the majority of Israelites, who were peasants, Schmueli claims that the social location of prophecy was closer to the free peasantry and the political order, their ideal being the restoration of simple agricultural life, which was ensured by political stability ("The Pariah People," 228, 232, 236–39, 244). The prophets' national hopes, according to Schmueli, prevented them from taking a "purely religious" standpoint, and this is what led them to repudiate the kings, as Weber suggested (pp. 232, 240–42). Nor were the prophets in opposition to the priests, or specifically anticultic, as Weber claimed, because, according to Schmueli, this would have contradicted their national interests (p. 231). Finally, Weber does not allow to monotheism "the decisive influence which it deserves," because he focuses only on its connections to the covenant-idea and to its effects on the "theodicy of misfortune," rather than seeing it as a force for national unity (pp. 242–44). These criticisms are pointed, but they are also somewhat obscure. Weber defined his problem differently than Schmueli, who seems to have different historiographical questions. Weber specifically inquired into what the significance of Judaism was for the individual Jew, whereas Schmueli is concerned with a different problem, namely the survival over millennia of the Jews as a "national" group, in his own terms. Schmueli's whole problematic is motivated by Zionist presuppositions, which look back into history for precursors to national peoplehood, in a very modern sense. Ultimately Schmueli's dispute with Weber has less to do with the empirical veracity of the Weber thesis than with how to define the uniqueness of the Jews as an object of historiography.

35. Weber, *Economy and Society,* 493. Schmueli's claim ("The Pariah-People," 176–77) that the distinction between the Indian and the Jewish case, in *The Religion of India,* is "novel," breaking with Weber's sociology of religion, in *Economy and Society* (which was written earlier), is thus incorrect.

table], and therefore are held to be ritually "impure." When such ritual barriers against a guest people exist, we shall, for our present purposes, use the expression *pariah people*. As far as the Hindus are concerned, the term would be quite incorrect. The Pulyian or Parayan (pariah) caste of Southern India by no means represents the lowest stratum of outcastes, as Abbe Raynal believes. A caste of ancient weavers (and today also farmhands), first mentioned in the inscriptions of the eleventh century, they did not rank high socially and have had to live outside the village, but they had, and have, fixed caste privileges. The leather-workers (Chamar) and streetsweepers ranked lower. And lower still are the castes like the Doms and others who mainly represent the dregs of the castes.

We use the term pariah here in the usual European sense, much the way the term Kadi is used in Kadi-justice. The term pariah people in this special sense should not be taken to refer to any tribe of workers considered by a local community "strange," "barbaric," or "magically impure" unless they are at the same time wholly or predominantly a guest people.

The purest form of this type is found when the people in question have totally lost their residential anchorage and hence are completely occupied economically in meeting demands of other settled peoples— the gypsies, for instance, or, in another manner, the Jews of the Middle Ages.[36]

In *Economy and Society* Weber says that he considers Jewry in the European Middle Ages to be "the most impressive historical example" of a pariah people.[37] Elsewhere Weber says that what distinguishes the Jews from the Indian case is that, while the religious outlook of the Indian Hindu attaches him psychologically to the existing social order, since he looks forward to reincarnation into a higher caste, the religious outlook of the Jews perpetuates the social distance between the Jew and all others.[38]

---

36. Weber, *The Religion of India,* 12–13.

37. Weber, *Economy and Society,* 933–34.

38. Ibid., 497. Cf. also: "Jewry [segregated] voluntarily (*freiwillig von sich aus*) and not under pressure of external rejection" (*Ancient Judaism,* 417). "The Jewish people remain[s] in its self-chosen situation as a pariah people as long as and as far as the unbroken spirit of the Jewish law, and that is to say, the spirit of the Pharisees, and the rabbis of late antiquity, continued and continues to live on" (ibid., 424). Cf. also: "The specifically urban, yet unassimilable and international character of Judaism . . . was the same in ancient and in later times" (*Economy and Society,* 1202).

This suggests that Weber is using an analogy not to the Indian pariah castes literally, but to a *metaphor* that has been, at best, inspired by knowledge of the Indian caste system. Ultimately he means by this that the case of the Jews is the *source* of sociological analogies and, to anticipate, these analogies are from the case of the Jews to "national" minorities and ethnic groups of all kinds, and to forms of what he calls "religious rationalism" of all kinds. It is important to note that, while the term *pariah*, "in the usual European sense," is a *description* of a certain social situation, Weber's sociology of the Jews is designed to go beyond this by offering an *explanation* of this situation.[39] The statements quoted above suggest that, for Weber, the Jews represent a paradigm for persistent separate social identity of a minority in society, where the fact of social difference is explained by the exclusiveness of the minority's attitude toward the majority.

Weber is not arguing that Judaism made the Jews into an especially passive people; their acquiescence in degradation, so to speak, is an active one. Thus it will not do to argue against Weber that because there is much evidence that the Jews retained their "pride" in the face of adversity, that the pariah-people concept does not apply. Joseph Maier advanced this criticism at the 1964 Weber Centenary meetings (as had Salo Baron earlier): "psychologically, there is a great difference between the pariah's acquiescence in and the Jew's rejection of his degradation. Jewish separateness was interpreted in antiquity preponderantly in norms of Jewish pride and arrogance. In short, in its precise scientific meaning, the term 'pariah people' is not applicable to the Jews."[40] But just this "pride and arrogance" is promoted by Judaism, according to Weber. He stresses Jewish persistence— and its tragedy, which is what, in Weber's eyes, Judaism and the Jews ultimately amount to in historical terms.[41] According to Weber, Judaism causes both Jewish separateness and Jewish social degradation to become positively valued as a means of salvation. Therefore, both Jewish pride and

39. Note that "subjective acceptance of an inferior, non-political status" (Momigliano) is not specified by the Weber thesis; to the contrary, Weber affirms that Judaism looks forward to a messianic restoration of the Jews' political sovereignty. Obviously, Weber's thesis anticipates the Jews' subjective rejection of inferiority, even if it is imposed on them. The Weber thesis would also, in principle, explain the collective ("national"?) survival of the Jews (re: Schmueli).

40. In Stammer, *Max Weber and Sociology Today*, 193.

41. In 1917 Weber closed what Honigsheim called his swan song, "Science as a Vocation," with the poetic evocation of Hebrew exile quoted in the epigraphs to this book.

Jewish valorization of suffering can exist at the same time; indeed, together they account for the exceptional solidarity of the Jewish community through the ages. The effect of religion on social relations is the most extreme and clear-cut in the case of Judaism and the Jews, in Weber's sociology.

In light of the empirical criticisms of the Weber thesis, many have gone on to link Weber in one way or another with the Jewish question, the problem of the causes and consequences of Jewish social integration, which was a common concern when he wrote. For example, Ephraim Schmueli asserts that the pariah-people concept "applies to the realities of perhaps only one short period—the beginning of the emancipation period in Europe."[42] Weber's claim that a sense of "honor" and frustration was the primary motive for the Jews' failure to integrate into majority society applies most clearly to the time "when Weber was writing his studies"; it was a peculiar perspective taken by "members of the majority society" at the time.[43] Holstein concludes that Weber's interpretation of the Hebrew Bible was a priori,[44] and beyond this, that his methods are rooted in some way in his cultural values. Holstein is led to this final point against Weber by the language of the Weber thesis, which is cast in terms such as "our interest" in the problem of the Jews, and the bearing this has had on Weber's setting of the problem. This is further confirmed for Holstein by some passages in essays on methodology written by Weber, where Weber explicitly states that cultural values have a guiding role in formulating historical problems.[45] Holstein thus tentatively links the logical structure of

42. Schmueli, "The Pariah-People," 169.

43. Ibid., 195.

44. Ibid., 169: "He sought corroborative data to justify his ideal types because, in effect, he already knew the essential qualities of biblical thought *before* he consulted the text." This has to do largely with critical biblical scholarship's dating of the biblical texts into various narrative layers. This originated in Protestant biblical criticism in Weber's day, but has never been completely accepted within Jewish studies. Although these issues are beyond the purview of the present study, the significance of the categories of the so-called critical view of the Bible promoted by Wellhausen for Weber's thesis at the time he was writing is not. This will be considered in chapter 8.

45. This makes somewhat facile Holstein's criticism of Weber for failing to "furnish detailed information about his cultural structure so that a reader would be in a position to understand his thought," and for failing to preface his studies with the admission "that *his* cultural ethos shaped and determined them" ("Weber and Biblical Scholarship," 168). The so-called methodological essays Holstein refers to rather show that Weber was quite aware of the role of cultural values in his scholarship. On this see chapter 4.

Weber's thesis to the climate of opinion in which he wrote. Similarly, Fleischmann has concluded that some of Weber's occasional remarks on Zionism and Jewish assimilation are characteristic of a negative image of the Jew developed in his sociology, where "the problem of Jewry has shifted from the realm of facts to that of moralism." Fleischmann concludes that the pariah-people thesis casts a shadow over Weber's well-known promotion of political liberalism.[46] These comments, especially the last one, suggest that the significance of Weber's sociology of the Jews does not lie in its empirical claims, but rather in the social outlook that it reflects.

It was, perhaps, inevitable that the critical literature on Weber's pariah-people thesis and the wider polemic over whether Weber's work anticipates fascism or liberalism would be brought together. The most pointed attack on the status of the Weber thesis has done just this. Richard Rubenstein's recent essay looks for "anticipations of the Holocaust" in Weber's work.[47] Rubenstein subjects Weber's pariah-people thesis to a "retrospective re-reading" in light of the events of World War II, which he cautions "is *not* intended as an effort to discover *causal connections* between Weber's thought and those events."[48] Somewhat contradictory conclusions follow from this perspective for Rubenstein. Although he says that "Weber used the term pariah in a completely non-pejorative sense," there is nevertheless a "hint of contempt which is intermingled with value-free analysis" in the Weber thesis.[49] Rubenstein is not interested in evaluating the veracity of the Weber thesis per se. His interest is, rather, in the image of the Jew and Judaism in Weber's work; to use his own words, in "what Weber's analysis may reveal about the situation of Germany's doomed [Jewish] community in

---

46. Fleischmann, "Weber und das Ressentiment," 281–83. Fleischmann's critical review of the Weber thesis is specifically devoted to setting the thesis in the context of contemporary concern about the Jewish question, claiming that Weber constructed his own *Judenbild* in light of various intellectual inspirations that were themselves direct responses to this wider social concern (p. 265). Unfortunately, the review Fleischmann has produced is only a sketch of some of the historiographical precedents for Weber's thesis (Sombart and Nietzsche are stressed) and does not meet the promise of the purpose he laid down at the beginning.

47. Rubenstein, "Anticipations of the Holocaust in the Political Sociology of Max Weber." Rubenstein's essay is in two parts, the first considering the pariah-people thesis and the second looking at Weber's concepts of value-freedom and political leadership. But no attempt is made to connect the two discussions. I will deal with the first part only.

48. Ibid., 166.

49. Ibid., 167.

the period of the Weimar Republic." Accordingly, he brings a number of passages from Weber's sociology of the Jews together to show that Weber constructed a portrait "of (a) Judaism as an institutionalized expression of a pariah people's thirst for vengeance and of (b) that people's long-range aim to overturn existing social hierarchies," and he concludes that this portrait "might have reflected a perception concerning Judaism among educated, nonextremist Germans that, given the embittered political atmosphere of post–World War I Germany, could easily have been distorted by others into National Socialist accusations that all classes of Jews without exception were a principal agent in the political, cultural, and economic disasters that beset the Germans in World War I and its aftermath."[50] Weber's ideas, Rubenstein goes on to say, even though they could never have been used to support racial anti-Semitism, did give "enhanced credibility and scientific dignity" to the myth of the Jewish aspiration for world domination found in the *Protocols of the Elders of Zion*, disseminated during the Weimar period. Finally, since "Weber regarded *ressentiment* and messianic revolutionary aspirations as intrinsic to Judaism and hence not subject to reforming amelioration," Rubenstein wonders whether his ideas could have been unintentionally used to "render plausible" the Nazi program for elimination of the Jews from society.[51]

Rubenstein's paper received two rejoinders that, while emphatically rejecting some of the obvious vituperative overtones of his exposition, still leave some questions unanswered. Gordon Zahn points out that the notion of "anticipations" Rubenstein used is overloaded with suggestions of causal links, notwithstanding Rubenstein's disclaimers. While Zahn rightly wants to discount the possibility that Weber bears any historical responsibility for the Holocaust, considering this a logical fallacy at the least, his revision of Rubenstein's claims concedes a large part of the point Rubenstein originally made.[52]

---

50. Ibid., 168.

51. Ibid., 170.

52. "Weber's treatment of Jewry as an 'alien' and 'pariah' people . . . [is] an accurate presentation of the 'definition of the situation' prevailing throughout Europe, a definition that had been in force long before he ever appeared on the academic scene. Even Jewish writers pictured their own people as in 'diaspora,' 'alien' to, and 'set apart' from the populations and cultures in which they were living. Zionist literature, while not necessarily accepting the invidious connotations of the term *pariah*, recognized the *reality* of that status and drew heavily upon it to support its appeal to the yearnings for a 'homeland.' Weber's only contribution (crime?) was to translate what was already established in common sense knowledge and practice into objective sociological usage" (ibid., 185).

In contrast to Zahn, Guenther Roth considers his disagreement with Rubenstein to be "total."[53] Contrary to Rubenstein's suggestions that Weber's thesis aided Nazism, it is demonstrable that the Nazis did not look to Weber for inspiration or legitimation, they condemned him as a liberal. Thus far Roth is on solid ground. He goes on, however, to fault Rubenstein for not taking into account the comparative purposes of Weber's study of Jewry: "Weber wanted to explain the distinctiveness of the ethical rationalism of the Judeao-Christian tradition and found the beginnings of Western rationalism in the ethical prophecy of ancient Judaism." In other words, Rubenstein has misrepresented Weber's scholarly views: "The passages to which Rubenstein refers have almost nothing to do with the position of German Jewry in Weber's time."[54] This implies a claim about the original meaning and inspiration for the work in its original context. According to Roth, Weber's interest was exclusively in the origins of Western civilization as a whole, and his sociology of the Jews was guided by that interest, not by the Jewish question of his own time. However, Roth stopped short of suggesting how the question of the nature of Weber's interest could be decided, beyond an internal examination of his work. In the end, therefore, Rubenstein's less vituperative claims are left unsubstantiated, but also unrefuted.

In the foreword to a recent collection of critical essays on Max Weber's study of ancient Judaism, Wolfgang Schluchter has addressed the question of criticisms of the Weber thesis in a way that nicely summarizes the issues that remain outstanding. Schluchter points to three lacunae that exist in the evaluation of Weber's sociology of the Jews. The first is the place of this part of Weber's sociology in his sociological system as a whole; Schluchter notes that Weber's sociology of the Jews "forms one of the pillars upon which his theory of Occidental, especially modern Occidental rationalism rests." The second lacuna for anyone wishing to evaluate Weber's studies of Jews and Judaism is to remedy the inevitable shortcomings that any "out-dated" piece of research comes to possess in time. The third lacuna, Schluchter explains, has to do with the values that guided Weber and his time.

Between Weber and ourselves lies National Socialism, and this cannot help but have consequences for our view of Judaism in general and

---

53. Most of his criticism is directed at the second part of Rubenstein's essay, on Weber's political sociology.

54. Ibid., 187–89. Other criticisms of Rubenstein's representation of Weber's views are made in chapter 9.

Weber in particular. Recall that Weber stood aloof from the anti-semitism of many of his contemporaries. Nevertheless, the concepts with which Weber approached post-exilic and especially Talmudic Judaism, concepts like pariah-people situation (*Pariavolkslage*) or the morality of resentment (*Ressentimentsmoralismus*) appear to us today as extremely pejorative. That Weber could propose an analysis of Judaism, especially of ancient Judaism, that even today remains pointed in that it is accompanied by values (*Wertideen*) that are bound to his personal, class and historical situation; that the viewpoint and concepts of this analysis must appear to us today to be extremely partial and ambivalent; this constitutes an ideological and philosoph-ical lacuna. Criticism [of Weber's study] is called for here above all.[55]

A review of the critical literature on Weber's sociology of the Jews leads to a different assessment of his second lacuna than Schlucter's own. Weber's sociology of the Jews is not merely out of date; it is, rather, fundamentally flawed because it is guided by the need to select and interpret evidence so as to confirm a thesis that cannot be sustained. In other words, the Weber thesis ought to be considered to be conclusively discredited, rather than to be marred by mere shortcomings that have to do with the limited evidence that might have been available to Weber.

Schlucter's first and third lacunae are, I think, intimately connected. That is to say, the values that inform Weber's sociology of the Jews are rooted in a social outlook that informs Weber's sociological system as a whole. Each of these two lacunae need to be addressed and to be brought into some relation with each other. This defines the problem of this study. My main aim is to locate Weber's work in its original social and intellectual setting, and so to work toward conclusions regarding the meaning his work had both for him and for his contemporaries.

Ultimately, I think, such conclusions ought to have implications for the meaning Weber's sociology has for us as well. For this reason I am also interested in the systematic implications for general sociology that Weber drew from conclusions he thought he had established in his sociology of the Jews, and the systematic sociological considerations that in part led Weber to those specific conclusions in the first place.

---

55. Schluchter, *Max Webers Studie,* 9 and passim. Notwithstanding Schluchter's suggestion that this last lacuna is one that has become conspicuous because of the tragic events for Germans and Jews that the distance of time has left us with, Schiper's, Guttman's, and Baron's criticisms, all written originally before the Hol-ocaust, show that these misgivings are not determined by this knowledge.

III

Weber's treatment of the Jews reveals a strong and fundamental bias against a pluralistic society, a society that tolerates many minority groups as a matter of principle and even regards such pluralism as a virtue. Moreover, the antipluralist social outlook reflected in Weber's work on the Jews is central to an understanding of his thought as a whole; it is not just an embarrassing footnote to a project in social theory that is otherwise informed by exemplary liberal values. This same antipluralist social outlook was applied by Weber to the criticism of other minority groups, such as peasants, ethnic Poles in Germany, and German Catholics. Weber was, as is well known, part of a broad movement of progressive intellectuals. But the progressive aspects of their social views went together with definite conditions they put on their conception of citizenship in the fullest sense. Weber's "progressive" antipluralism, and its place in the movement of liberal nationalism in Germany, determined basic features of his entire outlook on the nature and prospects of modernity, the central topic of his life's work. Weber's analyses of contemporary social problems and his general analysis of world history (and not just his sociology of religion) interact intimately in his scholarly approach to the Jews. This part of his work provides a window on the whole. Otherwise obscure aspects of Weber's general perspective come into sharp focus when viewed through his sociology of the Jews and its social and intellectual background.

The heart of the following study shows that Weber was reluctant to address the topic of Jews and Judaism, due to the sensitive social and political issues surrounding the question of the conditions and consequences of Jewish emancipation in his own time, the Jewish question. In his most famous study, connecting the Puritans to the rise of capitalism, Weber made some remarks in passing aimed at debunking the common association made between the Jews and capitalism, but he was finally impelled to undertake a full-scale investigation of this question only after his friend and colleague, Werner Sombart, sought to refute Weber's Protestant ethic thesis and prove that there really was a causal connection between the Jews and capitalism. This provided the animus for Weber's sustained attention to Judaica. For Weber now had to show exactly what the role of the Jews in history had been and what impact their religion had on this role, in order to sustain his original thesis on the significance of the Protestant ethic. In these efforts Weber appropriated nearly all the anti-Jewish imagery Sombart had developed—not without precedent, to be sure—and made this imagery a central feature of his sociology of law, the economy, group-formation and "societalization" (the incorporation of neighborhood, kin, and ethnic groups into a larger, integrated society), and political authority, as well as of the sociology of religion. Weber argued that precisely those aspects of social exclusiveness that Sombart had emphasized made it impossible for Jews, so long as they adhered to their religion, to become effective participants in a modern economy and a free labor market. Rather than contributing to the rise of modern capitalism, the Jews insisted upon remaining a pariah people, an insistence that was dictated by invidious social perceptions of the Gentile rooted in Judaism itself.

The role of the Jews and their religion in the rise of capitalism, however, was a side issue alongside a more important issue that provided the wider context for Weber's and Sombart's statements on Judaica. This deeper issue was the nature of modern social development, and especially its implications for modern national identity. A group with such segregationist tendencies as (in Weber's view) the Jews possess could not be tolerated in a society based on a strong national culture. Weber's historical claims led to the conclusion that Jews could never be integrated into such a society so long as they adhered to Judaism, however reformed. For Judaism, according to Weber (and to many of his contemporaries), is marked by centuries of resentment of the Gentile, based on acts of persecution against Jews and on Jewish powerlessness, enforced by Gentiles. In making such claims, Weber, Sombart, and other non-Jewish scholars and publicists were not simply studying some putatively objective entity, but were instead actively constructing a "Judaism" (and a group, "the Jews") the nature of which was, in significant measure, conditioned by their own sociopolitical connections, historic moment, and practical goals, as well as by the language and stereotypes available to them.

Max Weber was probably as close to tolerant liberalism as majority Germany could offer at the time. He, like many on the left, used class analysis mentally to exclude minorities from society. The left's use of class analysis concealed a basic premise that determined how such an analysis would be used. The unity of society, according to the belief of the left-wing liberal intellectuals, is based on an integral culture, an idea they occasionally expressed explicitly, but more often referred to obliquely with the notion that society is a *Kulturstaat*. In a later chapter, I will show how Weber's preference for a class analysis of modern society was first developed to give intellectual support to his practical policy proposals for excluding Poles from eastern Germany and resettling the east with "German" peasants, proposals derived from the *Kulturstaat* ideal. However, Weber was far from proposing a restoration of the historic peasantry in the east. His proposals carefully limited the power of the estate owners and put the program for the amelioration of German peasants under the control of the state. His wider aim was to see a more open economic struggle between landowners and landworkers so as, ultimately, to eliminate both groups as intermediate social orders between state and society. Not only did Weber call for prior elimination of Polish Germans from the competitive struggle, he advocated national class struggle as a means of cultural assimilation.

The principle of intolerance of foreign and *ständisch* elements within the state, a principle that informed Weber's view of the proper aims of social policy in a modern society, also informed his social theory. The problem of the place of Jews and Judaism in history, which he would take up later, was just another occasion for Weber to work out the implications of this principle, this time in the context of a far more developed system of comparative sociology.

IV

As is well known, Weber's comparative historical sociology is designed to construct an image of modernity, an interpretation of the situation of individual and society under conditions of secularization, open economic opportunity, and the resulting eclipse of the authority of traditional status by economic class. Yet Weber's sociology represents an important failure to come to terms with some features of modern reality that are just as important as these. Those features of modernity that Weber failed to address adequately in his sociology are those we now refer to with the idea of *social pluralism.* Historically, Weber's life and work coincides with a crucial phase in the history of modernity, one whose unresolved social dilemmas are in many ways still with us. The destruction of the authority of the *ancien régime* ushered in by the French Revolution was justified by the new scope given to the individual to form opinions about both private and public affairs and to act accordingly. These rationales for self-assertion have their roots in the religious struggles of the seventeenth century in Europe, but ever since they have provided a grounding for the emancipatory aspirations of ever-different kinds of individuals who, by associating themselves with an ethnic, religious, or "national" group, have demanded social inclusion on terms that dissent from the majority's understanding of society.[56] During

---

56. An eloquent treatment of this historic process is presented by Rabil, "Pluralism (1690–1960) and the Meaning of the 1960s." For the latest phases of this process, cf. Bodley, "The Self-Determination Revival," in *Victims of Progress,* 152–78.

Weber's lifetime, the principles of equality and freedom used to justify the individual's new authority came to be interpreted by members of minority groups in ways that diverged sharply from the majority's understanding of these terms. The freedom to be Jewish, Catholic, or Polish, in addition to being a German citizen in the fullest sense, was claimed as a civil right by leaders of each of these minority groups at this time. Toward the end of the nineteenth century, outspoken Jews in particular used the term *self-determination* in a quite literal sense to mean autoemancipation (rather than in the collectivist sense often meant today). Religious philosophies and practices, historical traditions, and social and aesthetic preferences were so many resources for the pursuit of *Bildung,* or self-cultivation. They came to see in their civic duty a responsibility to maintain their religious and even ethnic distinctiveness, in order to enhance the vitality of the German nation.[57] Such a view found few, if any, sympathetic ears among majority German intellectuals. Even liberals like Weber, who believed in autoemancipation in principle, did not think that Jewish self-assertion counted as a legitimate choice. Most non-Jewish Germans looked upon the Jews of their own time as pariahs, no matter how liberal their social views. They were still perceived as a group that was only partly, outwardly, attached to German culture in order to reap the social and material benefits of citizenship but who nevertheless had not contributed and could not contribute to creating that culture as Jews.

This view of the place and prospects of the Jews was in error and was based on a fundamentally fantastic image of Judaism and the Jews, an image to which first Sombart, then Weber, tried to give scholarly authority. Although it is important to show this, Weber's scholarly error hardly justifies a thorough examination of the background and original meaning of this aspect of his work. Rather, the suppressive function of his work, and the possibility that contemporary uses of Weber retain this function, is what should draw our interest and concern. By suppressing the experience and the just-emerging voice of his Jewish fellow-citizens, Max Weber succeeded in fashioning a monovocal and, in some ways, invidious construction of modernity as a whole. This construction is a litmus test for Weber's response to the de facto pluralism of modernity, to the problems of social inclusion and exclusion as the basis for coherent societies and individual identity in a modern world. This is ultimately also a test of the validity of his work as social theory.

---

57. Tal, *Christians and Jews in Germany,* 118–20, 180.

Is there, then, no reality to which Weber's sociology of the Jews corresponds? There is a corresponding reality, a pariah situation of a different sort than the one Weber defined. It is a historical situation created not by Jews but by anti-Semitic constructions of the Jew contemporary with Weber's analysis. Weber did nothing to remedy this situation, notwithstanding his philosemitic efforts. Instead his contribution to the discussion of the Jewish question could only exacerbate this situation, if it was to have any effect at all. It is the constructed Jew—"Jewish rationalism" (which is the object of Weber's analysis) and all the "Jewish" characteristics loaded into this idea—that Max Weber sought to explain, and by so doing Weber left the actual reality unexamined, uncriticized. The primary phenomenon is anti-Semitism, which creates the situation into which the real Jew is thrown, and which defines the limits of his freedom and his responsibility, as Sartre made clear in a trenchant analysis we would do well to take as a point of departure.[58]

Of the Jew Sartre writes, "It is pointless to ask him to hasten [his] integration, which always recedes before him; as long as there is anti-Semitism, assimilation cannot be realized."[59] "Jewish rationalism" is a consequence of the belief held by non-Jews that "behind a feigned adaptability, there is concealed a deliberate and conscious attachment to the traditions of his [the Jew's] race. The truth is exactly the contrary: it is because he is never accepted as *a* man, but always and everywhere as *the* Jew that the Jew is unassimilable."[60]

From this situation there is no escape for the Jew, at least not in the foreseeable future, for the end of anti-Semitism, of stereotypes of the Jew, is not in sight. It is only within this situation that Jews have choices, and Sartre argues that these choices are of two possible kinds. The Jew can be authentic or inauthentic. He can flee from this situation, by suppressing the constructions that cover over his concrete being by friends and enemies alike. He can do this by undertaking extraordinary efforts to prove his productivity, his loyalty, his sensitivity, his honesty, etc.—all characteristics which his social environment denies him. In this case, "his effort is to constitute himself a martyr, in the proper sense of the term, that is, to prove *in his person* that there are no Jews."[61] He can do this also by adopting a passion for a sort of universal humanism, by denying that there is any

---

58. Sartre, *Anti-Semite and Jew.*
59. Ibid., 144.
60. Ibid., 100.
61. Ibid., 95.

political subject other than anonymous Man, "humanity without race."[62] This was in fact the project of the Jews of Germany for most of the nineteenth century, for many of the proponents of a modernized Judaism, whether liberal or neo-orthodox, as well as for those few who sought to join humanity via the baptismal font.

But Sartre recognizes another response to his situation, taken by the authentic Jew:

> Jewish authenticity consists in choosing oneself *as Jew*—that is, in realizing one's Jewish condition. The authentic Jew abandons the myth of the universal man; he knows himself and wills himself into history as a historic and damned creature; he ceases to run away from himself and to be ashamed of his own kind. He understands that society is bad; for the naive monism of the inauthentic Jew he substitutes a social pluralism. He knows that he is one who stands apart, untouchable, scorned, proscribed—and it is *as such* that he asserts his being. At once he gives up his rationalistic optimism; he sees that the world is fragmented by irrational divisions, and in accepting this fragmentation—at least in what concerns him—in proclaiming himself a Jew, he makes some of these values and divisions his. He chooses his brothers and his peers; they are the other Jews. . . . The inauthentic Jew flees Jewish reality, and the anti-Semite makes him a Jew in spite of himself; but the authentic Jew *makes himself a Jew,* in face of all and against all. . . . At one stroke the Jew, like any authentic man [*sic*], escapes description.[63]

It was in the 1890s that a great awakening to their situation hitherto suppressed by the Jews of Germany gathered momentum, initiated with the first Jewish defense movement and later with Zionism, which was antagonistic toward domestic Jewish defense. Both Zionism and the assertion of Jewish defense against anti-Semitism and social exclusion, however opposed these two sides of the German Jewish community were, represented "Jewish authenticity" in Sartre's sense.

An already constituted Christian Jewish defense organization reacted to this change with only slightly veiled hostility, intent in actuality on maintaining the situation Jews had suffered since their legal emancipation, under the auspices of a progressive worldview. None of the non-Jewish progressives

---

62. Ibid., 97–99.
63. Ibid., 136–37.

(and few of the Jews in the university, who still aimed at proving with their persons that the Jew could be rehabilitated), including Max Weber, ever suggested suppressing anti-Semitism in any concrete way as a solution to the Jewish question. There is no analysis of anti-Semitism in Max Weber's work, and no mention of the then generally acknowledged anti-Semitic speaking campaign undertaken by Sombart in the wake of his book on the Jews. Instead, Weber sought in his own way to suppress the Jew, the real Jew, and to take the construction of the Jew forward by making it more internally coherent and compatible with his progressive outlook, which implied radical assimilation. In this way, so he thought, Weber could make the pariah situation of the Jews universally understandable to anti-Semite and philosemite alike.

Both anti-Semites and philosemites thought that the Jews' status as pariahs was due to their persistence in identifying with an alternative culture, the culture of the Jews, the culture of their unemancipated forebears. Majority liberals could concede that this identification was not necessarily a conscious one. It persisted, however, as perhaps an unwanted consequence of the Jews' continued attachment to Judaism, a religion that was unsuited to a modern, national society, no matter how far it was reformed or modernized. Protestant liberals considered liberal Judaism to be in marked contrast to Christianity itself which, inasmuch as it was based on an ethic of unconditional love, was eminently compatible with modern principles of national identification, bringing together regions and groups that had hitherto been severely segmented and hostile to one another. Secular majority liberals like Max Weber found it difficult to identify with the Protestant liberal ideal. However, inasmuch as some forms of Christianity were thought to depart from this ideal, especially Catholicism, they too came under attack from both Protestant and secular liberals, from the standpoint of cultural nationalism. The most charitable evaluation of what was supposed to be the fundamentally invidious character of Judaism might trace its roots to the long history of religious persecution of the Jews at the hands of the church, but the objectionable character of Judaism remained. Attempts to reform Judaism, without renouncing these assumptions, were further evidence that the Jews were pariahs in a foreign land.

There are historical and sociological reasons for this widespread perception of the Jews as pariahs in Germany. The timing of Jewish emancipation, at the beginning of the nineteenth century, led German Jews to adopt the ideal of *Bildung,* the belief that each individual has the power to form his character and widen his moral education, as the ideological vehicle for assimilation. *Bildung* is the ideal of self-development, an ever-renewed seeking of a progressive personal stance toward the forces of change, a stance that embraces modernity as so many opportunities for personal growth and social enrichment through collective personal growth.[64] Following the Napoleanic conquests in the first part of the nineteenth century, the *Bildung* ideal was the original vehicle for German liberalism as a whole. The *Bildungsindividualismus* of German Jews, however, prevailed long after it became outmoded in its original form among the liberal majority, who became cultural nationalists in the course of the nineteenth century. The central bearers of *Bildungsindividualismus* had always been schoolteachers and university-trained civil servants, as well as the professoriate, but by the end of the century nationalistic German idealism became the preserve of a closed, castelike elite of "mandarins" in the university.[65] In the course of this development, and especially after 1871, the *Kultur* toward which the individual's *Bildung* was to lead him was interpreted by Protestant and secular liberal intellectuals to mean identification with the German nation and an antipathy to the West in all but its functional achievements. Among them *Bildung* became a vehicle for nationalism and fell away from its origins in a truly liberal movement. Under these conditions, German Jews' persistence in clinging to the old *Bildung*-ideal long after the turn of the century was bound to be perceived as parasitical. This impression was enhanced by Jewish striving and success in society. In the nineteenth and early twentieth centuries the term *pariah* was used to describe the social situation of assimilating Jews in a philosemitic, sympathetic, but nevertheless pejorative way, and often from a progressive point of view. The more successful and the more liberal the German Jewish community became, the more it looked to the majority like a group of social pariahs. The German-Jewish symbiosis, which held such promise at the beginning of the nineteenth century, had collapsed by the century's end.

Weber's attempt to understand the pariah situation of the Jews reflects this divide between two groups' discourse about society and progress. His effort lacks the "concrete liberalism" that Sartre proposed:

> By that we mean that all persons who through their work collaborate toward the greatness of a country have the full rights of citizens of

---

64. Sorkin, "Wilhelm von Humboldt: The Theory and Practice of Self-Formation (*Bildung*), 1791–1810," 55–73.

65. Ringer, *Mandarins;* Hajo Holborn, "German Idealism in the Light of Social History."

that country. What gives them this right is not the possession of a problematical and abstract "human nature," but their active participation in the life of the society. This means, then, that the Jews—and likewise the Arabs and the Negroes—from the moment that they are participants in the national enterprise, have a right in that enterprise; they are citizens. But they have these rights *as* Jews, Negroes, or Arabs—that is, as concrete persons.[66]

Weber's outlook prevented him from hearing what many German Jews were saying plainly, and so from seeing that Jews were, in reality, often the primary bearers of just this concrete liberalism—liberal pluralism—in Germany during Weber's lifetime. The Jews were caught between the homogenization and self-effacement counseled by progressive philosemites and the formal as well as de facto exclusion demanded by anti-Semites. The demand for individual "self-determination" made by Jewish leaders in Germany around the turn of the century represented a faithful development of Enlightenment liberalism, at a time when the nationalism of majority liberals made them unsympathetic to the language of the eighteenth century. Both sides, even though they talked past each other, never really communicating, employed an individualistic rhetoric to express their respective social outlooks, but the majority progressives used an aristocratic individualism to exclude those who did not meet their standards of citizenship, which they held out to all. This fits nicely with David Sorkin's recent characterization of German Jews' *Bildungsindividualismus* as a "subculture" of Enlightenment (*Aufklärung*) in nineteenth-century Germany and helps explain why, in his words, that subculture "made them both cognitive insiders and outsiders; they had a definite place in German culture, yet somehow were not at one with it. In other words, while they commanded the majority society's culture, they nonetheless remained somehow outside its system of values, even when self-consciously affirming it."[67] Germany's Jews never really did command the majority society's culture, although they thought they did. This is what makes the ultimate fate of the German Jews, after 1933, tragic in a way that the same, more massive fate of their brethren to the east is not.

---

66. Sartre, *Anti-Semite and Jew*, 146.
67. Sorkin, *The Transformation of German Jewry*, 177.

V

A good part of the story I tell in the pages that follow depends upon a distinction I have been making between two kinds of liberalism, a classical form that is open to pluralism on the basis of individualistic (not group) rationales and was championed particularly by Jews in Germany, and a nationalist liberalism associated with majority Germans and, among the *Gebildeten,* especially cultural nationalists. This is a distinction I see as helpful in characterizing the modern liberal movement as a whole, in order to represent an internal conflict that continues to plague liberalism as a coherent set of rationales today. The following kind of dilemma is at the center of modern liberalism: is the state a liberator of individuals from local tyranny and from the tyranny of the majority, or is it the arm of that tyranny unless it pays obeisance to pluralistic principles designed to promote the emancipation of the individual? The specious notion of group rights has no place in this dilemma, except perhaps as a tactical slogan ultimately rooted in emancipatory, and thus individualist rationales. The denial of the individual's own preference for group affiliation, however, is a violation of liberal pluralism. The protection of intermediate ethnic and religious differences is a means of promoting individual emancipation, by providing options for individual identity and so for growth and development of the individual that would be otherwise threatened by national homogenization or upper-class cultural hegemony.

These issues came to a head at the end of the nineteenth century and the beginning of the twentieth century in Germany, on account of the collision between demands for the protection of minorities with those of liberal nationalism. During Max Weber's lifetime those who stood on the respective sides of the liberal dilemma corresponded closely with minority and majority. Both sides were using the same language for the most part, but meant widely different things. The reason for this is that divergent social outlooks informed the respective uses of liberal rationales in Germany. What I want to show is, first, that the language of majority liberals was much more exclusive than we would expect of liberals, and in particular much less inclusive than most students of Weber's thought have come to expect from him and, second, that an exclusivist, antipluralist discourse marks Weber's sociology in important ways, notwithstanding his explicit scholarly interest in universalism and universal history.

The modern nation-state has infrequently been the friend of social pluralism. Wherever the state has been tolerant of social pluralism in principle, the principles have had to be supplied by liberal ideology and imposed and sustained by a successful politics. Weber's career coincided with a turning point in the history of modern liberalism in Germany, a point where the ideology of freedom and equality was pressed into service by minorities to preserve subsocietal social identity in the face of the homogenizing forces of the modern secular society. It was a failure for German liberalism, however, because the majority intellectuals failed to rise to the occasion and were either unsympathetic to minority claims or unable to hear minority voices. It was a historic moment in which Max Weber's sociology of the Jews was deeply implicated. For Weber's sociology of the Jews is a necessary element in a fundamental outlook on modern society and its leading developmental trends, trends which hold out no hope for Jewish survival, as well as a method for applying this perspective on modern society systematically to comparative and historical topics of many different kinds. Weber seems to have assumed that social pluralism (not class pluralism) is inherently medieval or premodern. The case of the Jews and their religion is, for him, a single case in a much larger problem of the origins and foundations of an open, class-based society.

The Weberian vision of modernity is invidious. This is the effect, and partly the design, of a too-narrow class analysis of modern societies which Weber employs throughout his work. This is obscured by the real breakthroughs his work represents against the background of reformist mandarin political commentary and politically relevant scholarship of his time and place. The main trends of progressive social thought, tending to define the limits of possible positions, were the state-socialism and paternalist ameliorationism in the *Verein für Sozialpolitik und Sozialwissenschaft*, "Christian-Social" activism of the kind promoted by Friedrich Naumann and Ernst Troeltsch, and the socialist sympathies of, for example, the early Sombart and Weber's student, Robert Michels. But Weber's breakthroughs, in this context, were themselves limited by his inability or unwillingness to take seriously the traditional language for individual emancipation of the classical liberal movement, poorly represented by the socialist movement in Germany but, beginning in the 1890s, haltingly articulated by liberal Jews, Catholics, and German Poles who demanded "self-determination" for minorities within society or "minority rights."

VI

An examination of the development of his sociology from the 1890s, through the initiation of his sociology of religion with *The Protestant Ethic*

31

(1905), up to the construction of his pariah-people thesis on the Jews after 1911 in *Economy and Society* and the revisions in *The Protestant Ethic* this required, will show that at each point Weber brought the social outlook of his generation and his class into direct relation with his scholarship. Weber was motivated to take up sociological topics during this period by his interest in social problems that were directly related to these topics. These social problems were, respectively: the influx of Poles into eastern Germany; the conflict in Germany between a type of society structured along lines of historical status groups (*Stände* such as Junkers, peasants, religious-congregational communities) and a modern type of society structured along lines of economic-class interests (working class, capitalists, perhaps educators or scientists); the *Kulturkampf* against the Catholics; and the problem of Jewish assimilation and integration in society.[68]

Weber also contributed directly to an intellectual project in which most of the German mandarins had great interest. Around the time of *The Protestant Ethic*, Weber elaborated a complicated set of methodological rationales for universal history that were designed to give an account of how distinctive "cultural values" help define the objects of inquiry in the *Geisteswissenschaften*. This side of Weber's early methodological essays has often been obscured by those who, enamored of the image of Weber that came out of his personal circle, have taken the rhetoric of objectivity (which is also developed in those essays) at face value.[69] Notwithstanding this rhetoric, Weber sought to build on the "willing, feeling, acting" capacity

---

68. This list by itself shows that the social outlook that informs Weber's sociology cannot be derived from his sociology of the Jews alone. Weber's sociology of the Jews does imply a specific attitude to the Jewish question, but this attitude was developed first in the context of his approach to Poles, Catholics, Junkers, and peasants.

69. For example by Hughes, who sees Weber attempting "to combine the Germanic sense for history and philosophy with Anglo-French and positivist notions of scientific rigor" (*Consciousness and Society*, 287, where an important critique follows). In truth, Hughes was following Talcott Parsons in his evaluation here. And Ringer (*Mandarins*) built on Hughes, suggesting a great circle of interpretation beginning with Parsons's reception of the image of the liberal Weber, still fresh from the portraits constructed by Weber's circle and his wife. I would replace the word "combine" in the quotation from Hughes above with "accommodate" and stress that in many ways the worth of history as a means of constructing social identity—the Germanic sense for history—was primary for Weber, and that conventional canons of veracity—from the Anglo-French?—were to be accommodated to the former from Weber's point of view. Chapter 4 is devoted to developing this thesis.

of a scientific investigator (in Lotze's phrase) and to "universalize" the practical, judgmental stance of the progressive majority intellectuals of his time into a coherent perspective on history and society. The burden of my thesis is to show that Weber's views on Judaism and the history of the Jews grow naturally out of his total approach to history and current events, and that both his wider discourse and his particular statements on Judaica reflect an underlying social outlook or image of the ideal society that informs his scholarly work as a whole and that was readily understandable among his contemporaries.

A serious and thoroughgoing inquiry into the connections between and contexts for Max Weber and the Jewish question requires that we take up the development in Germany of educated opinion about national unity and the place of minorities in society, the role of academic knowledge and the academic class—the so-called German mandarins—in the development of national social policy, and the contribution Max Weber sought to make to these developments by constructing a universal history of religions, social groups, and social authority. Such an inquiry, in short, requires a study of Weber's social outlook in the context of his time and social location and how that outlook determined both the purposes and the content of his thought. These are the goals of this book.

PART ONE

Society and Science

2

Majority and Minority Consciousness in Nineteenth-Century Germany

At the center of the intellectual map on which we must locate Max Weber lies an ideology and a constellation of events on which the ideology was brought to bear. German idealism, the ideology, was the product of efforts to answer the question, "What social authorities were necessary for the life and continued cultivation of the new spirit, and what social circumstances could be disregarded?"[1] This question was the touchstone for the German Enlightenment at the beginning of the nineteenth century, and the new spirit it sought to cultivate was the spirit of German nationalism. However, because the political structure of German-speaking central Europe was so fragmented, this problem remained confined to the realm of philosophical discourse for the most part. The question was given concrete form by the political unification of the North German Confederation in 1871, which culminated events since 1860 involving the war with France and the annexation of Alsace and the northern territories by Prussia. The creation of the confederation was conceived as the founding of the modern German Reich, renewing the idea of the Reich last realized by Charlemagne a millennium ago.[2] This presented German idealism with its principal dilemma, which was felt especially acutely by the liberals and neo-Kantians, who sought to be German idealism's principal bearers. They wanted to lead a movement to unify socially the disparate regional, status, and class groups that had been brought together only formally by the political unification in 1871. The desire of the idealistic intellectuals and activists to play a role in this process was heightened by their regret at having been denied a role in the political unification itself, which was imposed militarily. Among them, conservatives and liberals disagreed widely on how this sub-

---

1. Holborn, "German Idealism," 4.
2. Tal, *Christians and Jews in Germany*, 19–20.

stantive unification of the German nation ought to be achieved, but none doubted that it was the most pressing task of the day, on whose completion would hang the value of the historic events that led to 1871. For its answers German idealism reworked the ideological foundations it had been built on nearly a century before.

The notion of self-cultivation (*Bildung*) became the ideology of emancipation in Germany as a result of the neohumanist appropriation of the Enlightenment in the decades around the turn of the eighteenth century. The concept of *Bildung* was informed by the autonomous education of Rousseau's *Emile,* for example, and Shaftesbury's notions of "inward form" and "self-breeding," which connected aesthetics, morality, and the "public good," were consistently translated as *Bildung.*[3] Under the influence of Wilhelm von Humboldt, the Enlightenment's faith in individual reason was translated into an image of civil society both as a social sphere providing the means to self-development and as the product of a reconstructed political life. Along these lines Humboldt sought to define both the duties of the citizen and the measure of appropriate state action. In his *Limits of State Action* (1791–92) Humboldt outlined the ideal of a liberal society as one where the individual, of his own free will, identified himself with the state: "He who has been thus freely developed should then attach himself to the state; and the state should test itself by his measure. Only through such a struggle could I confidently hope for a real improvement of the national constitution, and banish all fear of the harmful influence of civil institutions on human nature."[4] Men were transformed into citizens through *Bildung,* and *Bildung* would lead to a spontaneous union of citizens in the state.

The development of this philosophy by Humboldt and other German Idealists took place in association with German Pietist pastors at the universities, and by the end of the first decade of the nineteenth century, *Bildungsindividualismus* had become the vehicle for the secularization of the ideals of German Protestantism, a movement transcending the visible churches. By playing a central role in the reform of higher learning in Prussia the *Bildung* ideal soon came to have a specific class basis.[5] From 1794, with the Prussian General Code, members of university faculties were

---

3. Sorkin, "Wilhelm von Humboldt," 67n.43.
4. Quoted in ibid., 68–69.
5. Holborn, "German Idealism," 13–20; Ringer, *Mandarins,* 21–22; Sorkin, "Wilhelm von Humboldt," 66. The following discussion is based on Ringer, *Mandarins,* chapters 1 and 2; Ringer, "The German Academic Community"; Ringer, "Differences and Cross-National Similarities among Mandarins."

granted the privileges of intermarriage and regular social intercourse with the nobility, despite their plural, non-noble origins. These provisions reflected the social accomplishments of a newly emergent class of intellectuals and civil servants trained in the universities. This was actually the first phase of the drawn-out process of German modernization, distinct from but parallel with openings to upward social mobility through the economic sphere for those of non-noble background in other European countries. Indeed, in Germany the traditional disrepute in which the laboring classes were held by the European elite generally was reasserted by this new class of the educated (*die Gelehrten*) as part of their own campaign to elevate their social status. They adopted a common ideology to justify their status as an elite estate. In this way *Bildungsindividualismus* became the classical foundation of German liberalism, the ideology of a noncommercial middle class.

Although it began as a democratization of higher learning, by the 1870s the proponents who powered the movement for the elevation of learning had succeeded in so homogenizing their social origins from among their own class as to constitute a closed social elite. Throughout the first half of the nineteenth century, *Bildung* was the banner for a kind of social insurgency for a new culture-bearing class, an insurgency that would end in the formation of a new elite group.[6] Higher officials, pastors, and the learned in universities and *Gymnasien* took on the role of a modern aristocracy in a quite literal sense. There were, in the early part of the century, always plans for encouraging the working class to embark on the path of *Bildung,* but these wider aspirations were ambivalent, always in conflict with a general skepticism that the masses truly possessed the capacity for self-development. Of course, in theory, every individual possessed this capacity, but in practice, once the program of insurgency into the elite that was powered by the idea of *Bildung* became successful, so creating a new social class, *Bildung* itself was treated as a preserve of this class, and they took responsibility for creating and maintaining *Kultur* for the nation as a whole. Max Weber looked dimly upon the aspirations of the educated in Imperial Germany for just this reason, and he used his image of their caste spirit to construct many of the features he later attributed to the Chinese mandarins. Building on Weber's insight, Ringer has shown how the German mandarins, in concert with the Prussian state, closed off the field of secondary and vocational schools, classing these with technical institutes, from the field of

---

6. I am indebted to conversations with Fritz Ringer for this and the following points. Cf. Bramsted, *Aristocracy and the Middle Classes in Germany,* 71ff., 85ff.

classical preuniversities (*Gymnasien*) and universities admitting only Gymnasium graduates. Faculty in the Gymnasium came uniformly from the university; all other secondary school faculty had almost always never been admitted to the university. Nearly one-quarter of Gymnasium students' fathers were low civil servants and lower teachers.[7]

Education as an avenue of upward mobility was not just directed ultimately to the university, but it had an even wider significance on account of its links to the bureaucracy. Holders of the *Abitur,* prerequisite for university attendance obtained from a Gymnasium (only occasionally from a modern secondary school [*Realgymnasium*] as well), almost always moved directly into the university. In 1885 of those who did not, over four out of five chose the military or the civil service for their careers, rather than agriculture, commerce, or industry.[8] At the higher levels of achievement in both fields, ranks in university and government were understood to bear rough equivalency. This is indicated by frequent intermarriages between families with higher bureaucratic officeholders and *Gymnasium* and university instructors. Thus those schools offering the *Abitur* took on the character of preparatory schools for a nearly hereditary *Bildungsbürgertum.*

At the end of the nineteenth century the social backgrounds of students became only slightly more plural. Statisticians, for example, continued to break down their figures along old academic and "public" lines, as against new productive, modern "bourgeois" groups, so lumping together bankers and grocers, as against doctors and higher teachers.[9] So while students after 1890 saw some historically new faces, the status categories themselves had actually hardened. Under these conditions, the newcomers from the rising economic classes, who could now afford the expenses of university education, were bound to be seen by many as part of the trend toward an intrusion of "materialism" and "disenchantment" with traditional culture in Germany.

The peak of Germany's industrial revolution came in the period between 1890 and 1915, outstripping its previously more prominent Western neighbors.[10] This, together with the educational movement that had been oc-

---

7. Ringer, "German Academic Community," 74–75 and 71, table 2.1.

8. Ringer, *Mandarins,* 40. Friedrich Paulsen, historian of the German university, emphasized the distinction of the *Abitur* by noting that its holder was considered to have "the potential right of academic citizenship" (quoted in ibid., 35).

9. See also, for statisticians' use of the category "academics" (*Die Akademiker*), O'Boyle, "Liberal Political Leadership in Germany, 1867–1884," 345–46.

10. The percentage of population in communities with less than 2,000 members dropped from 1871 to 1910 from 64 percent to 40 percent, but the machine industry increased its employment over threefold from 1882 to 1907.

curring throughout the century, crystallized the formation of three mutually antagonistic groups contending for the leading social status in German society: the commercial *Bürgerthum,* the new mandarins—public officials and teachers in the classical track as well as bureaucrats—and the uneducated old nobility.

For our purposes it is important to identify two different roles the ideology of *Bildung* played in the period after 1871. On account of the new competition among the old and new leading classes, and most importantly, in order to address the problem of national unity in the Second Reich, the ideology of *Bildung* was pressed into service retrospectively, as it were, to construct a sharp distinction between German modernism and western European and American modernism, respectively. The aim of *Bildung* was the development in the individual of *Kultur.* By contrast, education in the utilitarian traditions of the Anglo-French orbit led to an individual's acquisition of mere *Zivilisation,* a polished manner that lacked inner character. Given the political security of the nation, the reduced role for "culture" as a force for unification especially threatened the prestige of the German intellectuals in society. The intellectuals themselves, however, located the origin of this threat in the West European Enlightenment, and its creators, the English, the French, and the Americans, displayed all the worst effects of secularism and antispirituality that supposedly resulted from utilitarian thinking. By 1890 the mandarin intellectuals felt the need to "restate exactly what they stood for."[11] They adopted a strategy for expressing their aspirations for national leadership that began with a German critique of the Enlightenment, which they identified as "Western," that is, Anglo-French. This went back to Immanuel Kant's essay "What is Enlightenment?" (1800), in which Kant commended rigorous analysis without preconceptions. He called this "rationalism," but carefully distinguished this from "utilitarianism," an intellectually shallow tendency that was understood to follow from the principle of Enlightenment only in the West. "Utilitarianism" to German intellectuals meant the use of rational inquiry solely for purposes of controlling the environment in order to enhance the average of material prosperity and personal comfort for a whole nation, regardless of differences in how far different persons and groups deserve such benefits, and especially with a complete disregard for how such measures might enhance or debilitate one's spiritual cultivation. The crucial question was how rationalism might further "culture." This, it was understood, meant

---

11. Ringer, *Mandarins,* 82.

German culture, no longer the cosmopolitan humanity of classical *Bildung,* and the sense of urgency given to the "cultural tasks of the nation" was the way in which concern for the problem of how to unify the nation socially was expressed. Thus, by the turn of the twentieth century, *Aufklärung* had been completely detached from Western Enlightenment and the French and Anglo-American rationales for liberalism and had become assimilated, through a retrospective reworking of Kant, into the new mandarin nationalist consensus on the meaning of "idealism."[12]

The intellectual map on which German Jews located themselves was slightly different from the one outlined so far, and this brings us to the second role that the ideology of *Bildung* played in the period after 1871. Because the promise of their own emancipation was held out to them by the civil authorities during the German *Aufklärung,* around the turn of the eighteenth century, the Jews of Germany, like the early *Gelehrten,* adopted classical *Bildung* as the ideology of emancipation. *Bildungsindividualismus* played a parallel role in secularizing Judaism, in the language of the Reform movement in the early decades of the nineteenth century, as it did in secularizing German Pietism. George Mosse has recently sought to explain this early identification with the philosophy of classical German liberalism and the particular direction it took:

> That German Jews so wholeheartedly accepted the ideal of *Bildung* as a new faith suited to their German citizenship was a result of their social structure. German Jewry contained a small upper class which corresponded to the various levels of the gentile middle class, but most Jews were poor (Jewish beggars were not unknown), and others lacked a steady source of income. Perhaps because they were without roots in any established class or occupation, it was relatively easy for them to embrace the ideals and goals of the bourgeoisie into which they had been emancipated. However, unlike the German middle class, Jews had no organic or family ties to the lower classes and no experience with German popular piety and German popular culture.[13]

This difference in approach to a common ideological heritage on the part of the Jewish minority and the Protestant majority had foreboding con-

---

12. See also Willey, *Back to Kant.* Weber's relationship to the neo-Kantian revival of his day is considered at length in chapter 4. Some comments on Weber's explicit identification with "idealism" are made at the end of chapter 3.

13. Mosse, *German Jews beyond Judaism,* 4–5.

sequences from the very beginning of the movement for a liberal society in Germany.

The liberal approach to the Jewish question in Germany was laid down by Wilhelm Dohm in his "On the Civil Betterment (*bürgerlich Verbesserung*) of the Jews" in 1781. It was based on an optimistic environmentalism, rooted in the faith in individual natural reason of the *Aufklärung*. Dohm started out by conceding to all critics of Jewish emancipation "that the Jews may be more morally corrupt than other nations," but he went on to argue that these immoral traits "are influenced by the climate, the food, and most of all the political conditions under which a nation lives. If, therefore, the Jew in Asia is different from the Jew in Germany, this will have to be regarded as a consequence of the different physical environment. . . . any other group of men, under such conditions, would be guilty of identical errors."[14] By holding out an "equal, impartial love" to the Jews with the granting of the privilege of freedom, the state can create the conditions under which the inherent goodness of the individual can be perfected. This indirect approach, by controlling the social environment, will, over time, eliminate the "flaws" in the Jewish character. For Dohm this was part of a long-term social process leading to the end of religious affiliation for all groups. The balance between civic character and private character would ideally leave no remainder.[15]

---

14. Ackerman, *Out of Our People's Past*, 232. Dohm's implicit reference here (the influences he lists have "been clearly recognized in our time" as determining national character) is Montesquieu's *The Spirit of the Laws* (1748). Two years later, in *Jerusalem*, Moses Mendellsohn explicitly traced Dohm's environmentalism to Montesquieu and himself adopted that strategy to argue that the purely religious separateness of the Jews is a necessary means of preserving theism. Modern conditions of tolerance otherwise threaten to dissolve all religious communities (cf. Meyer, *The Origins of the Modern Jew*, 50). However, in England John Toland had already argued as early as 1714, without immediate consequences (the Jew Bill of 1753, making possible naturalization of Jews, was passed for utilitarian reasons, and was soon repealed in response to opposition) that Jewish political allegiance was not a function of internal ethical attitudes, but was more malleable, dependent upon the political and economic conditions established for Jews by their host state (Katz, *Out of the Ghetto*, 40; Katz, *From Prejudice to Destruction*, 38–40, 69).

15. Dohm said Jewish flaws "are so deeply rooted that they will only disappear entirely in the third or fourth generation. But this is no reason not to start reform with the present generation, for without it the improvement will never be achieved" (Ackerman, *Out of Our People's Past*, 233; see also Katz, *Out of the Ghetto*, 63–64).

Dohm's environmentalist rationale for tolerance looks forward to the complete erosion of Jewish identity; unconditional equality is an instrumental strategy to achieve this end. This became the basis for the liberal attitude toward the Jewish question in Germany and is to be distinguished from overt anti-Semitism by the fact that negative Jewish characteristics can be remedied in the liberal view, but they are ineradicable, for example divinely caused or racially conditioned, for the anti-Semite. Also, although both views employ a stereotypical image of the Jew, the liberal view does this in order to promote assimilation (*bürgerliche Verbesserung*), the anti-Semitic view does this to promote the Jew's elimination from legitimate society, usually through legislative means. Thus either implicitly, as with environmentalist rationales for tolerance, or explicitly, Jewish emancipation was conditional from the start, rather than, for example, constitutional. The condition for full emancipation was complete assimilation of the Jew, and the fact that assimilation was not forthcoming as expected gave rise to the Jewish question in Germany.[16]

At the beginning of the nineteenth century in Germany, intellectual justifications for intolerance toward Jews took the form of skepticism that Jews could in fact ever achieve *salonfähigkeit,* or social respectability.[17] Earlier, the stereotype of the Jew had always been directed at the traditional "ghetto Jew." "The locus of animosity now shifted to the Jew's spinelessness, hopeless mimicry, lack of respect and character. If anything, the new view despised the Jew because he wanted to leave the ghetto, not because he was of it," according to Steven Ascheim. "The Jew who before was blamed for being a product of the ghetto was now castigated for his pretensions to transcend it."[18] The acculturated Jew was only just becoming a common experience in Germany. The feeling that he was a vulgar upstart, philistine, and interloper was illustrated in drama and comedy by highlighting his reliance on Yiddish to express his innermost thoughts, and his

---

16. Cf. Ruerup, "Jewish Emancipation and Bourgeois Society," 67–91; Schorsch, *Jewish Reactions,* 1–16, "The Price of Emancipation," and 84, for the 1890s. The actual legislative process of emancipation of Jews in Germany was halting and inconclusive until 1871, when the Reich (federal) constitution was imposed on all member states. For this see Pulzer, "Why Was There a Jewish Question in Imperial Germany?" 133–46.

17. At the popular level, resentment toward the movement of Jews into society culminated in riots in 1818–19. Such events would not be repeated in Germany until the 1880s (discussed below) and, after that, the 1930s.

18. Ascheim, *Brothers and Strangers,* 63.

inability to avoid unrefined mannerisms. The Jewish question in this context referred to assimilated Jews. Anti-Semitic portraits of the Jew made a clear distinction between the traditional, "uncultured" Jew and the "cultured" Jew, and invested the former with the romantic virtue of rootedness in an appropriate social context, and so considered him to be familiar, accessible to immediate understanding. The cultured Jew, by contrast, stood out precisely because he had renounced his tradition yet could not escape his outsiderdom. Indeed, outsiderdom was defined specifically as a property of the "new" German Jew.[19]

These sentiments were given their most elaborate intellectual expression yet in the 1840s, when Bruno Bauer introduced the phrase *die Judenfrage* with a pamphlet war he initiated between Christians and Jews in Germany. Bauer, speaking from the standpoint of the radical left-Hegelians, took the monopoly on defamation of Jews away from conservative proponents of the Christian state. Against defenders of Jewish emancipation, he argued that, if Jews were under pressure by their social environment, they must have provoked it by their determination to retain their identity. Jews, he said, will never be good citizens so long as they look forward to a messianic social state. Jewish history, according to Bauer, ended with the Talmud, five centuries after Jesus, when the Jews became "a collection of atoms," no longer a people.[20]

By the 1870s the tone of the discussion of the Jewish question had changed completely, compared to what it had been when the century opened. Now it was the acknowledged *success* of Jews in assimilating to favored positions in society that was the object of scorn by critics of emancipation. The injection of anti-Jewish arguments into the public realm coincided with the movement of Jews away from their traditional social roles, outside the cities, and with their movement into the cities, where they broadened their social stratification.[21] However, this demographic and occupational change occurred in the absence of real social or political in-

---

19. Ibid., 63–68. See also Toury, "The Jewish Question—A Semantic Approach," 85–106.

20. See Carlebach, *Karl Marx and the Radical Critique of Judaism,* 125–47; Bauer quoted here from 132. Marx's essays, "On the Jewish Question," were only superficially a response to Bauer, and he did not take up the Jewish question directly. I will return to Marx's essays, and their possible relation to Weber, in the last chapter.

21. Gilam, "A Reconsideration of the Politics of Assimilation," 109. See also Stern, "The Burden of Success: Reflections on German Jewry."

tegration.[22] This provided the background, on the Jewish side, for the new public urgency of the discussion of the Jewish question after the unification of the Reich in 1871. The conservative critique of Jewish emancipation, which had traditionally proceeded from the standpoint of the Christian state, now became more and more overshadowed by completely secular and often radical rationales for anti-Semitism. Thus Wilhelm Marr's influential racist pamphlet of 1879, "The Victory of Judaism Over Germanism" (*Der Sieg des Judenthums über das Germanthum com nicht confessionallen Standpunkt*), took its point of departure from "the historical fact," as he put it, "that Israel became the leading social-political superpower in the nineteenth century."[23] In the effort to explain the widespread suffering caused by the great bankruptcy of 1873 and the depression afterward, which lasted until 1896, a press campaign developed linking the state with Jewish control of economy and society. For the most part a guarded tolerance had prevailed among educated circles, who were committed to Enlightenment. But by the middle of the decade the arch-conservative *Kreuzzeitung,* though conceding that Jewish emancipation could not simply be eliminated, openly proclaimed that "Still we want to keep such elimination always in view and prepare the way for it, and ultimately complete it . . . by gradual legislative repeal."[24] This marked the beginning of what contemporaries would identify as an anti-Semitic "movement" (*Bewegung*), by which they meant a widespread desire for social change, based on a critical image of an alternative society.[25]

The association of Jews and the financial swindling that occurred from the 1870s on is only a surface phenomenon, however, and does not explain the rise and subsequent wavelike character of the anti-Semitic movement in modern Germany. The other religious minority, the Catholics, were subjected to persecution after 1871 as well. As Uriel Tal has argued, the repression of the Catholic church in Germany, the so-called cultural struggle

22. Pulzer, *The Rise of Political Anti-Semitism in Germany and Austria,* 78.

23. Mendes-Flohr and Reinharz, *The Jew in the Modern World: A Documentary History,* 272a-b. Marr's pamphlet came out in February and went through twelve editions before Treitschke would publish his articles. Marr is credited with authorship for the word "anti-Semite" after his League of Anti-Semites, formed in 1880.

24. Quoted in Katz, *From Prejudice to Destruction,* 254.

25. Ibid., 245–46. Treitschke used the term, for example. Katz criticizes the preference in current-day historiography for treating anti-Semitism exclusively as an explicit ideological trend or as centered around the history of specifically anti-Semitic political parties.

(*Kulturkampf*), and modern anti-Semitism are connected as outcomes of the German majority's anxiety about the social constitution of the modernizing German nation. The *Kulturkampf,* lasting from 1871 to 1887, was perhaps the most overtly illiberal period in the political life of Imperial Germany.[26] In 1864 Pope Pius IX published the Syllabus of Errors, condemning most of the principles of liberalism, and in 1870 this was followed by the Vatican Council's adoption of the doctrine of papal infallibility, which was reluctantly subscribed to by a majority of the German Catholic clergy. After conciliation with the church failed, Bismarck came out against the Catholics, who had returned about seventy deputies to the parliament in 1871, making them the second largest party after the National Liberals. By 1875 various antichurch laws had been passed, including the censoring of Catholic pulpits, expulsion of the Jesuits and some related orders, dissolution of monastic orders, intrusion of nonclerical inspectors for the Catholic schools (especially in the Polish districts), requirement of German university degrees for Catholic clergy, and the arrest of bishops who refused to comply with the requirement of state approval of clerical appointments and state control of church discipline. This latter measure resulted in the vacancy of parishes for nearly one-quarter of Prussia's 8.8 million Catholics, who were thereby deprived of regular pastoral care. Most of these laws remained on the books until 1887, when Bismarck's relations with the pope had warmed and he enacted a final "peace law," rescinding some antichurch measures and liberalizing enforcement of others, allowing the pope to declare the *Kulturkampf* had ended.[27] Bismarck's aim had been to nationalize the clergy by making them a part of the state system of education and to create a means for combating "Polonization," that is, the spread of the Polish population and culture within German borders. But he settled for a political truce that eventually brought the Catholic Center Party (*Centrum*) to his support. After 1887 the Catholic *Centrum* became a conservative anchor in the government's ruling coalition.

Protestant and Liberal support for the *Kulturkampf* was based on the supposition that the "ultramontanes," those within the Catholic church who supported, however ambivalently, the papal rulings, were interfering with the free will of the German citizen, which would, without clerical

---

26. For a convenient source of documents relating the course of the *Kulturkampf* and representative historiographical treatments, see Helmreich, *A Free Church in a Free State?* esp. 58–82.

27. The anti-Jesuits Act (1872) was only partly rescinded in 1904, and not fully repealed until 1917.

imposition, come to accept and identify with the authority of the state. "Ultramontane" Catholics were those who stubbornly persisted in identifying with the authority of Rome, and the epithet indicated obscurantism and intolerance. These religiously conservative Catholics—who were by far the majority—were standing in the way of the nascent process of social unification within the newly formed Reich. To the Catholics' criticism of this view, that political sovereignty does not reside in the state, but rather in principles that transcend the state, Treitschke for example responded, in his *Lectures on Politics:* "one must deduce the moral judgment concerning the state from nature and from the vital ends of the state and not from the individual." This represented a change in Treitschke's thinking, coinciding with the time of German unification, from Hegelian emanationism to the historical and ethnic understanding of *Volksgeist* and *Volkswesen.*[28]

The *Kulturkampf* presented the leaders among German Jews with a dilemma, which they experienced because of their liberal and pluralist commitments. The *Kulturkampf* had been initiated under the principal of the separation of church and state, which the Jewish leadership supported, but they also lobbied for nonintervention by the state in the private affairs of the individual. They used the principle of individual freedom to justify the continued and revitalized existence of Jewish communal institutions. Their vision of an integrated liberal society included a lively social pluralism consistent with the separate existence of minority religious groups within society. For this reason, the Jewish leadership had to regard the growing power that the anticlerical laws gave to the administration with increasing trepidude. On the issue of the *Kulturkampf,* however, their desire to identify with the majority German Liberals usually won out over their fidelity to the principle of liberal pluralism. Nevertheless, in the first year of antichurch legislation a prominent liberal Jewish organ, the *Allegemeine Zeitung des Judenthums* condemned German liberal enthusiasm for the *Kulturkampf* as forced equalization and social leveling (*Gleichmacherei* and *Nivellierung*) and called it a threat to every religious minority, and so shortsighted. Referring especially to Rudolph Virchow, a Progressive enthusiast for the state's anticlericalism and a highly regarded physiologist at Berlin University, it censured "scientific liberalism" for its secularizing aims and charged that it was motivated by imitation of the French.[29] This was obviously in part posturing, using a stock rebuke close to the *Bildungsbürgethum* in order to

---

28. Tal, *Christians and Jews,* 106n.68.
29. Ibid., 107–9.

criticize and remain identified with them at the same time. However, this charge against German liberalism was motivated by something more than strategic considerations. A small group, associated with the *Wissenschaft des Judenthums* movement, a vanguard for liberal Judaism, claimed at this time that Judaism was unique in being an "historical-religious individuality," not a church, and called toleration of such an individuality a test for liberalism.[30] When German Jews criticized the corrosive effects of liberalism, they were using the standard of social pluralism to promote an alternative version of liberalism they faulted German progressives for being blind to.

The Catholic leadership fought for minority rights in Germany until 1887. After their integration into the power structure, however, they ceased to promote liberal policies and became known as proponents of conservatism. From this time Catholic leaders adopted anti-Jewish positions in order to distance themselves from their earlier *grossdeutsch* sympathies with Catholic Austria and (in their words) "to find a common language with the Protestant community and with the masses."[31] They also reprinted in the 1890s and 1900s some of the more vehement anti-Jewish statements from the first days of the *Kulturkampf*, which pinned responsibility for the state persecution on the Jewish influence in society.[32] Yet Catholic leaders did not always abandon liberal pluralist arguments. For example, the Center Party leader, Ernst Lieber, argued against anti-Jewish legislation in the Reichstag in 1895, on the grounds of minority rights for all, but he also noted that he did this despite the pillory of Catholics by Jews during the *Kulturkampf*, which he said continued even at the time of his speech.[33] The Jewish leaders were indeed bringing out again many of their speeches condemning "ultramontane" Catholics, in response to the resurgence of anti-Semitism in the 1890s, as a defense measure designed to show allegiance to German liberalism and the leading class of German intellectuals among whom liberalism predominated.[34] In this way the fundamental issues of identity and authority underlying the *Kulturkampf* were kept alive long after its official conclusion.

By the turn of the century other developments among the Jewish leadership helped to revive these same issues. An inversion of the goals of liberalism and traditional religious identification, respectively, had occurred,

---

30. Ibid., 109n.82.
31. Ibid., 95–96.
32. Ibid., 88, 92–93.
33. Lieber's speech is translated in Massing, *Rehearsal for Destruction*, 295–96.
34. Ibid., 101n.56; also Katz, *Prejudice to Destruction*, 361n.7.

for religious conservatives were now often found defending minority rights while the liberals were in the main interested in the erosion of any basis for religious separatism.[35] This state of affairs, together with the incorporation of the other religious minority, the Catholics, into the state, led some liberal religious leaders among German Jewry, as well as proponents of *Wissenschaft,* to see a historic mission for the Jews, not as earlier in the nineteenth century, to preserve a pure form of monotheism, but rather, in Tal's words, "to preserve their status as a minority as a value in itself, as an ideal expression of the moral obligation of the citizen in the modern national state, the obligation to preserve his distinctive individuality while adapting himself to his environment."[36]

This coincided with the rise of the Jewish defense movement in Germany, from 1898 to 1906, which was at the time a novelty in public life.[37] A basic purpose of the Jewish defense movement was to remedy entrenched discriminatory practices in German society. For the first time prominent Jewish spokesmen openly and actively sought to ensure full participation for Jews in both the normal institutions of German society, such as the university, the military, and the judiciary, and in the growing German nationalist movement. However, the nationalist movement no longer possessed a primarily political cast among majority liberals; more and more it took on a cultural cast.

The Jewish defense movement came into immediate conflict with the Gentile organization, the Association to Combat Anti-Semitism (*Verein zur Abwehr des Anti-Semitismus*), founded in 1892 by Progressives and National Liberals under the leadership of Heinrich Rickert, Sr. Partisans of Rickert's association and liberals generally accused the Jews of aspiring to create a "Jewish *Centrum,*" as they called it, indicating that the issues of minority loyalty to the state aired during the *Kulturkampf* were, from their point of view, not far below the surface.[38] In fact, the aim of Rickert's association was characteristic of a concern shared generally by liberals within the German Protestant majority, namely to curb the alienating influences of the vulgar,

---

35. For the conservative religious resurgence among German Jews in the last quarter of the nineteenth century, see Liberles, *Religious Conflict in Social Context.*

36. Tal, *Christians and Jews,* 119.

37. Schorsch, *Jewish Reactions*; Marjorie Lamberti, *Jewish Activism in Imperial Germany: The Struggle for Civil Equality* (New Haven: Yale University Press, 1978), 55.

38. In addition to Lamberti (*Jewish Activism*), cf. Suchy, "The Verein zur Abwehr des Antisemitismus, II."

"rabble-rousing" anti-Semites, who they thought were standing in the way of the otherwise natural assimilation of the Jews. From their beginnings in the 1890s the Association to Combat Anti-Semitism conceived their purpose explicitly as a mission to the Jews, parallel to the traditional Christian stance. Their intention was to secularize this stance, which they considered now transposed onto the historical duties laid upon the liberal movement, the bearers of German idealism in modern times.[39] This was fully compatible with their approach to the fight against anti-Semitism, the purpose of their association. In the 1890s the *Abwehrverein* looked upon anti-Semitism as a threat to the *Rechtstaat* ideal, not as a distinctively Jewish problem but as the most dangerous challenge to the principle of civil equality for all. It was on this basis that Rickert denied the fight against anti-Semitism was a Jewish matter to be left to Jews.[40] After 1900, political anti-Semitism declined and forms of social and occupational exclusion of Jews multiplied. This prompted the *Abwehrverein* for the first time to turn its attention to institutional discrimination, but for universalistic reasons, to fight all forms of particularism and divisive status- and interest-group formation. They thought this call for unity was a further implication of the defense of the *Rechtstaat*.[41] The persistence of Jewish distinctiveness was anathema on the basis of these views, the survival of a medieval caste and, to that extent, an objective (even if exaggerated) cause of anti-Semitism.[42]

The *Abwehrverein's* weekly, *Mitteilungen des Vereins zur Abwehr des Anti-Semitismus,* published a pamphlet in 1900 called "Antichristian Anti-Semitism," which reprinted an 1872 statement by the Council of Jewish Communities in Germany, saying that

> Precisely because Protestantism's traditional religious strength is steadily decreasing in this era of industrialism, rationalism, and science, . . . the secular energy of liberal Protestantism emerges boldly as a large educational and ideological factor in the German nationalism of the Reich. . . . Their [liberal Protestants'] opposition to the idea of the Christian state derives from a far more profound and inclusive concept of Protestantism . . . which they view as being at once a spiritual force, a means of educating the people, and an epistemological criterion to be consciously employed.[43]

---

39. Lamberti, *Jewish Activism,* 153.
40. Schorsch, *Jewish Reactions,* 85, 90.
41. Ibid., 90–92.
42. Ibid., 84, 96.
43. Quoted in Tal, "Liberal Protestantism and the Status of the Jews in the 'Second Reich,'" 23–41, 30.

51

As this statement indicates, this staunchly liberal association supported a secular common culture, "steeped in a thorough identification with the Gospel."[44] Rickert himself addressed the association, in late 1899, in the following terms: "While as true liberals we will never deny the Jews' right to exist, still the continued existence of liberal Judaism seems incomprehensible to some of us."[45]

The social outlook of majority anti-anti-Semitism was already by this time causing alarm among some liberal Jewish leaders. For example, Ludwig Phillipson argued in 1898 that the liberal Protestant outlook was a far more serious threat to the Jews than "manifest" political anti-Semitism, insofar as the former grew out of "a great sea" of "*Gefühlsanti-Semitismus.*"[46] Similarly, after publication of Adolph Harnack's lectures, "On the Essence of Christianity" (1902), the *Allegemein Zeitung des Judentums* stepped up its criticism of the social-leveling tendencies of German secular liberalism and liberal Protestantism, arguing that they amounted to a form of extreme rationalism, connected to French revolutionary rationalism and scientific rationalism. In this German liberalism stood opposed to Anglo-Saxon liberalism, with its tolerance of individual, group, and national distinctiveness.[47]

In a 1906 pamphlet, "Jews and Christians," the umbrella organization of German Jewish associations, the *Verband der Deutschen Juden,* said in the official statement of its annual congress that the Jews of Germany had become "the true proponents" of "the original ideals of liberalism," that the religious and scientific trends of German liberalism have come together to promote "religious indifference," thereby endangering the basis of Jewish existence in Germany, "for Jewish uniqueness lies only—and we stress only—in their being members of a different faith."[48] Majority liberals, among whom German academics played a prominent role, offered tolerance to German Jews, but only on the condition that they made progress toward the goal of total assimilation, which meant effacing their religious identity. Liberal German Jews understood this and reacted by defining their group

---

44. Ibid., from the *Mitteilungen.*

45. Quoted in ibid., 36. A similar statement is quoted by Tal from the 1899 Symposium of Friends of *Die Christliche Welt,* with whom Ernst Troeltsch and Max Weber were associated.

46. Ibid., 33n.35, where there is a long quote.

47. Ibid., 32. This ideological struggle among the religious denominations was an important context for Max Weber's *Protestant Ethic and the Spirit of Capitalism* in 1905. See chapter 6.

48. Quoted in ibid., 33.

identity precisely in those terms majority liberals ultimately could not tolerate. And *liberal Judaism* was least tolerable to these non-Jewish liberals.

There is, then, an important difference in real contexts that accounts for the difference between Jewish *Bildung* and majority *Bildung:* the latter was marked, at least by 1870, by institutional competition, which resulted in a sort of game of closure and privilege, keeping Jews and others out and those whose family backgrounds were already from the *Bildungsbürgerthum* in. By contrast, Jewish *Bildung* remained utopian because it was unconnected to such concrete institutional advantages; throughout the nineteenth century, Jews were excluded from numerous institutions in Germany.

II

Where does Max Weber fit in these events and clashing social views? One way to answer this question is to look at how Weber responded to events that were in fact evidence of an emerging pluralism in Germany, events that called for some response from those who, like Weber, were socially conscious and sought to be politically astute. Some of these events and Weber's response to them are surveyed below, others are analyzed at greater length in subsequent chapters. At this point a general orientation can be achieved by reviewing the background of Weber's early intellectual development.

In many important ways Weber's life and work are the product of the developing place in Germany's class structure of the social type his own ancestors best reflect. The progressive but socially exclusive aspirations of that stratum, and how these helped define their understanding of the historical moment, provides one of the most general but important contexts for understanding Weber's thought. Within this stratum, Weber adopted and performed a historic role in Germany, the role of the scholar-politician; the social and intellectual context of that role is what gives much of his life and work their original meaning.

The role of the scholar-politician was one that Weber's father was close to, and he brought examples of it home to young Weber regularly. Both through his mother's and his father's family connections, Max Weber would have naturally identified with the ideal of political leadership of the *Gebildeten*. When he came of age it was becoming more and more difficult to combine politics and scholarship harmoniously in one role. Still, Weber was successful in performing the role. Despite his own personal, and obscure, psychological maladies, Weber continued throughout his life to develop a role that was common enough in Germany, highly esteemed, and appropriate to the class Weber was born to and to the aspirations that formed its historically specific outlook.

Marianne Weber's biography links Max's leading character traits to his grandfather's, seeking to portray Max as having "social and democratic views developed in opposition to the political heritage of his ancestors" on his father's side.[49] Now Max Weber's father (Max Weber, Sr.) was a National Liberal deputy to the Reichstag for a time whom Marianne Weber understands as standing on the right wing of his party. Ms. Weber's interpretation has the effect of portraying Max Weber, Jr., as exceptionally liberal (in some unspecified sense), but more important for our immediate purposes, it obscures how typical both Webers were of the transition among educated majority Germans in the nineteenth century from classical liberalism to liberal nationalism. The following sketch of events important for understanding the early development of Weber's social and political views is based on Marianne Weber's biography, which uses numerous family letters and (presumably) interviews with family members over the years of her marriage to Max, but with more attention to the larger context of the growth of the liberal movement in nineteenth-century Germany.

Max Weber's maternal grandfather, Georg Friedrich Fallenstein (1790–1853), was born of the earliest mandarin class in Germany. Fallenstein's own grandfather was assistant principle of the Gymnasium at Herford, and his father was once director of a seminary at Kleve.[50] Fallenstein himself studied at a university and became a follower of Friedrich Jahn's *Burschenschaften,* the nationalist fraternity movement. "His mind was filled with the Teutonic and libertarian ideals of the time," according to Marianne Weber.[51] He went to Paris as a soldier during the war in 1815 and preferred the Napoleanic laws to those of the Rhineland (under whose authority he fell as a Heidelberg resident after 1847) because he thought their repeal

---

49. Marianne Weber, *Biography,* 31.

50. Ibid., 2. Ms. Weber says Fallenstein's father married "a wife who was descended from a Huguenot family," and later she reports that Fallenstein's second marriage was to "Emilie Souchay, the daughter of a refined, wealthy, patrician Frankfurt family . . . descended from a Huguenot family, Souchay de la Dobossiere," who had fled France on account of their aristocratic origins. Some of the family, she reports, went to Hanau to work as goldsmiths, another branch went to Frankfurt, where they founded a commercial firm there and in Manchester and in London as well (p. 7–8).

51. Ibid., 3.

"would alienate the Rhineland from Prussia."[52] In 1816 he became a government secretary in Düsseldorf, in 1832 a government counselor at Koblenz, and finally an officer for the Ministry of Finance in 1842 before retiring to Heidelberg. Fallenstein's commitment to a "libertarian" reordering of society led him to look to the Prussian state to lead the way in liberalizing policies he hoped the more provincial states would follow. These views were characteristic of German nationalist liberals up to and after 1848, who generally supported a wider German state (either *Grossdeutsch* or *Kleindeutsch*) as a means to promote emancipation for individuals.[53] Although German liberals often expressed hope that "independence" would lead, as Kant described it, to the development of "civil personality," they actually considered these personal characteristics to be preconditions for membership in society.[54]

Fallenstein's surviving children, four daughters, married typical mandarins, with the exception of Max Weber, Sr.: Hermann Baumgarten, Strasbourg and Karlsruhe historian; Adolph Hausrath, pastor and church historian; and E. W. Benecke, professor of geology at Heidelberg and later Strasbourg. The first two became leading figures in the liberal movement in German politics. These were Max Weber's maternal uncles. In sharp contrast to their respective male spouses, both Weber's grandmother and mother were passionate followers of the then-emerging movement of liberal Protestantism, marked by its rejection of orthodox dogmatism and its pursuit of a strong social mission. Both women came under the personal influence of Georg Gottfried Gervinus, professor and publicist for the movement and former member of the revolutionary National Assembly in 1848.[55] It was through these women that he was introduced to the Evangelical-Social movement of Adolf Stoecker and to Weber's contemporary, Friedrich Naumann, who founded the Christian-Social movement that grew out of Stoecker's movement.

Weber's father was a lawyer and official in the Berlin city government. He engaged Helene Fallenstein a few months after her rape as a teenager by Gervinus, after she confided in him.[56] Weber's paternal ancestors had founded a large linen firm in Bielefeld and were Pietists. Max Weber, Sr., left this life to become active in Prussian politics as a National Liberal, at

52. Ibid., 12.
53. Cf. Holborn, "German Idealism"; Sheehan, *German Liberalism,* 39.
54. Sheehan, *German Liberalism,* 26–27.
55. Marianne Weber, *Biography,* 20.
56. Ibid., 20–21.

a time when the liberals saw the rising star, Bismarck, as "the corrupter of liberty and unity." Weber, Sr., thought this "liberty and unity" could be achieved by means of (in the words of the Constitutional wing within the National Liberal Party) "a strong Hohenzollern kingdom and full recognition of the rights guaranteed to the people."[57] Bismarck's challenge to national unity was most dramatic, from the standpoint of liberal-nationalist ideology, in his turning away from the *Kulturkampf* and eventually embracing the Catholic Center Party. The liberals' discouragement led at length to an antistatist mood that Weber, Jr., joined later.[58] Weber, Jr., remained a moderate monarchist out of traditional liberal distrust of the masses, although his disdain for the National Liberal Party's identification with commercial elites after 1893 kept him on the margins of political activity for most of his life.[59] Nevertheless, both Webers were equally committed to the spread of national sentiment, although naturally their evaluations of the best means by which to promote this varied with changing political and social conditions.

Weber, Sr., became the magistrate of Erfurt, probably in 1863. Max Weber, Jr., was born in Erfurt the following year. In 1869 the family moved back to Berlin, where Weber, Sr., answered a call to become city councillor and soon became a member of the Budget Committee in the Prussian Diet, as a specialist in education. They soon moved to the suburb of Charlottenburg. Weber, Sr., became a member of the Reichstag and entertained many of the luminaries in the party, including a number of professors under whom Weber, Jr., would later study.[60] These events surrounding his father apparently stimulated the young Weber to become engrossed in the history and genealogy of the Merovingians and Carolingians, writing essays while in Gymnasium on these topics and others, such as "Observations on the Ethnic Character, Development, and History of the Indo-European Nations." In this essay, of which Marianne Weber provides a lengthy summary, a millennial antipathy between East and West is said to dominate world history, with the Semitic branch of the Caucasian race

---

57. Ibid., 31. Marianne is wrong to characterize this as the right wing of the National Liberal Party. Weber identified with the mainstream development of the majority German liberalism of his father's generation, and to a large extent of his father's particular social circle.

58. Sheehan, *German Liberalism*, 137, 194–95.

59. Ibid., 266–71 for the political context; for Weber's relative political impotence, cf. Portis, *Weber and Political Commitment*.

60. Marianne Weber, *Biography*, 33, 39–40.

and Christianity among those on the side of the East, generally suppressing the forces of Greek and Aryan culture on the side of the West. This, the young Weber wrote, has been a process of "Semiticization": Marianne Weber quotes from the essay, "Semitic despotism and religious fanaticism, he says, have repeatedly endangered the Indo-European realms."[61]

Weber joined the dueling fraternity of his father, the Alemanni, upon enrolling in Heidelberg University in 1882, on the heels of the Berlin *Antisemitismussstreit* that had begun two and one-half years earlier, and had by then made the anti-Semitic movement the dominant force in the life of the dueling *Verbindungen*.[62] He soon received the perfunctory facial scars (*Schnisse*) and he continued later in life to advocate dueling as a form of dispute settlement quite vociferously.[63] These sentiments grew out of the revival of masculinist fraternity customs (*Komment*) under the impact of the renewed nationalism that accompanied the spread of anti-Semitism among students. The most militant of these forces organized themselves as the German Students Association (*Verein Deutscher Studenten*) which, in addition to excluding Jews from their ranks, sought to carry the movement forward by lobbying for "emergency laws" against Jewish participation in public positions, and they rejected racial mixing as a "solution" to the

61. Ibid., 46–47.

62. Cf. Norbert Kampe, "Jews and Antisemites at Universities in Imperial Germany (II)," 43–101. The *Antisemitismusstreit* is treated at length in chapter 3.

63. Marianne Weber, *Biography*, 66–70, 431; letter at 436; a dueling challenge issued by Weber in 1912, 443ff.; cf. also 70, on "the choral singing of those magnificent student and patriotic songs" Weber learned in the Alemanni: "their melodies accompanied Max Weber to the end of his life." On the ritual *Bestimmungsmensur*, cf. Jarausch, *Students, Society, and Politics in Imperial Germany: The Rise of Academic Illiberalism*, 244–47, 261f. (hereafter cited as *Students, Society, and Politics*) Weber's later condemnation of the aspiration for the *Mensur* among *business school students*, at a 1911 speech to the Congress of Teachers in Higher Education, shows his own desire to preserve the distinctiveness of his class rather than a criticism of the practice per se (see Shils, *Max Weber on Universities*, 23–30, and Marianne Weber, *Biography*, 426–28). Weber increasingly spoke out against the utilitarian approach to acquiring corporation colors, the *Mensur*, and reserve membership in the Officer Corps, because this necessarily diluted the elite spirit of the university. His dismay eventually led to his resignation from the Alemanni, but this did not mean, as Weber explicitly said in his resignation letter, rejection of "the cultivation of manliness," which "must seek other ways and means." The full letter is in Mommsen, *German Politics*, 312–13n.114; cf. also 94–95. I think Weber's identification with the dueling corporations is far more ambivalent than Mommsen says (ibid., 4).

Jewish question.[64] A small group of fifteen students at Berlin formed a "Committee" against anti-Semitic student agitation which became the *Frei Wissenschaftliche Studierenden* (FWV) in mid-1881, quickly growing in membership and becoming over half Jewish.[65] A movement toward cultural and self-defense associations specifically for Jewish students began soon thereafter, its first group forming in the winter of 1883 at Berlin.[66] In the same year *Reformburschenschaften* began to actively oppose the anti-Semitism of the corporations. The polarization of student life around the Jewish question was described in 1882 by Max Spangenberg, the Christian chairman of the FWV, in these terms:

> It is precisely the diabolical effect of these brutal practices not only to create a difference between Jews and Christians but likewise between Christian and Christian; and not least among students, for whom the question has become one of social life. In obscure corners of the Wiener Cafe, on the open promenade of the Unter den Linden, wherever one goes, the first question on seeing an acquaintance is: Is he Christian? Is he Jewish? Is he pro-semitic? Is he antisemitic?[67]

When he was an associate professor Max Weber supported a philosemitic "Sozialwissenschaftliche Studentenvereinigung" formed by students in Berlin in 1893 that was, in accordance with university regulations, and understood in contrast to the anti-Semitic and new Jewish *Vereine,* nonpartisan. It aimed at promoting discussion of "the social problem and to support reforms if the class struggles that threaten to tear apart the nation are to be eliminated and revolution is to be avoided."[68] This group was part of

---

64. Kampe, "Jews and Antisemites," 52n.45; Jarausch, *Students, Society, and Politics,* 266ff.

65. Kampe, "Jews and Antisemites," 63–64. After 1887 nearly all members were Jewish.

66. This led finally to an umbrella union in 1896, the Kartell-Convent. Under the influence of Russian Jewish students, a Zionist "Verein judischer Studenten an der Universität Berlin" formed around 1900, and a "Bund Judischer Corporationen" in 1902 (Jarausch, *Students, Society, and Politics,* 272–73).

67. "The Standpoint of the Berlin University FWV on the Jewish Question and *Wissenschaft,* Two Lectures, July 4, 1881 and October 30, 1882" (Berlin, 1882), quoted in Kampe, "Jews and Antisemites," 71.

68. From E. Schultze's address to the Association, *Die Studentenschaft und die Sozial Frage,* quoted in Jarausch, *Students, Society, and Politics,* 275–76. In 1895 a one-year ban was imposed on the association because the rector agreed with another faculty member's petition that, "especially now, when social issues are the focus of controversy, it will hardly be possible to avoid dragging the related political questions into the debate," so "endangering academic discipline."

a movement among nonaffiliated students that had begun in Berlin in 1892, forming various *wissenschaftliche* associations to oppose the dominance of the uniformed corporations and the dueling ethic in the name of a "renewal and transformation of academic life on the basis of modern principles." The independent student movement sought to revive and advance the classical liberal "ideals of self-cultivation and education" of the *Burschen-schaften*.[69]

Dueling was a problem for Catholic students, because the church had prohibited dueling ever since the 1850s. So the *Mensur,* and the related policy of dismissal from the military, including the Officer Corps (to which Weber was admitted), for refusal to answer a challenge, excluded Catholics, and they said so from the 1890s on. This was especially important in light of Georg von Hertling's speech at the 1896 Catholic Congress in Constance on "the causes of backwardness (*Zurückbleibens*) of German Catholics in the area of *Wissenschaft,*" which caused a long-term debate over the "inferiority" of Catholic representation in the university and the Catholics' call for "parity."[70] The new Jewish student associations also rejected the code of honor of the traditional corporations in the 1890s, as did other independent student groups, and for that matter the majority of students generally, making the power position of the uniformed fraternities increasingly anachronistic.[71] Weber's continued support for the code of honor was, under these conditions, insensitive at the least.

---

69. Ibid., 250ff., 281f., 287–88. The movement soon spread to Leipzig, Halle, Königsberg, Bonn, and Marburg, founding a national organization in 1900, *Deutsche Freistudentenschaft.*

70. Evans, *The German Center Party, 1870–1933,* 141–48. The parity issue is at the center of "the Spahn case" in 1900, and the related debate over "academic freedom," which Weber later intervened in (see Shils, *Max Weber on Universities,* 14–23). The liberals Theodor Mommsen, Lujo Brentano, and later, Max Weber all rejected the state's program of concessions to the Catholic Center Party "in the continuing effort to raise the Catholic population from its second-class citizenship," Mommsen even going so far as to suggest "that a Catholic world-outlook disqualified a man for a university history position," in Evans's words. Brentano introduced the slogan "the presuppositionlessness of *Wissenschaft*" to justify the liberals' rejection of Catholic parity. This issue also provided the context for Weber's opening lines in *The Protestant Ethic and the Spirit of Capitalism* in 1905. On this see chapter 6.

71. Kampe, "Jews and Antisemites," 88. However, the early Jewish corporations, founded to combat anti-Semitism and thereby prove their worthiness for assimilation, observed the code militantly, including training in sword-fighting (see ibid., 84, and Reinharz, *Fatherland or Promised Land?* 30–34. Cf. also chapter 3, note 95).

Weber was on the border of both liberal and illiberal organizational currents in student life. Norbert Kampe reports that "the *Alte Herren* of the old traditional corporations looked with displeasure at student politicization by the 'Jewish Question,' and sought to differentiate the nationalism of their own student days by speaking of 'modern nationalism,' " which they applied to "student" or "academic anti-Semitism."[72] Max Weber took over this perspective from his student days without, however, ever expressing sympathy for the more cosmopolitan liberalism of the independent student movement, or the pluralist liberalism of the Jewish student associations fighting anti-Semitism in the university. His philosemitism was based on the same "liberal" anti-anti-Semitism of the *Reformburschenschaften,* which stopped short of developing a positive concept of minority protection, remaining committed instead to the nationalist liberal principle of "disappearance of Judaism by amalgamation with the German race."[73] As we know from his well-known sloganizing later in his career, Weber also took over the university authorities' perspective, that the Jewish question was off limits as a topic for discussion from any side, since it involved partisanship and so violated the regulation that ethical neutrality be observed within the university community. This meant in practice that, in the university, liberal nationalism was the "politically neutral 'normal position' " among the "parties."[74] This was also the perspective of the *wissenschaftliche* student groups. The concept of *Wissenschaft* was primarily theoretical in the mandarin tradition, contrasted with "empiricism" in the sense of technical and "practical." The classical educational reformers of Humboldt's

---

72. Kampe, "Jews and Antisemites," 58.

73. From an 1890 statement in the first issue of the *ADB Correspondence,* an organ of the umbrella organization of *Reformburschenschaften,* the *Allgemeiner Deutschen Burschenbund* (cited in ibid., 85). Compare Struve's discussion of Weber's youthful "contact with such discontented and pessimistic old liberals as the historians T. Mommsen and H. Baumgarten. Both Mommsen and Baumgarten had come to consider the tragic fault of German political life to lie in an absence of leaders and in the 'political immaturity' of the nation. . . . Baumgarten had even decided that the 'great tasks' of politics could only be solved by a nobility. Weber never abandoned their idea of a special group of political leaders" (Struve, *Elites against Democracy,* 125).

74. Kampe, "Jews and Antisemites," 70, on Rector Hoffman's views. The operating assumption of this perspective, as Weber was to put it in his own sophisticated terms in 1913 at a meeting of the *Verein für Sozialpolitik,* is that "the unconfined rigor, matter-of-factness and sobriety of the lecture declines, with definite pedagogical losses, once it becomes the object of publicity" (Shils, *Weber on Universities,* 49).

generation accordingly defined "Lehrfreiheit," or the "freedom of learning," in a way that "was always at least partly informed by the conviction that geist must not be asked to descend from the realm of theory in order to involve itself in practice," according to Ringer.[75] It was this spirit, and not a more positive pluralism, that informed the Sozialwissenschaftliche Studentenvereinigung and other *freie wissenschaftliche* groups at Berlin and other German universities.

The same kind of instrumentalist rationale for equal rights for minorities that stood back of the majority liberals' philosemitism can be seen in Weber's early skepticism of the antisocialist laws. These laws opened the new Reich by outlawing members of the Social Democratic Party from positions in the civil service and universities. Weber criticized these laws for their "exceptional" nature, indicating that he thought the radicals ought not to be so singled out for special treatment from the rest of the citizenry, even if this was punitive treatment. This was inconsistent with the principle of the *Rechtstaat,* the universal applicability of the laws. In the process he revealed important clues concerning his commitment to "equal rights" and "public freedom," phrases Weber used. For also in this youthful analysis of politics was a criticism of Bismarck's action *rescinding* the antisocialist laws and, for tactical reasons which Weber astutely recognized (to create a counterweight to the power of the National Liberals), instituting universal suffrage. "The cardinal fault is the Greek gift of Bismarck's Caesarism, universal suffrage, the veriest murder of *equal rights for all in the true sense of the word.*"[76] Like the Trojan horse, Bismarck had imposed universal suffrage, without the participation of Parliament, and thereby in the guise of a gift forestalled the social and political struggle within society that might have forced all parties, especially the until now disenfranchised proletariat, to develop an active social outlook and so achieve a personal sense of political responsibility. This was a view he would develop at great length in the years to come.

The nationalist side of Weber's social outlook comes through more clearly in his attitude toward the *Kulturkampf.* His support for the anticlerical movement was motivated by a commitment to the characteristic form that *Bildungsindividualismus* took among majority German liberals, who derived cultural nationalism from the *Bildung* ideal. On the occasion of Bismarck's

---

75. Ringer, *Mandarins,* 111.

76. Marianne Weber, *Biography,* 117–18, all emphases in original. This was in 1884, when Weber was twenty years of age.

truce with the Catholic church in 1887 Weber protested, as did many German liberals:

> this unceremonious "peace" is sad, and in any case it is a confession of an injustice, a grievous injustice, if one says today that there were only "political" reasons for the struggle on our side. If it is true that for us it was not a matter of conscience but only one of expediency [as it had looked from Bismarck's "capitulation"], then we really have done violence to the conscience of the Catholic people, as the Catholics say we have, for reasons that were of an external nature. For most of the Catholics it surely was a matter of conscience, and in that case it was not a matter of conscience against conscience, as we always reminded them. We have acted *without* conscience, then [if Bismarck was correct], and are the losers morally as well. This is the worst part of our defeat [n.b.], for it prevents us from ever resuming the struggle the way it must be resumed if it is to lead to victory.[77]

The following year, looking ahead to the future of Germany after the death of Crown Prince Friedrich, Weber saw the new coalition, "the Prussian Junkers in concert with the ultramontanists," as threatening "the decline of the national elements in Central Germany."[78]

Weber did not recognize as altogether legitimate the ecclesiastical identification of German Catholics with church authority, however ambivalent, and he tried to justify tolerance toward Catholics by separating out their "piety" from their relation to religious authority, something many religious Catholics could not countenance. In a 1908 letter Weber counseled Nau-

---

77. Ibid., 121 (letter to Baumgarten). Cf. Mommsen's commentary on this letter, *German Politics*, 13: "He unequivocally shared the liberal viewpoint during the *Kulturkampf*, but, like [his uncle and National Liberal deputy, Hermann] Baumgarten, he supported the struggle for its own sake and not as a means to achieve other goals. When in 1887 Bismarck again watered down the *Kulturkampf* laws, Max Weber protested that some National Liberals now accepted the fact that only 'political' goals, the objective conditions of which no longer existed [i.e., the unification of the Reich was now firmly in place], had made the actions against Catholicism necessary." Ms. Weber's apologetic: "he rejected the *Kulturkampf*, just as he later opposed the Prussian language policy for the Germanization of the Poles" (*Biography*, 120), is without basis as a suggestion of Weber's social pluralism. Weber's changing attitude to the Polish question is examined at length in the next chapter; see especially section VIII for Weber's later position on the language question, which Ms. Weber refers to here.

78. Marianne Weber, *Biography*, 122.

mann to use the occasion of "the 'tolerance motion' of the Center Party [which they both opposed] to demand (1) the elimination of *any* compulsory *religious* instruction, and (2) the elimination of *any* privileged status for a *church* (treatment in accordance with the law governing associations!), to demand at least the former as a 'basic right.'. . . In this area the Center Party must be democratically trumped."[79] By this last statement, Weber indicates his desire to see Catholics disaffected from religious authority, not merely to separate religious authority from civil authority. Weber's understanding of "democracy" in this passage assumes the kind of social leveling Catholic and Jewish leaders alike explicitly denounced on many occasions. Catholics needed these provisions (and similar issues concerning state support for religious institutions concerned both liberal and conservative Jewish religious leaders) to revive their apathetic congregations. Similarly, a 1909 letter from the Weber papers links state bureaucracy and "the virtuous machinery of the Catholic church" as the two powers that in the future "have the best chance to dominate everything else. *In spite of* this, indeed *because* of it, I regard it as a demand on my humanity to fight these public powers, with the notation of course that the specific Catholic form of piety in all of its richness, is quite a different thing from what I have designated above as the 'machinery' of the church—in truth it is antagonistic to this machinery, and has only a meager chance for the future."[80] For Weber the establishment of the authority of a German "culture" was the higher purpose of political action, and this purpose was in conflict with the authority of the Roman church over the hearts of German Catholics. His tolerance of the German Catholics is justified with an instrumentalist rationale that looks forward to a form of assimilation that entails renouncing the church.

It has already been suggested that Weber's identification with the German mandarins was ambivalent. On the one hand, he shared their aspiration

---

79. Reprinted in ibid., 401–2.

80. Cited in Mommsen, *German Politics,* 123; Mommsen's conclusion: "He [Weber] was never able to forsake totally the emotions of the *Kulturkampf,* which had been of such import for him as a young man." The actual course of the *Kulturkampf,* which was marked by the progressive galvanizing of Catholic opposition to the German state, belies Weber's judgment. Such a view has, however, been very influential for historiography. For corrective historical arguments, cf. Anderson and Barkin, "The Myth of the Puttkamer Purge and the Reality of the *Kulturkampf,*" 647–86; Tal, *Christians and Jews,* chap. 2. The sharp distinction between formal religious authority and an inward religious piety subsequently became a cornerstone of Weber's sociology of religion. This will be discussed in chapter 8.

to have a directive role in society by virtue of their monopoly on expert knowledge (*Wissenschaft*). This aspiration was an important motive in the mandarins' nationalism. But, on the other hand, he had nothing but disdain for the conservative intellectuals' inclination to identify with aristocratic society, to guarantee the social influence of the mandarins as a class by cultivating an aristocratic life-style. This, he thought, revealed a parvenu mentality in the worst sense. In 1893, in a letter to Marianne, Weber expressed "little respect for the so-called 'intellectual training' (*geistige Bildung*)," referring to the arrogance he often found within the mandarin class. These remarks, however, were coupled with a characteristic expression of the late nineteenth-century liberal mandarin criticism of "artificial self-limitation."[81]

His disdain for mandarin conservatism was one reason Weber found it necessary to break rank with the mainstream of social activism among the generation of his university teachers and to aspire to lead his own, younger generation on a new path. Another reason was that the conservativism that dominated academic activism up to 1890 placed definite limits on the mandarins' effectiveness, because their reform efforts were directed to the imperial court, the bureaucracy, and the landowning nobility at a time when an industrial mass society was fast emerging, and the circle of public opinion was beginning to widen. Thus the new path Weber's generation of intellectuals embarked on included both a progressive ideal, in contrast to the accepted conservativism of the academics, and a new style of realizing this ideal, by reaching out to a wider audience than the court and its bureaucracy. Two examples will illustrate how Weber combined these commitments to academic separatism, national unity, and progressive modernism.

Weber's close association with Friedrich Naumann began in 1892 with Weber's request, in the name of the Freiburg branch of the *Evangelisch-soziale Vereinigung,* that Naumann speak on the topic of the "duties of the educated to the lower classes," and specifically on the dangers of "economic patriarchalisms."[82] However, Weber's own faith in the power of the individual to freely attach himself to the state, once detached from other social allegiances, was so uncompromising as to make him unable to adopt a religious standpoint in social policy. Despite his active support for Naumann's left-wing Lutheran reform movement, the higher value of his version of *Bildungsindividualismus* led him to raise this demurrer about Naumann's efforts, in the 1894 meetings of the Evangelical-Socials:

81. Marianne Weber, *Biography,* 187–88.
82. Letter of 29 April 1892, cited in Mommsen, *German Politics,* 124n.135.

We are not engaging in social politics in order to create human happiness. . . . Last night Pastor Naumann's address reflected an infinite yearning for human happiness, and I am sure all of us were moved. But our pessimistic attitude leads us, and me in particular, to a point of view that seems of incomparably greater importance to me. I believe we must forgo the creation of a positive feeling of happiness in the course of any social legislation. We desire something else and can only desire something else. We want to cultivate and support what appears to us as *valuable* in man: his personal responsibility, his basic drive toward higher things, toward the intellectual and moral values of mankind, even where this drive confronts us in its most primitive form. Insofar as it is in our power, we wish to arrange external conditions not with a view toward people's wellbeing, but in such a way as to preserve—in the face of the inevitable struggle for existence with its suffering—those physical and spiritual qualities that we would like to maintain for the nation.[83]

Weber subsequently published a sympathetic critique of Naumann's views under the title "What Does 'Christian-Social' Mean?" where he distanced himself from Naumann's religiously inspired socialism by pointing out that societal impersonalism in employer-employee relations was the condition given by the trends of "modern evolution."[84] This indicated the pro-industrial and class-analytic basis of Weber's liberalism, in contrast to Naumann's religious liberalism. Specifically, Weber was interested in promoting the economic-class identification of the German citizenry as the surest means of getting the individual to detach himself from subnational group allegiances and to participate in the national life without reserve. Further criticism of Naumann came in 1896, when Naumann attempted to get a new party of "National-Socials" off the ground. Weber's rationale for rejecting this effort was that Naumann was directing its appeal to "the educated" but he defined the party's program as an arm of the worker's movement. In Weber's view this was to mix social strata that ought to be kept apart for maximum effectiveness. He asserted that the idea of a "class party" of the educated was a contradiction in terms; to work for the interests of the proletariat one must enter their social circle.[85]

---

83. Marianne Weber, *Biography*, 136–37, remarks at the Fifth Annual Evangelical Social Congress in Frankfurt.

84. Mommsen, *German Politics*, 124.

85. Ibid., 128. Weber nevertheless became an active supporter of Naumann's party from this time up to at least 1908; see chapter 5, note 22.

This characteristic model of social openness, the class-polarized society, was employed by Weber later, on the occasion of the fortieth anniversary of the *Verein für Sozialpolitik* in 1912, when Weber tried to organize a demonstration with Lujo Brentano, a liberal and free-trader, that would stimulate the general public's interest in progressive social policy. This was designed to lead ultimately to the founding of a social policy association that would promote propaganda for this cause. To this end Weber opposed Brentano's insistence on bringing up the problem of free trade because it would alienate conservative and even Catholic academics, and because the free-traders in Germany had traditionally been enemies of social policy. Notwithstanding his desire to include academics of all stripes, he wrote to Brentano that he considered himself among those "on the left" within this group.[86]

Weber's goal transcended the interests of the *Verein* as a particular body; he wanted a statement by all the "big name" academics who were identified with *Nationalökonomie* as a "discipline."[87] This statement would, as he put it in a memorandum to thirty-four members of the planning group who met in Leipzig, "reject, partly in principal and partly as inadequate, the point of view of master rule or patriarchalism, the bonds of welfare institutions and those who would treat the worker as an object for bureaucratic regulation, and insurance legislation that merely creates dependency." The statement would also "affirm the strengthening of [the workers'] organizations, which spearhead[s the] effort [to promote equality 'in the collective determination of working conditions']; we see the comradeliness and class dignity that develops in this way as a positive cultural value."[88] In the end Weber succeeded only in alienating Brentano, which dashed all hopes for the collective statement. But the episode shows that "social policy" was above all "worker" policy and was, for Weber, informed by economic-class analysis, and specifically by Weber's belief that economic class polarization was an appropriate means to achieve national social unification.

---

86. Ibid., 122n.131. Some years earlier he wrote to his brother Alfred that, at the 1905 convention of the *Verein* at Mannheim, he (Max) had to carefully restrain his support for the workers' cause, "in case the enemies take the position of treating us as 'decorations' and as swaggering radicals." Among the enemies the moderate Schmoller figured prominently. Weber considered Schmoller's aim was to preserve a "Verein for socially respectable social policy" (letters to Alfred Weber and Brentano, cited in ibid., 132nn.165, 166). "Socially respectable" for Schmoller meant an anti-industrial, even state-paternalist policy (see Ringer, *Mandarins,* 159).

87. Mommsen, *German Politics,* 118–22.

88. Quoted in ibid., 120.

Weber's agenda, then, was *Bildung* for all in this sense: he wanted a vitalization of the German citizenry, but at the same time he detested the *Bildung*-game of the established elite of *Kultur* as a form of mimicry of the traditional aristocracy, which he thought was in truth the opposite of *Kultur*. That is, Weber thought that imitation of an aristocratic life-style, and the use of an ideology of privilege to guarantee the status of that life-style, was wrong. In his view, *Bildung* and *ständisch* paternalism were both ideologies, in the pejorative sense, and amounted to the same thing. Notwithstanding this, Weber had his own *Bildung* agenda. Although he was critical of the mainstream use and effects of the ideology of *Bildung*, for him as well as the majority in general, the emancipatory implications of *Bildung* were hedged about by cultural conditions. The masses (and other social outsiders) must assimilate or achieve a level of dignity before they can embark on the path of healthy and beneficial citizenship through the personal pursuit of *Bildung*. Thus it remained for Weber, as well as those he criticized, an elitist ideology that is only formally universal.

III

We have no evidence that Weber expressed as direct a position on the Jewish question as he did on the *Kulturkampf* or on the legitimacy of full participation in society for the working classes. We must, instead, infer his position from occasional remarks and from the stand he took on other central social issues that involved the same principles as did the Jewish question. Many of these evidences will be considered in the chapters that follow, in connection with my examination of parts of Weber's scholarly work. For now it will suffice to give a general indication of his evaluation of the place of Jews in German society. Weber looked forward to the full admission of the Jews to German society. What he perceived as their vestigial desire for social distinctiveness and perhaps ethnic solidarity he considered to be a tragic element of their contemporary existence. This was because he knew from his own experience that the surrender of Jewish distinctiveness was de facto the necessary condition for the Jews' full membership in German society, especially for positions of leadership.[89] But this evaluation also grew directly out of his liberal nationalist perspective on the events of his day. This perspective led Weber to see these de facto conditions

---

89. Cf. for example statements on these questions late in his career, reprinted in ibid., 310f.n.105, 326; Marianne Weber, *Biography*, 648f.

for Jewish integration as symptomatic of principles of general social evolution which for him defined modernity. This, in turn, made it impossible for Weber to criticize these conditions, for he saw them as set in the nature of things, and so irremediable.[90] Rather than leading him to sympathize with his Jewish fellow citizens' real plight, and their arguments for liberal pluralism and principled tolerance, Weber's nationalist liberalism led him to view such arguments as coming from the voice of pariahs within the liberal movement and to support tolerance as a means to the long-term radical assimilation of the Jews.

The approach he took toward social questions in Germany put Weber at a distance from his Jewish fellow-citizens and many of his Jewish colleagues and students, despite his own intentions, which were the opposite of this for the most part, and apart from his own awareness of this distance. This was characteristic of the general failure of rapprochement and symbiosis between German Jews and majority Germans in this period, a failure that was especially poignant within the German liberal community because it so contradicted the desires of both sides. Both sides wanted deeply to identify with what they considered the authentic sources of German culture in order to bring about a wider national community than had ever before existed in their history. This common aspiration and the divide that it ultimately led to can be seen in the divergent interpretations that German Jews and Protestant German liberals gave to Goethe's literary achievement, for example. Compare the significance Goethe had for Walter Benjamin, who was just coming of age when Weber had become a leader in the dominant generation, and Weber's own evaluation of Goethe. The young Benjamin is reported to have identified strongly with the statement that, "above all, in a study of Goethe one finds one's Jewish substance."[91] This, at the time, was characteristic of the German Jews' belief that they could, by forming a Jewish identity, contribute most to the development of an authentically German national culture. This, they felt, was an expression of German idealism. The young Weber, who supposedly read all forty volumes of the current edition of Goethe in his early teens, denigrated Goethe's treatment

---

90. Weber's outlook is quite close to Brentano's, as expressed in the following statement, from the latter's Rectoral Address in November 1901 at Ludwig-Maximilian University in Munich: "All efforts to influence social life can be successful and just only insofar as they do not run counter to the actual nature of things or to the requirements of a natural (progressive) development" (quoted in Ringer, *Mandarins*, 161).

91. Mosse, *German Jews*, 14.

of the hero as "limited" in contrast to the treatment he found in the Greeks. He wrote to his cousin Fritz Baumgarten that "The real purpose of a heroic epic like the *Aeneid,* on the other hand, is the utmost glorification of the hero; in addition it should give pleasure with its beautiful depiction of details."[92] At age twenty-three he argued that one ought not look for norms for personal development in Goethe. The shortcomings of Goethe lie in the centrality he gave to a model of humanity:

> People, particularly those who occupy themselves with literature a great deal, are having their taste for Schiller spoiled by the exaggerated exclusive adoration of Goethe, and this makes them so unjust toward everyone else that I have often had occasion to be annoyed, for example with [my brother] Alfred and people his age. For what good is it to me if people tell me today how all-encompassing Goethe's poetic conception is and how one can find in it the entire contents of human life from A to Z, if afterword I find one side, and the most important one, hardly touched? For in general people's conception of life is not that the only thing that matters is for them to have a sense of well-being and to find a side of life that they can enjoy. Nor do people face only the question as to the road on which they can or cannot find happiness and inner satisfaction. But if one looks at things soberly and closely, this question is the deepest that one can derive from Goethe's works, including *Faust,* and everything, even the knottiest ethical problems, is illuminated from this standpoint [alone].[93]

Weber continued throughout his life to use Goethe as a touchstone for his own outlook on life, even occasionally in his scholarly work, but always emphasizing the gloomy side of Goethe, the places where conflict and struggle come to the surface. For German Jews, in contrast, George Mosse has written "Goethe's emphasis on individual freedom, his ambivalence toward all forms of nationalism, and, finally, his belief in *Bildung* seemed to foster Jewish assimilation. More important, unlike Schiller, Goethe was the embodiment of the ideal *Bildungsbürger* of the period of Jewish emancipation," a feeling that led German Jews to write numerous Goethe biographies and to play leading roles in the Goethe societies of the time.[94]

---

92. Marianne Weber, *Biography,* 51–52. Weber was fourteen years old at the time.

93. Ibid., 154–55, letter to Weber's girlfriend, 1887.

94. Mosse, *German Jews,* 44–45.

This contrast symbolizes the divergent paths that the ideology of *Bildung* had reached by the beginning of the twentieth century within the German Jewish and Protestant liberal intellectual communities in Germany, respectively. Although they used the same language when they spoke of their common liberal aspirations for the future of the German nation, Germans and Jews repeatedly talked past each other and would, in the course of time, become more and more frustrated by the absence of any echo from the other side. Before there was outright frustration, however, there often existed only a benign silence. When Walter Benjamin discovered his Jewishness in 1912, at the age of twenty, he was moved to valorize the Jewish literati (*Literatenjuden*) as central forces for change in German society.[95] At the same time, Max Weber was working out an explanation for why such men were so maligned: the perhaps half-conscious remnants of inherited religious sentiments was at the root of their desire to hold in reserve a part of themselves from German society. These men, then, brought malice upon themselves.

This indicates the wider cultural context within which Weber's sociology of the Jews is located, a context that Weber himself was, perhaps, only partially aware of. When the identification of German Jews in the first decades of the twentieth century with the ideology of *Bildung* had become stronger than ever, the ideology of the German majority had become antipluralist nationalism.[96] Because of their deep sense of responsibility for national development, the ideology of majority German liberal intellectuals had become a specific form of cultural nationalism, one which defined the "cultural tasks" ahead in a way that was both all-inclusive, and so universalist, and also exclusivist. With his own life and works Max Weber sought to play a central role in this development. How this aspiration, and especially the outlook on which it was based, determined the direction of his sociological studies in particular areas, is a question to which we now turn.

---

95. Ibid., 66.
96. Cf. ibid., 17, top.

3

Liberalism, Nationalism, and the Problem of Minorities

Max Weber had an abiding interest in the problem of so-called national minorities, and his efforts to address this problem provided occasions for him to both express his social outlook and develop his scholarship. In the late 1890s Weber's acute frustration with the German political climate, which he had labored hard to affect since the beginning of the decade, together with the onset of his nervous breakdown in 1898, led him to withdraw from politics and devote himself to purely scholarly pursuits. Up until this time, Weber saw no conflict between political activism and a teaching vocation. For example, he looked upon his first appointment to a full faculty position, to Freiburg in 1894, as a means to have a political impact in lieu of a position of party leadership, which he had hoped for earlier.[1] His criticism of Treitschke much later for combining the roles of

---

1. In 1892 Weber revealed (in a letter to his girlfriend) that he was more attached to the tasks of teaching than of pure scholarship in the university, undoubtedly for the forum it gave him for expressing his strong social and political views (Marianne Weber, *Biography,* 35). A letter to his uncle, Pastor Adolph Hausrath, in 1896, in response to the news that he was being considered for a chair in *Nationalökonomie* in Heidelberg, is also important for assessing Weber's early ambivalence about the academic vocation (see ibid., 126–27). Nevertheless, until his participation in drafting the Weimar constitution, after 1918, Weber willfully confined himself to political observation and commentary and assiduously avoided political participation of any kind. Compare Wolfgang Mommsen's judgment: "Weber's will was too boundless. He greatly surpassed his politically active contemporaries both in his actions and in the sharpness of his critical judgment. He could not feel comfortable with the unavoidable daily petty struggles in politics, the constant compromises, and the tactical corner-cutting. His volcanic temperament could not long be contained by the tactical bonds of partisan and factional politics, which he himself described so perceptively. He was very conscious of this and was therefore ultimately repelled whenever the opportunity for active political involvement occurred" (*German Politics,* 131).

scholarship and partisanship probably reflects in part a self-criticism in light of his own change of role.[2] At any rate, his interest in social and political questions did not lessen on account of his academic appointment, and by 1905 he was again immersing himself in social policy debate, this time in conjunction with the activities of the *Verein für Sozialpolitik,* in which he was taking a leading role.

At the center of Weber's concerns in the 1890s was the "Polish problem," the displacement of both Junkers and the German peasantry east of the Elbe by ethnic Poles. Weber's efforts to "solve" this problem, in lectures to clergy and students and in public addresses in political and intellectual societies, influenced the government to adopt more stringent anti-Polish measures, ultimately expelling Poles and putting harsh financial obstacles in the way of Polish progress. These were measures Weber called for in his speeches. These efforts reached a climax in his inaugural address at Freiburg University. In the address he calls for political economy (*Nationalökonomie*) to take an activist role in the political education of the nation. All his arguments here are designed to rehabilitate the image of liberal political scientists who, according to Kenneth Barkin, "were regarded as the outcasts whose vague theoretical solutions were no longer in tune with the problem of a developing nation."[3] This is why Weber tries to justify the younger academics' interest in social reform (with which he identified deeply) by specifying the national rather than the abstract nature of their work. "The aim of our social and political work," he said of himself and his colleagues, "is not world happiness but the *social unification* of the nation, which has been split apart by modern economic development, for the severe struggles of the future."[4] This concern, to consummate the military and political unification of the *Reich,* achieved by the state in 1870, with the social and

---

2. Weber's evaluation of Treitschke is considered at length at the conclusion of this chapter.

3. At this time the German state had taken the lead in promoting industrialization and was regarded by public opinion as the progressive force in society, in contrast to academic social scientists (Barkin, *The Controversy over German Industrialization, 1890–1902,* 37, hereafter cited as *Controversy*). This was, of course, in sharp contrast to the tradition of academic activism Weber and his peers felt heir to, and which many of them aspired to reform.

4. Max Weber, "The National State and Economic Policy (Freiburg Address [1894])," 447 (hereafter cited as "National State"); and an excerpt, "Economic Policy and the National Interest in Imperial Germany," in Runciman, *Weber: Selections in Translation,* 267; emphasis in original. I have combined the two translations. See also below, notes 107 and 108.

cultural unification of the German population was a characteristic preoccupation of liberal nationalists in the Imperial period. The way in which Weber brought this concern to bear on the Polish problem reveals a central and perhaps irresolvable conflict between the liberal and nationalist aspects of his social outlook.[5]

Weber's liberalism lies in his pro-industrialism, a commitment to the positive features of an industrial society that Weber consistently adhered to throughout his career. Weber's pro-industrialism was based on a class analysis of political and economic evolution he shared broadly with the radical tradition in German social thought established by Marx, without himself taking seriously the dialectical evolutionism or the one-sided advocacy of the proletariat of Marxism and the socialist labor movement.[6] This left Weber with a positive evaluation of the industrial capitalist open-class social order, and set him against both Marxist progressives and the agrarian conservatives in Germany. Weber can nevertheless be termed a progressive in a specific sense. He promoted the development of what he took to be the natural trend in his own time toward a liberal economic order and toward political representation based on some sort of universal franchise. These views, especially in light of the sophistication with which Weber was to develop them later, were rather distinctive at the time. They cannot, however, be separated from his views on national unity, because the conditions for national unity had to be met before class struggle could fully develop, according to Weber. Indeed, for Weber *cultural* unity actually promotes class struggle; failure to achieve cultural unity is, accordingly, an obstacle to the full development of class struggle.

If Weber's particular brand of liberalism was distinctive, his nationalism was not. Weber's nationalism is based on a version of the theory of the *Kulturstaat,* the theory that modern societies must be based on a common

---

5. Cf. Mosse, "The Conflict of Liberalism and Nationalism and Its Effect on German Jewry," 125–39, for a general discussion; also Mosse's paper in Leo Baeck Institute, *Perspectives of German-Jewish History in the Nineteenth and Twentieth Centuries.*

6. See Mommsen, *German Politics,* 96, 102–23, and the evaluation of J. Schumpeter cited ibid., 103n.56. For comprehensive reviews of Weber's relation to Marx and Marxism, see Mommsen, "Max Weber as a Critic of Marxism," *Canadian Journal of Sociology* 2 (1977): 373–98; Kilker, "Weber on Socialism, Bureaucracy, and Freedom," 76–95; a brief review in Keith Tribe's introduction to Weber, "Developmental Tendencies in the Situation of East Elbian Rural Laborers," 177–205. Weber's relation to Marx and the Marxist position on the Jewish question is considered at length in chapter 9.

culture. "Unification" (*Unificierung*) and "social leveling" (*Gleichmacherei*) were terms used interchangeably in German political discourse from the time of the *Kulturkampf* into the twentieth century to describe a public policy that promoted national unity consciously at the expense of the social differences among various ethnic or religious groups in the Second Reich.[7] Similarly, for Weber "social unification" meant integration of all groups, notwithstanding *economic* conflicts, into a common *Kulturstaat*. *Kulturstaatliche* social thought was itself a form of integral nationalism, a position signaled by valorization of *Deutschtum* or "Germanism." The family of discourse this belongs to includes the anti-Semitic, philosemitic, and Jewish-apologetic uses of the contrast between *Deutschtum* and *Judentum* ("Judaism," "Jewry"), the contrast between *Deutschtum* and the Roman Catholic church (or Catholics), and the contrast between *Deutschtum* and *Polentum* ("Polonism," Polish culture). In all these cases, *Deutschtum* is part of an invidious contrast designed, from the standpoint of the majority, to better define German national identity.

The conflict between liberalism and nationalism in Weber's thought may be obscured by Weber's role in the controversy over German industrialization, which began two years after the Freiburg address. Karl Oldenberg's 1897 lecture to the Evangelical Social Congress on "Germany as an Industrial State," which employed the agrarian critique of industrialism to express disdain for social inequities in society, brought strong criticism from Friedrich Naumann, the activist theologian, and Weber, thereby bringing the conservative critique out of the academy and into the arena of public debate over social problems. It also thrust Weber himself into the forefront of the left wing of academic social activists. However, the form of the debate, which was focused on economic issues, masked the broad agreement of both sides, conservative and liberal, on the general values embodied in Weber's own cultural nationalism. Given this broad consensus, there was no reason to bring these ideas into the debate, and so Weber's progressive modernism is naturally highlighted whenever we look at his critique of the agrarians. Finally, Weber's unwillingness to compromise on the *Kulturstaat* ideal was the primary reason for his inability to identify with many extreme nationalists in his time.[8]

---

7. Tal, "Liberal Protestantism and the Status of the Jews in the 'Second Reich,' 1870–1914," 25n.10, 33. See also Jarausch, *Students, Society, and Politics*, 161ff.

8. Barkin, *Controversy*, 4, 186–207. On the idea of the *Kulturstaat* among German intellectuals at the time, see Ringer, *Mandarins*, 115–27, 134–35, 146ff. Note that Ringer's most important primary sources who write about the origins

In this chapter I shall examine various interlocking contexts for Weber's analysis of the Polish question in Germany, culminating in his 1895 Freiburg address. These include the legitimacy of Marxist analysis in the academy, the *Kulturkampf,* the Jewish question, and various constructions of the concept of race, as well as the role of peasants and Junkers in the development of the nation. A full understanding of Weber's position on the Polish question allows us to locate Weber among those who took contrasting positions on the question of the social constitution of modern German society. By negating various alternatives, such as racial or religious constructions of state and society, and by specifying his identification with the principle of "culture," Weber's case for excluding the Polish minority is one of the clearest indicators of his antipluralism.

II

Weber's attacks on academic conservatives mark him in many ways as a "modernist" and brought him close to Marxists, who were beginning to become prominent among the academics of his generation.[9] At the same time, Weber's nationalism kept him from fully identifying with the internationalism and historical optimism of the Marxists, who in many ways represented the model of modernism. This requires us to look closely at the kind of modernism to which Weber was committed.

Academic conservatism in Imperial Germany was defined by a patriarchal tradition of social criticism. The agrarian favoritists Karl Oldenberg, Adolph Wagner, and Max Scring were the most prominent leaders in this tradition at the time Weber was writing.[10] Wagner helped found the *Verein für Sozialpolitik* in 1872, whose idealistic members came to be known as the *Kathedersozialisten,* or "socialists of the lectern." This epithet, which this group of academics accepted for themselves, indicated their willingness to undertake agitation through lectures and writing to effect legislative initi-

---

of *Bildungsliberalismus* and *kulturstaatliche* ideals in the period around 1800 are in fact writing retrospectively from the time of the war or the Weimar period (especially Meinecke, Troeltsch, Spranger, and Rickert).

9. The characterization of Weber as a "modernist" has been most forcefully and comprehensively developed by Ringer, *Mandarins.* More recently, Lawrence Scaff has offered a modernist reading of Weber as an existentialist, in *Fleeing the Iron Cage.*

10. The following sketch of the conflict between anti- and pro-industrialists among German intellectuals around the turn of the century follows Barkin, *Controversy,* chapters 4 and 5.

atives for social reform. In his address to the first meeting of the *Verein*, Gustav Schmoller, a central figure among the *Kathedersozialisten,* decried the modern division of labor because it threatened traditional independent producers on the land and in the city. He called attention to the supposed "moral factors" that independence produced, in order to highlight the shortcomings of the wage contract: "Does it sufficiently educate the youthful elements? Does it bring about diligence, thrift, honesty, family life among adults so that here too progress besides the economic [kind] is probable?"[11] Weber agreed broadly with these social goals but, as we will see, he objected strenuously to Schmoller's view that *ständisch* independence was the appropriate means to achieve these ends.

Oldenberg's conservative activism brought him into contact with the Evangelical Social Congress, under the sponsorship of the court preacher Adolph Stoecker, and the government's "Die innere Mission der evangelischen Kirche," which became more and more oriented to propagandizing to the proletariat throughout the 1890s.[12] Stoecker led the established Lutheran clergy in reform efforts, working in concert with the *Kathedersozialisten* and sharing their animus against Social Democracy, which Stoecker saw as weaning away the working class from Christianity. Stoecker himself had firm sympathies for the agrarian cause and its ideal of benevolent paternalism. Max Weber, who had been participating in the Evangelical Social Congress since 1890, thought that Stoecker's group was filling a vacuum left by the increasingly traditionalistic tone of the *Kathedersozialisten*'s agitation, although he could never accept Stoecker's paternalistic and openly anti-Semitic social views.[13]

Like Oldenberg and Schmoller, Adolph Wagner was critical of Bismarck's government for its economic liberalism, which he thought had unchristian and inhumane effects on the working class, who were put at the mercy of the entrepreneurs and speculators (among whom he thought Jews predominated). Wagner was shocked by the economic dynamism of Berlin, where he joined the faculty in 1870. He would have agreed with Oldenberg's criticism of Marxism, in an 1891 article for the *Evangelische Soziale Zeitfragen,* that its ideal for society would result in a heightened bureaucratic impersonalism. By 1877, however, his abrasive single-mindedness obliged him to resign from the *Verein* and to join the smaller *Zen-*

---

11. Schmoller's remarks quoted in Mitzmann, *Sociology and Estrangement,* 146n.

12. Barkin, *Controversy,* 135–39.

13. Marianne Weber, *Biography,* 130–37; Massing, *Rehearsal for Destruction,* 117–18.

tralverein für Sozialreform. This organization merged with Stoecker's Lutheran reform movement in 1879, and by 1881 Wagner became its president and editor of its journal, *Der Staatssozialist,* Stoecker having directed his energies to religious revival among workers and to political anti-Semitism. Wagner's critique of industrial capitalism differed from that of the radical Social Democrats only in the image of the ideal he held— agrarian harmony rather than an ultimate working-class hegemony. This made him pessimistic rather than optimistic about the future.

A dissenting tradition among the activist-minded academics had begun in the 1880s. Heinrich Braun started a version of Schmoller's *Jahrbuch* in 1888 that distinguished itself from the older *Kathedersozialisten* by its lack of faith in state socialism. Braun spoke for those of the younger generation, like Sombart and Weber, who wanted to broaden the social-problem orientation of the older academics. Although he was considered to be a Marxist, Braun distinguished himself from the utopian internationalism of orthodox Marxism. Braun (like Sombart) identified himself with the German Social Democratic Party, which was openly Marxist, in support of the working class. Together with Weber and Sombart and other reform-minded younger academics, Braun felt that agrarian partisanship had to give way to a more comprehensive program designed to encourage national identification among the German masses. Both the successful bourgeois classes, who seemed to pursue a misguided desire for ennoblement, and the working classes, who threatened revolution in the view of many activists on both the right and the left, had to be addressed by a broad-based nationalist social policy. Such a policy was considered a "cultural task" among the modernists, and the rhetoric of "culture" and the mass social program it represented distinguished the modernists from the traditionalist academics and the aristocratic agrarians with whom many of the older generation of academics sided with. This modernist current was to become sympathetic to, and was even to collaborate with, revisionist (nationalist) socialism later, especially after the 1903 elections when revisionism began to dominate the Social Democratic Party.

In his introduction to the first issue of his *Archiv für soziale Gesetzgebung und Statistik* Braun pointed out that social legislation was needed that addressed the problems of all the working classes. The task of scientific inquiry into social problems therefore had to include statistical research into these classes "and of social conditions generally."

> The fulfillment of this need found a decided opponent in the state [according to Braun's statement]. Only with resistance, under the force

of circumstances, and almost always only in reference to the momentary needs and goals of its legislation and administration did it allow to statistics the solution of that task. The scientific viewpoint of a non-party representation of the social conditions of the people, seeking only the truth, thus gave way to political [partisan] interests.[14]

Sombart, who as early as 1891 had attacked the patriarchal exploitation of cottage-industry workers in Braun's journal, expressed similar dissenting views in the 1899 meeting of the *Verein*. This precipitated a near break with the older *Kathedersozialisten,* one that was averted only by Schmoller's flattering closing remarks. Schmoller described Sombart's speech as both informed by "the materialist conception of history," with which "not all members of the *Verein* could agree," and as "one of the most brilliant masterpieces of eloquence and spirit that I have ever heard. And I was proud that I could count him [Sombart] among my students . . . even though I find myself on essentially different ground."[15] Sombart's support for Marxist Social Democracy, which his views were taken to reflect, had already become notorious as a result of the publication of his 1896 lectures on "Socialism and the Social Movement in the 19th Century." Sombart's specific polemic against the older *Kathedersozialisten* had already been published, too, in an 1897 article in Braun's journal, as "Ideals of *Sozialpolitik.*" Here he rejected Schmoller's view that social policy should be designed to reconcile traditional and modern interests with state-national goals; Sombart favored instead a free struggle among conflicting groups in society.[16]

---

14. Quoted in Mitzmann, *Sociology and Estrangement,* 147.

15. Ibid., 159. This moderated the chairman Otto von Gierke's more direct rebuttal of Sombart's claim that traditional and patriarchal social forms are "obsolete and diseased and whenever possible should be the object of a mercy killing so that [they] end earlier" (p. 158). Actually, Sombart's view was that it was possible, on the basis of a scientific analysis, to identify the "progressive" classes or groups in society; their development ought to be promoted by state action and at the expense of the historically "regressive" social forms. At this time Sombart's standard for "progress" was economic productivity and efficiency, so as to reduce the individual's bond to unhealthy work and increase his leisure and the quality of family living.

16. Ibid., 159–60, 168–70. Beyond this, in the 1897 article Sombart anticipated Weber's radical distinction between science and values (under the influence of neo-Kantianism), the attribution of the creation of value to the individual will (under Nietzsche's influence), the association of value-setting with freedom of the will (both Sombart and Weber used this the criterion for a critique of Stammler's historical teleology), and finally the need for the scientist to pursue the task of "clarification of the situation" of social and political life from the standpoint of a

These differences being constructed between the older and the younger academics, notwithstanding the argument on the surface for the purification of scientific methods (to which Braun's journal committed itself), were designed to heighten the social activism of university intellectuals, not to lessen it. The real difference between the two wings of academics lies in the positive approach to things "modern" among the younger scholars, in contrast to the near absolute rejection of modernity by the older generation. Their modernism, however, went hand in hand with a selective and not altogether wholeheartedly sympathetic reception of Marx and Marxism. Weber's efforts to rehabilitate the image of the professorial activists thus meant breaking with agrarian conservatism first, but also maintaining a calculated distance from Marxism. In 1894 Weber decisively distanced himself from both religious and paternalist social-ethical motives for reform with the striking statement, "Lasciate ogni speranza [Abandon hope all ye who enter here]: these words are inscribed above the portals of the unknown future history of mankind. So much for the dream of peace and happiness."[17] These words from Dante's *Divine Comedy* would have been especially striking to those familiar with Marx's *Contribution to the Critique of Political Economy* (1859). The preface to that book, which included the concise statement of the materialist theory of superstructure and substructure that even then had become a *locus classicus* of Marxism, ended with these words: "at the entrance to science, as at the entrance to hell, the demand must be posted: 'Qui si convien lasciare ogni sospetto; / Ogni vitta convien che qui sia morta.' ['Here all mistrust must be abandoned / And here must perish every craven thought.']"[18] Both Weber's and Marx's words contain an

---

coherent *Weltanschauung.* Because the latter task ultimately involves the exercise of "his will" rather than "his perception," "just for that reason he [the social scientist] should draw the line between science and action so much the sharper" (quoted in ibid., 170).

17. Weber, "National State," 437; cf. Mommsen, *German Politics,* 38; Marianne Weber, *Biography,* 216–18.

18. Tucker, *Marx-Engels Reader,* 6. The *Divine Comedy* figures prominently in the *Problemstellung* of *The Protestant Ethic.* Weber's remark is also close textually to a remark made by Engels in 1872, in criticism of anarchism. Engels argued that the need for centers of authority, and so the coordination of individuals, will not go away simply on account of a successful social revolution. He uses the example of the "authoritarian way" in which factory production is organized, in a statement that strikingly presages Weber's description of the "iron cage" of industrial work: "At least with regard to the hours of work one may write upon the portals of these factories: *Lasciate ogni autonomia, voi che entrate!* [Leave, ye that enter in, all autonomy behind!]" (ibid., 731).

appeal to progress and a dark willingness to step out into the tepid air of modernity, in sharp contrast to "the interested prejudices of the ruling classes."[19] Both, too, were addressing their explicit critiques toward classical political economy. But by Weber's time "Manchester" economics had fallen into low repute and had become for all intents and purposes a straw man. Weber's critique was now directed just as much against Marxism's optimistic embrace of transnational class solidarity in the future, a future which, in sharp contrast to Marx, Weber here calls "unknown." Marxism was also widely perceived to be ultimately striving for an unheroic "happiness" for the masses and was looked upon dimly for this reason by even the farthest left of the academic activists, like Lujo Brentano.[20] Weber's statement attacking both Marxism and Manchesterism thus put him in good stead with the mainstream reformist wing of the Kathedersozialisten.

III

Weber's inaugural dissertation on ancient Roman agrarian history (published in 1891) had led to his commission by the Verein in 1890 to take part in a survey of agricultural workers in eastern Germany, which eventually resulted in a series of scholarly essays and addresses on "the landworker question" that would become the vehicle for expressing Weber's nationalist social philosophy and launching his interest in the origins and development of capitalism.[21] Just as Sombart had earlier, Weber argued in his first major report for the Verein, in 1892, that the relative independence attached workers once enjoyed under feudalism was impossible under the influence of rural capitalism. Fixed allowances or salaries were now the only means of achieving independence, but this came at the expense of the long-term viability of both sides' (but especially the workers') economic situation. For the landlords quickly made use of cheaper Polish migrant labor, further

---

19. Weber, "National State," 437.

20. So also Sombart, who in his lectures of 1900, *Dennoch!*, criticized as "utopian" "the old Robespierre talk of the dictatorship of the proletariat," which he finds in Lassalle, the English classical economists, and Marx. But he takes over Marx's valorization of English progress, calling it *"Kultur,"* in order to argue for a peaceful struggle for a new, harmonious social order through a combined trade-union and political-social movement (Mitzmann, *Sociology and Estrangement,* 179–82).

21. For Weber's writings on the landworker question I have relied mainly on Mommsen, *German Politics,* chapters 2 and 3, and Mitzmann, *Iron Cage,* part 1.

driving German peasants off the land.[22] Actually, the factors leading to the rural labor shortage were more complex than Weber admitted. He was certainly right about the landowners' propensity to land speculation at the expense of the workers' standard of living, a theme he would mercilessly exploit. The German Customs Union (*Zollverein*), by limiting import trade in grain, wool, and meat (as well as iron) and promoting the exploitation of new internal markets had kept prices highly favorable since midcentury, leading to a progressive inflation in land prices. Since the 1820s agrarian reforms in most German states had allowed landowners to appropriate the smaller holdings of serf families and to deny all commons privileges; many of the remaining smallholders sold out to their landlord under the impoverished conditions that resulted. After 1861 Prussia granted freedom of movement across all borders, obviating the need for burdensome applications to the respective state authorities to emigrate. Together with the American Homestead Act of 1862, German farmworkers could at last act on their longstanding dissatisfaction, and an exodus to German ports to take advantage of cheap steamship fares to the New World ensued.[23]

Weber's writings on the landworker question would become more and more explicitly anti-agrarian. But in this 1892 report Weber bows to the "political instincts" of the Junkers which, he argues, the rising bourgeoisie will need further "education" to attain. His praise for the Junkers is actually a disguised means to elaborate a liberal program for reform based on acceptance of the working class's striving for independence. However, the disguise brought him praise from the conservative *Kreuzzeitung,* and this greatly embarrassed Weber.[24] On the other hand, a Silesian landowner had attacked the report in the Parliament as typical of the National Liberals' bias against rural capitalism. These responses compelled Weber to develop a sharper and more rigorously grounded statement of his views. A series of articles and lectures followed in which Weber elaborated on a brief and seemingly unnoticed conclusion here: "The patriarchal estates sustained the nutritional level of the agricultural working class and conserved its military

---

22. Cf. also Weber, "Developmental Tendencies," 177–205.

23. Barkin, *Controversy,* 21–32.

24. Cf. letters to Otto Baumgarten and Lujo Brentano of February 1893, cited respectively in Mitzmann, *Iron Cage,* 97n, and Mommsen, *German Politics,* 25n.15. In the latter Weber says he "repress[ed] my native liberal antipathy for the eastern landlords," and vowed to correct the *Kreuzzeitung's* misinterpretation of his study at the upcoming convention of the *Verein.*

fitness; today's capitalistic estates exist at the expense of the nutritional level, the nationality, and the military strength of the German east."[25]

Weber's position derived in part from his experience in Posen, where he had his military training in 1888. During this time he had become familiar, through the district magistrate whose guest he became, with the government's 1886 Colonization Commission, set up to buy Polish estates to resettle German farmers on them and so alleviate the "Polonization" of the east.[26] The establishment of the Colonization Commission culminated a longer struggle over minority rights in German-controlled schools in the east that grew out of the *Kulturkampf*. The *Kulturkampf* had replaced priests with bureaucrats among elementary school supervisors. In 1873 and 1874 administrative decrees substituted German for Polish in all Posen elementary and secondary schools. In 1876 the same was done for all citizens' regular communication with the state, so requiring a translator in official affairs for the common people. Initiated by the state, the liberals and progressives had joined the *Kulturkampf* not for religious reasons, but (in William Hagen's words) because "they could agree in uniting against Catholic influence in education [in order to] . . . uphold the legitimacy of the solution of 1871, the unity of the Reich, and the ideal of Imperial German nationality."[27]

Despite their collaboration over Germanization policy in the east, Bismarck's aims were always different than those of the independent bourgeois left. Bismarck looked forward to neutralizing the power of the Polish gentry. Ever since the 1863–64 Polish insurrection against Russia, the Polish gentry had presided over a nationalist movement that grew up in response to Prussian oppression.[28] By attacking the Polish gentry Bismarck sought to weaken the ability of the Polish people to withstand Prussian hegemony. After 1878–79 the government became openly conservative and antiliberal.

---

25. Quoted in Mommsen, *German Politics*, 24–25.

26. See Marianne Weber, *Biography*, 146–49; Mitzmann, *Iron Cage*, 41.

27. Hagen, *Germans, Poles, and Jews: The Nationality Conflict in the Prussian East, 1772–1914*, 127 (hereafter cited as *Germans, Poles, and Jews*). Information on government actions in the following paragraphs comes from Hagen's study.

28. The Polonophobia of German popular literature after 1848 reflected the increasing competition between the industrial and commercial bourgeois classes of the respective minorities, with Germans and Jews in the east on one side, Poles on the other. Polonophobia caused the Poles to withdraw from nationally mixed organizations and to create a separate economic and cultural life aspiring to national independence (on the basis of the pre-Napoleonic prepartition borders). The political struggles over Germanization are sometimes a weak echo of these other struggles.

From 1878 to 1890 a ban on socialist agitation and association was put into effect, eliminating the Social Democratic Party. From 1883 to 1885 summary expulsions of Austrian and Russian citizens who had settled in Berlin and the German east were ordered; two-thirds of the deportees were Poles, one-third were Jews. Bismarck's most ambitious project, the Royal Prussian Colonization Commission, capped these events. The project was undertaken in conjunction with the National Liberals, who demanded parcelization of land purchased from failing Polish gentry to German peasants for resettlement, not to the Junkers, as Bismarck would have preferred.[29] In 1886–87 there followed more laws Germanizing schools in the Polish regions, ultimately banning the Polish language altogether from Polish-German schools. But the 1886 Colonization Commission represented the first positive program in Prussian *Polenpolitik* toward full-scale Germanization, an action that, in its intent, went well beyond Bismarck's negative goal of suppressing "Polonism."[30]

After 1890, when Bismarck stepped down, his successor, Caprivi, ended the settlement program and reopened the borders to Polish migrants. (This benefited the East Elbian and Upper Silesian industrialists, but also the Polish gentry.) A rapprochement by the Polish gentry toward Berlin brought concessions from Caprivi of a few hours of Polish-language instruction in the schools, and permission for land-hungry Polish peasants to take part in estate parcelization and colonization programs newly established in 1890–91. Polish votes in the Reichstag got Caprivi an important army bill in 1893, but this made enemies of the upper bureaucrats, who had become bourgeois liberal nationalists and imperialists, as well as the German agrarians. Many among the *Bildungsbürgertum* had adopted an extreme ethnic

---

29. The Progressives did not follow the National Liberals in this. For example, Ruldolph Virchow complained in the Reichstag that, because Germans with Polish wives would not be settled, according to Bismarck, the commission had arrogated to itself "the right to say who is and who is not German." H. Rickert, however, described the process of Germanization more benignly, as "the reconciliation of the nationalities" (quotes in ibid., 156 and n. 129 there). The Progressives struck out ahead of the National Liberals (Weber's party and the party of which his father had been a deputy) at this point by voting against the Colonization Commission as an "exceptional" law that violated the *Rechtstaat* principle, the same rationale they used to oppose the expulsions of 1883–85. The liberals moved away from their support of minority rights of Poles prior to 1871, when they thought a Polish-Prussian alliance against Russia was necessary. Now the Poles themselves were regarded as a "cultural" enemy (See ibid., 150–57).

30. Ibid., 120–36, 167.

nationalism. Such feelings led to the founding in 1893 of the Farmer's League, which agitated for higher farm duties, to a campaign by the Pan-German League in 1894 against Caprivi's Polish policies, and in the same year to the founding of the Society for the Support of Germans in the Eastern Marches, or "H-K-T Society," representing commercial, Junker, and German-Posener interests against the Poles. All these groups demanded a more vigorous Germanization program in Posen.[31]

In 1895 Weber would make reference to his own experience in Posen by claiming that "anyone who has observed the civilizing effect of colonization on the spot" could see that "a few dozen villages with a dozen German farms each will eventually *Germanize* many square miles."[32] This put him on the side of the bourgeois nationalists and their demand that *Polenpolitik* be conceived as an ethnic struggle. His papers on East Elbia in the 1890s are designed to isolate this position from agrarian loyalism. In a lecture to the 1893 meeting of the *Verein* Weber made their disinterest in Germanization the fulcrum of an unmitigated criticism of the Junkers. The Junker, he said, has renounced his traditional responsibility to protect those he employs in order to pursue profits first. The landworker wants only one thing, namely liberation from the Junker's now intolerable patriarchal authority, which is being used to retain the worker's obedience while the landlord imports cheap migrant labor. Germany's ability to compete internationally in grain was already lost; therefore social policy regarding the land question should abandon the attempt to prop up the eastern agricultural interests. The eastern landlords are, at any rate, posing a greater threat to the nation by their importation of cheap Polish labor than by their declining competitive position on the world market. They have become "the most dangerous enemy of our nationality" precisely because they have become "our greatest Polonizer."[33] "It is precisely the *decline* of competitive ability that creates a situation . . . where small farms are more capable of survival than large, market-oriented establishments." Weber expressed alarm at this consequence, which he called "denationalization." In order to halt this process the government ought to embark on a settlement policy that goes far beyond the 1886 commission. For this it would be necessary to oppose both the landowning interests, by "emphasiz[ing] *peasant* colonization alone" (against the pro-agrarian views of von der Goltz and

---

31. Ibid., 169–76. For the latter group, see Tims, *Germanizing Prussian Poland.*
32. Weber, "National State," 449n.5; cf. Mommsen, *German Politics,* 39.
33. This and the following quotes are taken from Mommsen, *German Politics,* 28–29. See also Mitzmann, *Iron Cage,* 99–100.

Sering), and "the instincts of those who defend Manchesterism and free trade."[34] In other words, the Junkers have something less than the national interest at heart, for they, too, use the free-trade argument to justify access to the cheapest labor while arguing for the protection of grain tariffs.[35]

Weber closed his 1893 lecture to the *Verein* by outlining "the most important political tasks of the state: in the first place the preservation of German culture in the east, the defense of our eastern boundaries, of German nationality, even in peace. The big landowners . . . have become uprooted and worthless for the state—not through their fault, I repeat, but through overpowering national changes of a material and psychological nature."[36] Weber finally calls for a new equivalent of the landowners' "political intelligence" that is appropriate to the changed conditions of Germany's development:

It is the weighty curse of decadence that burdens this nation, from the masses to the highest circles. We cannot revive the verve and enthusiastic energy that inspired the generation before ours. . . . They built us a solid house, and we were invited to live in it and enjoy its blessings. We face different tasks. We cannot appeal to the common sentiment of the nation, as was done when the creation of national unity and a free constitution were the issues. We are a different breed of men. We are free from the countless illusions that formed our fathers' enthusiasm. Colossal illusions were necessary to create the German Reich, illusions that fled with the honeymoon of German [political] unity and that we cannot recreate artificially or theoretically.[37]

In "Developmental Tendencies in the Situation of the East Elbian Landworkers," which appeared in Braun's *Archiv* in 1894, Weber was even less restrained in his social criticism. In a clear indication of the early Marxist influence on his thought, he develops the view that capitalism would free

---

34. The latter position distanced Weber from Brentano, to whom he wrote in the same year that, under the conditions, free trade posed "a cultural danger" (letter of February 20, 1893, cited in Mommsen, *German Politics,* 30n.34).
35. Mitzmann, *Iron Cage,* 102–3.
36. Quoted in ibid., 104–5.
37. Quoted in Mommsen, *German Politics,* 31; compare Mitzmann, *Iron Cage,* 106–8.

the rural workers to engage in "class struggle."[38] Weber now asks if there are analogies in the east to what he thinks the urban proletariat show are the preconditions for successful class struggle. The question had been raised in the debate following Weber's 1893 lecture to the *Verein*, by the socialists Bruno Schönlank and Max Quarck. Schönlank argued that Polish labor could not be kept out of Germany as long as the German landworkers were forbidden to organize. Quarck criticized Weber for concentrating on how the landlords' needs for labor could be satisfied, as if this was an adequate solution to the landworker question as a whole.[39] Weber's 1894 article is in part a response to these criticisms.

Weber wants the state to provide a resettlement scheme that will institute the more "developed," "businesslike exploitation" he says has been lacking in the east, by leveling the gradations of status among landworkers, concentrating them regionally, and bringing the whole arrangement under the rule of law. Indeed, the breach in the traditional approach to profit on the part of the Junkers has already begun, by virtue of the competition of lifestyles between them and their urban counterparts. And the landworkers are already showing that flight is preferable to the "brutal personal domination" they face from the landowners.[40] Therefore, state-sponsored emigration to designated centers of rural production in the east will both solve the Polish problem and forestall the imminent economic demise of private landowning in the east.[41]

Weber's juxtaposition of "national unity" and "Polonization" in the east is less descriptive than tactical, as is his reference to a "political consciousness" which supposedly has had a hand in creating "the unity of the Reich." Weber knows that the Reich organization of Germany has been imposed by the state, and he recognizes that the aspirations of eastern German

---

38. Weber, "Developmental Tendencies," 191; cf. Mommsen, *German Politics,* 19–20, 26. Weber's sympathy for Marxist terms of analysis, notwithstanding his rejection of Marxist theory, would always stand in the way of his ability to identify with the theologian's efforts toward social reform, such as his close friends Göhre and Naumann.

39. Mitzmann, *Iron Cage,* 132–33.

40. Ibid., 101–2, criticizes Weber's analysis for disregarding the workers' declining standard of living as an important factor explaining the changes occurring in the east. This more palpable motive for leaving the countryside is acknowledged by Weber, but he nevertheless chooses to put all his emphasis on the landworkers' idealistic striving for freedom.

41. Ibid., 129, 133–36.

peasants are hardly driven by nationalism. National unity is an aspiration for Weber and his colleagues; it is something they think that Germany now lacks. Weber intentionally obscures this by calling the Junkers "Polonizers" and by describing the threat their actions pose as "denationalization" of the east. These are all rhetorical ways of expressing his own aspirations by negation. In the process, however, Weber develops a series of positive metaphors for these aspirations: culture, nationality, race, and *Deutschtum*.

IV

After 1895, under Chancellor Hohelohe, anti-Polish Prussian policies were sharpened. Poles were rejected from parcelization and settlement programs, expulsion of non-naturalized Poles resumed, as did suppression of Polish-language instruction. In 1898 the Colonization Commission was given an additional 100 million marks by the Landtag, largely because German colonists had been providing so little return on the commission's past investments in them. The creation of a German ethnic stronghold in the east to counter the putative "efforts to Polonize" those provinces (in the words of the 1886 colonization bill) was, in the second half of the 1890s, a nationalist goal agreed upon by liberals, industrialists, German landowners, the landed peasantry in the east, and conservatives, all of whom *Polenpolitik* radicalized at this time.[42]

Weber's strong support for the state and its responsibility for the modern development of the nation convinced both the government, who controlled all academic appointments, and the generally state-socialist academics of his abilities, and in 1894 he was called to his first full faculty position to Freiburg University as a full professor in political economy, *Nationalökonomie*.[43] With full support from the authorities Weber decided to make his inaugural address at Freiburg the occasion for the sharpest formulation of his views on social policy yet. In the Freiburg address of 1895 Weber says the landworker question is no more than "a *single example* to make clear the role played by racial differences of a physical and psychological nature,

---

42. Hagen, *Germans, Poles, and Jews,* 176–80.

43. This was in contrast to economic history, the field in which he had received his doctoral degree and his habilitation (cf. Oberschall, *Empirical Social Research in Germany, 1848–1914,* 26–27). Weber's Freiburg address probably influenced positively the state's refinancing of the Settlement Commission some three years later.

as between nationalities, in the economic struggle for existence."[44] In fact the address is much more; it is no less than a program for overhauling the state's social policy from the standpoint of the primacy of ethnic-German nationality. Accordingly, the Polish question is put in the forefront of the discussion, and all the previous analyses of the landworker question are now organized around this problem. As in the earlier analyses, *Staatsraison* is the primary principle of social policy, but here the most pressing task of the state is to determine "what *social strata* are the repositories of 'Germanism' (*Deutschtum*) and 'Polonism' (*Polentum*) in the country districts," and to promote the former at the expense of the latter.[45] Compared to his earlier articles and lectures on this topic, the landworker question is transvalued from an economic struggle to a struggle between two "nationalities," and purely economic change has shifted from an end to a means to achieve the victory of Germanism over Polonism. Weber's commitment to the national idea is worked out in greatest detail here and, despite his later misgivings about aspects of this lecture, he remained committed to its national image of society to his last days.[46] One aspect of this image, reflected in Weber's concern with "racial differences," calls for special consideration before we can turn directly to the address itself.

Weber's understanding of the concept of race is based on constructions of the Darwinian notion of natural selection designed to apply to the German nation's struggle for survival. Around 1870 such constructions were used to justify Prussia's victory over France, and immediately thereafter neo-Darwinian notions were further stimulated among liberals by the *Kulturkampf*. Weber may have been influenced by Nietzsche's widely influential "Outline Concerning History and Historical Studies" (1867) which asked, "What is there in history except the endless war of conflicting interests,

---

44. Weber, "National State," 428.

45. Ibid., 429; also "we wish under this slogan of 'reason of state' to raise the demand that for questions of German economic policy . . . the ultimate and decisive voice should be that of the economic and political interests of our nation's power, and the vehicle of that power, the German national state" (p. 439).

46. See Struve, *Elites against Democracy*, 119. See the 1911 letter reprinted in Marianne Weber, *Biography*, 411: "In my Freiburg inaugural address, immature though it may have been in many respects, I most outspokenly supported the sovereignty of national ideals in the area of all practical policies, including the so-called social policy, at a time when a great many of the colleagues in my field were being taken in by the fraud of the so-called social kingdom."

and the struggle for self-preservation?"[47] Majority liberals took this supposed truism to explain the failure of Enlightenment ideals to provide answers to the problem of national unity. Proponents of biological racial theories took this same principle of historical struggle to justify the rejection of culture as a socially integrating force altogether, and this is what divided them from the liberals. Biological racialists argued that all morality and culture would be superceded by the emergence of an ever-growing human group possessed of vital physical energies, now concentrated in the German people. This view only stimulated liberals to expound in more elaborate terms their alternative model of a society rooted in "culture," by which they meant an ethnic mentality rooted in common memory rather than biological inheritance.[48] To the degree that they could not or would not be expected to identify with a common historical memory of the German nation, Jews for example were characterized as a "foreign racial tribe," as for example by the brothers Grimm.[49]

In the Freiburg address Weber adopts this nonbiological concept of race, arguing that hereditary physiological characteristics of a given population are one among a number of different aspects of race. What is primary is the *historical* link of memory and the authority this confers on historical generations for the identity of their descendants. The ability of those for whom we become "forefathers" to recognize a continuity in their social identity across the ages is what defines racial identity.

> If . . . we could arise from the grave thousands of years hence, we would seek the distant traces of our own nature in the physiognomy of the race of the future. Even our highest, our ultimate, terrestrial ideals are mutable and transitory. We cannot presume to impose them on the future. But we can hope that the future recognizes in our nature the nature of *its own ancestors*. We wish to make ourselves the forefathers of the race of the future with our labor and mode of existence.[50]

---

47. Quoted in Tal, *Christians and Jews,* 177, where family archives, reporting "talks in intellectual circles in Berlin, Frankfurt, [and] Leipzig" where Nietzsche's statement was taken seriously, are also cited.

48. Ibid., 46.

49. Ibid., 54–55. Philological and folkloric studies made the evolution of the German language central to the development of the German nation, but with the same implications for the Jews.

50. Weber, "National State," 437.

In a long note Weber denies that biological-racial characteristics themselves *determine* behavior and notes that his interest is all in the other direction, how "we" can shape racial characteristics, in the widest sense, for the future. He notes that anthropological investigations into biological race are as yet very inconclusive, although they "deserve more attention than they have been given, irrespective of all the reservations that have to be made."[51]

Weber's stress on the variety of factors that have to be taken into account in the formation of the nation was based on the theory that the nation is a *Mischvolk,* a theory that many intellectuals on both the right and left of the political spectrum used to oppose biological racialism. For example, in 1872 Ruldolph von Gneist opposed theories of the virtues of racial purity, claiming instead that language, customs, legal systems, and religion—that is, historical and cultural factors—form national character, not blood. From a biological-racial point of view, the culture of a nation is a *"mixtum compositum,"* and the intermixture of different racial origins actually promotes cultural growth and vitality. Von Gneist's remarks were originally published in 1872, but perhaps would have been more familiar to Max Weber through Hugo Preuss's later discussion of them in an important essay in *Die Nation* in 1887.[52] In the same year, 1887, von Gneist's speech of 1881 against political anti-Semitism was reproduced in the collection,

---

51. Ibid., 448–49n.4. Weber remained very interested in the possibility of racial explanations of social action to the end of his career. In 1908, in connection with his Protestant ethic thesis, he wrote essays on "The Psychophysics of Industrial Work" in which he made a sharp separation between "biological heredity," which might depend on "comparative racial neurology," and "environmental conditions" uncovered by "sociological and historical investigation," as two different kinds of factors to be taken into account in an explanation of work-discipline and productivity. In this article, and thereafter, he concluded that, for the present, our information on the former type of factor was too inconclusive to give sustained attention to the problem, and that for this reason all social research ought to be confined to the latter type of factor. See Oberschall, *Empirical Social Research in Germany,* 123–25, where reference is also made to similar remarks of Weber's in scholarly papers in 1913 and 1920. See also Max Weber, "Die protestantische Ethik," 24n; *The Protestant Ethic,* 30. There is no reason to think that Weber's better-known later elaborations of the concepts race, nation, and ethnicity depart in any important way from his position here. See his extended exchange with Alfred Ploetz at the 1910 meetings of the German Sociological Society, translated in two parts: "Max Weber on Race and Society"; "Max Weber, Dr. Alfred Ploetz, and W. E. B. Du Bois."

52. "Nationalität und Staatsgedenken"; Gneist's remarks originally came out in *Annalen des Deutschen Reichs;* all cited in Tal, *Christians and Jews,* 64n.

Kulturkampf (Berlin), which Weber was almost certainly familiar with, given his great interest in the *Kulturkampf*. In this speech von Gneist concluded, "When the Jews will give up their distinctiveness, we shall witness the final consummation of the emancipation."[53]

Throughout the 1880s and 1890s opponents of political anti-Semitism, including for example university professors Rudolph von Jhering and Albrecht Weber, used the *Mischvolk* argument about culture to justify the conclusion that Jewish identity should all but disappear, leaving only a small orthodox group. This, they thought, was consistent with the doctrines of liberalism as they understood them. Scholars who subscribed to racial doctrines, like Werner Sombart and the anthropologist from the University of Berlin, Felix von Luschan, used the *Mischvolk* argument in a closely related way, insisting on the complete effacement of ethnic and racial identity in order to strengthen the nation. Thus the idea that the nation is a *Mischvolk* was widely accepted by the mandarins on the right as well as the left, by social conservatives such as Hans Delbrück and liberals like Friedrich Meinecke.[54]

Another key to understanding Weber's use of the concept of race in promoting the national ideal is the term *Germanism,* which he uses to identify and isolate what he considers problematic, namely *Polonism.* In fact the issues of *Deutschtum,* nation, race, national minorities, and the Jewish question could hardly be separated. The most notorious immediate precedent for the by then common language of Germanism came during the *Antisemitismusstreit* that broke out in the 1880s in Berlin in the university and the press on account of Heinrich Treitschke's agitation for legislation that would exclude Jews from prominent positions in social life, on the assumption of the Christian character of the German state and society. Two of Weber's most prominent teachers, Treitschke himself and Theodore Mommsen, who took an important role in Weber's own dissertation defense, became major actors in these events. As a result of this debate Treitschke was compelled to work out his own position further in his annual course of lectures at the University of Berlin in the following years, including the year 1887, when Weber attended these lectures.[55] It is therefore worth pursuing the contemporary debate about anti-Semitism, a debate that took the form of arguments about the relation between Germanism and Judaism.

---

53. Quoted in ibid., 78f.
54. Cf. ibid., 64n.
55. Cf. Marianne Weber, *Biography,* 81–82.

This excursus will also provide an indication of the range of opinion at the time on the nature and significance of race, nationality and minorities, and the position of liberalism among German intellectuals within this range of opinion.

Treitschke published a series of four articles in the conservative *Preussische Jahrbücher,* of which he was editor, starting at the end of 1879 and, with replies to his Jewish critics, ending in early 1880. These articles were collected as a pamphlet later in 1880 as "A Word About Our Jewry" and reprinted four times by 1896.[56] The immediate context for Treitschke's articles was provided by the agitation of the court preacher Adolph Stoecker. Having attracted a poor showing for his reform speeches to workers in the previous year, Stoecker took a cue from the thousands of newspaper articles, pamphlets, and books written on the Jewish question in the seventies and initiated the anti-Semitic mass meeting in Berlin. In his first speech on "What We Demand From Modern Jewry," in September 1879, Stoecker castigated the Jews for misunderstanding the nature of their emancipation. It was not a license for them to behave as equals to Germans or even to surpass them. They are tolerated strangers, he said, and ought to conduct themselves accordingly.[57] While Treitschke could not agree with Stoecker's state-socialism (which Stoecker developed under Adolph Wagner's influence), nor with his religious rationales for reform, Stoecker's attempts to win the lower classes for church and monarchy was something Treitschke felt ought to be furthered. Taking up Stoecker's strategy of anti-Semitic demagoguery, Treitschke made Jew-baiting respectable among the highest circles by his personal initiative and participation in the dispute that followed. In particular he gave an important stimulus to the racist anti-Semitism of the student fraternities, even though he himself denounced racism.[58] By the end of 1880, both in and outside Berlin, insulting speeches

---

56. Excerpts from this and from the primary sources mentioned below by Marr, Stoecker, and Mommsen are translated in Mendes-Flohr and Reinharz, *The Jew in the Modern World.* I have relied mainly on Meyer, "Great Debate on Antisemitism," 137–70, and Liebeschütz, "Treitschke and Mommsen on Jewry and Judaism," for Treitschke's and Mommsen's roles in the *Antisemitismusstreit*; Liebeschütz's is a study of the *Judenbild* of each author in the context of their historiography as a whole, while Meyer's is a close study of the chronology of the events. For the general background of anti-Semitic thought and sentiment I have relied mainly on Katz, *Out of the Ghetto,* and *From Prejudice to Destruction*; and Ascheim, *Brothers and Strangers.*

57. Katz, *From Prejudice to Destruction,* 262.

58. Meyer, "Great Debate," 145–46; Massing, *Rehearsal for Destruction,* chapters 2 and 3; Liebeschütz, "Treitschke and Mommsen," 173.

in the streets as well as an increasing flood of anti-Jewish literature were agitating bands of hoodlums to stop Jewish-looking people from entering cafes and to provoke brawls and window-smashing in the name of German idealism; this continued into the following year, when a synagogue in Neustettin was burned down.[59]

Although Treitschke was a proponent of benevolent monarchy (as well as modern nationalism), the attitude he expressed toward Jews contains both liberal and anti-Semitic elements. As the concluding part of the *Preussische Jahrbücher* November current events summary, Treitschke's first article opens by asking whether all this agitation is nothing but "a momentary outburst, as hollow and irrational as the Teutonic anti-Semitism of 1819?"[60] His answer is negative, and he suggests instead that polite restraint about anti-Semitism amounts to a "*reverse* Hep-Hep call,"[61] referring to the rallying cry against the Jews that took its name from the 1819 riots. In western Europe this restraint might be understandable, because there are so few Jews there.

> But our country is invaded year after year by multitudes of assiduous pants-selling youths from the inexhaustible cradle of Poland, whose children and grand-children are to be the future rulers of Germany's exchanges and Germany's press. This immigration grows visibly in numbers and the question becomes more and more serious how this alien nation can be assimilated.[62]

The problem is compounded by the fact that western European Jews, who have for the most part successfully assimilated, are of Sephardic origin. "We Germans, however, have to deal with Jews of the Polish branch, which bears the deep scars of centuries of Christian tyranny. According to experience they are incomparably more alien to the European, and especially to the German national character."[63] These charges against the Jews were essentially the same as Stoecker's as well as racists' like Marr. What is important for our purposes, however, is that they involve a subtle blurring of attributes of the traditional Jew and the assimilated Jew, respectively,

---

59. Massing, *Rehearsal for Destruction,* 30, 40; Meyer, "Great Debate," 169.
60. Mendes-Flohr and Reinharz, *The Jew in the Modern World,* 281a.
61. Ibid., 280a.
62. Ibid., 281a.
63. Ibid., 281b.

into a single image.[64] Thus many of the old, Christian-inspired charges were freely combined with new, essentially secular fears of national diversity, by Treitschke and by many others of quite different explicit ideological bents. Treitschke himself had enjoyed close friendships with Jews for some time without speaking out against the Jews in general.[65] But when faced with the anti-Semitic movement he felt bound to justify it and felt no contradiction with these friendships, or with his support for Jewish emancipation, which remained intact:

> There is no German city which does not count many honest, respectable Jewish firms among its merchants. But it cannot be denied that the Jews have contributed their part to the promoting of business with its dishonesty and bold cupidity, and that they share heavily in the guilt for the contemptible materialism of our age which regards every kind of work only as business [i.e., a means to an end] and threatens to suffocate the old simple pride and joy the German felt in his work. In many thousands of German villages we have the Jewish usurer. Among the leading names of art and science there are not many Jews. The greater is the number of Semitic hustlers among the third rank talents. And how firmly this bunch of literateurs hangs together! . . . There can be no talk among the intelligent of an abolition or even of a limitation of the Emancipation. That would be an open injustice, a betrayal of the fine traditions of our state, and would accentuate rather than mitigate the national contrasts. What made the Jews of France and England harmless and often beneficent members of society was at the bottom nothing but the energy of the national pride and the firmly rooted national way of life of these two nations which look back on centuries of national culture. Ours is a young nation. . . . we are in the process of acquiring these qualities. . . . It is not possible to change the hard German heads into Jewish heads. The only way out therefore is for our Jewish fellow-citizens to make up their minds without reservation to be Germans. . . . The lack of . . . respect in many of our Jewish fellow-citizens in commerce and in literature is the basic reason for the passionate anger in our days.[66]

---

64. Ascheim, *Brothers and Strangers,* 68–69. Cf. also Katz's thesis that "In the crystallization of the anti-Semitic movement, the criticism of religion played no decisive role. The antiJewish motivations alone did the trick" (*From Prejudice to Destruction,* 267).

65. Meyer, "Great Debate," 143.

66. Mendes-Flohr and Reinharz, *The Jew in the Modern World,* 282–83.

In this statement can be seen both the instrumental environmentalism that goes back to Dohm's rationales for tolerance, and a justification for the intolerance that had become the predominant mood of the time. Nevertheless, Treitschke himself is less than intolerant; we find him conceding that "a complete solution" to the problem is impossible. "There will always be Jews who are nothing else but German speaking orientals," and Treitschke expresses his willingness to live with this situation, so long as the excesses he cites are sufficiently remedied.[67]

The first comprehensive response to Treitschke came from Moritz Lazarus, professor of ethnic psychology and a Jewish Reform community leader, in December of 1879.[68] In "What Does 'National' Mean?" Lazarus rejects Treitschke's unitary ideal of culture (*Einheitskultur*) for the ideal of a diversity of cultural values, arguing on this basis that Judaism strengthens the German national spirit. Lazarus was at the time engaged in an attempt to revive religious identification among the masses of apathetic Jews, and he sought to justify this program now by arguing that "Judaism is German just as Christianity is German."[69] In his response to Lazarus, Treitschke claimed that "Judaism is not as German as Christianity, for, unlike the latter, it has not through the centuries been 'intertwined with every fiber of the German character,'" as Lazarus had held. The medieval historian and right-wing liberal Harry Bresslau responded with a scholarly refutation of Treitschke's historical claims about the Jews in an open letter in 1880, "On the Jewish Question." Bresslau also rejected Treitschke's cultural monism, and noted German culture's de facto diversity from a long-term historical perspective. Bresslau made no claims for a special cultural role or religious value for Judaism. He faulted Treitschke for his failure to set forth proposals for acculturation, as all previous "anti-Jewish literature" had done, and asked Treitschke what the Jews ought to do.[70] In his response to Bresslau, Treitschke expressed surprise that his colleague on the Berlin faculty had (as had Levin Goldschimidt) become a Jewish spokesman instead of supporting his views.[71] Treitschke held out the hope that "the

---

67. Ibid., 283b.

68. Unless otherwise noted, the account below follows Meyer, "Great Debate," 145ff.

69. Tal, *Christians and Jews,* 56.

70. Among the many Jewish comments on Treitschke that followed, none questioned Bresslau's turning to Treitschke for advice.

71. Treitschke never doubted these men's Germanness, and thus his surprise (Meyer, "Great Debate," 144). Goldschmidt was Weber's dissertation advisor and a National Liberal deputy to the Parliament.

reconciliation of racial contrasts" would be accomplished by conversion and intermarriage, but nevertheless registered a note of skepticism in light of the fact that conversions had declined with the progress of emancipation. (In fact conversions annually doubled in 1880 over the previous five-year average.)[72] Hermann Cohen, the well-known neo-Kantian philosopher, entered the debate in order to speak out against this last point, for at this time he looked forward to religious amalgamation in a common Germanism, which he equated with Kantian ethics. Cohen argued for the equality of Jewish monotheism and Protestantism on the basis of the Kantianism they shared, a view that Treitschke harshly denounced later, in his *German History in the 19th Century* (1885).[73] Still, Cohen sided with Treitschke, arguing "physical unity [is] to be achieved by mixed marriages." Treitschke was pleased, but the Jewish press felt betrayed, especially by Cohen's demand that Jews acknowledge the historical significance of Christianity for reforming Jewish religion, and his expressed desire to look in complexion German rather than Jewish.[74] Ludwig Bamberger's statement, "Germanism and

---

72. Ibid., 166; Katz (*From Prejudice to Destruction,* 176) reports that conversions among Jewish intellectuals in the 1830s amounted to about two-thirds.

73. Liebeschütz, "Treitschke and Mommsen," 159, 173.

74. Actually, Cohen's view was more ambiguous: monotheism constitutes a common religious principle between Christians and Jews; Lutheranism has achieved the principle of internalizing the moral imperative, but historical reality has tied Judaism to German Christianity, making "religious differences" "inherent" in Germany's "historical tradition." These differences can be preserved "without detriment to the homogeneous national culture." Cohen said "we have no need to acknowledge the gospel of the Son of God, for we know that with all the need for humanizing morality there is also the need to preserve the original core of the God of the prophets, which no amount of humanization (*Vermenschlichung*) could eradicate. . . . all Christians are children of Israel." This brought him into conflict with Lazarus and Graetz, who thought Cohen was challenging the continued existence of a separate Jewish community. In response to them Cohen wrote that "the preservation of monotheism as a separate mission until a purer form of Christianity arises" is justifiable under present conditions, "but after the attainment [of this pure form, it will] be the common mission of all the monotheists." Cohen did not say how long the temporary need for Jewish religious and communal consciousness would last (Tal, *Christians and Jews,* 60–63). Later, Cohen left open a theoretical possibility that Germanism might not justify assimilation, when he said, "A Germanism which would demand from me that I divest myself of my religion and my religious inheritance,—such a Germanism I would not acknowledge as an ideal peoplehood with the right to the power and dignity of statehood. . . . Were I born into such a peoplehood or such a statehood, I would then regard myself as entitled to claim 'a publicly and legally insured home,'" referring with

Judaism," followed, setting forth a comprehensive theory of symbiosis of the two cultures. They shared common, ethnically conditioned features, such as spirituality, and an inclination for the cosmopolitan, the abstract, and for business, as well as complementary differences. Among the latter the German "deliberate, solemn, reverent, earnest, dutiful character contrasts with an amazingly versatile, sarcastic, skeptical, undisciplined spirit" of the Jews. Bamberger thus rejected the unitary ideal but, with Cohen, acknowledged the historical superiority of Christianity over Judaism for the Germans as a whole. The German-Christian state that Treitschke argues for is a lesser evil than socialism.[75]

Not far in the background in these discussions was the *Mischvolk* idea. Lazarus, Bresslau, Goldschmidt, Cohen, and Treitschke can all be seen as proponents of the idea, notwithstanding the fact that the pro-Jewish spokesmen all opposed Treitschke's political anti-Semitism. They actually interpreted the concept in a cultural way from the beginning, as referring to the mixing of cultures, in contrast to Treitschke (and Cohen), who saw racial mixing as a means of strengthening the common culture. Both Treitschke and Cohen thought that miscegnation would enhance German culture by making it unitary. Treitschke himself, therefore, is not a proponent of race purity. He clearly looks forward to benefits he thinks will accrue to "culture" once the biological types within the German population fully mix. His proposals for legislative exclusion of Jews are designed in part to accomplish this goal. However, the *Mischvolk* idea was also used to oppose political anti-Semitism by both Jewish spokesmen and non-Jewish liberal intellectuals. There remained, nevertheless, an important difference between the Jewish and non-Jewish liberals' use of the idea. Rabbi Manuel Joel, for example, attacked Treitschke by asking him whether he could "testify under oath that he is the direct descendent of the Germans who lived in the oak forests of Germany," some 1,800 years ago, and whether the English were not "a great nation . . . precisely because they are mixed?" Since Treitschke favored miscegnation, he could for his part find nothing to disagree with in Joel's anticritique. He responded to Joel by declaring, "the emancipation had a positive effect in that it deprived the Jews of all cause for justified complaints; but it also made miscegnation difficult, at all times the most effective means for the neutralization of tribal differences. The number of

this last phrase to the Basle platform of the Zionist Congress (quoted in Schwartzchild, "The Democratic Socialism of Hermann Cohen," 438).

75. Meyer notes that "the Jewish press was unqualified in its favorable opinion of [Bamberger's] article" ("Great Debate," 154).

converts to Christianity was greatly reduced, but intermarriages between Christians and nonconverted Jews will continue to remain exceptional as long as our people will regard Christianity with reverence." Harry Bresslau used outwardly identical language to counter Treitschke's claims about Jewish exclusiveness, when he said, to the contrary, that most German Jews were ready and willing "to be absorbed into the German nation." But Bresslau had in mind, in Uriel Tal's words, "a union of mutual interest and benefit between Judaism and Germanism and their reciprocal cultural influences," not the amalgamation of the Jews into the German ethnic group through miscegenation and so their eventual disappearance.[76] Even those more interested in the strictly biological aspects of race, such as Sombart and von Luschan, supported the conclusion that majority liberals drew from the *Mischvolk* principle, that the nation's vitality would be enhanced, this time by means of the intermingling of the different types of blood.[77]

However, a deeper issue underlay the differences between pro-Jewish spokesmen on the one side and majority liberals and conservatives on the other. This was their respective understandings of the nature of "culture" and its role in unifying the nation. All of these parties proceeded on the assumption that national social unity was one of the most, if not the most, pressing needs of the time. But minority and majority divided over the question of whether national "culture" is pluralist or unitary.

In one of his 1879 articles Treitschke had made a point of identifying Heinrich Graetz, the historian of the Jews, as typical of "a very influential segment of our Jewry" that resists assimilation. Graetz's response, in an open letter to the *Schlesische Zeitung* in the beginning of December, was vociferous, provoking Treitschke's rejoinder and another response by Graetz before the month was out. Treitschke had taken up the last part of Graetz's final volume of his *History of the Jewish People,* dealing with the period 1750 to 1848. Graetz's *History* was widely read as non-(German) nationalist and, worse, as asserting Jewish nationality. In this part of the *History,* Graetz expressed "his resentment against the Romanticism in Berlin, which had caused a wave of conversions," and as a radical, his "disappointment with the development of Germany's political affairs."[78] Ludwig Phillipson, a liberal and Reform Jewish leader, who had published all the previous volumes in his series, rejected this final one and rushed to repudiate its

---

76. Tal, *Christians and Jews,* 65–66.

77. Ibid., 64f.

78. Liebeschütz, "Treitschke and Mommsen," 173.

Jewish nationalism.[79] Jews who were indifferent about their religio-ethnic identity, like Cohen, Bamberger, Bresslau, and the jurist and economist H. B. Oppenheim, now tried even harder to distance themselves from Graetz's views, which Treitschke had caused to be regarded as representative.[80] In fact, only the religiously conservative rabbis came to Graetz's defense, even while they attacked his lack of piety. They alone among the Jewish parties of the 1880s realized that no matter how Jews changed socially or religiously, continued identification with the Jewish people or religion was inappropriate for a full-fledged German citizen in the eyes of German non-Jews.[81] Nevertheless, as a result of the internal reexamination of Jewishness caused by the controversy all parties rejected the concept of "nation" to describe persistent Jewish self-identification. Both Lazarus and Cohen defined Jewish identity through religion, as a sentimental attachment to the traditional faith; Bamberger saw it as a less voluntary attachment, rooted in heredity. Even the conservative rabbis insisted on a strictly eschatological identification with Zion, which for the foreseeable future was perfectly consistent with German loyalty. Bresslau argued that the Jewish question might be solved if "the conception of the Jew" were to be constructed on the basis of the characteristics of the majority of Jews, modest city inhabitants "who live in peaceful, middle-class diligence without the pretentious luxury of the moneyed aristocracy and without the filthy degeneracy of usury and peddling." But Christian Germans are too little acquainted with the Jewish majority, because "aside from the relationships of business and public life, [the Jewish community] is essentially confined to itself and restricted to intercourse within its own circle." Bresslau said this self-imposed isolation was the result of "many a bitter experience" of Christians' prejudice, which intimidated Jews.

Most Jewish respondents argued that anti-Semitism was an affront to each of them precisely as Germans, and they expressed their duty, in response to it, not to emigrate. Their general strategy was to publish non-Jewish critiques of Treitschke, which were considered for this reason "fully accredited witnesses." Internally, their advice was consistently that

---

79. On Phillipson, see Tal, *Christians and Jews,* 39–40 and passim.

80. Bamberger went so far as to call Graetz a "Stoecker of the synagogue," while Cohen, a former student of Graetz, in an address to students, called Graetz's judgments on "the German spirit" perverse and emotional, calling on the students to cultivate their German manner and sympathy for German greatness if they wished to become scholars (Meyer, "Great Debate," 156–57).

81. Cf. Liberles, *Religious Conflict in Social Context.*

Treitschke's views were a small minority and the German people would come to the Jews' defense. But there was also self-criticism. For example, Lazarus lectured his fellow Jews: "I rebuke [the Jews] for their lack of pride and self-consciousness. The absence of both manifests itself in conceit and ostentation, in pushing one's way into the higher levels of society where one pleases not according to what one is, but wants to please according to what one seems to be. I ask for more pride—from genuine pride comes true modesty."[82] By the end of 1880 the organization of liberal Jewish congregations, the *Deutsch-Israelitischer Gemeindebund,* issued rules for comportment, cultivation of character, and attitude to Gentiles. Read also among Christian circles, these suggestions, according to Meyer, "were welcomed as an indication of Jewish recognition of their shortcomings and desire for betterment."

The anti-Semitic movement made the charges of Jewish separateness into a self-fulfilling prophecy, an irony that would be repeated many times in the decades to come. To the reluctance to engage in uninhibited social intercourse noted by Bresslau was now imposed for the first time formal exclusion of Jews, by the student fraternities, ethical culture societies (the Masonic lodges), political associations and the formal parties, except the Libertarians (*Freisinnige*) and socialists (Social Democrats), and a further hardening in all areas of public administration, including the army and the universities, was imposed.[83] The street incidents and public defamations fueled by Treitschke's and others' activity continued throughout 1880 and reached a crescendo in November of that year, when the leading Berlin newspapers all published a declaration protesting the anti-Semitic actions that had occurred in its wake, signed by seventy-five Berlin notables following the mayor, and including seventeen professors and members of the Academy of Sciences (including Theodor Mommsen and Max Weber, Sr.),[84] and government officials, legislators, Lutheran clergy, and industrialists. This changed the climate decisively, for up to then three different protests from the Berlin Jewish community from as early as October 1879 to the Minister

82. Quoted in Meyer, "Great Debate," 164.

83. Katz, *From Prejudice to Destruction,* 270–72. Compare Katz's conclusion: "The exclusion of the Jews from such positions, perhaps even more than their social and political segregation [in centuries past], demonstrated their exceptional and precarious situation, recalling once again the notion of the pariah."

84. The list of signatories is published in Liebeschütz, *Das Judentum,* appendix; Meyer, "Great Debate," 168, has seventy-three signatories, based on contemporary reprints in the Jewish press.

of the Interior had received no reply. Now, under Moritz Lazarus's leadership, 200 Jewish notables of Berlin assembled on December 1, 1880, followed by a December 16 meeting of some 600, most of whom broke with their previous disinterest in Jewish affairs to condemn the charges of collective responsibility for financial improprieties and of national separateness. Other important non-Jewish groups met in protest. To preserve the honor of the capital 2,500 Berlin Landtag electors adopted a resolution on January 12, 1881, expressing indignation at the anti-Jewish excesses; 3,000 Berlin workers followed suit; a student committee was formed at Berlin University to fight anti-Semitism. In August, in the wake of the first Russian pogroms, the emperor himself ordered the authorities to apply the full force of the law to quell the anti-Semitic movement. This seemed to discredit the movement, for eight Jewish deputies were elected to the Reichstag the following October and the conservatives and anti-Semites lost ground. Finally, Bismarck broke his official silence to declare that he was no enemy of the Jews, and quiet returned to Berlin.[85] However, the aftermath of the anti-Semitic agitation, especially the linkage made between the alien Jew of the east (*Ostjuden*) and the dual loyalty of the German Jew, included the expulsion of Poles that took place from 1884 to 1887 under Bismarck's authority. Although the official orders applied to non-German Polish nationals, they in fact had incorporated the anti-Semitic demands by instructing border patrols to keep out "persons who looked undesireable." At an 1882 cabinet meeting Interior Minister Eulenberg had used this phrase, and Bismarck added that usurers should be expelled, thus clearly using the Polish question as a means of addressing the Jewish question, as Treitschke (and others) had done.[86]

Theodor Mommsen issued a statement on the Jewish question following the November declaration of the seventy-five notables. Mommsen's statement is important because it shows the limits of German liberalism at the time on the question of so-called national minorities. Mommsen's own liberal standpoint compares, in its general features, favorably with Max Weber's, upon whom Mommsen had a significant influence. Mommsen attacked Treitschke's suggestion that citizenship ought to be conditional on ethnic-German descent or on religious fidelity to orthodox Lutheranism. In fact, Mommsen suggests, Treitschke wants to limit genuine citizenship

---

85. Meyer, "Great Debate," 167–70; Liebeschütz, "Treitschke and Mommsen," 174, 176n.42.

86. Stern, *Gold and Iron,* 60–61.

to those who support the program of the current coalition of landowners and the clergy, as he does.[87] Against this, Mommsen points to the ethnic diversity of Germany's origins and the positive consequences of such diversity for the future:

> Our nation . . . would have to do without a lot more than just the Children of Israel if its current stock were to be corrected according to Tacitus' *Germania*. . . . only the central states are of truly Germanic descent, while *la race prussienne* is a mass actually made up of depraved slaves and other human refuse; it so happened that *la race germanique* and *la race prussienne* later combined to become the trailblazers for the German nation, and that all those who were retreating before them did not seem to notice any difference between them. Anybody who is really familiar with history will know that transformation of a nationality is a gradual development with numerous and manifold transitions.[88]

Treitschke had used Mommsen's claim, in his *Roman History,* that the Jews were a "ferment of national decomposition," to further his anti-Semitic argument, in his own response to the declaration of the seventy-five, but Mommsen here argues that its application to modern conditions actually shows the opposite:

> Just as the Jews were an element of national decomposition in the Roman state, so they doubtlessly are an element of tribal decomposition in Germany. That is why in the German capital, where the tribes mingle more freely than elsewhere, the Jews hold a position for which they are envied in other places. Such processes of decomposition are often necessary, but they are never pleasant. Their consequences are inevitably negative, in Germany less so than in Rome, because our nation is no pale chimera as the nation of the Caesars used to be. I am not so estranged from my homeland, however, that I do not painfully feel the loss of something I used to have and that my children will miss. But the happiness of children and the pride of men do not go together. A certain amount of mutual adjustment on the part of the tribes is necessary, resulting in the formation of a German nationality in which no tribal ingredient will be dominant. . . . I do not consider it at all unfortunate that the Jews have been active in this

---

87. Liebeschütz, "Treitschke and Mommsen," 175.
88. Mendes-Flohr and Reinharz, *The Jew in the Modern World,* 285a.

direction for centuries. It is my opinion that Divine Providence, much more so than Stoecker, has understood very well why a few percent of Israel ought to be added to the Germanic metal.[89]

Although Mommsen appears here to be a principled pluralist in his concept of nationality, a closer look reveals otherwise. For Mommsen, ethnic pluralism seems to be a transitional phase in the development of modern nations. On the one hand, the Jews play a providential role insofar as their cosmopolitan influence breaks down particularistic groups. But on the other hand the Jews, too, must relinquish their historical distinctiveness in order to finish the social task of unification that has begun in the political dimension.[90] The process of forming one nation of the many nations now contained in Germany puts certain demands on the Jews, notwithstanding the equal protections of the law, which Mommsen does not question.

> We cannot, however, protect the Jews from the estrangement and inequality with which the German Christian still tends to treat them. There is danger in this, as the present moment shows, for the Jews as well as for us—the danger of a civil war waged by a majority against a minority; even the possibility of such a war would be a national calamity. This, in part, is the fault of the Jews as well. The word *Christianity,* in our day no longer means what it used to mean; nevertheless it is the only word which still defines the entire international civilization of our day and which numerous millions of people of our highly populated globe accept as their intrinsic link. It is possible to remain outside these boundaries and yet live within the nation, but it is difficult and fraught with danger.[91]

The existence of "specifically Jewish societies," for philanthropy for example, societies that are not for "purely religious ends," Mommsen finds intolerable: "I view their separate existence as nothing more than an anachronistic phenomenon from the days of protected Jews [*Schutzjudenzeit*]. If such anachronistic feudal phenomena are to be abolished on the one side, they will have to disappear on the other side as well; and on both sides there

---

89. Ibid., 286a-b.

90. Compare Liebeschütz, "Treitschke and Mommsen," 176: "In Mommsen's view the amalgamation of the diverse groups joined together to form the 'Reich' was by no means complete. A campaign appealing to those instincts in man which produce antagonism and conflict in human society, is necessarily contrary to the most vital purpose of national policy." Cf. also Tal, *Christians and Jews,* 52.

91. Mendes-Flohr and Reinharz, *The Jew in the Modern World,* 286b.

is still much to be done."[92] "The people of Hanover, Hessen and Schleswig-Holstein," districts that were annexed in 1871, "are prepared to pay the price" of their separate group identity, and the Jews should be no different in this regard. Mommsen therefore calls on them to convert to the diluted form of Christianity he has described, in order to "tear down all barriers between themselves and their German compatriots."[93]

> He whose conscience—be it for positive or for negative reasons—does not permit him to renounce his Judaism and accept Christianity, will act accordingly, but he should be prepared to bear the consequences; issues of this nature can only be resolved in privacy, not in public. It is a notorious fact, however, that a great number of Jews are prevented from conversion not by their conscience, but by quite different emotions which I can understand but not justify.[94]

Mommsen turns out to be no more pluralist than Treitschke, because he shares the latter's underlying ideal of a nation ultimately based on a unitary culture, a secular national culture that has no room, in the end, for transitional, "anachronistic" subnational groups cultivating their own ethnic culture, on whatever grounds.[95] He seems to feel that religious distinctiveness, if it persists over generations, will become a ground for ethnic dis-

---

92. Ibid., 287a.
93. Ibid., 287b.
94. Ibid., 286b.
95. Compare Liebeschütz's conclusions, "Treitschke and Mommsen," 179–80. Graetz drew similar conclusions at the time about Mommsen and was roundly criticized by Bresslau, in a letter of 1885 to one of the heads of the Jewish *Gemeindebund*: "In his [Graetz's] judgment personalities like Treitschke and Mommsen are in complete agreement. The latter relegates Graetz's 'talmudic style of historical writing' to a literary corner and puts it . . . on the same level as ultramontane historical falsification" (quoted in Tal, *Christians and Jews,* 54n). Mommsen's position in the *Antisemitismusstreit* was read by liberal students as showing that there had to be "a merging of the less in the greater, of the worse in the better." They looked upon the resistance to this ideal represented by Jewish student corporations and *Vereine* as evidence of a general mentality of separatism, showing that the Jews bear primary responsibility for the Jewish question. The following statement is characteristic: "even today [the Jews lead] a pitiful separate existence and as a contribution to the perpetuation of the Jewish Question to all eternity, comes the very latest creation, the *Vereine Israelistischer Studenten,* which is gradually emerging at the universities"; from an anonymous article in *Die Grenzboten* in 1899, which Kampe says "was reprinted or discussed innumerable times throughout the corporation press" ("Jews and Antisemites," 85 and n. 168 there).

tinctiveness. Mommsen differs from Treitschke only in applying his unitary ideal critically to Christianity as well as to Judaism, for he says "if such anachronistic feudal phenomena are to be abolished on the one side, they will have to disappear on the other side as well." However, this reference to Christianity is probably confined to Catholicism, for in another article in the same month Mommsen likened modern anti-Semitism to the *Kulturkampf* and the class war as another stage in the struggle necessary to defend the German nation and culture.[96] His general point is that, if the effect of religion in promoting separate solidarity within the state is not remedied, then the demagoguery of a Stoecker or of a Treitschke threatens to escalate the antagonism of groups by appealing to irrational instincts and leading to a national calamity.

V

The same attitude toward minorities held by Treitschke and Mommsen is expressed in Weber's analysis of Polonism in the Freiburg address, and the address is motivated by the same overriding concern with social unification of the nascent German nation that impelled liberal demands, however gradualist, for complete Jewish assimilation. The Freiburg address represents a similar commitment to Germanism but in another context.

Weber's Freiburg address begins with a lengthy demonstration that Polonization is confined to the hilly regions and the districts dominated by large Junker monoculture farms (sugar beets or grain). This demonstration is based on an equation of religious affiliation (Catholicism and Protestantism) with nationality (Polish and German, respectively) and on the "language map" of the east. This shows that the Poles are the majority in the hills and the large estates and, on account of their exceptional rates of childbirth, they are fast increasing in numbers. Weber concludes from this that Poles have a superior "ability to adapt" to the poorest soil conditions and the most servile social conditions, on the large estates where they are housed in barracks. Both emigration and internal population increase are rooted in "*a lower expectation of living standards,* in part physical, in part mental, which the Slav race either possesses as a gift from nature or has acquired through breeding in the course of its past history."[97] On the other

---

96. Tal, *Christians and Jews,* 56. Weber was in the student corps at the time; for their reponse to pluralism, cf. above, pages 57ff.

97. Weber, "National State," 432.

hand, "Economic advance (*wirtschaftliche Kultur*), a relatively high standard of living and *Deutschtum* are in West Prussia identical."[98] A brief theory Weber proposes on minority assimilation suggests that, in the east, German Catholics are becoming Polish through intermarriage:

> Now a shift in the boundary between two nationalities can occur in two ways, which are fundamentally distinct. It may on the one hand happen that the language and customs of the majority gradually impose themselves on national minorities in a nationally mixed region, that these minorities get "soaked up." This phenomenon can be found as well in eastern Germany: the process is statistically demonstrable in the case of Germans of the Catholic confession. Here the ecclesiastical bond is stronger than the national one, memories of the *Kulturkampf* also play their part, and the lack of a German-educated clergy means that the German Catholics are lost to the cultural community of the nation.[99] But the second form of nationality-displacement is more important, and more relevant for us: *economic extrusion.* And this is how it is in the present case.[100]

The consequences of changes in the east are ethnic and cultural, but the causes of these changes are not. They are the result of processes that can be controlled by national social policy.

> Why do the German day-laborers move out? Not for material reasons. . . . The reason is as follows: there are only masters and servants, and nothing else, on the estates of his homeland for the day-laborer, and the prospect of his family, down to the most distant of his progeny, is to slave away on someone else's land from one chime of the estate-bell to the next. In this deep, half-conscious impulse towards the distant horizon there lies hidden an element of primitive idealism. He who cannot decipher this does not know the magic of *freedom.* . . . And why is it the *Polish* peasants who are gaining the land? Is it their superior economic intelligence, or their greater supply of capital? It is rather the opposite of both these factors. Under a climate, and on a soil, which favor the growing of cereals and potatoes above all, along-

---

98. Ibid., 430.

99. One of Bismarck's actions in the *Kulturkampf* in the 1870s was to impose western German Catholic clergy on the Polish parishes in the east, but with little success.

100. Weber, "National State," 432.

side extensive cattle-raising, the person who is least threatened by an unfavorable market is the one who brings his products to the place where they are least devalued by a collapse in prices: his own stomach. This is the person who produces *for his own requirements*.[101]

It is not just a matter of German competition with migrant labor; even the Polish independent peasant is at an advantage, for unlike his German counterpart, he lacks the industriousness to introduce a greenhouse and produce a surplus for the market. "The small Polish peasant gains more land [as a group], because he as it were eats the very grass off of it, he gains not *despite* but *on account of* the low level of his physical and intellectual habits of life."[102]

The conclusions for social policy are therefore clear: a free market policy, including open borders in the east, is the worst possible policy at this point, because this will only sustain the unfavorable outcome of competition with the German landworker. On the other hand, continued protection of the Junkers' estate-farming will exacerbate this outcome even further. "The rise of sugar-beet cultivation and the unprofitability of cereal production for the [international] market are developments running parallel and in the same direction: the first breeds the Polish seasonal worker, the second the small Polish peasant."[103]

There are, it follows, "two demands which in my view should be posed from the standpoint of Germanism." These are the closing of the eastern border, and a new program whereby the state would purchase good farmland specifically earmarked for colonization by German peasants. Both of these proposals, Weber thought, would further German "culture" in the east, by which he meant an increase in German-speaking Protestants at the expense of Polish-speaking Catholics.[104] In other words, Weber's proposals are designed to regulate the ethnic composition of the *Reich,* which he feared was being diluted.

The argument then quite noticeably changes tone. Weber has now twice explicitly distanced himself from the "economic class standpoint" of the "vulgar materialists," as well as from the free-trade standpoint, first with

---

101. Ibid., 432–33.

102. Ibid., 434.

103. Ibid., 435.

104. Note that the vast majority of the Poles were German citizens; they were not *Gastarbeiter.* For further background, cf. Hauschildt, "Polish Migrant Culture in Imperial Germany."

his conclusion that superior "physical and psychological qualities" (of Germans over Poles) do not necessarily lead to success in economic competition, and second, by noting how ironic it is that the "class conscious" Junker Bismarck closed the eastern border in the 1880s "in the interests of the maintenance of our nationality," but the bourgeois Caprivi opened them again, "in the interests of the big landowners, who are the *only people* to gain from this influx" of foreigners. Only a policy of cultural unity will make "national" economic success possible. For example, the success of the English and French nations had little to do with their early acceptance of free-trade or distributive models of the national economy. The English and French were successful, rather, because the important social classes in those countries early on achieved "political maturity," the willingness to act on "power instincts" to preserve the nationality of the state. Socialists and Progressives in Germany who emulate the revolutionary ideals of the Jacobin Convention lack such "instincts," and have therefore actually misunderstood those ideals:

> they are infinitely more harmless than they appear to themselves, for there lives in them not one glimmer of that Cataline energy *of the deed* which agitated the halls of the Convention. By the same token however they possess no trace of the Convention's tremendous *national* passion. Wretched political manipulators—that is what they are. They lack the grand *power* instincts of a class destined for political leadership.[105]

Weber makes a similar judgment about the "German proletariat," who he considers to be "politically uneducated philistines."

> Why is the proletariat of England and France constituted differently, in part? The reason is not only the longer period of *economic* education accomplished by the English workers' organized fight for their interests; we have once again what is above all a *political* element to bear in mind: *the resonance of a position of world power.* This constantly poses for the state great power-political tasks and gives the individual a political training which we might call "chronic," whereas with us the training is only received when our borders are threatened, i.e., in "acute" cases.[106]

---

105. Weber, "National State," 446. For Weber's repeated arguments for the harmlessness of the Social Democratic Party, cf. Mommsen, *German Politics,* 108ff.
    106. Weber, "National State," 446.

Turning to the Junker aristocracy, Weber scores their abuse of power, on account of which "the word 'Junker' resonates harshly in South German ears," and judges that nothing can "bring back their old social character."[107] Nor can the German bourgeoisie play the part of the leading class today, because it has assumed the "miserable countenance" of satisfaction with mere political unification.[108] The absence of "political maturity" in all the classes of German society sets the task for *Nationalökonomie:*

> there is an immense labor of *political* education to be performed, and no more serious duty exists for us than that of fulfilling *this* task, each of us in his narrow circle of activity. The ultimate goal of our science must remain that of cooperating in the *political* education of our nation. The economic development of periods of transition threatens the natural political instincts with decomposition; it would be a misfortune if economic science also moved towards the same objective, by breeding a weak eudaemonism, in however intellectualized a form, behind the illusion of independent "socio-political" ideals.[109]

It is difficult to overlook the allusion to anti-Semitic discourse in Weber's use of the metaphors of "decomposition" and "misfortune" to describe economic modernization in this passage; the first metaphor was introduced by Mommsen's discussion of the economic role of the Jews in antiquity, and was subsequently used by Treitschke to support his slogan, during the *Antisemitismusstreit,* that "the Jews are our misfortune." And yet Weber's concern for the political immaturity of the German classes (the main point

---

107. The decline of the Junkers is symbolized by "the partial failure" of Bismarck, who "intended to lead [us] not just to the external but to the inner unification of the nation, and, *as every one of us knows,* this has not been achieved" (ibid., 443, emphasis added).

108. See ibid., 444: "And after the nation's unity had been achieved, and its political 'satiation' was an established fact, a peculiarly 'unhistorical' and unpolitical mood came over the growing race of German bourgeois, drunk as it was with success and thirsty for peace. German history appeared to have come to an end. The present was the complete fulfillment of past millennia." Weber counters this with an alternative vision: "Over our cradle stood the most frightful curse history has ever handed to any race as a birthday-gift: the hard destiny of the political *epigone.*" The conflict Weber sets up here between competing transcendental meanings of the present is conspicuous, and always occurs at the points where he elaborates on the relation between the *Gründungsjahre* and the "demands" of current events.

109. Ibid., 447.

of the passage) was not unusual on the left, and was commonly expressed among those who spoke out against anti-Semitism. For example, Ismar Schorsch relates that

> [i]n 1892 Theodore Barth, a Progressive Deputy in the Reichstag, asserted that the real problem was not the inaction of the authorities but the exaggerated reliance of the people upon the government in the formation of their opinions. It was this extraordinary dependence upon authority that led Germans to conclude that an anti-Semitic demagogue must be at least partially right if the authorities ignored him. Barth insisted that freedom of speech requires a certain lack of sensitivity, a tolerance for the preposterous, a capacity for judgment without the paternal guidance of government. Germans were still wanting in the courage and maturity to exercise the right of free speech without official guidance.[110]

VI

In the course of his plea to the university community to undertake "an immense labor of political education," Weber offers the beginnings of a sophisticated construal of *Nationalökonomie* as something other than an abstract science. Looking back to Heinrich Braun's editorial essay for his own *Archiv* and forward to the editorial essay Weber himself will write upon taking over co-editorial responsibilities for Braun's journal in 1904, Weber proposes that *Nationalökonomie* can and should be based on cultural values, and these values are not, as critics have often charged, the values of eudaemonism, or the utilitarian principle of the greatest happiness for the greatest number.[111] Those who believe this, and are optimistic because

---

110. Schorsch, *Jewish Reactions*, 85.

111. "Certainly, the vulgar conception of political economy is that it consists in working out recipes for making the world happy; the improvement of the 'balance of pleasure' in human existence is the sole purpose of our work that the vulgar conception can comprehend. However the deadly seriousness of the population problem prohibits eudaemonism; it prevents us from imagining that peace and happiness lie hidden in the lap of the future, it prevents us from believing that elbowroom in this earthly existence can be won in any other way than through the hard struggle of human beings with each other" (Weber, "National State," 436). Note that the possibility of military conflict is completely lacking from the context.

of that belief, are captives of an "illusion." Weber seeks to shatter this illusion.

> As a science of explanation and analysis political economy is *international,* but as soon as it makes *value judgments* it is bound up with the distinct imprint of humanity we find in our own nature. . . . The economic policy of a German state, and the standard of value adopted by a German economic theorist, can therefore be nothing other than a German policy and a German standard. . . . We have witnessed a hitherto unimaginable growth in the present generation's interest in the burning issues of our field of science. Everywhere we find an advance in the popularity of the economic method of approach. Social policy has become the central preoccupation instead of politics, economic relations of power instead of legal relations, cultural and economic history instead of political history.[112]

Those who share the recent enthusiasm for *Nationalökonomie* have perhaps been led to expect some added power from its abstract method of analysis, over more traditional and direct analyses of policy. Such a view is misleading, for even the most abstract economic method harbors fundamental values which become the basis for explanation and analysis of events. Because these fundamental values remain implicit in the seemingly pure economic point of view, they go unanalyzed. The "national" political scientist cannot avoid such judgments of value; which judgments he will adopt is the only choice he has.

> A method of analysis which is so confidently forging ahead is in danger of falling into certain illusions and exaggerating the significance of its own point of view. This exaggeration occurs in a quite specific direction. . . . it is not the general rule, in fact it is well-nigh exceptional, for the maker of a judgment to clarify for others and *for himself* the nature of the ultimate subjective core of his judgments, to make clear the *ideals* on the basis of which he proceeds to judge the events he is observing; there is a lack of conscious self-inspection, the internal contradictions of his judgment do not come to the writer's notice, and where he seeks to give a general formulation of his specifically "economic" principle of judgment he falls into vagueness and indeterminacy. In truth, the ideals we introduce into the substance of our science are not peculiar to it, nor have we worked them out inde-

---

112. Ibid., 437 bottom, and 439.

pendently: they are *old established human ideals of a general type.* Only he who proceeds exclusively from the pure Platonic interest of the technologist, or, inversely, the actual interests of a particular class, whether a ruling or a subject class, can expect to derive his own standard of judgment from the material itself.[113]

Manchesterite economists had based an optimistic utilitarianism on the belief that, under modern conditions, principles of equitable social justice were called for and that, indeed, they were built into the method of free-market analysis. Economists of a more progressive mind sought to go beyond this and apply principles of distributive social justice in their analyses. Both trends developed in response to what were considered fundamentally changed conditions that warranted a departure from the selfish national conception of an economy whose ideal was closure. This led to protectionism and to disastrous results on occasion. Such negative consequences justified economists in searching for new ideals. Weber rejects this construal of the methodology of political economy completely:

> Has the situation perhaps changed since economic development began to create an all-embracing economic community of nations, going beyond national boundaries? Is the "nationalistic" standard of evaluation to be thrown on the scrapheap along with "national egoism" in economic policy? Has the struggle for economic survival, for the maintenance of one's wife and children, been surmounted now that the family has been divested of its original function as an association for production, and meshed into the network of the national economic community? We know that this is *not* the case: the struggle has taken on *other forms,* forms about which one may well raise the question of whether they should be viewed as a mitigation or indeed rather an intensification and a sharpening of the struggle. In the same way, the world-wide economic community is only another form of the struggle of the nations with each other, and it *aggravates* rather than mitigat[es] the struggle for the maintenance of one's own culture, because it calls forth in the very bosom of the nation material interests *opposed* to the nation's future, and throws them into the ring in alliance with the nation's enemies.

Weber considers it imperative to resist world market forces insofar as their free play threatens nationality, but also to constantly respond to these same

---

113. Ibid., 439–40.

international forces insofar as they can be used to enhance nationality. The maintenance of "national character" takes precedence over a policy of improved average economic well-being. Economic policy ought not to be designed to ensure economic autarky. This much of what progressive and Manchesterite economists have said Weber accepts. But for him the national ideal in economic analysis is not discredited, only misconstrued. The legitimate purpose of a national economic policy, Weber argues, is to achieve cultural autarky. This requires full participation in the international market to achieve that measure of national power that will allow Germany the "elbow room"—the political and economic conditions—to develop its particular culture.

> We do not have peace and human happiness to bequeath to our posterity, but rather the *eternal struggle* for the maintenance and improvement by careful cultivation of our national character. And we should not abandon ourselves to the optimistic expectation that we have done what is necessary once we have developed economic progress to the highest possible level, and that the process of selection in the freely conducted and "peaceful" economic struggle will thereupon automatically bring the victory to the more highly developed human type.[114]

Weber did not need to disabuse his audience of the "illusion" of an internationalist, cosmopolitan social ethic; the abstractness of "pure economic" analysis was already in disrepute and the social ethics of "Manchester*ism*" were already hotly debated. Weber dwells on these things mainly for rhetorical force. The real point he wants to drive home to his audience is a methodological one, and this is new: the alternative in social analysis is not between utilitarian economics and no political economy at all; we should not reject social science for its shortcomings and then feel free to speculate on the ends of social policy. Nor ought the problem-oriented social sciences be made free of values in order to purge from them the baneful effects of utilitarianism. Knowing that he has so far come close to reciting platitudes in flowery language, Weber continues:

> And is it so unnecessary for us, the younger representatives of the German historical school, to keep in sight these extremely simple truths? By no means, for we in particular are liable to fall victim to a special kind of illusion: the illusion that we can *entirely do without*

---

114. This and the last quotation are continuous from ibid., 437–38.

conscious value-judgments of our own. The result is of course, and the evidence is quite convincing on this point, that we do not remain true to this intention but rather fall prey to uncontrolled instincts, sympathies, and antipathies. And it is still more likely to happen that the point of departure we adopt in analyzing and *explaining* economic events unconsciously becomes determinant in our *judgment* of the events. We shall have to be on our guard lest the very qualities of the dead and living masters of our school to which they and their science owed its success turn in our case into weaknesses.[115]

Having demonstrated that "conscious value-judgments of our own" are implied in economic analysis, Weber now asserts, "There is only one *political standard of value* which is supreme for us economic nationalists," and that is the idea of "political maturity." As applied to economic-class analysis, the idea refers to a class's "understanding of the lasting economic and political interests of the nation's power and [its] ability to place these interests above all other considerations if the occasion demands." Power is necessary to exercise in order to ensure "elbow room," not in any simple territorial-imperialist sense, but rather in the sense of securing the territorial conditions under which *cultural* development can flourish. With these concepts in mind, the two "illusions" mentioned previously are now brought together: "one of the delusions which arise from the modern over-estimation of the 'economic' in the usual sense of the word [occurs] when people assert that feelings of political community cannot maintain themselves in face of the full weight of divergent economic interests, indeed that very possibly these feelings are *merely* the reflection of the economic basis underlying those changing interests."[116] It is true that "in normal times this political instinct sinks below the level of consciousness for the masses" and must therefore become the responsibility of a specific class. But "great moments," such as war, show that "the national state rests on deep and elemental psychological foundations within the broad economically subordinate strata of the nation as well, that it is by no means a mere 'superstructure.' "[117] It is these deep foundations that, for Weber, both arise from and must be nurtured by "cultural" development.

---

115. Ibid., 440.
116. Ibid., 442.
117. Ibid.

VII

Weber's Freiburg address came at the height of a debate over closing the eastern borders to "Poles" (*Grenzschluß*). An occasionally stated and more often tacitly understood purpose of *Grenzschluß* was to stop *Ostjuden* from migrating into Germany, in the wake of pogroms in the east, and to hasten the integration of German Jews through miscegenation. Treitschke had argued this in 1880, expressing regret at what he thought was the slow pace of Jewish intermarriage. As a result of the *Antisemitismusstreit,* up to 1895 and beyond, it was impossible to take up the problem of *Grenzschluß* without directly taking a position on the *Judenfrage*. In 1895 the expulsion of nonnaturalized Poles resumed, after an open-border respite under Caprivi.[118] In the same year the radical anti-Semite Hermann Ahlwardt proposed *Grenzschluß* in the Reichstag with the following words:

> The Jews have lived here for seven hundred to eight hundred years, but have they become Germans? Have they ever placed themselves on the soil of labor? Have they ever dreamed of doing such a thing; as soon as they arrived they started to cheat and they have been doing that ever since they have been in Germany. . . . The Jew is no German. If you say he was born in Germany, he was nursed by a German wet nurse, he abides by German laws, he has to serve as a soldier . . . then I say that all this is not the crucial factor with regard to his nationality; the crucial factor is the race from which he stems. Permit me to make a rather trite comparison which I have used elsewhere in my speeches: a horse that is born in a cowshed is far from being a cow.[119]

Ahlwardt was a racist, and accordingly this kind of rhetoric closed the door to Jewish assimilation and thoroughly blurred any distinction between *Ostjuden* and German Jews. But this was hardly new; Treitschke had already given clear expression to the association of "Jews" and "Poles," and that association was echoed over and over in the popular pamphlet literature and in speeches. The anonymous and inflammatory *Israel und die Gojim* in

---

118. Hagen, *Germans, Poles, and Jews,* 176–77.

119. Ascheim, *Brothers and Strangers,* 75–76. The speech is reprinted in full in Massing, *Rehearsal for Destruction,* 300–305. In the Reichstag session the Catholic deputy Ernst Lieber spoke out against the motion to close the border to Jews, pointing out that this was intended "to be but the first step toward a general solution to the Jewish question" (ibid., 295).

1880 supported border closing in the east by reference to the Talmud's injunction to hate the Gentile.[120] A halt to immigration of alien Jews was a major demand in the 1881 Anti-Semite's Petition.[121] In 1885–86 the *Ostjuden* were in fact expelled from Prussia. Reichstag member Pickenbach called this "a first step toward the solution of the Jewish question."[122] The liberals also supported these actions, but as a means to encourage the gradual assimilation of German Jews. The same reasoning had been applied to Germanization of the Poles in the east, which the Progressive deputy Rickert described in 1886 as "the reconciliation of the nationalities."[123] The linkage among assimilating German Jewry, *Ostjuden,* and the Polonization of the east had therefore changed little in the 1890s.

With the Freiburg address Weber injected a new argument into the debate over the closing of the eastern border. Weber's contribution to the debate over *Grenzschluß* takes the typical liberal view of racial mixing, but it remains unusual in that he fails to mention the Jews at all. The main point of Weber's arguments on the landworker question is to isolate the purely economic aspect of the "denationalization" of the east. He is not talking about the whole of Germany. And at this time he apparently sees no threat from the Jews to German nationality east of the Elbe. Polonization is the unforseen result of a competition among the *peasantry* in the east, brought on by shortsighted protectionism. Against the background of the anti-Semitic movement, therefore, the significance of Weber's arguments and polemics leading up to the 1895 Freiburg address is that they clearly *distinguish* the Polish question from the Jewish question. Much later, he showed he was concerned with the *Ostjudenfrage* when, during the war, he wrote to Franz Eulenberg, arguing against the incorporation of Poland explicitly to avoid "free movement of those Jews across our borders."[124] Weber was probably in agreement with Eugen Ehrlich, a legal scholar and Jew, who wrote in *The Tasks of Social Policy in the Austrian East* (1909) that

---

120. Cited in Ascheim, *Brothers and Strangers,* 61–62.

121. Ibid., 60.

122. Ibid., 77.

123. Hagen, *Poles, Germans, Jews,* 156. As should be apparent by now, Weber was not as gradualist as this on the Polish problem.

124. Mommsen, *German Politics,* 220n.109. At this time, Weber may have shared the common view that "Russians" and "Jews" were identifiable; on this cf. Ascheim, *Brothers and Strangers,* 46. For example, Weber regarded Georg Lukacs "as a typical product of the Eastern European political sphere and cultural milieu" (Vermes, "Buber-Lukacs Correspondence," 369–78).

the movement of *Ostjuden* westward threatened to interrupt the assimilation of German Jews.[125] However, in 1895, by focusing all his attention on the competition among the peasantry, Weber detached the Polish question from the Jewish question. The problem in the east, he argues implicitly, has to do with a Polish-German, not a Jewish-German struggle.

It would be a mistake to take this as demonstrating a moderation in Weber's nationalism. Rather, it shows the opposite. Thus, when Weber joined the Pan-German League in 1893, he did not oppose its volkish nationalism; he was looking for support for his position on the Polish question. He was able to labor successfully within the League for inclusion of his policy proposals on border closing and a new settlement policy, which they adopted at their first convention in 1894. When he broke with the pan-Germans in 1899 it was because of the demagoguery of Heinrich Class, which led the League to call for repressive measures against the Poles, not just the economic ones Weber proposed, and because, under Class's leadership, the pan-Germans had begun to ally themselves with the agrarian conservatives. Weber felt that this last move made the League unable to be " 'uncompromisingly' national on the Polish question," as he put it.[126] Much later, in 1911, he distanced himself from the extreme and, as he called it, "entirely empty and hollow sorts of purely zoological nationalism" of the fraternities for similar reasons. The students' nationalism represented "a lack of conscience on all great cultural questions," and their demonstrations poorly compensated for "the total lack of any cultural ideal and the shameless narrowing of their spiritual horizons."[127] Yet in his own

---

125. According to Ehrlich, if the migrations did not "at every moment carry a new, uncomfortable problem to the West, no one would be thinking about the Jewish problem" (Ehrlich quoted and discussed in Ascheim, *Brothers and Strangers,* 47).

126. Mommsen, *German Politics,* 54–56. Weber's letter of resignation, where he makes this case, is reprinted in Marianne Weber, *Biography,* 224–25. The first president of the Pan-German League was Ernst Hasse, a professor and National Liberal who in the 1895 Reichstag denounced the anti-Semites. Cf. H. Ahlwardt's rejoinder, reprinted in Massing, *Rehearsal for Destruction,* 300–305. Also, despite their populist aspirations, the pan-Germans adhered to the mandarin elitism Weber shared. See Chickering, *The Pan-German League,* 300: "The Pan-German League never abandoned the view that academic education, *Bildung,* and direct access to German culture entitled the men who had it to precedence and authority in the public realm."

127. Letter to the Freiburg faculty, quoted in Mommsen, *German Politics,* 65–66.

position supporting Germanization in the east, Weber's twin commitments to liberalism and nationalism are characteristically mixed. On the one hand, his commitment to an open-class struggle, within a regime brought under the rule of law, led Weber to propose that the state create the economic conditions for free competition of peasants in the east. But these must be "German" peasants, not "Polish" peasants; Weber would even exclude *naturalized* Poles. Here the liberalism of Weber's proposals reaches its limit, a limit defined by his nationalism.

We may well ask whether Weber's position on the Polish question is not rooted in the same values, more precisely, the same ideal for society, as Treitschke's and Mommsen's positions on the Jewish question, whatever other differences exist among them. Their *Einheitskultur* ideal is a common element among many otherwise strongly differing parties to the disputes over social problems in Imperial Germany. The recognition of this underlying agreement was even expressed by Weber himself, in his critical evaluation of Treitschke. The usual interpretation of Weber's relation to Treitschke lays great stress, after Marianne Weber, on the young Weber's denunciation of Treitschke's inflammatory lecture style, and the putative effect this had on the mature Weber's strenuous appeal for "value-freedom" in scholarship and in scholarly presentations, especially from the lectern.[128] However, Weber always had great admiration for Treitschke, despite the fact that his repugnance for Treitschke's tactical use of anti-Semitism was very real. In the letters he wrote to his uncle, Hermann Baumgarten, while attending Treitschke's lectures in 1887, Weber argued that, if one could bracket the public mood of "brutality" Treitschke was so adept at—and shamelessly—appealing to, his "idealism" was really quite admirable.

> . . . then the countless, often glaring instances of one-sidedness, the vehemence of the struggle against other views, and the predilection for what is today called Realpolitik . . . would not be the only things that students derive from Treitschke's lectures. They would reserve their judgment on such things, or they would regard them as disagreeable excesses; but in all this, and sometimes even in these very

---

128. Thus, for example, Liebeschütz, "Treitschke and Mommsen," 173–74. See Marianne Weber, *Biography,* 119–20, 317–318. In the latter place Ms. Weber cites, significantly, a passage from Max Weber's 1913 paper on "value-freedom" that mentions *both* Treitschke *and* Mommsen as among "the most passionate" scholarly orators. Interestingly, in the passage it is not they who come in for the brunt of criticism, but rather those academics who are *less* explicit in their personal judgments.

excesses of political passion and one-sidedness, they would discern the man's great and ardent striving for an idealistic basis, and some of this they would carry away with them.[129]

It was not just the uncontrollable emotionalism that Treitschke's anti-Semitism led to that Weber took issue with. Like Barth's denunciation of anti-Semitism, Weber says that Treitschke's style obscures for students the most pressing political tasks for the nation that lay ahead: "my admirable generation," he wrote sarcastically to his uncle, "limits its regard for such matters either by making common cause with anti-Semitism . . . or, and this is the higher level, they think it meaningful to style themselves as 'Bismarck sans phrase.' "[130] The young Weber's reaction to Treitschke is, then, a mixed one; he condemns the method of conveying the message, but defends the ultimate aims of the message.

The same evaluation of Treitschke can be found in the mature Weber. I have already referred to Weber's 1913 statement.[131] In "Parliament and Government in a Reconstructed Germany," written in 1917 and revised in 1919, Weber made explicit reference to Treitschke's "unitary ideals" in the context of a discussion of the *Reichsgründerjahre*. He asserts that the National Liberal Party's commitment to such ideals set them against Bismarck on the question of constitutional reform at the time, and he expresses regret that "we have abandoned [such ideals] in the meantime, in part for nonpolitical reasons." Finally, referring to the actual unification of the Reich, Weber concludes: "At any rate, the later developments have *completely vindicated* the basic political premises of the National Liberals."[132] That is, the hope of National Liberals during the *Reichsgründerjahre*, that political unification would lead to a wider commitment to German "culture," had in Weber's mind been vindicated by national developments up to and

---

129. Marianne Weber, *Biography*, 120. The letters are excerpted in Mommsen, *German Politics*, 8–9, including the one quoted at length by Marianne Weber, ibid.

130. Cited in Mommsen, *German Politics*, 8.

131. However, the context is as much tactical—the preservation of the prestige of German learning—as it is a straightforward demand for objectivity in science (see on this Ringer, *Mandarins*, 352–66). For the background to Weber's concept of "objectivity" itself, see the next chapter.

132. In the appendix to Weber, *Economy and Society*, 1388 (emphasis in original). Roth's clarifying footnote to this passage, detailing the constitutional debate at the end of the 1860s, rather obscures the significance of this as an expression of basic identification with Treitschke's social values.

especially including World War I. These statements suggest strongly that Weber always considered there to be a kernel of truth buried in Treitschke's often insulting statements on national policy, and that this kernel was his secular integral nationalism.[133]

VIII

German *Polenpolitik* forced the Poles into a position of national solidarity against German oppression and helped create a following for the Polish nationalist movement after 1890. It made it respectable for the movement to become increasingly pan-Polish, inspired by a revolutionary hope for a restoration of a unified Poland across the Austrian-, Russian-, and German-occupied territories. Although most Poles in eastern Germany continued to look to their gentry and clergy for leadership and to the demand for home rule rather than irrendentism, the nationalist movement, powered by Germanization policy from the west, succeeded in discrediting the Polish conservatives as collaborationists at worst, at best as compromisers with the German government. The radicals' call for a Polish revolution, however, only hardened the German government's attempts to force the Poles off the land, and this in turn heightened nationalist aspirations among all classes of Poles.[134]

After the turn of the century, von Bülow's regime presided over another wave of repression, replacing Polish with German in even the teaching of religion in elementary schools, where alone it had been tolerated since 1898. Waves of language conversion efforts, followed by more and more massive strikes by Polish elementary school students, marked the period up to 1907. Meanwhile the colonization effort floundered due to competition with the Poles' own parcelization and credit institutions, as well as their boycott of German business. This successfully kept land in Polish hands, drove up land prices, and forced the Colonization Commission to target Junker estates for reparcelization to German peasants. The net result was that Polish landholdings in Posen expanded at German expense. In exasperation, the government sent a law for forcible expropriation of the Polish gentry to the Reichstag in 1908, passed with the support of the National Liberals, Free Conservatives, and agrarian Conservatives, but opposed by both the Pro-

---

133. Other commonalities between Weber and Treitschke, supporting this conclusion, are brought out by Factor and Turner, "The Limits of Reason and Some Limitations of Weber's Morality," 317–19.

134. Hagen, *Poles, Germans, and Jews,* 225–38.

gressives and the Catholic Center Party as an "exceptional law," a law violating the *Rechtstaat* principle. Both international and domestic criticism of this blatantly repressive measure forced the government to postpone the law's application until 1912. But the government's *Polenpolitik* had definitely turned from the Bismarckian conception of Germanization as a struggle between Prussian and Polish gentries, to the ethnic-nationalist conception that Germanization primarily meant ethnic hegemony over the region. This change in the terms of the Polish question, in Hagen's words, "justified depriving the Poles of national toleration and stripping away their civil rights as Prussian and Reich citizens."[135] These were precisely the terms Weber had laid down in 1895, and these aims were his aims as well. Within ten years of the Freiburg address, the government's *Polenpolitik* had shifted completely from Bismarckian to Weberian grounds.

Wolfgang Mommsen has argued that, after the Freiburg address, a "basic reversal in his position on Poland" can be found in Weber's writings. This occurred, according to Mommsen, because Weber became more and more committed to the *Machtstaat* and German imperialism, at the expense of his early commitment to the *Kulturstaat*.[136] However, the evidence Mommsen brings to bear on this thesis shows that the change in Weber's views was wholly tactical, motivated by the need to respond to changed circumstances.

The liberal nationalists who agitated for Germanization in the east were themselves westerners, they did not live in eastern Germany. They organized themselves in 1894 as the "H-K-T Society," or Hakatists, and Weber became a founding member, giving speeches at their meetings, as did many nationalist German academics then.[137] They did not control government policy, but rather developed a liberal ideology for its repressive actions. To this end they adopted nearly all the principles laid down in Weber's 1895 analysis and turned these into the slogans "large estates Polonize," "economic struggle" with the Poles in the east, and "industry Polonizes" (because Poles will work for lower wages than Germans).[138] This was a "liberal" ideological campaign because the Hakatists avoided racial terminology and, above all, because their stated goal was to promote the gradual assimilation

---

135. Ibid., 193–94.

136. Mommsen, *German Politics,* 53.

137. See Tims, *Germanizing Prussian Poland,* 261ff.; also Chickering, "Dietrich Shäfer and Max Weber," 334.

138. Cf. Hagen, *Germans, Poles, and Jews,* 266–84; and Marianne Weber, *Biography,* 135, for the last slogan.

of Poles by driving them out of their ethnic stronghold in the east economically. The strong arm of the state was a legitimate tool to achieve this; indeed it was their only hope. In contrast to these liberal nationalists, conservative agitation was directed against the Polish gentry, whose estates they wanted to expropriate, but not against the Junkers, in whose interests they sought to preserve Polish peasantry as a source of cheap labor. But the liberal German nationalist ideologues feared this would only galvanize the Poles' seemingly tenacious ethnic identification. Rather than forced expropriation, they conceived *Germanisierung* to be a policy that left the Polish masses no choice but to migrate westward, where they would become attracted to German culture and voluntarily assimilate. As one of their leaders put it in 1907:

> The issue is not the Poles' rights, but entirely justifiable German claims. We want to force the Poles out of their landholdings in the eastern marches as completely as we possibly can. . . . If they can't make a living here, they're entirely free to settle down somewhere else in the German Empire . . . where they will very quickly become Germanized.[139]

Germanisierung had become a program for assimilation of the Poles, their economic extrusion from the land had become the principle means to that end.

Weber remained associated with the Hakatists up to and during the war. One vehicle the Hakatists hoped would accomplish their goals was the German Cooperative Bank, established to prop up German business in the east, which suffered particularly from the Polish boycott, as well as to help the German peasantry. In 1915 its director was Leo Wegener, one of Weber's former students and a particularly strident Hakatist. In his *Wirtschaftlicher Kampf* (1909) Wegener argued, following Weber, that the government needed to help Germans win their economic competition with Poles in the east in order to preserve *Kultur*.[140] Marianne Weber reports that by 1915 Wegener had become "particularly devoted" to Weber, who no doubt offered his counsel.[141] But by this time a wide spectrum of

---

139. *Justizrat* Wagner, at an Executive Committee meeting of the German Society for the Eastern Marches, in Bromberg (quoted in Hagen, *Germans, Poles, and Jews,* 274).

140. Ibid., 274.

141. Marianne Weber, *Biography,* 244, 553; on Wegener, cf. Hagen, *Germans, Poles, and Jews,* 275, 375n.31.

nationalist intellectuals, like Ludwig Bernhard (whose *Die Polenfrage: Das polnische Gemeinwesen im preussischen Staate* [1908] was very influential) and Gustav Schmoller (who wrote in his *Jahrbuch* in 1913 of the Poles' intent to secede, with little basis in fact), as well as more actively Hakatist writers, were openly responding to their fear of the nationalist movement among the Poles.[142] Conceding the strength of Polish nationalism became even more important after August 1915, when Germany and Austria took Congress Poland from Russia. For then it became a question of winning Polish loyalty as a bulwark against Russia.

Weber had come to this position much earlier than other liberal nationalists. After the turn of the century, Weber studied the Russian Zemstvo liberals' attempts to promote Polish autonomy, which he thought was designed to extend the Russian empire. By 1908 Weber thought this strategy should be adopted by Germany as well, lest the Russians' westward imperial expansion succeed at the expense of Germany. At this time, because he thought it was a question of who was going to win the Poles' allegiance, Germany or Russia, he opposed the language laws as "morally and politically impossible" (a view both the Poles and the German Progressive Party took in much stronger terms in the 1890s, when Weber was on the opposite side of this question).[143] But he also continued to favor "the unlimited right of expropriation" in order to settle German peasants in the east. By this Weber meant that the state should be free to expropriate land from both the Polish gentry and the Junkers. He says that only if that is done can the Poles be "offered a national compromise involving recognition of their 'cultural autonomy.' "[144] Yet he had not backed away from the *Kulturstaat* principle. His later position on the Polish question amounts to an admission of failure in the "cultural" struggle, in the wider Weberian sense,

---

142. Hans Delbrück, University of Berlin history professor and Free Conservative Reichstag deputy, blew up at Weber's self-described "matter-of-fact" polemics against Bernhard's appointment at Berlin in *Nationalökonomie,* in the *Frankfurter Zeitung* in 1908, probably because he saw through Weber's prose to his antipathy for Bernhard's earlier blaming the Hakatists for Polish unrest, in *Die Polenfrage.* Weber's three letters to the *Frankfurter Zeitung* are in Shils, *Weber on Universities,* 4–14, with an extensive summary of Delbrück's response, "Academic Muddle," in the *Preussische Jahrbucher,* which he edited.

143. As Hagen shows, Polish activists used the idea of "self-determination" as a rationale to maintain their distinctiveness within Germany as a nation-state, to which they remained devoted. Weber never countenanced this principle, which conflicted with his cultural integralism.

144. Letter to Naumann in 1908, in Marianne Weber, *Biography,* 401–2.

and a turn to a fall-back strategy designed, as in the 1890s, to preserve "elbow-room" in Prussia. This was part of a larger strategy he proposed, to secure a ring of German satellite states against Russia, which he still called so many "cultural tasks in the east."[145] Consistent with this view, during the war Weber wrote that "a state [need] not necessarily be a 'nation state' in the sense that it [orients] its interests exclusively in favor of a single dominant nationality. . . . [It can] serve the cultural interests of several nationalities in a way that [is] in full harmony with the interests of the dominant nationality."[146] What had changed was the eastern Poles' economic tenacity, which was based on their successful creation of exclusively Polish economic institutions and their use of the boycott against Germans, and these actions were motivated by a new-found nationalist feeling. This consideration underlies Weber's change in thinking, which paralleled the changes the H-K-T Society itself went through, finally accepting the Central Powers' creation of a Polish Kingdom in November 1916, two years before the end of the war.[147] After the defeat, in November 1918, Posen went into civil war between Germans and Poles, and the Hakatist Society came to be widely blamed even among former members for long fanning the Poles' animosities toward Germans. In the spring of 1919 the Versailles Treaty awarded nine-tenths of Posen and most of West Prussia to the Polish Republic, including all the farm colonies and subsidized towns funded by the Royal Colonization Commission and H-K-T monies. Hakatism and shrill anti-Polish campaigns, including in particular the society's promotion of the language policy, was now thoroughly discredited.[148] This fact is

---

145. Mommsen cites a lecture Weber gave in Munich on October 22, 1916, "Search for Security in the West—Cultural Tasks in the East" (*German Politics*, 206; but cf. pp. 205–27 passim for the whole development of Weber's views on this during the war.

146. "Die Polen-Politik," from the *Frankfurter Zeitung*, February 1917, quoted ibid., 59. (The bracketed insertions are Mommsen's.) Weber proposed in this article a cooperative arrangement with Poland whereby "voluntary relocation of German settlers from the kingdom of Poland to Germany and the reverse" would be encouraged. Mommsen himself notes that elsewhere, even at this time, Weber proposed "demarcation of local settlement regions" in the east.

147. Tims, *Germanizing Prussian Poland*, 273–76. The leaders of the Hakatist Society early in the war wanted a *Polen-frei* "belt of German colonists . . . extending German domination into Russia's Baltic provinces" (p. 274).

148. Nevertheless, according to Tims, "the availability of the 'Polish corridor' as an inflammatory issue in German politics during the next twenty years [i.e., until at least 1939] was due in part to the intensive cultivation of German minds

probably the most important reason why Weber's views on the Polish question are generally obscured by his biographer and most of the memoirs written after Weber's death in 1920.

The changes in Weber's position from the 1890s to the war are due, therefore, to changing world conditions, not to any basic change in his social outlook. Weber's wartime position on the Polish question retains the ethnic definition of nationality, and the national definition of the state's purposes, although (as Mommsen argues) there is a less than absolute identification of state and nation as such.[149]

Weber's Freiburg address worked out a combination of modern nationalism and commitment to a modern open-class society that would animate his later contributions to a variety of areas of sociological analysis. On the one hand, Weber's rhetoric was distinctively liberationist: he argued for policies that would free persons from all kinds of secondary social groups that stood between the individual and the state. On the other hand, he had definite ideas about what this freedom was for and he did not often appreciate how far he was in fact proposing with these ideas a massive set of constraints on otherwise free citizens. Weber wanted individuals to be "free" to adopt the dominant ethnic-national identity, and if certain groups did not immediately appear to be disposed to such a choice, he thought that they should be encouraged, even forced, to make that choice by state policy. The liberation of the individual had this higher purpose, which Weber considered to be the great "cultural task" of his time. Even Weber's commitment to the power interests of the state was ultimately an instrumental one, motivated by his continued concern for preserving a national culture. The *Machtstaat* was the means for achieving the "elbow-room" that the *Kulturstaat* required. This view is nicely summarized by Weber in his 1916 article "Between Two Laws." Consistent with his Freiburg address, he argues there that, by the "laws of this world," which include

---

by the H-K-T movement in the generation that went before" (ibid., 278). See further for the unintended xenophobic effects of Hakatist education, Rosenthal, *German and Pole: National Conflict and Modern Myth,* 39–68.

149. In 1915, in an article on "The Triple Alliance and Russia," as summarized by Mommsen, "Weber rejected a return to the 'idea of the state,' as we now would call it; it would be impossible, he thought, since all culture was unavoidably nationally tied, to put the 'idea of the state' in the 'place of nationality.' Much as Weber emphasized the state's identification with power, he was not prepared to give up the state's *national* definition" (Mommsen, *German Politics,* 59–60). I view Mommsen's conclusion here as inconsistent with his claim that Weber's position on the Polish question underwent a "basic reversal."

"the possibility and unavoidability of wars for power for the foreseeable future, the preservation of national culture is linked necessarily to power politics."[150]

The idea of the *Kulturstaat* remained a fundamental presupposition of Weber's social outlook throughout his career. He never admitted the possibility of a civic culture that would embrace plural "ethnic" or "national" cultures. The full inclusion of a variety of ethnic or national groups within a common civic life was for him a contradiction in terms and conflicted specifically with his image of a modern society. For Weber, social unification in Germany had to be based on acceptance of a common culture and the hegemony of a dominant ethnic group. The achievement of this goal was, for him, no less pressing than economic and political liberalization. Weber's "solution" to this problem, more often implicit than explicit, is to tie the ethnic nationality of Germany to German *culture*. However, this is a more or less conscious intellectual construction, a theoretical ideal. For Weber's proposals for a nationalist social policy hold out the preservation of German culture as an *aspiration for the future*. German "national character," *Deutschtum,* which Weber wants to preserve, was at this time in the process of formation. Important conflicts remained unresolved among Catholics, Jews, Lutheran partisans of a Christian state, liberal Protestant activists, and mandarin intellectuals, as well as German Poles. All these groups, through their leaders, proposed respectively contrasting versions of German national identity, and the constitution of society. The particular image of modernity that informs Weber's scholarly discourse is one in which distinctions among ethnicity, culture, nationality, and citizenship are blurred or even collapsed. In the Freiburg address, as well as in many other of his political writings up to the end of his career, the discrepancies between this social ideal and reality are considered by Weber to be the result of ill-conceived interventions in the progress of social evolution, or to be unintended by-products of incorrect social policy. Later, this ideal gets worked into his sociology, which constructs a series of developments that either promote or hinder the growth of the culturally homogeneous national community.

---

150. Quoted in ibid., 65.

4

Weber's Idea of Universal History

If you want universal history, you must have some notion of the future and its goal; for only in the light of such a notion can the record of man be drawn together into a unity. How far that is possible, and in what sense it is possible, is one of the great burning questions of the day.

—Ernst Troeltsch, "The Idea of Natural Law and Humanity in World Politics"

Just after the turn of the century Max Weber published a series of studies designed to achieve a coherent construal of the methods of the historical and social sciences. Although it was intended to apply somewhat to all the *Geisteswissenschaften*, the construal of method Weber worked out in these essays applied most completely to the idea of a universal history.[1] These essays, in which this idea was worked out more or less systematically for the first time in his work, are important as much for what they tell us about what Weber thought he was doing as for what they tell us about his actual methods. In them Weber tried to explicate the difference between the "validity" of values that possess a universal quality, in a neo-Kantian sense, and the conventional validity of a causal explanation. Although he always held universal history to the canons of objectivity, Weber also wanted to ground the historical and social sciences in "universal" values.

---

1. See especially the 1920 "Author's Introduction" to Weber, *Religionssoziologie*, reprinted in Weber, *The Protestant Ethic*, 13ff. Schlucter has cited this passage as proof "that Weber did not indulge in the ethnocentrism that is nowadays found so frequently in modernization theories" (Schlucter and Roth, *Max Weber's Vision of History*, 22n.30). In the secondary literature, only Mommsen's work has pursued the possibility of links between the values that underlie Weber's scholarship, and Weber's self-conscious pursuit of the German genre of universal history (see Mommsen, *The Age of Bureaucracy*, especially 6–8 and 18–19). However, some of Mommsen's more recent statements severely compromise this linkage, and revert to a common attempt to valorize universal history as a distinctive personal philosophy of Weber's (cf. below, 170–71).

Weber uses the term *universal history* in a sense that is revised from its earlier nineteenth-century meaning, in light of the various contexts that determined the meaning of the humanistic disciplines at the turn of the century in Germany. These contexts, which all overlapped at times, included the changing social-problem focus of the recent *Nationalökonomie* concentration within the Historical School of German scholarship; this was linked to political and philosophical disputes between older conservatives (agrarians and monarchists) and younger modernist progressives (pro-industrialists and Marxists), wider disputes in which academics played prominent roles; the better known methods debate (*Methodenstreit*) in *Nationalökonomie* over the relative value of analytic and synthetic approaches in the humanistic disciplines; this stimulated independent work by neo-Kantian philosophers of value on the question of how far the *Geisteswissenschaften* possessed methods distinct from the *Naturwissenschaften,* and on what basis these differences lay; and the question of whether and how far the *Geisteswissenschaften* in general, and historical research in particular, involved the use of value judgments, and whether this compromised the systematic and scientific aspirations of these disciplines and thereby their place in the university.[2] However, "the social question" was in many ways the basis for these more intellectual disputes, especially for Max Weber. The social question included at least two distinct problems, and their possible relationship to a third: (1) the *agrarian* worker problem, (2) the *industrial* worker problem,[3] and (3) the decline of traditional and common values in the face of the rise of materialism, rationalism, and secularism, the problem of progress itself.

Weber addresses these issues from the point of view of his own agenda, which grew out of his concern with social problems in the 1890s and his identification with the role of the German man of knowledge. In Weber's methodological essays a modernizing agenda, signaled by the rhetoric of objectivity he uses, interacts with a preservationist agenda, Weber's desire to retain what he sees as the virtues of the traditional genre of universal history in nineteenth-century German scholarship. On the one hand, Weber

---

2. See Ringer, *Mandarins,* 143–99, for the general background; see also Oberschall, *Empirical Research,* 12–13, where "at least seven major issues" are listed differently.

3. The growth of an industrial proletariat was a problem insofar as it was thought to occur at the expense of both the declining nobility and the new middle class of professionals and civil servants, both of whom were tracked through the increasingly aristocratic bureaucratic and military services, by means of the humanistic educational system.

wants to incorporate the ideal of secular knowledge (*Wissenschaft*) and empirical research (*Forschung*) into the theoretical methods of the modern humanistic disciplines. That is, he wants to modernize the *Geisteswissenschaften*. On the other hand, his account of methods in the humanistic disciplines is designed to preserve their traditional links to cultural values. This part of Weber's construal builds on remarks he made in the Freiburg address about the presuppositions of *Nationalökonomie.*

Originally Weber's position on these issues was not that of the passionate and single-minded advocate of "objectivity," at least not in the simple sense for which Weber is well known. This is in good part an incomplete image we have of Weber's life and work, one that has come down to us from his role in the debates of the German Sociological Society (GSS). For example, in the *Methodenstreit* between the analytic instrumentalism of Carl Menger and Gustav Schmoller's wholesale rejection of the utility of concepts, due to their "unreality," Weber did not come down on one side. He took a position between those who rejected the injection of values into scholarship (Menger) and those who argued that judgments of value ought to be among the highest goals of humanistic scholarship (Schmoller and the Historical School).

> The function of concepts was assumed to be the *reproduction* of "objective" reality in the analyst's imagination. Hence the recurrent reference to the *unreality* of all clear-cut concepts. If one perceives the implications of the fundamental ideas of modern epistemology which ultimately derive from Kant, namely that concepts are primarily analytical instruments for the intellectual mastery of empirical data and can be only that, the fact that precise genetic concepts are necessarily ideal types will not cause him to desist from constructing them. The relationship between concept and historical research is reversed for those who appreciate this; the goal of the Historical School then appears as logically impossible, the concepts are not *ends* but are *means* to the end of understanding phenomena which are significant from concrete individual viewpoints. Indeed, it is just *because* the content of historical concepts is necessarily subject to change that they must be formulated precisely and clearly on all occasions. In their application, their character as ideal analytical constructs should be carefully kept in mind, and the ideal type and historical reality should not be confused with each other. It should be understood that since really definitive historical concepts are not in general to be thought of as an ultimate end, in view of the inevitable shift of [their] guiding value-

ideas (*Wertideen*), the construction of sharp and unambiguous concepts relevant to the concrete *individual* viewpoint which directs our interest at any given time affords the possibility of clearly realizing the *limits* of their validity.[4]

An *internal* criticism of the Historical School can be perceived in this statement. Although he rejects Schmoller's idea of an imaginary re-creation of the past and adopts Menger's "instrumentalism" ("the ideal type and historical reality should not be confused with each other"), he also turns Schmoller's position into a rationale for siding with Menger's "analytic" viewpoint.[5] (Weber uses the same strategy in this passage for evaluating the historicity of values, which he takes to be a good reason to adopt an analytic point of view, the opposite of the conclusion the historicists actually drew.) Against the background of other possible views, Weber's positions on methodological issues must have looked like an attempt to modernize the Historical School. Other proponents of science and the analytic ideal in the university were led to reject the methods of the Historical School altogether. In contrast, Weber's overall position reflects a deep, though critical identification with Schmoller, the chairman of the *Verein* and acknowledged leader of the Historical School.[6]

"Objectivity" is not an issue between the two sides of the *Methodenstreit*. It became an issue when Tönnies and Weber led in the movement for adopting the principle of "abstention from values" as the unifying theme for a new discipline, sociology. This principle would, as Tönnies said in closing the First Convention of the GSS in 1910, establish "a lasting and significant validity for our whole scientific life, and therefore also indirectly

---

4. The following abbreviations are used in the notes to this chapter: GAW = Max Weber, *Gesammelte Aufsätze zur Wissenschaftslehre;* RK = *Roscher and Knies: Logical Problems of Historical Economics;* OS = " 'Objectivity' in Social Science and Social Policy"; CS = "Critical Studies in the Logic of the Cultural Sciences." In view of the inconsistency of the different published translations, I have often used my own below. Both references from the published translation and from GAW are given in each case; when the latter reference is given first, this indicates my own translation.

GAW, 208–9 (OS, 106–7). Cf. also further comments on the Historical School in GAW, 42–43, 185–90 (RK, 93–4; OS, 50–112, 85–89).

5. For a fuller treatment, see Schön, "Gustav Schmoller and Max Weber," 59–70, especially 62; and section V below.

6. Cf. Ringer, *Mandarins,* 145. Weber's closeness to Schmoller's view of science did not mitigate their differences over other social and political values (see chapter 2, note 86).

[do the same] for our entire public life."[7] This movement was partly responding to the ridicule mounting outside the social sciences, both within and beyond the university, of the "disunity" and "confusion" of the field. This was expressed, for example, in a report in *Die Hilfe* on the 1910 proceedings: "Is it not to be feared that under the name of sociology the most heterogeneous of things come together, having nothing in common but that they simply have something to do with human beings?"[8]

The GSS had its origins in Weber's and Tönnies's participation in the meeting of the *Verein* in Vienna in 1909. There they argued that a scientific approach had to be "value free." But Weber affirmed the ethical and political focus of the *Verein,* and suggested that it carry on its mission, while another learned society might focus on scientific research, strictly conceived. This new society met in 1910 for the first time as the GSS. There was, just the same, much overlap between the *Verein* and the GSS. Most active members of the GSS shared broadly the social-problem focus of the *Kathedersozialisten,* and many were members of the *Verein,* which was the *Kathedersozialisten's* organization. Moreover, the leaders of the *Verein* themselves had a longstanding record of advocating "objectivity" in *Wissenschaft,* especially in *wissenschaftlich* inquiry into social problems. They tied the need for objectivity, just as Tönnies had, to the need for national social unity. In fact, Weber's formulations of the principle of value neutrality were probably influenced in no small degree by his uncle and intellectual confidant, Hermann Baumgarten, who as early as 1866 wrote an article for the *Preussische Jahrbucher,* "German Liberalism," expressing very similar views on the role of science. In Baumgarten's article, the principle of value freedom for science is advised so as to free politics from intellectualism, and to achieve national unity by fostering pan-Germanism and statism.[9] However, various parties to this debate operated with different images of what social unity ought to look like, and this provided the impetus for a quite open conflict of values and ideologies, notwithstanding everyone's rhetorical expression of a desire to expunge values.[10]

---

7. Dirk Käsler, "In Search of Respectability: The Controversy over the Destination of Sociology during the Conventions of the German Sociological Society, 1910–1930," 234. The following discussion is based on Käsler's account of the GSS. See also Turner and Factor, *Max Weber and the Dispute over Reason and Value.* At the 1910 meeting the principle of value neutrality was imposed on the GSS by statute, under Weber's and Tönnies's influence.

8. Quoted in Käsler, "In Search of Respectability."

9. Tal, *Christians and Jews,* 42.

10. So Käsler: "Everyone spoke against 'evaluations,' but continued just as

But the movement for "abstention from values" was also in part a reaction to the older *Verein für Sozialpolitik*, which was dominated by the state-socialism and paternalism of the *Kathedersozialisten*. As Weber put it at the second GSS Convention in 1912:

> We have not . . . the majority of old scholars of wide renown and therewith the help of the larger institutes for our work. Our members . . . are predominantly scholars who are active outside the university faculties or only in the future will be able to take their places there. Furthermore, our research is entirely objective in nature—not propagandistic . . . and we hope that our association will succeed in winning for sociological science the position it has long enjoyed abroad, and that, despite the perhaps deserved ill-repute of earlier years, our present achievements merit. I may observe in this connection that the directorate has decided to consider how the discipline of sociology, now entirely unrepresented in German scientific institutions of higher learning, may obtain its appropriate place and rank as a regular subject.[11]

Weber's portrayal of the older *Kathedersozialisten* as propagandists in contrast to their more sociologically minded successors was overdrawn purposely for the occasion. After all, the disagreement between the pro-industrialists and the older, state-socialist academic activists in the *Verein* revolved around the basic values that ought to guide research into questions that addressed social problems; there was no disagreement over the principle that values ought to provide the impetus for social research.

From the 1910 convention on, the principle of value neutrality was used to justify ideological critique of those styles of scholarship that the dominant members of the GSS thought would bring their work into disrepute. Nearly all members agreed that there was a great need to achieve "tranquillity" among the members, so as to enhance the general respectability of the emerging discipline. The principle of value neutrality sought to accomplish this by excluding "ideology" from the social sciences, and this primarily meant "the materialist conception of history" on the left, state-socialism

---

thoroughly to evaluate" (on the third convention, 1922; "In Search of Respectability," 240). Tönnies nevertheless continued to contrast "objectivity," which he praised, to "partisan passions." " 'Evaluations' and 'applicability' again were recurring themes throughout the debates of the fourth convention [in 1924], though without even the semblance of an emerging consensus" (ibid., 246).

11. Quoted from published proceedings in ibid., 235.

on the right.[12] Many, however, expressed reservations about the ability of objectivity to meet this need. For example, in the 1912 convention, Sombart supported a race-theory of groups on the principle of theoretical pluralism, a principle he promoted instead of value neutrality as the means of preserving "tranquillity."[13] The group led by Weber and Tönnies attempted to brand race-theory along with materialistic theory as one of the "ideologically determined approaches" to sociology. But this exchange shows that both the defenders and detractors of the principle of "abstention from values" were looking to modernize and so institutionalize sociology; they only disagreed over what was the best means of doing so. "Abstention from values," value neutrality, was therefore much more a battle cry in the formation of a new intellectual group than a methodological principle.

Beyond their shared interest in social problems, members of the GSS in actuality repeatedly became embroiled in questions rooted in alternative ideological positions, from its first meeting to its last in 1930. This very circumstance stimulated continual reference back to Weber's and others' arguments for "abstention from values" in scientific scholarship long after Weber was dead. In this way, the identification of Weber with the so-called principle of value neutrality became part of the reception of Max Weber's thought in the social sciences, and this identification has subsequently been developed even further as new occasions demand.[14] Originally, however, the debates over objectivity in the sense of value neutrality were

---

12. As the GSS developed, the principle helped formally unify the three different, modernist types of "sociology" represented in the GSS: formal (Simmel, von Wiese), cultural (Alfred Weber, Karl Mannheim), and Marxist sociology (Sombart, Michels, Adler) (compare ibid., 234, top). The principle that "neutrality" is the appropriate way to maintain "academic discipline" in the university had a long history (cf. above, pp. 58ff.).

13. Ibid., 236.

14. For the early part of this development, see ibid., 252, bottom (fifth convention, 1926), 255f., 258f. (sixth convention, 1928), 262, bottom (seventh and last convention, 1930). See also Factor and Turner, "The Limits of Reason and Some Limitations of Weber's Morality," 301–34, and Gerd Schroeter's response. It should also be noted, however, that outside the social sciences, especially in fields that continued to be influenced by neo-Kantianism, Weber's reputation *in the theory of value* had outstripped that of Rickert, originally regarded as his teacher, by the twenties (Schnädelbach, *Philosophy in Germany,* 189). In 1928 Meinecke extolled Weber's research methods as the *opposite* of the "separation of values from the logical essence of history," which he attributed to Rickert! (see "Values and Causalities in History," in *The Varieties of History,* ed. Fritz Stern [Cleveland: World Pub., 1956], 267–88, cited in Willey, *Back to Kant,* 169f).

much more restricted in scope. They were intended to justify the institutionalization of those types of social science that were being developed by a group of German historians, political economists, psychologists, and philosophers who, in the previous generation, would have been called *Kathedersozialisten,* mandarin social activists.[15]

Weber's contributions to the debate over value neutrality help us very little to understand his idea of universal history. On balance, when all his methodological writings are taken into account, Weber has a positive attitude toward the role of values in scholarship, although his position is also reformist and modernist, and therefore critical. Let us now turn from the problem of objectivity to a different problem Weber addressed, one he considered no less important: how is "universal" knowledge possible in the *Geisteswissenschaften?*

II

Weber's idea of universal history has its beginnings in the analysis of *Nationalökonomie* he presented in his Freiburg address. The Freiburg address, it will be recalled, rejected the axiomatizing goals of a purely value-free social science by pointing out that fundamental cultural values were at least implicitly built in to even supposedly asceptic Manchesterite classical economics.[16] Weber went on to argue there that we ought to make the cultural values that guide *Nationalökonomie* explicit, and employ these values more systematically. For *Nationalökonomie* in Germany these values are national, not Manchesterite ("eudaemonist"), according to Weber. In the context of the purposes of and audiences for the Freiburg address, this meant that modern social science ought to address the broad social and cultural issues that underlie the German striving for social unification within the second Reich.[17]

---

15. I therefore take the opposite view from Bruun (*Science, Values and Politics in Max Weber's Methodology,* 81), who says that the social question was "probably the immediate occasion rather than the fundamental cause of Weber's protests [against propagandizing by the older members of the *Verein*]. Of far greater importance was the 'controversy over method.' " In my view, the former was fundamental to Weber's construal of universal history, not the latter.

16. See chapter 3. In *Roscher and Knies* Weber specifically denied that "analytical knowledge of an object" of understanding is "value free" (GAW, 74 [RK, 133]).

17. The connection between the two discussions of methodological issues in the Freiburg address and the early methodological essays, respectively, has apparently been commonplace among early critics of Weber, as Hans Alpert complained in 1964, at the Max Weber Centenary convention in Heidelberg (Stammer, *Max Weber and Sociology Today,* 56f.; cf. also Marianne Weber, *Biography,* 216).

In " 'Objectivity' in Social Science and Social Policy" (1904) and "Critical Studies in the Logic of the Cultural Sciences" (1905) Weber defines universal history more generally than *Nationalökonomie,* as the investigation of the past in order to discover the causes for developments that have come to light only in modern times, and which "we" recognize. The objects of historical inquiry possess "universal significance" (*universal Bedeutung*) or "cultural significance" (*Kulturbedeutung*). This must be distinguished from "causal significance." Weber's construal of universal history tries to establish each of these, universal significance and empirical validity in causal statements, as absolute standards for the veracity of historical knowledge. But it also glosses over the obvious possibility of a conflict between cultural universality and causality.

It might be thought that what Weber is proposing is a type of "value relevance" that is often associated with the "universal value" of modern humanistic methods. This is based on the assumption that, to be truly universal, the core of our cultural literacy must be more and more inclusive. The topics that humanistic scholars take up must be designed to lead to knowledge that the largest audience can identify with. Humanistic knowledge ought to have the potential for humanizing particular audiences by confronting them with humanity, in the sense of the variety of human life that has flourished on our globe. One of the goals of humanistic methods in this sense should be to provide intellectual tools for sorting out particularity from general humanity, and for seeing general humanity in particularity. Modern humanistic social scientists have typically hoped that their knowledge would aid in everyone's efforts to find a meaning for his or her particular fate that brings one a little bit closer to those normally outside the sphere of one's personal experience. Thus a study of Samoan Islanders might be said to be valuable because it broadens the reader's social and intellectual horizons.

Is this the goal of "universal relevance" in Weber's usage? Let us look at some examples. Hellenic culture, according to Weber, possesses universal significance, but African cultures do not. The universal significance of Hellenic culture "could change only if some future age became only as capable of attaining a direct 'value-rapport' (*Wertbeziehung*) to those cultural 'creations' of antiquity as we are today in relation to the 'songs' and 'world view' of a central African tribe, which arouse our interest only as instances of cultural products [as such], i.e., as a means of forming [general] concepts or as 'causes.' "[18] It was nearly unthinkable to Weber that the modernization

---

18. See GAW, 259 (CS, 157; see note 4 above for list of abbreviations). Cf.

of social scientific scholarship should require that we treat different historical and cultural situations as of equal worth in some sense. Such a view of the tasks of historical studies was not unknown in Weber's time. He attacked such "modern" claims, which he found in a contemporary collection of studies in world history that aimed to abstain from judging between the ultimate worth of the Persian wars or "a scuffle between two tribes of Kaffirs or Indians."[19] What lies in back of such a goal, Weber thinks, is "the notion of a sort of 'social' justice which would—finally, finally!—take the contemptibly neglected Kaffir and Indian tribes at least as seriously as the Athenians and which . . . resorts to a geographical organization of the data." This approach to world history Weber judged to be "merely childish."[20] In another context, Weber confines "universal historical" interest in the history of the Aztecs or the Incas to purposes of generating general concepts that might help "us" better understand "our own" history. He then dismisses the idea that Inca or Aztec life might have intrinsic interest, or at least a "humanistic" interest in the sense just suggested, as a "logical" possibility only.[21] The same rationale is given for the merely instrumental value of studying the state formation of North American Indian tribal peoples, such as the Iroquois.[22]

---

also his more emotional statement during the war (in a letter to his mother): "We have proved we are a great cultural nation. People who live in a civilized milieu and are nevertheless able to rise to the horrors of war (no achievement for a black man from Senegal!) and to return as honorably as most of our people do—that is real humanity" (quoted in Mommsen, *German Politics,* 191; Also in Marianne Weber, *Biography,* 522–23 [the editor, Harry Zohn, points out that this is a reference to the military use of natives by the colonial French]).

19. See GAW, 273–77 (CS, 171–75).

20. CS, 172n (GAW, 274n).

21. GAW, 258 (CS, 155–56).

22. GAW, 234–35 (CS, 132–33). The following letter to *Time* magazine, by Mike Myers, administrator for the Onondaga Nation in Nedrow, New York, is an interesting counterpoint to Weber's perspective: "As a citizen of the Seneca nation, I am moved to comment on your presentation of Native Americans. The Iroquois Confederacy, of which the Seneca is a member, is among the world's oldest continuously functioning democracies. In 1784 and 1794 our government concluded treaties with your government that recognize the political integrity and separateness of our nations and that grant the U.S. land on which to live. These treaties formed the political basis of the Indian nations' relationship to the U.S. But beyond the political reasons for our steadfast refusal to be integrated are spiritual reasons. It is not a mistake that the creator of life put our people on the earth, gave us our languages and beliefs, and provided a model for our political orga-

It might be said that cultural-value biases are indeed a real danger of historical study, one that Weber ought to be commended for bringing to light. It could be said, further, that there is nothing especially interesting about the role of values as the basis for selective interests in historical reality. This is a necessary part of historical methodology, as Weber and others have shown. Moreover, Weber's demonstration that this places limits on our ability to achieve strict objectivity remains valid. Historical knowledge will always retain problematic features on account of this circumstance, and this insight ought to be derived from Weber's methodological arguments.

This might be called the weak view of the role of cultural selectivity in historical and social science research. The weak view considers such selectivity to be an impediment to objectivity that, with diligence and critical acumen, can be more or less remedied. Against this view, I think it can be shown that Weber's construal of historical methods as universal history, in his special sense, involves a strong view of cultural selectivity. Weber considers cultural selectivity to be a virtue for research, if properly handled, and he definitely rejects the notion that we can or ought to try to eliminate cultural bias from theory or research design in the historical and social sciences. In fact, he uses the distinction (after Heinrich Rickert) between "value judgments" and "cultural values" for this latter purpose, tying the abstention from value judgments to objectivity, and tying "cultural values" to the "universalism" of universal history and all the *Geisteswissenschaften*.

This move involves, I think, an essential blurring of the otherwise sharp distinction Weber makes between empirical validity (objective causal statements) and "universal significance." The standard of empirical validity implies that analytic conclusions and conceptual apparati ought to be able to be adopted by anyone, regardless of particular field of scholarly analysis, and regardless of any specific "point of view" or special angle according to which available data are selected. Weber seems to adopt this as his own standard when he says that empirical scientific conclusions ought to be able to be accepted by one who is Chinese.[23] But (as we will see) what he

---

nization that endures to this day. We are very clear about who we are and why we exist as part of the universe. Can Americans say the same?" (*Time* 130; no. 4 [July 27, 1987], 6c). It is quite possible that a non-Iroquois could share Mr. Myers's value for the separate dignity of his people, and be motivated thereby to undertake study of the history of the Iroquois. This possibility, however, is rejected on principle in the statements from Weber quoted above.

23. GAW, 155–56 (OS, 58–59).

ultimately requires of the Chinese, in order to accept the veracity of empirical claims in historical studies, is that they actually adopt the cultural values of the historian whose work they are reading, whether or not they agree with these values. Let us turn to the background of Weber's understanding of the term *values*.

III

The philosophical development of the concept of value, from Rudolph Lotze, through Wilhelm Dilthey (who in 1882 succeeded Lotze in Berlin), Wilhelm Windelband (Lotze's most accomplished student), and Heinrich Rickert, is the most important intellectual background both for Weber's discussion of "value-theoretical interpretation" in the "cultural sciences" and for his position of "abstention from value judgments" in sociology, in the GSS debates.

The expression "values have validity" entered German philosophy in the 1840s from political economy through Rudolph Lotze, whose works Weber read avidly while in *Gymnasium*.[24] From Lotze to Weber and beyond, the question of value was bound up with personal *Bildung*, which Lotze had characterized as the development of a "point of view" and an "unprejudiced soul," in order to achieve universalism in outlook. Lotze was also the first to identify the concept of value with the concept of individuality. The development of a personal "point of view," through *Bildung*, was what made it possible for a person to perceive the individuality of things; the manifestation of values in perception is the individuality of phenomena. Lotze introduced the expression, the "sense" (*Sinn*) of things, in his *Mikrokosmos* of 1813, to refer to the meanings which the "unprejudiced soul" perceives and evaluates.[25] In a sense, we perceive things by perceiving value in them. From Lotze, Windelband developed this idea into his theory of "idiographic," "individualizing" sciences. It was from

---

24. This paragraph is based on Schnädelbach, *Philosophy in Germany*, 169–80. For Weber's early difficulty with Lotze's *Mikrokosmos*, see Marianne Weber, *Biography*, 67–68.

25. See the quote in Schnädelbach, *Philosophy in Germany*, 173, where "reflections which undertake, by a comparison of particulars, to distinguish the essential from the inessential, the constant from the transitory, the valuable from the indifferent" are said to lead to *Bildung*, which is "precipitated out of the experience of life, as the outcome of that sensory observation."

Windelband that the language of "axiology," as distinguished from ontology, came, a language also adopted by Weber.[26]

Heinrich Rickert, Jr., was the first to show how scientific knowledge in the *Geisteswissenschaften* could be construed as an outcome of the operation of "values." His demonstration, which Weber drew on in part, is formally a solution to the problem of selecting an object for investigation. The importance of this is established for him, as for Weber, by the circumstance that the totality of reality cannot be comprehended. By making this consideration fundamental, Rickert and Weber can dispense with a variety of problems that arise when the ontological character of reality is addressed. They both wanted to head off general denials that any type of objective, "analytic" explanation was appropriate in the humanistic disciplines because of the nature of their subject matter, as argued by irrationalist theorists of introspection. The irrationalists looked mainly to the veracity of an immediate experience of human situations or a sympathetic reliving of historical episodes to ground the understanding of events. Such subjective grounds were then often thought to be capable of providing a basis for generalizations about all human experience.

The neo-Kantians took a wholly different approach to these problems because they looked upon "experience" precisely as a central problem.[27] Both they and the irrationalists agreed that individual consciousness is primary, and so by "reality" they all mean "experienced reality." But for the neo-Kantians, and for Rickert, experience by itself is essentially undifferentiated.[28] On the assumption that "experience" is undifferentiated, methods of arriving at knowledge are solutions to the problem of selection: *which* experiences are to be chosen as the *object* of knowledge?

Following Windelband, Rickert believed that the idiographic approach was a logical result of our *evaluating* a particular field of inquiry. Where we do not approach a field with evaluations, there the generalizing method is appropriate; where we do, the individualizing approach is prescribed.[29]

---

26. Cf. ibid., 179–83. In his 1914 *Introduction to Philosophy*, Windelband distanced himself from the concept of "universally valid values" that had come down from Lotze, as leading to relativism. He proposed instead to ground "absolute values" in "the voice of common consciousness in the individual consciousness."

27. See Willey, *Back to Kant*.

28. In the first edition of his *Logical Investigations* (1901–2) Husserl characterized experience in this way, as a "stream of perceptions," and this language was also influential for Weber.

29. Cf. Ringer, *Mandarins*, 325ff.

Their interest in the *genera* of phenomena enables the natural sciences to have direct access to their objects without the mediation of values. This left the problem of ensuring objectivity where an object is defined by its indivisible individuality. Rickert's efforts to solve this problem reveal a subtle transvaluation of the idea of the universal.

This is where the first volume of *Limits* left off. It was published in 1896 and was limited to concept formation in the natural sciences. With the second volume, in 1902, Rickert turned to the historians as a sort of proof case for the individualizing approach to scientific knowledge. He tried to solve the problem of objectivity in history by translating it in light of the idea of universality, which he now develops. History renders its concepts "universally significant" with respect to their evaluative origins. By virtue of their "willing, evaluating, and committed" nature, humans bestow uniqueness on the particular.[30] Historians are no different in this regard. The objects of historical interest, however, must be determined by something more reliable than mere value judgments. Practical evaluation itself must be transformed into an operation, one that confers a formal, theoretical *value relation* on the object. Rickert uses the term value relation (*Wertbeziehung*) consistently to describe the outcome of this operation, in order to maintain a distinction between it and value judgment (*Werturteil*), which is the product of purely subjective evaluation. Both the objective operation abstracting the value relation a thing possesses and the subjective evaluation of the thing employ values. But by calling the first a "relation" to value and the second a "judgment" of value Rickert can assert that a description of value relations leaves open the question of which practical attitude should be taken toward the object.

The distinction between the objectivity of a value relation and the practical, subjective, and so capricious nature of value judgments is one side of Rickert's argument. Another side holds that the objectivity of the value-relating operation in history depends on making the actual values employed theoretically general. Values can provide a valid basis for selection if they are generally recognized. "Scientific" for Rickert includes this sense of "general."[31] To show how historians employ values Rickert proposes as a meth-

---

30. Quoted in Brunn, *Science, Values and Politics,* 89. Rickert draws on Dilthey's language here.

31. Thus history for Rickert "is a science of *reality* insofar as it has to do with uniquely individual realities as such; it is a *science* of reality insofar as it takes a standpoint of mere consideration that is valid for everybody, and hence makes individual realities into the object of its presentation, realities that are rendered meaningful only through relation to a general value" (quoted in ibid., 90).

odological category, the idea of culture. Rickert's construal of historical research methods took an authoritarian turn when he went on to assert that "culture" provides a foundation for objectivity only when it is defined in terms of obligatory and therefore, he thought, transcendent values.[32] According to Bruun, Rickert finally confined objectively valid history to cultural history, "in the sense that it must be concerned with human behavior oriented toward one or more cultural values, toward *culture*." "Cultural values," more specifically, are exemplified for Rickert by "politics, art, religion, literature, etc." and these values, in turn, are determined with authority for all members of any whole society (Rickert used both *Gemein-* and *Gesellschaft*). The concept of culture refers to that which "all members of a society should attach great importance to (*am Herzen liegen*) and whose cultivation can be *demanded* of them."[33]

This blatant turn to the substantive content of values should not obscure the more fundamental development of the idea of universality. This idea, properly elaborated, provides a standard for the *objectivity* of the process of historical selection, according to Rickert. Rickert actually proposed two standards for objectivity in this sense, both of which are no more than criteria for ensuring that historical objects are "universally significant." (1) Historians' initial evaluation of the phenomena can be rendered generally valid by being shared by their public, by representing "a common concern of the members of [one's] community."[34] A correct historical presentation sublimates value judgments, giving the object a higher, more abstract value relation.[35] This is apparently to be distinguished from a judgment about how to act, which is "practical" rather than "abstract." However, even if we confine ourselves to objects that possess only a value relation, there may still be an element of randomness in the selection process, in Rickert's view. Therefore, in order to achieve objectivity he requires in addition that (2) "The leading values of concept formation for an 'objective' scientific representation are always to be taken from the historical material itself."[36] This means that "generally valid" value relations can be achieved in history only when they coincide with evaluative standpoints that are contemporary with the time and place being represented. Criteria of objectivity are legitimate only when they satisfy both of these two standards. By making the second

---

32. Cf. Bochenski, *Contemporary European Philosophy*, 95–96.
33. Bruun, *Science, Values and Politics*, 94; see also 92, 129, 132–33.
34. Quoted in ibid., 92.
35. Ibid.
36. Quoted in ibid.

condition just as binding as the first, Rickert feels the strength of the overall criterion of objectivity has been ensured, since a necessary connection between the object and the method of historical science (a concern of the proponents of *verstehen*) has been established.[37]

Interest in "the particular" seems at this point to take on much more than a purely methodological significance for Rickert. He seems to want the principle of individuality to ground "human" studies ontologically, and preserve them from the challenge of modern science methods. Our interest in "the particular" makes possible a realm of common values from which criteria for "meaning patterns" (*Sinngebilde*) are drawn. These patterns are actual historical relationships which, in and of themselves, mediate "objectively" between the realm of values and the realm of facts.[38] The principle of "interest in the particular," then, defines historical knowledge and justifies it transcendentally. Taken together the twofold relationship to "values" constitutes the "universal significance" of history's objects of inquiry. While always maintaining a conceptual distinction between his two criteria for universal values, Rickert nevertheless held that they were transcendentally ("logically") linked by virtue of their common underlying reason in the fact of human interests.

Although Weber may have been repelled by the authoritarian tone of Rickert's project of grounding the cultural-value construal of humanistic methods transcendentally, he did adopt Rickert's understanding of "universality." Weber isolated Rickert's discussion of theoretical value relation, how "valid values" can be made a basis for scientific validity, from other parts of Rickert's system, and anchored his construal of method there. This is perfectly compatible with Weber's more well known position, that no scientific analysis can *establish* the "validity" of values.[39] However, because

---

37. Far from abandoning this last position, Rickert only emphasized it all the more in the fifth edition of *Limits* (1929), when he said that the idea that certain kinds of material demand an individualizing treatment was "in truth . . . the central idea of my positive teaching on history, and which makes it possible to recognize the connection between form and content" (quoted in ibid., 96n.11).

38. Bochenski, *Contemporary European Philosophy,* 96.

39. This is the meaning of a passage in *Roscher and Knies* that Willey misinterprets: "The epistemology of history confirms and analyzes the meaning of 'relating to values' for historical knowledge, but for its own part does not establish the validity of values" (GAW, 27n.1, cited in *Back to Kant,* 162). This passage does not differ from Rickert's and other neo-Kantians' characterization of values as possessing validity. Weber departs from Rickert mainly in his effort to ground the discourse of "universality" in an analytic and so, he holds, "objective" analysis of

he rejected some of the philosophical foundations of Rickert's construal of science methods, the notion of value relation in Rickert as the basis for the "universal significance" of historical knowledge only proved to be a problem for Weber that had to be resolved.[40]

IV

Weber stressed the problem of selection because it supported his attempts to justify the dignity or scientific status of the humanistic disciplines in the German universities, by demonstrating their need for both "analytic" and traditional ways of knowing.[41] Weber's use and development of Rickert's neo-Kantian theory of value, and his efforts to solve epistemological problems, had practical significance for Weber in a way they did not for Rickert. If every science, whenever it employs clear concepts, can be said to be engaged in a process of selection of information from an otherwise undifferentiated flux, then to show the distinctiveness of the way this process of selection occurs in the historical and social sciences is close to legitimating their concepts as science. If culture, the origin of the principles of selection in the *Geisteswissenschaften,* is characterized by conflict (as Weber holds), not obedience (as Rickert holds), then theoretical disputes can be construed as occurring within the circle of a value relation, a connection to common values. Indeed, such disputes can be said to further the understanding of what those values are.

The context of Weber's most programmatic solution to the problem of selection, developed in his essay on " 'Objectivity' in Social Science and

the "cultural values" that inform "our" interest in history and comparative studies. However, Weber and Rickert are in agreement that values exist and that, to the extent that they are "universal," they are also "valid."

40. For evidence specifying Weber's positive reliance on Rickert: letters concerning Rickert's work to Georg von Below (July 17, 1904), L. von Bortkievitz (March 12, 1905), Gottl-Ottlilienfeld (March 28, 1905), Gottl (same date,) and Franz Eulenberg (September 8, 1905), cited in Bruun, *Science, Values and Politics,* 206, 85n.2, 95n.8, 119n.74, 206n.35, 210n.50; a letter to Rickert himself (June 14, 1904), cited in ibid., 207; draft notes to Weber's copy of Rickert's *Limits,* cited in ibid., 130n.40, 132; Marianne Weber, *Biography,* 260 (letter to his wife); GAW, 3n, 7n, 15 and note, 92n, 116n (RK, 211–12, 213n.9, 219n.25, 251n.47, 267); GAW, 146n (OS, 49–50); GAW, 263–64 (CS, 161). Cf. also Willey, *Back to Kant,* 161–63.

41. Similarly, Menger put Schmoller on the defensive, for fear that economic theory would claim the prestige of science at the expense of traditional historical research (see Turner and Factor, *Max Weber and the Dispute over Reason and Value*).

Social Policy" (*Sozialwissenschaft und Sozialpolitik*), suggests the practical nature of Weber's interest in the problem. The essay was written as a statement of editorial policy for the *Archiv für Sozialwissenschaft und Sozialpolitik* on the occasion of a change in editorship. Previously the journal had been the organ of the *Verein für Sozialpolitik*, founded in 1872 by Schmoller, Adolph Wagner, and Lujo Brentano. Weber was himself an outspoken younger member of the *Verein*. When he joined with Werner Sombart and Heinrich Braun in 1904 to take over editorial responsibilities for the *Archiv*, this represented both a break with the older *Kathedersozialisten* and an intent to maintain a certain continuity.[42]

Under Schmoller's and Brentano's leadership the *Verein* had pressed a clearly state-socialist line, and the *Archiv* had accordingly been committed to the scholarly examination of "the social problem" in Germany and to critical discussions of legislative solutions to its various aspects. Up to now, however, the mainstream of academic activists had sought some sort of accommodation by the state to the needs of industry and labor, without necessarily upsetting the traditional class structure which the state also sought to preserve, especially the leading role of the Junkers. When the editorial responsibilities of the *Archiv* changed hands, the title page of the new journal carried the banner, under the title itself, "New Series of the *Archiv für Soziale Gesetzgebung und Statistik*, Founded by Heinrich Braun." Braun's journal, since 1888, had been oriented to problems of the working class, specifically presenting itself as an alternative to the state-socialism of the older *Kathedersozialisten*, and had published some of Sombart's early articles on these questions. It was seen for these reasons as clearly sympathetic to Marxist socialism. (Braun was also an editor for the Marxist *Die Neue Zeit*.) The new banner, then, marked the new series of the *Archiv* as an organ of the younger generation of academic activists, and their progressive outlook.

Yet even the younger members remained committed to the idea of *Sozialpolitik*, a word they retained in the title of the *Archiv* even after announcing its new editorial policy. Fritz Ringer has shown how the anti-laissez-faire sentiment of German social theory became central to the social-problem orientation of the *Verein* and how, during Weber's participation, this united both older and younger members.[43] This common concern with

---

42. For the background for this and the following, see Ringer, *Mandarins*, 146–62. Cf. also Mommsen, *German Politics*, 15–20, 101–36; Marianne Weber, *Biography*, 278.

43. Ringer, *Mandarins*, 147.

defining and explaining the problems of progress for the educated public was reflected in the word *Sozialpolitik*. Against this background, Weber's essay can be seen as a careful balancing act between an expression of commitment to this orientation and a call for further modernizing its direction.

The "Objectivity" essay is broken into two parts, and there is a tactical relation between them designed to best express this modernizing motive in the climate of the methodological concerns shared by practicing social scientists influenced by the *Kathedersozialisten*. Part 1 alone is said to be representative for the collective editorial policy of the new *Archiv*. Its burden is to establish a more or less strict distinction between science and objective validity on the one hand, and values and value judgments on the other. The argument is often extreme because part 2 establishes the centrality of the role that the "highest values" play "in determining the focus of attention of analytical intellectual activity."[44]

Part 2 identifies *social problems* (questions of *Sozialpolitik*)[45] as the animating spirit for social science and for the special character of the *Archiv* in particular. Here Weber affirms continuity with the previous editors, but expresses criticism of the free-handed manner in which such ultimately moral questions were handled by academics, often ignoring the canons of science and thereby discrediting all scientific analysis of social facts. Still, he expresses sympathy with the previous editors' effort to avoid a moral tendency, by their openness to diverse viewpoints.[46] This is why it is so urgent to establish, in the first section of the essay, a commitment to objectivity. Beyond this, the language Weber employs is often unmistakably taken from Rickert in the first part; it is in the second part that Weber breaks with Rickert's terms.

Weber begins by outlining three purposes that a scientific discussion of policy or value questions might have. Criticism of values first implies "technical criticism," which is designed to "balance the unintended against the intended consequences" of actions. Second, beyond this such criticism can offer any person so concerned "*knowledge* of the *significance* of that which is intended itself. We can teach him to know such aims in their meaning-context (*Zusammenhang*) and their significance, aims which he desires and among which he chooses. We can do this first by showing and developing in a logically coherent fashion the 'ideas' which do or can underlie the

---

44. GAW, 155 (OS, 58) (". . . ordnende Tätigkeit des Denkens").
45. Once, at GAW, 159, "*politischen* Probleme."
46. Cf. GAW, 157–61 (OS, 60–63).

particular aim." Weber argues that such a task is within "the limits of a *science* that strives for 'intellectual ordering of empirical reality,' even if the means it employs are not 'inductions' in the usual sense of the word." But he concedes that this falls outside "the framework of the special discipline of *Nationalökonomie*. . . ; it has to do with the tasks of *social philosophy*."[47]

Thus the task of placing values within a wider context in order to clarify their meaning is, Weber contends, a proper task for all the human sciences, precisely in their capacity as sciences. This "scientific treatment of value judgments" does more than sensitize the "acting person" to the complexities of his own commitments; it can perform a third function related to the second, of promoting critical judgment. "*This* criticism, of course, can have only a dialectical character; i.e., it can only be a formal-logical judgment of the material present in the value judgments and ideas that are given historically, a test of ideals in terms of the postulate of the inner *consistency* of that which is intended." Bringing to light such ultimate criteria for the worthiness of an object of nevertheless diverse personal commitments is the most that the historian can accomplish this side of pure speculation.[48]

Weber next tries to distinguish individuals' value judgments from the "formal-logical" substance of values, using Rickert's idea of culture. That which is or can be the object of *general concern* is distinct from the substance of an individual's concrete decision to act with respect to that area of concern, according to Weber. We can speak of the former as the field of "culture" or "cultural significance." Within this field, the validity of the principles of individual commitment are subject to dispute, but the general cultural values they assume are not. Here it is best to follow Weber's argument in his own words:

> precisely those most inward elements of "personality," the highest and most ultimate value judgments which condition our action and give sense and significance to our life are regarded as "objectively" valuable. . . . However: to *judge* the *validity* of such values is a matter of *faith*, which is *perhaps* a task only for speculative consideration and interpretation of the meaning of life and the world, but it is certainly *not* a topic for an empirical science in the sense in which this will developed here.[49]

---

47. GAW, 150–51 (OS, 54); first emphasis added.
48. GAW, 156 (OS, 59).
49. GAW, 152 (OS, 55).

... around normative criteria themselves there can and *must* be dispute, since the problem emerges from within the domain of universal *cultural* questions. . . . [But] the more "universal" the problem involved, i.e., in this case, the broader its cultural *significance,* the less is it open to a single unambiguous response on the basis of the data of the empirical sciences, and the greater is the role played by the ultimate and highest personal axioms of belief and of ideas of value (*Wertideen*).[50]

... from the norms for the concretely conditioned conduct of the *individual,* the *contents of culture* cannot be clearly *deduced* as being desirable, and the more inclusive the contents are with which culture has to do the less is this the case. Only positive religions—or more precisely expressed: dogmatically bound sects—are able to confer on the content of *cultural values* the status of unconditionally valid *ethical* imperatives. Outside these sects cultural ideals which the individual *intends* to put into action, and ethical obligations which he *ought* to fulfill, have a status that is different in principle. . . . *The highest ideals,* which move us most forcefully, are always formed only in the struggle with other ideals which are just as sacred to others as ours are to us.[51]

"Ideals," then, can lead to either value judgments or to cultural values. They will lead to the former whenever they are pressed into service in the individual's attempt to resolve particular dilemmas, when they play a part in a particular context of ethical decision making. Cultural values, however, are more general, defining an area of dispute about the practical and imperative stance that should be taken toward the object of valuation. Because they open up questions of practical obligation without resolving them, cultural values can be distinguished from concrete ethical imperatives.

This is a logical distinction, not an empirical one. Because he wants to concede that value judgments often provide the strongest motives for knowledge, Weber says the theoretical direction of historical conceptualization ought to be provided by "the *logical* analysis of an ideal on the basis of its content and ultimate axioms." Such an analysis does not itself require any practical attitude to be adopted. To the contrary, its results can be valid for a Chinese, despite the fact that "he may lack the 'musical ear' for our ethical imperative, and that he can and surely often will refuse to accept

---

50. GAW, 153 (OS, 56).
51. Adapted from OS, 57 (GAW, 154).

the particular *value judgments* that follow from it." This does not "damage the scientific value of conceptual *analysis.*"[52]

In fact "the stimulus to posing *scientific* problems [in the social sciences] is actually always given by *practical* 'questions,' " according to Weber, and he has in mind such public issues as the Polish question, the social question, the Jewish question, and the landworker question. A conflict of value judgments concerning various solutions to social problems always attends practical questions like these, and this conflict provides an impetus for elucidating the contents of the cultural values that underlie these questions.[53]

There is, therefore, an empirical process—value conflict—that promotes the development of general (universal?) cultural values out of practical value judgments. This theory of the virtues of value conflict sheds light on the actual criteria for universalism in Weber's thought. Weber seems to have believed that a certain universality would come out of dispute, that the struggle over values was itself a means to universalism, providing that dispute was allowed to travel any and all paths of discourse that might arise immanently, as it were, from the disputants themselves. That is, free dispute would, of its own logic, uncover a universal object of dispute. This object would not be universal in the sense of "value free," but rather universal in the sense of socially general to the utmost degree. "Universal values" define a circle of disputation outside of which criticism is "logically" ineffective or unimportant. Weber's claim that a "value analysis," tacit or not, underlies the formation of concepts in the *Geisteswissenschaften* is rooted in a deep faith in the natural dialectic of dispute, a belief that the way to truth in matters of value (thus history and social problems) is only through the uninterrupted and unconstrained struggle among value judgments and "standpoints."[54]

---

52. GAW, 155–56 (OS, 58–59).

53. GAW, 156f., 158 (OS, 60–61). Cf. also GAW, 101n.2 (RK, 260n.57).

54. This conviction, that the universal objects of dispute will emerge in more clarified form as a result of a sort of dialectic of dispute, is expressed well in the often-quoted message Weber sent to Friedrich von Gottl-Ottlilienfeld at the time of his early methodological essays: "Please polemicize *as sharply* as you can against my views, at those points where we differ." This quote provides the frontispiece for the second German edition (1973) of Mommsen, *German Politics.* This was also Weber's operating assumption in the debates over the Protestant ethic thesis, some of which will be reviewed in subsequent chapters. In these disputes Weber's strategy is simply to elaborate on and further clarify his "point of view" on the place of individual commitment in the rise of capitalism, and then to call attention to discrepancies between his own and his opponents' "points of view."

Weber's effort to connect a social-problem focus and universal history is part of his affirmation of the older "social policy" orientation of the *Verein*, which introduces the second part of Weber's essay. Weber now wants to show why that orientation provides good grounds for selecting an object for analysis in history. The careful denial that science seeks to confer "meaning" on the world in part 1 now gives way to an inquiry into the way in which scientific problems are given meaning. His strategy is to develop an extreme version of a nomological construal of economics, which he can then show fairly easily is unable to account for how historical problems are conceptualized. His thematic argument is that all empirical sciences, including generalizing ones, presuppose problems that are defined prior to the explanations they aim to undertake. Weber's favored way of expressing this is to say that they presuppose the prior *meaning* of problems, and he wants to show that especially in the *Geisteswissenschaften* this meaning is grounded in cultural values. These disciplines ought to be called *Kulturwissenschaft*, because in order to do a thorough empirical analysis of causes of the social problem ("i.e., the place of the modern working class in the present social order") one is invariably led to consider "the general cultural significance of the social-economic structure of life in human communities (*Gemeinschaftsleben*)."[55] The inadequacy of the nomological construal of concept formation for these disciplines can then justify a reassertion of the legitimacy of the social-problem focus that has always provided the direction for the *Archiv*.

German social science in the late nineteenth century has actually developed in this way toward a universalization of theoretical viewpoints:

> The more the practical treatment of labor conditions became a permanent object of legislation and public discussion in Germany [from the 1880s], the more the accent of scientific work had to be shifted to establishing more universal contexts within which these problems received a hearing. It had thereby to culminate in the analysis of *all* cultural problems that have arisen from the nature of the economic bases of our culture and which are, in that sense, specifically modern.[56]

Within such a broadened context social science is legitimately and intentionally "one-sided" when it adopts the narrow perspective of a concern for economic factors. Yet the initial integration of economic analysis into

---

55. GAW, 164f. (OS, 66–67).
56. Ibid.

the "natural law and rationalistic *Weltanschauung*" of the eighteenth century "*obstructed* the discovery of the *problematic* character of that standpoint."[57] Actually there are no objectively economic events apart from the cultural meaning we ascribe to events in such terms.[58]

Weber finds (after Rickert) that the meaning of problems is ultimately based on "the investigator's *Wertideen*" (value ideas). This finding is then linked up to the earlier discussion (also Rickertian), where *Wertideen* were said to be the product of a "formal-logical" analysis. *Wertideen* establish a "universal *Zusammenhang*" circumscribing scientific interests in the *Geisteswissenschaften,* and so perform a selective function. Weber uses the problem of selection tactically, to disarm aspirations for a closed system of theories and concepts, and to open the possibility of a more traditional construal of humanistic methods. For example, it had often been claimed that the nomological clarity of its concepts reflected the "presuppositionless" status of economics or, later, of psychology, which some proposed could on this account become the basis for historical research. Against this view Weber says that a nomological concept of an isolated factor like the economic does not provide criteria for isolating specific historical events that need to be explained.[59] Not only is the initial interest in such events determined by our values, but other values determine the wider theoretical significance within which the relevance of economic concepts themselves must be set in any particular research problem. Even if we possessed "an immense casuistry of concepts" that were directly relevant to a given problem, we would still be "helpless in the face of the question: how is the causal explanation of an individual fact possible, in general?, since even a *description* of just the smallest slice of reality is never intellectually exhaustive."[60] At the same time, this very demonstration of the role of values in historical reasoning provides an occasion for Weber to bring the analytic ideal back in, with his Rickertian theory of value analysis.

All the following statements separating the methods of the "cultural sciences" from the nomological ideal are designed to highlight the former disciplines' reliance on values, and to establish that "culture" is an important

---

57. GAW, 185 (OS, 85).

58. GAW, 161, 169–70 (OS, 64, 71). This point was also prominent in Weber's Freiburg address.

59. GAW, 182 (OS, 82 is in error). See also GAW, 169–70, 176–77 (OS, 71, 77).

60. GAW, 174, 177 (OS, 75, 78).

basis of theory. This, for Weber, was the key to solving the problem of selection he thought Rickert had isolated so well, if inconclusively.

A chaos of "existential judgments" about countless individual events (*Wahrnehmungen*) would be the only result of a serious attempt to analyze reality "without presuppositions." And even this result is only seemingly possible, since every single perception (*Wahrnehmung*) discloses on closer examination an infinite number of constituent perceptions which can never be exhaustively expressed in a judgment (*Wahrnehmungsurteil*). Order is brought into this chaos *only* on the condition that in every case only a *part* of concrete reality is interesting and *significant* to us, because only it is related to the *cultural values* (*Kulturwertideen*) with which we approach reality. . . . [These parts] alone are objects of causal explanation.[61]

This is true even for the person who views a *particular* culture as a mortal enemy and who seeks to "return to nature." He can acquire this attitude only after *relating* the culture in which he lives to his values (*Wertideen*) and finding it "too soft." This is the *purely logical-formal* fact which is involved when we speak of the logically necessary rootedness of all historical individuals [i.e., objects of historical inquiry] in "Wertideen." . . . we *are* cultural *beings,* endowed with the capacity and the will to take a deliberate *attitude* toward the world and to endow it with a *meaning.* Whatever this meaning might be, it will lead us to recognize that we *judge* certain phenomena of human existence in its light, and to respond to them as (positively or negatively) *significant.* Whatever the content of this attitude, these phenomena have cultural *importance* for us, and on this alone rests their scientific interest.[62]

All *Wertideen,* Weber says, are "subjective." What is important to know, moreover, varies with historical periods themselves.

But it obviously does *not* follow from this that *research* in the cultural sciences can only have *results* which are "subjective" in the sense that they are *valid* for one person and not for others. Only the degree to which they interest different persons varies. In other words, *what* will be the object of investigation, and how far this investigation attempts to penetrate into the infinity of causal connections, is determined by

61. GAW, 177–78 (OS, 78).
62. GAW, 180–81 (OS, 81). Also GAW, 182, top (OS, 82).

the *Wertideen* that dominate the investigator and his age. . . . A system of sciences of culture, even in the sense of a definitive and objectively valid systematic fixing of the *questions* and the *domains* of inquiry it would be called upon to treat, would in itself be pointless. The attempt to achieve such a thing could issue forth a collection of numerous specifically particularized, heterogeneous and disparate viewpoints, continually strung together in a topsy-turvy manner, in the light of which reality only occasionally becomes "culture," viz., by being or having been meaningful in its consequences.[63]

There are two senses of the universal in Weber's conception of the humanistic disciplines so far. On the one hand, their explanations strive for universal validity in the same sense as any empirical science. Another sense of university, however, is associated with the significance of their theoretical concepts. For this sense Weber adopts Rickert's first formulations of a solution to the methodological problem of selection, by developing the concept of culture. Although Weber concedes that "culture" is perhaps never actually experienced apart from potentially invidious moral attitudes, he asserts nevertheless that "culture" is the source of theoretical concepts in the *Geisteswissenschaften*. Nevertheless, in Weber's presentation, as in Rickert's, the "universality" of culture has important limits. It ultimately refers to the breadth of the group or community that will find a theoretical problem compelling. It is always a definite social circle, and not a set of empiricist rationales, that grounds Weber's sense of "universal relevance."

The concept of "cultural" or "universal significance" is crucial for understanding Weber's construal of historical concepts as ideal types. According to Thomas Willey, "his ideal types are unquestionably the progeny of Rickert's 'theoretical relating to values.' "[64] The choice of term *ideal type* is meant to indicate that the criteria of theoretical selection are at least implicitly contained in the "ideas" we bring to history. The ideal type thus illustrates Weber's theory of the link between culture and concepts, as the following examples will show.

The idea of the medieval "city economy" is not a general concept. It makes use of a concept of the "city economy" in general, but then alters this in certain ways according to our particular, culturally grounded interest in the medieval, occidental city.[65] The ideal type is therefore comparative

---

63. GAW, 183–84f. (OS, 84f.).
64. Willey, *Back to Kant,* 163.
65. GAW, 190–91 (OS, 90).

in the following sense: against the background of a general class of phenomena (city economies), "peculiarities" are put into relief whose significance is established by the historian's values. The historian's values lead him to view certain features of an example of a city economy as more or less striking in comparison with other examples. How are these specific features distinguished? In this case, according to Weber, interest in *the medieval occidental city* actually guides inquiry into other cities.

Similarly, the distinction between a "church" and a "sect" can be legitimately employed to conceptualize a certain kind of social formation in terms of what is common to all instances of each class. But if "I wish to formulate the concept of 'sect' *genetically,* e.g., with reference to certain important cultural significances which the 'sectarian spirit' has had for modern culture, certain characteristics of both ['church' and 'sect'] become *essential* because they stand in an adequate causal relationship to *those* influences."[66] Failure to make the initial outlines of an object of interest explicit in this way has, as the "inevitable consequence" for the historian, either that he "consciously or unconsciously uses other similar concepts without formulating them verbally and elaborating them logically, or that he remains stuck in the realm of the vaguely 'felt.' "[67]

The ideal types of the medieval occidental city, and of church and sect, like all empirical-scientific concepts, are supposed to provide empirically consistent models that can be tested against the historical record.[68] This is not why they are "universal," however. The universalism of universal history has to do with the historian's description of the specific features of the ideal type and his presentation of possible historical links between these *specifica* and subsequent developments that are of value "for us." Such tasks of the historian are, according to Weber, all logically prior to historical explanation.

The importance of the historian's values is further emphasized in Weber's explication of the attempt to conceptualize ideas held in the minds of historical contemporaries, which "involves a somewhat complicated construct." For example:

Those components of the spiritual life of actual individuals living during a particular period in the Middle Ages, for example that which

66. GAW, 194 (OS, 93–94); last emphasis added.
67. GAW, 195 (OS, 94). The same point is made in the Freiburg address, quoted chapter 3, page 111.
68. So, e.g., GAW, 198–99 (OS, 97): "the synthesis is an 'idea' which *we* have created"; it remains subject to "*comparison* with and the *measurement* of reality."

we would call "the Christianity" of the relevant individuals, would, *if* we were capable of bringing them fully into a representation, naturally constitute a chaos of infinitely differentiated and most contradictory intellectual and emotional patterns of all kinds, despite which the medieval church was certainly capable of bringing about the unity of faith and morals to a particularly high degree. If we now ask, what then in this chaos could be *the* "Christianity" of the Middle Ages—for which we must still continuously employ a fixed concept—and in what does this "Christianity" that we find in medieval institutions lie—as soon as we ask such a question it becomes apparent that even here, in this individual case, a construction of pure thought, created by us, is being used. It is a combination of articles of faith, church-legal and moral norms, maxims for the conduct of life, and countless individual patterns which we put together into an "idea." This is a synthesis that we would be unable to achieve with any consistency without the use of ideal types.[69]

This example is meant to emphasize the fact that our access to the past is mediated by our own intellectual and evaluative concepts of history. But it goes further, to elevate what might be a precautionary methodological consideration to a foundation for knowledge.

The "Objectivity" essay concludes with a brief outline of Weber's construal of the growth of knowledge in the human sciences. Weber's conclusions here are meant to contrast with the ideal of a linear accretion of knowledge into a unified universal theoretical scheme, which usually accompanies a stress on generalizations as a methodological paradigm. In contrast to such an ideal, Weber says the human sciences are characterized by a variety of universal schemes, and their respective diverse value bases would all have to be reconciled before we could hope for an overarching system encompassing these schemes. "In the cultural sciences the formation of concepts depends on the setting of the problem (*der Stellung der Problem*), and this varies with the content of culture itself."[70] For this reason it is unlikely that there will be any rational progress in knowledge in these sciences. This is not the case in the short term, however. Once a particular *Problemstellung* has led to the establishment of a particular subject matter and a practical approach to the field, investigation proceeds without conscious reference to the field's underlying *Wertideen* and, indeed, researchers

---

69. GAW, 197 (OS, 96).
70. GAW, 206–7 (OS, 104–5).

in the field become unaware that it is anchored in such principles.[71] However, because "the eternally onward flowing stream of culture perpetually brings new *Problemstellungen*" to the cultural disciplines,[72] a longer term theoretical discontinuity prevails: "The greatest advances in the sphere of the cultural sciences are *substantively* tied to the shift in practical cultural problems and they take the form of a critique of concept-formation."[73] This, finally, ties the formulation of problems in society to the formation of concepts in the social sciences logically, as well as historically. Theoretical dispute on Weber's view is really criticism of the way a historical concept (ideal type) selects out phenomena from history; such criticism really addresses, if only implicitly, the value basis of a given historical theory rather than its strictly empirical veracity.

V

According to advocates of the analytic ideal at the time, reliance on the ability to "understand" human events in a way not possible in the natural sciences has to be given up for the sake of modernizing the *Geisteswissenschaften*. Their opponents held up the "irrationality" of "understanding" as the distinctive advantage of the *Geisteswissenschaften* over the natural sciences. Weber rejects both these views in their extreme, uncompromising forms, and offers his cultural-value construal as a way of harmonizing these views and preserving the virtues of each. Both psychological and analytical types of understanding are forms of interpretation ultimately rooted in "valuations" (*Wertungen*), and this allows the objects of each type of interpretation to achieve "general (= universal) significance."[74]

Weber's solution to the problem of understanding is very similar to Dilthey's. Dilthey's efforts, like Weber's, grew out of an attempt to bring together the Kantian critique of knowledge and the methods of the Historical School.[75] Only while Dilthey's construal of *geisteswissenschaftlich*

71. GAW, 214 (OS, 112).

72. GAW, 206 (OS, 104).

73. GAW, 208, top (OS, 106).

74. GAW, 254, top (CS, 152). With reference to this context, Ringer (*Mandarins*, 332–33) also shows how Weber's theory of the methodological role of "culture" represents a revision of the theory of *verstehen* that is designed to both de-mystify the ideal of empathy and to accommodate the legitimate aspects of the analytic ideal in the *Methodenstreit*.

75. Cf. Manfred Riedel, intro. to Dilthey, *Der Aufbau der geschichtlichen Welt in den Geisteswissenschaften* (1910; Frankfurt, 1970), cited in Schnädelbach, *Philosophy in Germany*, 122.

knowledge was psychologistic—that is, the object of understanding depends on the human act of understanding—Weber followed the Baden neo-Kantians in their efforts to develop a transcendental (nonpsychologistic) theory of historical knowledge. A comparison of the two construals of understanding shows that Weber's effort is less universalistic than Dilthey's.

Dilthey's psychologism grew out of his holism, "a historical and psychological concern with the whole of man . . . in the multiplicity of his powers, this willing, feeling, representing being." On this basis, Dilthey's "critique of historical reason" seeks to ground knowledge in "the history of our development, which proceeds from the totality of our being."[76] Dilthey drew on the terminology of the historian J. G. Droysen (1808–84), who had undertaken a similar analysis of hermeneutics. Droysen's aim was to separate history from philology by distinguishing among three methods of understanding, "heuristics," "critique," and "interpretation." The first makes historical material available, the second is the equivalent of source-criticism in philology. The third is historical understanding, and it has two aspects, the act of understanding, which "is like an immediate intuition" (and in fact draws on the other two "lower" methods of understanding), and a procedure that can be subjected to methodological norms. The purpose of these distinctions is to support a construal of the psychological process as an understanding of empirical *expressions,* expressions of all sorts and not just texts, as in philology. In Droysen's words:

> It is merely an extension of what has been said that the works of industry, the foundations of cities and their fortification, the building of harbors and roads, that justice, law, state, church—in short, all human efforts to impose form on their lives, even if the common will of many created or reshaped them, are of the same sort, expressions of the human spirit and intelligible to the human spirit, just as they come to be empirically observable to it. In a word: nothing which has stirred the human spirit and found sensuous expression could not be understood, nothing which can be understood which does not lie in the domain of our common spirit, which we have recognized as belonging to historical experience, in the domain of the ethical world.[77]

---

76. Dilthey, preface to *Introduction to the Human Sciences* (1883), quoted in Schnädelbach, *Philosophy in Germany,* 54–55.

77. Droysen, *Grundrisse der Historik* (1868), quoted in Schnädelbach, *Philosophy in Germany,* 120.

Dilthey extended this analysis, holding that history is life interpreting itself by understanding the objective expressions of spirit, a revision of Hegel's philosophy of history. The act of understanding in just this way becomes universal rather than subjective; that is, it becomes "scientific."

> If we grasp the sum of the achievements of understanding, then there becomes visible in it, in opposition to the subjectivity of experience, the objectification of life. Besides experience, the observation of the objectivity of life, its externalization in manifold connections, becomes the basis of the human sciences. The individual, the communities and the works into which life and spirit have been transferred form the outward kingdom of the spirit.[78]

For both Droysen and Dilthey, understanding is both a meeting of the minds across time, and a synthetic act of the historian.[79] All three, Droysen, Dilthey, and Weber, distinguish philology from hermeneutics or historical interpretation in a similar way; in Dilthey's terms philology is the artistic interpretation of texts, while interpretation is "the science of this art," culminating in exposition, which is itself a technique for understanding.[80] For Weber, however, our immediate understanding of action and events is not of the form of a meeting of the minds, if only because this type of understanding requires analysis, or observational confirmation, both of which take us out of the immediacy of lived experience.[81] Both everyday and historical understanding are "continuously 'revised' by means of 'empirical knowledge' in exactly the same way as the hypotheses of the 'natural sciences' are."[82] The analytic ideal is just as important, Weber wants to say, in the cultural sciences as in natural sciences. He does not want to

---

78. Dilthey, *Der Aufbau*, quoted in Schnädelbach, *Philosophy in Germany*, 56.

79. The characteristic combination (and confusion) of these two aspects is expressed by Dilthey in these terms: "By 'external expression of life' (*Lebensäußerungen*) here I understand, not only those expressions which are intended to mean or signify something, but also those which, without such an intention, as expressions of something spiritual make it intelligible for us. The manner and results of understanding differ according to the classes of external expressions of life" (*Der Aufbau*, quoted in Schnädelbach, *Philosophy in Germany*, 124). Schnädelbach goes on to suggest that "the concept 'expression' thus acquires the same kind of key function [in Dilthey's system] as the concept 'lived experience' (*Erlebnis*)" (ibid., 125).

80. Dilthey quoted in ibid., 126.

81. See, e.g., RK, 168–69 (GAW, 109–10); compare Weber, *The Protestant Ethic*, 232–33n.66.

82. GAW, 102 (RK, 159–60).

concede that the cultural sciences are distinctive in any way that will violate the analytic ideal.

But there is a stronger reason for denying that a meeting of the minds is possible across cultures. Since the most immediate form of understanding is practical value judgment,[83] based on the values of the investigator and his age, there is no sense in which we have access to the "native's point of view," except through our common rationality.[84] In Weber's view, the understanding of human action presumes some form of rationality, and this presumption is based at least as much on the historian's *Wertideen* as on objective demonstration. As with historical knowledge more generally, "universality" of values and empirical validity are each necessary conditions of historical understanding. But—and this is where Weber differs from some of his prominent predecessors in the Historical School—inasmuch as culture, for Weber, defines the circle within which value analysis can occur, the meaning of events and historical development is primarily an artifact of our common values. Cultural values condition our capacity for understanding, and so also the degree of "universality" of our understanding. Weber's aspirations for the *Geisteswissenschaften* are less universalistic than Dilthey's or even Droysen's, each of whom thought nothing was inaccessible to understanding in principle.

Notwithstanding his criticisms, Weber does not want to deny that immediate understanding of some kind is possible in the *Geisteswissenschaften.* In fact, he affirms the common, pro-*Geisteswissenschaften* view, that this is what makes these disciplines distinctive. He does want to deny, however, that immediate understanding makes possible universal access to, or universal sympathy for, all human life. Despite the formal weaknesses Weber points to in their arguments, this claim at least redeemed the theorists of *Nacherleben,* like Dilthey and others Weber criticizes. But it is just this part of their construal of historical knowledge that Weber attacks, in order to clarify his own cultural-value construal. It is not our psychology, but our culture, Weber suggests, that gives us the ability to understand things immediately.

The view that we have immediate access to the meaning of human events through our human psychology, a view Weber calls "intuitionism," was built upon and developed into an extreme analytic model by Wilhelm

---

83. E.g., RK, 184 (GAW, 124, bottom): " 'valuation' is the normal *psychological* transitional stage for 'intellectual understanding.' "

84. See Weber's explication of *"Evidenz"* in immediate understanding, in RK, 174–76 and 186–91 (GAW, 114–17 and 126–31).

Wundt, who Weber criticized. In his *Grundriss der Psychologie* (1896–1922) Wundt argued that the science of psychology ought to be the basis for the *Geisteswissenschaften*.[85] Wundt's view remakes the methodology of the cultural sciences in the image of a completely axiomatized science, the universal comprehensiveness of whose laws should be the goal of concept formation in these sciences. This view makes two errors in Weber's view. First, it supposes that the natural sciences all seek to arrange their findings in relation to a single body of laws, but this is so only in extreme cases, like physics. Second and more importantly, it completely ignores the de facto value the objects of historical inquiry possess, that which makes the purely unique and distinctive features of those objects possible (according to Weber's theory of value). Such features are not explicable in terms of axioms of psychology or any other discipline. They are meaningful only in terms of *Wertideen*. In addition to being psychologistic, Wundt's view that the empirical process of thinking explains the nature of thought is too formalistic for Weber, because Weber wants to make room for the cultural basis of concept formation which Wundt would deny. He does not deny that the psychological aspects of "understanding" which the intuitionists have identified are important, he only proposes to construe these processes as "resonation with values" (*Wertbeziehungen*).

Practically and psychologically, judgments of fact or of what has occurred originate in the committed character of one's immediate attention to or focus on the thing so judged (*das stellungnehmend Actualität*). Ordinarily, we do not undertake an abstract, discursive interpretation of actions. Rather, evaluation of a thing produces in us "nascent feelings and actions that are immediately 'practical,'" not conceptual or theoretical.[86] The intuitionist construal of "understanding" possesses this kernel of truth: our relatively unreflective synthesis of human events regularly makes use of "value-concepts whose 'meaning' we ourselves continually 'experience,' in act and feeling, as committed subjects."[87] Lived experience is the basis of immediate understanding, but it is not a reexperience from the other's point of view, nor is it a privileged means of access to the other. It is only the most immediate aspect of the application of one's own point of view. Moreover, as an intellectual act, understanding occurs on a continuum, from imme-

---

85. Cit. Schnädelbach, *Philosophy*, 241n.9. Schnädelbach goes on to show how Wundt's priority for psychology threatened the identity of established humanistic disciplines as science (p. 74).

86. GAW, 94 (RK, 152); cf. also notes 49–53.

87. GAW, 91 (RK, 151).

diateness to analytic distance. Normally our immediate understanding of the meaning of a statement spoken by someone else (its "noetic" content) is confirmed by "an actual, observational 'agreement' with the author." Where this is impossible, for example when one tries to understand the objective sense of a written military command that is drawn up ambiguously, it is necessary to intellectually interpret the motives or purposes of the commanding officer, to find out what motives could account for the content of the command. "Therefore, the *causal* question—how has the order *arisen* 'psychologically'?—will, with regard to the purpose, be opened up in the process of solving the 'noetic' question regarding its 'meaning.' Here *theoretical* 'interpretation' (*Deutung*) of personal action and eventually of the 'personality' (of the commander) appears in the service of everyday practical purposes."[88] This is an analytical operation, not the product of immediate experience.

Although the two aspects of cognition, the object of "commitment" and the content of valuation, are actually experienced together, in an unbroken consciousness of the world, they can be separated analytically. Once this is done, by subjecting a "commitment" to scientific analysis, "the theoretical *relation* to value takes the place of 'valuation' (*Wertung*), [while] the causal 'understanding' of the interpretive historian takes the place of the 'commitment' of the experiencing subject."[89] In this way, a dogmatic, immediate understanding of the sense or meaning of a thing gives way to an "interpretive understanding" (*Deutung, deutend Verstehen*) of meaning in a wider sense. This process of abstraction, called "value analysis" in the essay on "Objectivity," extracts the *Wertideen* from *Wertungen,* where they originate, according to Weber.

VI

The theory of value analysis is developed further, completing Weber's scheme for the types of historical interpretation and leading to his characterization of universal history on the basis of this scheme, in his critique of Eduard Meyer.[90] The main burden of this 1906 essay is to show that

---

88. GAW, 95 (RK, 154).

89. GAW, 90 (RK, 149). See also RK, 255–57n, points 2 and 3 against Gottl, for the priority of selecting the essential features of the object in order to understand its meaning. I will return to this below, when discussing Weber's critique of Eduard Meyer.

90. CS, especially part 2.

Meyer's construal of historical methods neglects the distinctive role of values in the *Geisteswissenschaften*. Meyer proposed a single, simple and universal formula for deciding what is "historical" as against what is historically superfluous. He held that the role that events have in a subsequent development give them "historical" status. Because the developmental connections over time are at the center of the historian's attention, all forms of interpretation fall short of the historical because they are "static," they represent a constellation of events frozen in time. Meyer's main example of nonhistorical, "static" concept formation in history was the philological interpretation of a document or artifact. This was not truly "historical" research because the causal relation to subsequent important events was left out of account. "Interpretation," Meyer concluded, is not a legitimate historical method.

Meyer also claimed that what is "historical" is unpredictable, and that the unpredictability of historical events is due to the peculiarly "irrational" quality of human action. Meyer said that "irrationality" in the sense of the unpredictability of an individual's action is the product of a universal human quality, the freedom of the will. Human behavior does not conform to nomological laws; free will overcomes causal laws. The "universality" of a historical explanation, finally, he said is based on the universality of free will in human action.

What lies back of this view is not so much an interest in a privileged means of access to human history, as in intuitionism; Meyer is interested, rather, in devaluing access to history through the analytic ideal. This is why Meyer stresses the recalcitrance of human events to nomological and interpretive understanding. (Thus Meyer talks about the distinctive method of "explanation" rather than "understanding" in history.) Weber rejected Meyer's view that the unpredictability of singular events is distinctive to historical explanation. The same logic applies to meteorology and geography, for example. Also, historical processes are just as "rational" as natural processes, according to Weber, if by "rational" we mean the events are susceptible in principle to nomological explanation.

Weber makes these demurrers in order to stress all the more his agreement with Meyer's developmental understanding of universal-historical causation.[91] Even though the hypothetical expectations we frame on the

---

91. "In my opinion only the form in which he [Meyer] has substantiated his standpoint is untenable" (GAW, 263 [CS, 161]). Also CS, 131 (GAW, 233): "Since Eduard Meyer failed to confront these issues he was able to 'feel' what is

basis of nomological knowledge are central to historical explanation, the reason why historians are so often dissatisfied with a purely nomological account (e.g., today: psychobiography, econometric or ecological explanations) is that historians specify their objects of inquiry by reference to the unique aspects of those objects. This assumption also underlies Meyer's understanding of universal-historical causation, with which Weber expresses strong agreement. But Meyer was wrong to construe historical explanation as "irrational" in contrast to nomological explanation. Meyer was actually describing a very important feature of historical accounts, one that he emphasizes in his work, namely their selective focus on those events that seem to go against the grain of history, to stand out against the field of our general expectations. This is what the "uniqueness" of an event or historical development refers to.

The logic of causation is general, applicable to all sciences interested in "genetic explanations" (e.g., history, geography, astronomy). But the *principles of selection* for the parsing out of a "causal chain" are, in *history,* rooted in cultural values. Such causal chains are supposed to be consistent with nomological knowledge; in Weber's terminology, such chains are constructed "using the category of objective possibility, which itself evaluates our imagination, oriented to and schooled by reality, to be [empirically] adequate."[92] So the "causal relevance" of facts in a historical account is of the "objective" type, in the strict empiricist sense. (Weber's statement suggests a series of probabilistic claims.) But what the facts are causally relevant to is determined by "possible 'relations to values' (*Wertbeziehung*)," and Meyer has neglected this.[93] Both criteria, "causal relevance," and "value relevance" are to be applied in evaluating a historical account; each is a necessary condition for the veracity of such an account.

Weber explains this at length in the first part of his "Critical Studies" essay, in the same terms that were used in the essay on "Objectivity." In the course of this analysis he employs the examples of African and Mesoamerican cultures cited at the beginning of this chapter. Thus, "it is our *interest* which is oriented towards 'values' and not the objective causal

---

correct in regard to the role which these 'laws' governing events play in historical research, but he was not able—as it seems to me—to give it an adequate formulation. This task will be undertaken in a special section of these studies [i.e., CS, part 2]." For Weber's high estimation of Meyer as a universal historian, see also Tenbruck, "Max Weber and Eduard Meyer," especially 242–44 and 259.

92. GAW, 193–94 (OS, 92,) emphasis removed.
93. GAW, 26of. (CS, 158).

relationship between our culture and Hellenic culture which determines the range of cultural values which are controlling for a history of Hellenic culture."[94] In other words, the connection we construct between ourselves and the Greeks is distinct from the actual causal connections between Greek life and our life. This is what Weber means when he says that the *Wertbeziehungen* of events turn them into "historical individuals," a term first introduced by Droysen to describe the focus of universal history.[95]

In order to get a sense of Weber's understanding of the logic of an explanation in universal history, let us look at a "rather extensive formulation of a simple matter" (this also pertains later to his construction of the history of the Jews):

If . . . Eduard Meyer judges that a theocratic-religious development in Hellas at the time of the Battle of Marathon was "possible," or in certain eventualities, "probable," this means . . . that certain components of the historically given situation were *objectively* present; that is, their presence is ascertainable with objective validity, and that there were, when we imagine the Battle of Marathon as not having happened or as having happened differently (including, naturally, a host of other components of the actual course of events), positively "capable," according to *general empirical rules* (*Erfahrungsregeln*), of producing such a theocratic-religious development. . . . The "knowledge" on which such a judgment of the "significance" of the Battle of Marathon rests is, in the light of all that we have said hitherto, on the one hand, knowledge of certain "facts" ("ontological" knowledge) "belonging" to the "historical situation" and ascertainable on the basis of certain sources, and on the other—as we have already seen—knowledge of certain known empirical rules, particularly those relating to the ways in which human beings are prone to react under given situations ("nomological knowledge"). . . . it is clear that in order to demonstrate his thesis, which is decisive for the "significance" of the Battle of Marathon, Eduard Meyer must, if it is challenged, analyze that "situation" into its "components" down to the point where our "imagination" can apply to this "ontological" knowledge our "nomological" knowledge, which has been derived from our own experience and our

---

94. CS, 156 (GAW, 259).

95. GAW, 257–58 (CS, 155); cf. also GAW, 124–25 (RK, 183–84). On Droysen's use of "historical individual," cf. Schnädelbach, *Philosophy in Germany,* 121.

knowledge of the conduct of others. When this has been done, we can render a positive judgment that the joint action of those facts— including the conditions which have been conceived as modified in a certain way—"could" bring about the effect which is asserted to be "objectively possible." This can only mean, in other words, that *if* we "conceived" the effect as having actually occurred under the modified conditions we *would* then recognize those facts thus modified to be "adequate causes."[96]

This makes the logic of a genetic explanation in universal history appear to be the same as that of a nomological proposition, i.e., a proposition of an "if-then" form, however complex. But note what unannounced assumptions are involved here: why is the Battle of Marathon important to know about? Because the "theocratic-religious development" it made possible has had effects on *modern* life that "we" consider to be important or valuable. Thus the effect of concentrating, for purposes of methodological polemic, on the intricacies of events around the time of the Battle of Marathon, is to obscure the great leap of faith that is involved in thinking the "great battle" important in the first place. For this involves assumptions about *our own time,* including the respective roles of Judaism and the branches of Christianity in the development of modernity, and the very nature of each of these religions, as well, perhaps, as a number of assumptions about how "religion" affects the everyday life of human populations and the institutions humans create to regulate their lives and make them meaningful. Such assumptions, whether well demonstrated or not, are built into the "historical individual" or *Geschichtsbild,* that provides the occasion for historical "causal" analysis in the first place.

In the passage above Weber stresses all the ways in which "nomological knowledge" is used in this analysis in order to counter Meyer's denial that a "natural-science" model of explanation has any role in history.[97] The uses of generalizations fall into two classes, following the threefold scheme that Weber develops throughout all his early methodological essays. On the one hand, generalizations are used to obtain "ontological knowledge" knowledge of raw facts, "ascertainable on the basis of certain sources," as in philology.

---

96. Adapted from CS, 174–75 (GAW, 276–77).

97. Almost immediately following this part of his discussion, Weber turns to the opposite tactic, by saying that Ranke, the paragon of "objective" historiography, actually " 'divines' the past" by relying on his personal " 'intuitive' gift" for perceiving causal connections in history (CS, 176 [GAW, 278]).

This involves a preliminary "causal interpretation" of the historical situation. On the other hand, generalizations are employed to examine a particular point on the "causal chain," to determine if it is a "crucial" point, so to speak. This involves an "explanation," a demonstration of a necessary connection, or causal link, between two sets of events separated in time. But in the middle, between these two kinds of nomological explanation in a sort of logical sense, lies the object of interest (here, the "theocratic-religious development" Weber talks about). Its construction (which may also be very complex, especially if integrated into a systematic perspective on history and society) is covered in Weber's terminology by the concept of the "historical individual" we met above.

Weber concludes that Meyer has failed to make a "distinction between two types of interpretation," a "value analytical" interpretation of a historical individual, and the type of interpretation involved in philological analysis of a text.[98] "The correct kernel" in Meyer's construal of method lies in his description of the "static" character of value analysis, which distinguishes it from causal explanation. "Even the historian, e.g. Eduard Meyer, in his own works, must in order to weave his design, take his point of departure in certain 'given' beginnings which he describes 'statically' and he will, in the course of his exposition, repeatedly group the 'results' of 'developments' into 'static' cross-sections." Such descriptive episodes in historical writing are the product of and occasion for value analysis, the construction of the *Zusammenhang* that guides historical research.

> "value analysis" deals with facts that are neither (1) themselves links in an historical causal sequence, nor (2) usable as heuristic means for disclosing facts of category (1). In other words, the facts of value analysis stand in none of the relations to history which have been hitherto considered [viz., as instances of a class, as illustrative analogies, or as a conventional "cause"]. In what relations then do they stand, or does this value analytical approach have no relationship whatsoever to any type of historical knowledge?[99]

Weber's answers to this last question try to go somewhat beyond his earlier formula for value analysis in the "Objectivity" essay. In the earlier essay, the formal-logical significance of value analysis, as opposed to the

---

98. CS, 146 (GAW, 248).

99. CS, 147 (GAW, 249); for the bracketed insertion, cf. CS, 141–43 (GAW, 244–45).

"practical" significance of value judgments, was said to lie in uncovering "possible" evaluative positions, or value judgments, without actually making a value judgment. So also here.[100] But now such "possible relationships to values" are said to be possible "for us," that is, for a definite social circle that shares values. This makes those within the circle receptive to a certain "value relation" the historical facts possess. A clear "understanding" (*Verständnis*) of these value relationships is sought by the historian, beyond knowledge of the historical origins of the facts in question. The historian of Marx's *Das Kapital* "investigates [the book] with regard to its *intellectual* content and expounds its *intellectual*—but not its historical—relationship to other systems of thought concerned with *the same problems*." This type of investigation "takes its point of departure in the character [of the facts] as 'values' independent of all purely historical-*causal* significance, and to that extent [has] a status which is for us, beyond history."[101] Meyer's construal of historical knowledge as strictly causal knowledge leaves this aspect of history out completely.[102]

Again, the psychological operation of cognition (the neo-Kantian's "judgment") involves both "philological" and "value" types of analysis in an unbroken process. The former type of analysis is involved when it becomes necessary to inquire into the origin of certain facts to ascertain their objective sense. But it is bound up with value analytical "understanding" in the normal case. So to interpret the sentiment expressed in some of Goethe's letters, or in *Faust,* the Sistine Chapel paintings, as well as Marx's *Das Kapital,* "numerous nuances and turns of thought and sentiment remain 'incomprehensible' when the general conditions are unknown—e.g., the social 'mileau' and the quite concrete events of the days on which those Goethe-letters were written—and when the historically given 'problem-situation' of the time in which Marx wrote his book, and his development as a thinker remain undiscussed."[103] Value analysis synthesizes factual

---

100. ". . . value analysis teaches us to 'understand' the intellectual or spiritual content of [a thing]; it explicates that which we 'feel' dimly and vaguely and raises it to the level of explicit 'evaluation.' For this purpose, interpretation is not at all required to enunciate or to 'suggest' a *value judgment.* What it actually 'suggests' . . . are rather various *possibilities* for *relationships* of the object to values . . . [or] *possible* 'standpoints' of 'evaluation' as well as judgment's 'points of attack' " (GAW, 246 [CS, 144]).

101. GAW, 249 (CS, 147).

102. GAW, 251 (CS, 149, top).

103. Adapted from CS, 147–48 (GAW, 249–50); cf. also CS, 143, middle, 145, 146n.

knowledge, according to what is important to know for certain purposes, into an interpretation.[104] This synthetic interpretation "reveals the 'valued' components of the object, the causal 'explanation' of which is the problem of [another] type of analysis." "The former creates the points of attachment from which there are to be regressively traced the web of causal connections and thus provides causal analysis with the decisive 'viewpoints' without which it would have to operate, as it were, without a compass on an uncharted sea."[105]

VII

Let me summarize the main points I have sought to establish in this chapter, and bring these points together with some of the conclusions from previous chapters.

Weber's militant promotion of "abstention from values" occurs in a quite different context than his discussion about universal history. The context of the debates about objectivity among those associated with the GSS, where there was a premium on emphasizing the new and distinctive features of social science methodology, obscures analyses of the role of "cultural values" in concept formation Weber worked out in his earliest methodological essays, where he develops his idea of universal history. In these essays Weber constructs a continuity with the *Kathedersozialisten* and argues that their style of scholarship ought to be modernized in some sense. The issue of objectivity plays a different and less prominent role in these texts. It's difficult to appreciate this because our image of Weber is tied to his role in the GSS, where he gave passionate briefs in defense of the principle of "abstention from values" in all scientific scholarship.

Weber considered the problem of achieving universal relevance for historical and social scientific knowledge to be fundamental. However, the standard of "objectivity," which Weber also put in the foreground at various times, stands in a problematic relationship to the problem of "universality." At times Weber links "universal relevance" and objective validity together in a necessary way, as in this statement: "The 'objectivity' of the social

---

104. Cf. CS 174; CS, 118 (GAW, 277, 338).

105. CS, 149 (GAW, 251). See also, on the technical significance of a "causal regress," GAW 257–61 (CS, 155–59 [Rickert's "primary" versus "secondary" historical facts," i.e., "historical individuals" versus empirical causes]); GAW, 269n (CS, 167–68n.35 [Mills's "method of difference" describes the causal explanation of a "historical individual"]).

sciences depends . . . on the fact that the empirical data are always related to those evaluative ideas which alone make them worth knowing, and the significance of the empirical data is derived from these evaluative ideas."[106] More often, however, Weber holds that these are two distinct criteria, conditions, or standards for the veracity of a historical account. In principle an analysis of values of some sort, designed to abstract their common object, grounds "universal relevance." A conventional empirical analysis of causes and effects, common to all empirical sciences, grounds the objective validity of a historical account. Causal explanation, objective in principle, both precedes and follows value analysis. Universal history is distinctive, perhaps, in the importance it places on achieving an "interpretive understanding" of a "historical individual" from the vantage point of "our" present interests. But universal history, like all other branches of history, must in principle conform to the canons of convincing causal explanation. But is the standard of objectivity consistent with Weber's idea of universal history?

The kind of universalism Weber argued for in the methodological essays we have examined meant taking relatively unreflective evaluations about history and current events to a higher level of abstraction, and so in some sense standing above them. It meant generalizing the inevitable biases we bring to the study of society so that they would be relevant for a community of interested readers. Weber's ideal of objectivity is almost wholly tactical from this point of view. For his primary concern is to arrive at a defensible (neo-Kantian) construal of something most intellectuals at the time agreed was an essential part of historiography, the value and evocative power of an "immediate understanding" of historical personalities, events, and epochs. This tied the *Geisteswissenschaften* to traditional methods that brought them closer to aesthetic criticism than the analytical ideal of modern science. For Weber aesthetic criticism and "interpretive understanding" were parallel. He held that an "artistic" interpretation of intellectual, aesthetic, or ethical creations is designed to give us an "immediate understanding" of the relation of these things to our values. "Interpretive understanding," unlike the kinds of "causal understanding" Weber reviews, is not necessarily a product of analysis at all (even though it remains subject in principle to revision on the basis of a more considered "value analytical" interpretation of the meaning of history).[107] Weber's formal construal of methods is de-

---

106. OS, 111 (GAW, 213).

107. GAW, 249 (CS, 147). Also GAW, 237 (CS, 134f.): concept formation is designed to help portray "the generic 'character' of certain artistic 'epochs.' "

signed to preserve this aspect of historical method while making room for analytical methods, which are more "modern."

By *universal* Weber means socially general. If he insists on making this sense of universal a condition of historical knowledge, Weber is guilty of psychologism, a position he argued against at great length because it compromises objectivity. Weber's idea of universality makes knowledge dependent on a social-psychological process, if not an individual psychological act. For, by enlarging the circle of consciousness, from individual to social consciousness of values, one does not turn this consciousness from subjective to objective. One turns it from personal to general. One might characterize Weber's methodological interest, in light of this, as a search for a way to incorporate *cultural psychology* into historical scholarship. This would help to explain Weber's vehemence in promoting abstention from particular or personal values. But his position still allows a kind of cultural psychologism in method, notwithstanding the rhetoric of objectivity.

Strangely, Weber's efforts to demonstrate that historiographical concepts (ideal types) possess "universality" and "validity" ignore the potential for conflict between these two standards as he himself defines them. When he said that the validity of an account will be just as compelling to a Chinese as to Weber's readers, despite the fact that "the Chinese" will not be as interested in the account as the intended reader is, Weber missed an obvious occasion to consider the potential for conflict between the strict norm of empiricism and the cultural values that supposedly define the object of interest. If "interpretation" of historical phenomena is possible only within the circle of "our" cultural values, outside this circle the account will not be "understandable." Does this mean "the Chinese" must give up the desire to criticize important aspects of a historical interpretation, perhaps its underlying assumptions? Or does the conflict among "points of view" toward history include this kind of criticism, allowing "the Chinese" to see aspects of historical events that are really there, but to which Westerners are normally blind?

Despite Weber's announced aspiration to pursue positive, realistic knowledge of the social trends that dominate our times, rejecting one-dimensional approaches informed by a "systematic" philosophy of history, such as the materialist philosophy of history,[108] this was not really his goal, at least not in any simple sense. For his aspiration to achieve "cultural relevance" represents another goal altogether, one that is inconsistent with the first. We-

---

108. Thus Karl Löwith, *Max Weber and Karl Marx,* 102.

ber's arguments for the universalism of the concepts of the social sciences mean something essentially more parochial than what humanistic scholars today usually understand by such aims. He was conscious of making assumptions based on his own cultural background which, while he subjected them to *analysis,* he did not always approach critically. A critical approach was not really his aim. His aim was, rather, to *systematize* cultural assumptions toward a "point of view," assumptions about the constitution a "modern" society ought to possess, including, for example, assumptions about the role of religion and ethnicity in society.

These assumptions may be analytic, but they are not value free. There is a background assumption for all these, that the circle of historical discourse is a definite social circle, defined as those who possess a common "culture." This suggests that the circles of "universal relevance" Weber talked about are meant to describe social borders. That Weber's discourse presupposes a more or less severely restricted social circle, that it in fact is partly designed to construct that circle, is something that, at any rate, now becomes our suspicion. Weber nearly says as much in his formal construal of methodology, and many parts of his sociology fit such a characterization.

It is usual to think of Weber's methodological arguments as justifying a more or less self-conscious pursuit of personal identity through scholarship. Weber is telling us, on this view, that one of the highest goals of scholarship in the *Geisteswissenschaften* is a kind of personal *Bildung.*[109] One such "humanistic" gloss on "the theory behind ideal types," counter to the reading I am proposing, has been offered by Wolfgang Mommsen: "In the last analysis interpretive sociology of a universal historical compass could serve to indicate the optimal form of conducting one's life according to one's own ultimate ideals. This required that our entire knowledge of the past be put into systematic order at any given time according to specific perspectives."[110] This synopsis is undeniably based on what Weber said could be achieved by universal history. But it leaves out the larger contexts in which Weber's discussions of the roles of "cultural values" and "value analysis" in identifying meaningful phenomena took place. In the form in

---

109. For example, Dieter Heinrich, *Die Einheit der Wissenschaftslehre Max Webers* (Tübingen: Mohr, 1952), 122, cited in Schlucter and Roth, *Weber's Vision,* 86n.55; Löwith, *Marx and Weber;* Schlucter, *The Rise of Western Rationalism,* chapter 3; see also Hennis's paper in Mommsen and Osterhammel, *Max Weber and His Contemporaries.*

110. Mommsen, "Towards a Reconstruction of Max Weber's Concept of History," 36.

which we have it here (in Mommsen and Weber) any kind of individual can employ universal history in the service of his or her identity construction, so to speak. In the "systematic ordering" of history one can work out one or more "specific perspectives."[111] But there are no criteria for "universalism" in outlook in these formulae. Any kind of person can use universal history to his or her benefit. Perhaps purely personal "ultimate ideals" could not provide the basis for historical selection; Weber says that the more general such ideals are, the more universal is the point of view from which history is ordered. But in practice Weber's "specific perspectives" were general within the German mainstream, progressive intellectual community, not outside it. In general, even the most liberal within this group were intolerant of the permanent growth and development of minority groups in society.

Jürgen Habermas also took up the connection between Weber's formal and actual methodology, and the evaluation of Weber's sociology he arrived at is apt (if we translate "value freedom" into "positivism"): "In his own work Max Weber did not keep within the limits set by positivism: he was, however, in agreement with the neo-Kantians, positivistic enough not to allow himself to reflect upon the connection between his methodological perspectives and rules, and the results of social analysis."[112] We should revise this slightly to read: Weber did not reflect upon the connection between his formal and actual methodology *as we would like.* On the other hand, he was reflecting upon the connection between his formal construal and the actual methods of the Historical School. He tried to go beyond this, however, to anticipate revisions in the historiographical perspectives demanded of this style of scholarship by a positive, progressive attitude to modernity.

But Habermas is essentially right. Weber's own methods of concept formation never approached measuring up to the degree of self-conscious elaboration of the underlying "cultural values" of the investigator and his age that he outlined in his methodological essays when describing value analysis. If they did, we would not need to recover the various interlocking

---

111. Compare GAW, 272, top (CS, 169f.): "history is exclusively concerned with the causal explanation of those 'elements' and 'aspects' of the events in question which, on the basis of specific points of view, are of 'general significance' (*allgemeiner Bedeutung*) and *hence* are of historical *interest.*"

112. Habermas's remarks at the 1964 Max Weber Convention, in Stammer, *Max Weber and Sociology Today*, 65. We need not follow Habermas beyond this, to his portrait of the "decisionist" politics he claims Weber's sociology leads to.

contexts which he addressed in order to understand the original meaning and coherence of his sociology. Rather, the evaluative basis of seemingly peripheral concepts like "pariah-people," and more obviously foundational concepts like "status" and "class," is tacit in Weber's presentations. In his sociology—and not just his sociology of the Jews—an ideal-typical portrait of historical phenomena looks like an exceedingly long chain of conditionals whose individual parts are often finely honed in a literary manner. Many of the steps in such a construction appear, by themselves, as quite "understandable" complexes of "typical" action under specified circumstances, lending the whole portrait the character of an intuitively impressive result. But this very intuitive impressiveness—we need always to ask: intuitively impressive for whom?—obscures the degree to which the chain itself might be a product of uncritical imagination. To support the veracity of an ideal-typical *Geschichtsbild,* Weber usually offered "thick description" without adequate documentary or secondary authority for his conceptual starting point. The veracity of his historical accounts are based as much on the fact that the values of others readily resonated with Weber's scholarly portrait (and for many continue to) as on the evidence. But the evidence in very many cases refutes Weber's theses, and the values that inform his theses are ultimately antipluralistic.[113]

The goals and methods of the social sciences are defined in Weber's idea of universal history so as to achieve a sense of self-identity. This much of the humanistic reading of Weber is correct. But quite contrary to the humanistic reading, in Weber's work methodology serves the purpose of identity construction by attempting to close the circle of "relevance" (*Bedeutung*), generalize personal evaluations to the widest possible audience within the circle, but finally to construct an invidious border between outsiders and insiders. Weber's universal history is an example of a discourse

---

113. One should not be misled by the following kind of statement, also very common in the literature: "In principle he [Weber] adhered to a pluralistic model of societal change" (Mommsen, "Personal Conduct," 40, bottom) All this means is that Weber tried to take account of many different kinds of changes, within a number of institutional fields (e.g., changes in economy, polity, religious beliefs, etc.), not that he made room in his sociology for perspectives that were fundamentally different from his own. As his polemics in the German Sociological Society show (and the aim of these is carried over to his better-known 1917 essay on value neutrality), Weber was quite ready to exclude such perspectives as "ideology," thus legitimating his own type of comparative and systematic sociology exclusively (see above, pages 58–61 and 131).

of closure, and his formal methodology can be read as a recommendation that such a discourse is the best way to develop a personal sense of self.

What is the status of Weber's sociological concepts? Are they universally valid, or (what is quite different) universally relevant? To whom is their relevance addressed, and is this relevance really universal, or is it restricted? If the relevance of his concepts is indeed restricted, how severely is it restricted, how exclusive is the circle for whom his "universal-historical" portraits are relevant? All of these questions are raised by both Weber's methodological arguments and his actual methodology, but none of them are explicitly addressed by Weber anywhere.[114] They remain unanswered questions, directing us to the social background of his work and, ultimately, to the soft underbelly of his actual comparative methodology. In the end, the status of Weber's sociology will be determined by an answer to this question: how far does the meaning and coherence of Weber's concepts depend on their original contexts, and how far is it possible to revise Weber's sociology in the light of other values, values Weber did not share and which are not embodied in his sociology in its original form and purpose?

These questions lead to the suspicion that the vast panorama of portraits in universal history Weber has left us is often of severely restricted relevance. In part this suspicion is an outcome of the historical approach to his texts I have adopted, with its emphasis on the purposes of the texts in light of various audiences, and with a view to the place of the text in the climate of intellectual and social problems. Nevertheless, both the original meaning of Weber's methodological rationales and many parts of his sociology seem more or less intentionally confined in their relevance to those who share a nineteenth-century view of the struggle of unified, politically and economically isolated nation-states for survival, the preservation of "national" cultural traditions, and who are also "progressive" in a certain sense. A large and, indeed, leading group of German academics and other German intellectuals shared this point of view. As Troeltsch said, universal history was a burning issue. Weber's universal history is designed to construct this point of view by constructing a history (and thus a destiny) from this point of view.

---

114. It is conspicuous that in all of Weber's methodological discussions, he never talks about historical or cultural bias as something to be responsibly identified, simply in order to allow the reader to judge whether the exposition succeeds in uncovering new truths about or empirically grounded perspectives on the world.

PART TWO

Religion and Society

5

Introduction to Part Two

After 1911, when Werner Sombart (1863–1941) published *Das Juden und die Wirtschaftsleben* (*The Jews and Economic Life*),[1] a dispute developed between Weber and Sombart over the role of the Jews in the development of modern capitalism. The dispute had to do with alternative theses they each brought to bear on the same body of evidence. This evidence, however, is of dubious validity; it has no basis in a critical use of sources, and it is skewed in a stereotypical direction by certain historiographical and theological questions it was designed to address, questions that were standard ones in the scholarship of the day but which have now been discredited. Neither Sombart nor Weber subjected this body of evidence to a critical examination. They only brought to the evidence sociological questions that were somewhat unique in the context of the time, each in a slightly different way. But their selection and use of this evidence was designed to construct an object, Judaism and the Jews, they both took as a common point of departure. Despite Weber's sometimes pointed criticisms of Werner Sombart's sociology of the Jews, Weber's own treatment of the Jews and Judaism differs very little from Sombart's.

Sombart's and Weber's respective versions of a sociology of the Jews culminated a long period of mutual scholarly identification that was rooted in similar social outlooks and similar academic interests. Weber originally presented his well-known essay on *The Protestant Ethic and the Spirit of Capitalism* (1905) in large part as a commentary on Sombart's work, recommending in particular the "pointed formulations" of Sombart's much-criticized *Modern Capitalism* (1902) and his *German Economy in the Nineteenth Century* (1903) as a good starting place for addressing the problem

---

1. Trans. as *The Jews and Modern Capitalism* (New York: Burt Franklin, 1913; reprint 1969).

of Weber's own essay. In the first part of *The Protestant Ethic* Weber expressed his indebtedness to Sombart in this way:

> Although the following studies refer back to the viewpoints of much older work, I should not have to emphasize how much they owe to the mere fact that Sombart's important works,[2] with their pointed formulations, have been put before us, even—*and especially*—where they take a different road. Even those who feel themselves continually and decisively disagreeing with Sombart's formulations, and who reject many of his theses, have the duty to do so only after a thorough study of his work. It must be indicated that the approach that German political scientists (*der deutschen nationalökonomischen Kritik*) have taken against these works is *frankly ridiculous*. The first and, for a time, unrivaled one, undertaking a thoroughly *factual* exposition of certain *historical* theses of Sombart's, was an historian (von Below, in the *Historische Zeitschrift,* 1903). However, what has been "achieved" against the specifically *nationalökonomischer* parts of Sombart's work by way of criticism could be reported all too politely with the expression, "trivial."[3]

These early works of Sombart's included an analysis of the role of the Jews in the history of the rise of a capitalistic spirit. He equated the spirit of the Jews with the spirit of the German economy, but this was incidental to the main burden of his thesis at this time. Especially in *German Economy,* the real burden of Sombart's arguments was a critique of the modern *German* spirit, which he thought had lost the virtues of beauty, wholeness, and community, in contrast to the German spirit of the past. After Weber published *The Protestant Ethic* in 1905, however, Sombart went on to develop his thoughts on the spirit of capitalism further, with the result that the role of the Jews became the most prominent. Weber had also mentioned the role of the Jews in the origins of a modern capitalist spirit a number

---

2. In the current German edition (*Die Protestantische Ethik I*), Johannes Winckelmann, the editor, has at this point put a reference to Sombart's study of "Der Unternehmer," originally published in the 1910 volume of the *Archiv für Sozialwissenschaft und Sozialpolitik,* without further comment. This is misleading, since it appears in neither the 1905 nor 1920 versions of *The Protestant Ethic,* and this footnote is itself preceded by a reference to Sombart's *German Economy* and is followed by a number of references to Sombart's *Modern Capitalism.* On Sombart's paper, see chapter 7.

3. Weber, "Die protestantische Ethik" (1905), 19–20n. The last three sentences were omitted in the 1920 version. Cf. Weber, *The Protestant Ethic,* 198n.14.

of times in passing, in *The Protestant Ethic.* But when Sombart came out with his *The Jews and Economic Life,* Weber felt compelled to reassert his original differences with Sombart by undertaking an exhaustive investigation of just the problem Sombart had turned to, the special characteristics of "the Jewish spirit" and its role in history, and the possibility that these things were rooted specifically in the distinctive character of the religion of the Jews. The questions Weber differed with Sombart on concerned the historical effects that the spirit of "Jewish rationalism" had on modern capitalism, but he never disputed the supposition that the Jewish people were marked for millennia by a uniquely rationalistic spirit. In other words, Weber accepted Sombart's basic claims about special Jewish characteristics and brought these to bear on a different thesis. This thesis was only subtly different from Sombart's own, and the differences were designed to support Weber's original Protestant ethic thesis.

It appears that Weber was very reluctant to undertake a sustained study of Judaism and the Jews. He did so only after he was goaded into this by Sombart, who challenged his thesis that Protestantism and capitalism were linked historically, by proposing that "Jewish rationalism," rather than "Protestant rationalism," as Weber held, was responsible for the rationalistic spirit of modern culture. Sombart's sociology, in Weber's judgment, was based on an unclear and inconsistent conceptual apparatus. Weber therefore undertook a clarification of Sombart's concepts from the standpoint of his own social outlook. In all his early work Sombart championed the proletariat, and his perspective on the rise of capitalism was accordingly antagonistic. Weber's pro-industrial modernism led him to look for the sources of what he came to call the "vocational ethic" of modern societies, the sources as well of the dynamic national unity he sought for his own country. The differences Weber had with Sombart, then, parallel differences in the progressive social outlooks of the two men. These differences, in turn, would be brought to bear on their respective approaches to a sociology of the Jews.

In the whole of this complicated interaction with Sombart's work, Weber's numerous differences with Sombart represent a thin veil covering a fundamental agreement over the legitimacy of common problems they both addressed. The combination of agreement and disagreement with Sombart is informed for Weber, however, by the methodological considerations he was elaborating on at the time he wrote his first response to Sombart, *The Protestant Ethic,* and which we examined in the last chapter.[4] Consistent

---

4. According to Marianne Weber, in the essays on *The Protestant Ethic,* "Weber

with his conception of historical social science methodology, Weber self-consciously grounded his definition of Judaism and the Jews in contemporary value-ideas (*Wertideen,*) values that he was led to clarify in contrast to what he perceived to be the confused underpinning of Sombart's treatment of the Jews. In his own mind his differences with Sombart were matters of detail and revision, and did not affect his deeper agreement with Sombart on the nature of "Jewish rationalism," and an important thesis they shared on the connection between the Jewish religion and "Jewish rationalism."

Weber defended his identification with Sombart's approach to the historical-sociological analysis of the Jews on these grounds to the end of his career. Sombart had introduced a valid problem in Weber's view, the problem of the significance of Jewish "religious rationalism," in light of the more general question of the role of religion in the rise of capitalism. Thus, in a footnote added to *The Protestant Ethic* in 1920 Weber defended Sombart's *The Jews and Economic Life* against factual criticisms brought by Lujo Brentano, some of which he conceded were quite justified, by saying that "Brentano does not himself seem to understand the real essence of the problem of the Jews."[5]

II

In his sociology of religion Weber is in part applying, in part developing, what he called a "philosophy of history" in his early methodological essays. Ernst Troeltsch used that term in the same way, in his lectures of 1901 on "The Absoluteness of Christianity," an expansive statement of the culture-Protestant point of view, toward which Weber helped push the Christian-Social movement since the early 1890s.[6] Weber is in fact something of a

---

consciously used for the first time the procedure of a cultural-sociological search for truth—a procedure he simultaneously analyzed in his logical writings" (Marianne Weber, *Biography,* 335–36). This is an overstatement, but probably accurately reflects the renewed focus that Sombart's challenge provided for Weber's efforts to express his social outlook in his scholarship.

5. Weber, *The Protestant Ethic,* 187. Fleischmann, "Weber, die Juden, und das Ressentiment," 271, has also called attention to this expression of support for Sombart, as an important indication of Weber's method (in contrast to Ernst Troeltsch's sociology of religion, for example). See also Liebeschütz, "Weber's Historical Interpretation," 46–52, for another treatment of Weber's relation to Sombart.

6. See Troeltsch, *The Absoluteness of Christianity,* 91ff. A long foreword to the 2d ed. accompanies the text; otherwise the 3d ed. is not substantially changed.

transitional figure between two groups of integral or cultural nationalists on the left who came closer and closer together in their social outlook as the nineteenth century came to a close. On the one side were those cultural nationalists of his father's generation, including liberal Protestants in the camp of Weber's uncle, Pastor Adolph Hausrath, popularizer of Richard Rothe, who established the main principles of an enlightened Protestant social ethic. Rothe wanted to subject the dogmas and rituals of Christianity to the test of rational criticism in order to distill from the Christian tradition principles that could guide enlightened citizens in a modern world. Rothe's social ethic was subsequently taken over by many who were active in the liberal nationalist political movement.[7] On the other side, there was a movement of liberal Protestant religionists close to the *Kathedersozialisten* but from Weber's own generation, such men as Naumann, Troeltsch, Martin Rade, his cousin, the chaplain and theologian Otto Baumgarten, and especially the pastor Paul Göhre. Weber's close association with this latter group, which had sought to inherit the mantle of the older group, shows how deeply Weber was imbued with the conscience of liberal Protestantism, which had been strongly modernist and reformist, as well as nationalist, since at least Hausrath's generation.[8]

For Weber, this association was not a great leap from his secular nationalism but was, rather, quite consistent with it. There were a number of important figures among the older generation of National Liberal political leaders and scholars who frequented the young Weber's father's house and who could have provided a natural bridge to liberal Protestantism. Among the most important was Rudolph von Bennigsten, whom Weber came to hold in high regard.[9] In 1888 at a discussion sponsored by the Association of German Protestants, Bennigsten defended the liberal Protestant point of view that state and citizenry should be permeated with Christianity, not in the sense of an autonomous church, but in its effects on each personality.

---

7. See Tal, *Christians and Jews,* 160–63. Rothe was an important participant in the *Burschenschaft* movement in the early nineteenth century, when he maintained philosemitic principles against the exclusivity of Arndt and Jahn, the main leaders of the movement (cf. above, pages 54–56).

8. Cf. Willey, *Back to Kant,* 158, for general recognition of this; Marianne Weber provides important evidence for this, drawn on below.

9. Marianne Weber, *Biography,* 39, 118, bottom. There is also a suggestive story about the young Weber's close relationship to an obscure liberal theologian who became a boarder in his family's house and a spiritual confidante (ibid., 144–45, 152–54).

Through a "consciousness of vocation" (*Berufungsbewusstsein*) that could inform daily conduct, Bennigsten argued that religion would cease to be imposed by the external authority of church or state.[10] Bennigsten's point of view was widely represented, for example, in *Die Christliche Welt,* the main organ of liberal Protestantism and a publication Weber became associated with.

The Association of German Protestants attracted a left wing within the Inner Mission, a state-sponsored association Weber participated in. The Inner Mission became an important focal point for the Christian-Social movement, which was becoming increasingly polarized between the partisans of a Christian state on the right, led by Stoecker, and the liberal Protestants. By the 1890s, liberal Protestantism was crystallizing as a social movement of modernist mandarins around these groups and the Evangelical-Social Congress. Their reasons for taking a position against the right wing of the Christian-Social movement are expressed nicely in a summary of discussions among left wing leaders at the 1895 Congress of the Inner Mission, provided by Uriel Tal:

> Despite many internal differences, there was general agreement on a number of basic issues: (1) Christianity is primarily concerned with the redemption of the soul and the welfare of the spirit; it is thus by its very nature apolitical, and the intrusion of politics in religion is prejudicial to its truthful exposition; Christianity is not confined to any one class or nationality, but has a divine commission to promote justice and to ensure the freedom of moral action under every regime and within every social reality; (2) to confer religious or suprarational validity on ethics, science, politics, or matrimonial affairs is unwarranted and can only lead to tyranny and the denial of religious liberty and freedom of conscience; the concern of Christianity is to foster man's love of God and his fellow man, whereas the state and politics are concerned with the consolidation of power toward the attainment of material ends and *terrena felicitas;* (3) since man's autonomous rational authority theoretically resides in morality, society, and the

---

10. Tal, *Christians and Jews,* 170–71. Concern for the "vocational spirit" was apparently longstanding within the German liberal movement: for example in 1861 *Die Grenzboten,* a popular periodical on the right of the liberal movement, warned against the growth of an "acquisitive and speculative spirit" at the expense of a "genuinely human and organically legal and moral occupational spirit (*Berufsgeist*)" (Sheehan, *German Liberalism,* 86).

state, it is common to all men and all citizens and therefore not restricted to the communicants of any particular church; (4) to make of Christianity a political instrument is to vitiate its religious purity; from an educational and even political point of view the extraneous intrusion of politics is injurious to religion and will of necessity provoke an atheistic reaction: "The result of the Christian state in the forties and fifties was Social Democracy." In this spirit Professor Rudolph Sohm at the Congress . . . stated that "the questions that dominate public life, prominent among which today is the social question, have to do with justice and the distribution of power, that is, questions of this world that cannot be solved by Christianity . . . which is concerned only with questions of the world to come. . . . Luther burned Christian law so that Christianity might be free. 'Away with Christian law' is the verdict of the Reformation. 'Away with the Christian state' is the verdict of world history. . . . The hatred of the masses against Christianity, against Christ, against the church . . . is the consequence of the idea of the Christian state."[11]

Similarly, *Die Christliche Welt* called for an ideological character, or *Weltanschauung,* to imbue character training among all classes of German citizens; they called this the application of the "Christian principle," in their specifically civic, nonchurchly sense.[12]

Weber shared the social values of these liberal Protestants, and he thought his active participation in the movement would offer a means of implementing the progressive social policy whose principles he developed from the 1890s on.[13] In a defense of Göhre in *Die Christliche Welt,* Weber said that the liberal Protestant groups in the younger generation had come together around the idea that spiritual independence needs to be promoted and cultivated among all classes of citizens: "Their [the workingmen's] intellect has emancipated itself from bondage to tradition, and we should not only understand this and view it with indulgence, but *take it into account* and recognize it as something justified."[14]

---

11. Tal, *Christians and Jews,* 174–75.

12. Ibid., 171–72.

13. This is the conclusion of Rita Aldenhoff as well, on whose highly informative article, "Max Weber and the Evangelical-Social Congress," in *Max Weber and His Contemporaries,* ed. Mommsen and Osterhammel, 193–202, much of my interpretation is based.

14. Quoted in Marianne Weber, *Biography,* 133.

Weber participated in the Evangelical-Social Congress from its founding in 1890. In 1892 he became a member of the executive Council of the Congress and, in 1894, a member of the local Council of the Evangelical-Social Union in Baden. He undertook to further the political education of clergy with lecture courses for the Congress up to 1897, including lectures in Berlin, where Weber debated the industrialization controversy with Wagner, Oldenberg, and others. He collaborated with Rade on *Die Christliche Welt,* wrote articles for the Congress's *Mitteilungen* and, with Paul Göhre, he extended his research into the social psychology of rural workers under the auspices of the Congress.[15] In all these activities, Weber enjoyed the sympathy of both the older and the younger generation of liberal religionists who, like himself, "wished to see social policy grounded in a recognition of the rights of working people to independent organization and self-determination. This was to include a recognition of their right to political and social representation."[16]

Throughout the 1890s and after the turn of the century, Weber developed his social and historical theory in the direction of the liberal, culture-Protestant social ideal. It was this agenda that led Weber to sign a petition to the Protestant High Commission in 1894, under Adolph von Harnack's instigation, calling for liberalizing the status of the Apostles' Creed in the religious service.[17] Harnack went on to successfully oppose Stoecker's agenda for "social monarchy" within the Congress, and to redefine the functions of the group as a forum for secular social policy debate. According to Rita Aldenhoff, "this new understanding of the Congress's functions . . . enabled Weber to present himself to some extent as a specialist in law and political economy willing to serve Protestant aspirations by carrying out his work of theoretical 'enlightenment.' "[18]

It was only after Weber became deeply involved with the Christian-Social's that he became associated with Friedrich Naumann. Naumann was chaplain to the Inner Mission in Frankfurt in 1892, when he spoke at the third Evangelical-Social Congress. At that time he was considered to be the leader of the younger generation in the Christian-Social movement, and he

---

15. Aldenhoff, "Evangelical-Social Congress," 194; cf. Marianne Weber, *Biography,* 135–37. Weber and Göhre presented the results of a new survey of rural pastors at the fifth Congress in 1894.

16. Aldenhoff, "Evangelical-Social Congress," 195.

17. Ibid., 197.

18. Ibid.

was called the "poor people's pastor."[19] It seems to have been Naumann's apparent ability for imminent success in reaching the proletariat with a program of "national" political education that kept Weber actively engaged in Naumann's pastoral and, later, political efforts. But it was Naumann who turned toward Weber much more than the other way around. When Weber's Freiburg address came out in print in 1895, Naumann was so strongly affected by it that he broke with the proletarian Christianity that had informed his thinking up to then and proposed a "national socialism" to takes its place.[20] We looked at Weber's first critique of Naumann, at the fifth Evangelical-Social Congress in 1894, in chapter 3.[21] Weber continued to have two basic criticisms of Naumann's political association, notwithstanding his active membership in it: (1) it was not manned by the working class; (2) it's "miserabilistic standpoint" (*Miserabilitätsstandpunkt*) provides no guarantee for "the preservation of national power interests" (the precondition for "cultural" "elbow-room," as Weber argued in the Freiburg address,) and Naumann's followers therefore waffle whenever a new "economic misery gets on their nerves." The "national viewpoint" is incompatible with the miserabilistic one.[22] In 1903, when Naumann, after his second failure to become elected to the Reichstag, dissolved the National-Social Party, and Weber had the opportunity to found a periodical

---

19. Marianne Weber, *Biography*, 133–37.

20. Theiner, "Friedrich Naumann and Max Weber," 302, bottom.

21. Cf. above, pages 64–65.

22. Marianne Weber, *Biography*, 222, a lengthy report on Weber's remarks at the founding meeting of the National-Social Association, organized by Göhre and Naumann in Erfurt, November, 1896. The lack of a "national viewpoint" to unify one's view of social policy and national development became Weber's definition of a "philistine" outlook (ibid., 224). A later judgment on Naumann applies to the philistine generally: "the past speaks to him far less than it does to us [Marianne and Max Weber]. He now feels too 'modern,' too social, and too economic"—i.e., too little "national" (ibid., 254). Nevertheless, none of these criticisms prevented Weber from remaining an active member of the National-Social Party. As late as 1908, after Naumann's party had been dissolved, he considered the Progressive People's Party (*Freisinnige Volkspartei*) to be "inferior allies" to Naumann, whom Weber still supported, because they seemed willing to move to the right to protect their personal interests. That is, this party possessed no independent commitment to national power. At this time Weber feared their coalition with the "power-hungry [Catholic] Center Party," which he considered to be "the ruling parliamentary party" and whose continued power threatened to create "a clerical regime everywhere, in all individual states, including Baden, and the Reich as a whole" (Letters to Naumann, in ibid., 398–403). This fear was quite unfounded, however.

on the party's activity, Weber decided to join Heinrich Braun's *Archiv* with Sombart instead.[23]

The Christian-Social movement took an explicit stand on the Jewish question, expressed occasionally in the 1890s and more often just after the turn of the century in a series of articles in *Die Christliche Welt* on "the spiritual struggle with enlightened [i.e., liberal, including Reform] Judaism." Their agenda of an integral national culture comes through particularly clearly in these statements. Liberal Protestants looked forward to attracting liberal Jews to their cause, the unity of the nation through the revitalization of the citizenry, and they considered "a peaceful and gradual fusion [of the Jews] . . . with the Christian nations" to be a test of the success of their efforts, according to an 1893 statement.[24] Such hopes were dashed, however. According to Tal,

> The desire of German Jewry to retain its identity was therefore a severe blow to the Liberal Protestant principle of unity, for it was precisely the educated and emancipated Jews who, despite their strong intellectual affinity with liberal Christians, spurned the consolations of the dominant faith and insisted on remaining Jews. That this unity to which the Liberal Protestants aspired failed to include the Jews as a separate body was prejudicial to the truthful exposition of their deepest convictions and productive of their deepest disappointment. Jewish recalcitrance had deprived them of a quick harvest of success and revealed the impotency and inadequacy of Christian liberalism. The main hope and purpose of Liberal Protestantism, namely, the national and cultural unity of the Second Reich based on historical and Christian principles, had broken against the stiff neck of Judaism. . . . they recognized this Jewish defection as demonstrating the weakness of Liberal Protestantism itself and as a challenge to its adherents to inquire into the foundations of their faith and the validity of its central ideal that looked forward to the day when "Germanism, the Reich, and the nation, state and society, that is, our whole public life, will be imbued with a vital ethical Christianity" [quote from Troeltsch's 1901 lecture].[25]

Weber's deep reservations about the ultimate value of confessional Christianity presented no obstacle to his identification with culture-Protestantism,

23. Ibid., 276–77.
24. Quoted in Tal, *Christians and Jews,* 164.
25. Ibid., 162–63, 176.

because the movement's own understanding of Christianity was tantamount to just that secular outlook of independent individual identification with the national culture that Weber wanted to promote. Weber ultimately came to think that a religious revival, however scientifically informed, was not a realistic means to the goal of creating and activating an independent citizenry. But he always remained sympathetic to the goals of the left-wing Christian-Socials, that "Jesus was to be resurrected as a man of the people, and the Christian ethos was to have a regenerative effect" on society.[26] Later Weber would give life to this image of Jesus in his sociology of religion, and the liberal Protestant idea of the regenerative effects of a worldly Christianity accounts in part for the direction in which Weber developed his Protestant ethic thesis and his sociology of religion.

The stimulus to think more seriously about the theoretical implications of his cultural-nationalist outlook, and specifically to use a comparative history of religions as a vehicle to do so, probably came in 1897, when Weber's association with Ernst Troeltsch began.[27] F. W. Graf has recently made a convincing case "that Troeltsch was Weber's adviser on the theological literature" he employed in his sociology of religion, and that, "[w]ith regard to his assessment of the history of Lutheran theology Weber is directly dependent on Troeltsch." But he overstates the novelty of Troeltsch's historical constructions, and so his priority for such positions Weber later developed as "the central position occupied by the concept of Law in all 'old Protestant' doctrinal systems, the attribution of ethical differences between the Protestant confessions to competing interpretations of God's law, the impotence of Lutheranism as a practical cultural force resulting from a specific version of the doctrine of grace, the adoption by late Lutheran orthodoxy, largely inspired by Melanchthon, of traditions regarding natural law that were at variance with Luther's teaching on Law, the rejection of Ritschl's critique (based on his own religious politics) of Lutheran mysticism and pietism."[28] These ideas, developed at length in *The Protestant*

---

26. Marianne Weber's characterization of Naumann's social ideal, *Biography,* 134.

27. Cf. ibid., 227ff. Although Troeltsch also participated actively in left-wing Christian-Social circles from the early 1890s, there is no evidence of a friendship with Weber before 1897. The available clues are surveyed by Graf, "Friendship between Experts: Notes on Weber and Troeltsch," 216–19, although Graf says "It is far from easy to determine the shared interests which brought Troeltsch and Weber together." I hope I have shed additional light on this question.

28. Graf, "Friendship between Experts," 222.

Ethic, were central to the critical-historical study of the Bible developed by liberal Protestant theologians from Adolph Hausrath to Paul Göhre, and were ideas with which Weber had been in contact since his youth, through his father's political associates and family connections. Troeltsch added little to the imagery of primitive Christianity of the liberals, but he did provide a stimulating sketch of a comparative analysis of religions, in his "Absoluteness of Christianity" in 1901.[29] In the latter Troeltsch asserted that religions could be compared according to how radically they separated two worlds, the world of the spirit and the world of "state, blood, and soil." Those "world religions" that were "inferior" in their ability to keep these separate suffered "the entanglement of divinity in the powers and phenomena of nature." "The religions of redemption are the ones that consummate this distinction between the two worlds. They sever men inwardly from the whole of existent reality, even from the nature of their own souls, in order to confront reality with divinely empowered men."[30] From within the "Jewish folk religion," one of "the ethnic religions of antiquity," a radical separation of religion and world was achieved by Jesus, along with his first apostles: "the spirit of this one man renews a weary world, leavens the state, family and business, science and art with new powers."[31] Such new men with such new powers, Troeltsch believed, along with the entire liberal Protestant movement, were to be the harbinger of modern society.

Weber's sociology of religion, according to Marianne Weber, "is connected with the deepest roots of his personality and in an undefinable way bears its stamp. . . . Evidently he concerned himself at an early age with the question of the world-shaping significance of ideal forces. Perhaps this tendency of his quest for knowledge—*a permanent concern with religion*—was the form in which the genuine religiosity of his maternal family lived on in him."[32] Ms. Weber is, I think, wrong about the organic roots of Weber's religiosity; at least we do not need to take this into account to understand this aspect of his sociology. This generally neglected feature of Weber's social outlook can be understood in terms of the concept of religion developed within the left-wing of the Christian-Social movement. Their social-ethical message was nearly identical, though not as rarefied, as the

---

29. See the analysis of the "world religions" in Troeltsch, *Absoluteness of Christianity,* 92ff., 108ff.

30. Ibid., 109.

31. Ibid., 128, 125f.

32. Marianne Weber, *Biography,* 335. Cf. also Honigscheim, *On Max Weber,* 111–12, for Weber's "religiously-based [philosophy of] autonomy."

social ethics of the Baden neo-Kantians Weber would soon link himself to intellectually.[33] This religiosity led directly into both his political outlook and his scholarship: at the 1909 meetings of the *Verein für Sozialwissenschaft* he and Alfred Weber, for example, argued that "the ultimate criterion for a social reformation was the question of what *type of personality* it promoted—a free, responsible person, or a politically and psychologically dependent one who bows to authorities and superiors for the sake of external security."[34] The opposite of Weber's social ideal was the "machinery" of industrial and political bureaucratic organization, what he called a potential "iron cage" at the close of *The Protestant Ethic*. The central thesis of *The Protestant Ethic*, however, was designed to identify, more precisely than the Christian-Socials or the neo-Kantians had done, the character of the "ethic" that had in fact ushered in the modern industrial form of society. It is to an examination of the genesis and development of that thesis that we must turn first to see how Weber applied his social outlook to the study of religions.

---

33. Cf. Tal, *Christians and Jews*, 71ff., 188ff. for the neo-Kantians.

34. Marianne Weber, *Biography*, 415, with a lengthy excerpt from Weber's speech.

6

Religion and Rationalism in
The Protestant Ethic

Weber's explicit interest in the Jews and Judaism appears for the first time in his writings with his essays on *The Protestant Ethic and the Spirit of Capitalism,* which came out in two parts, in separate numbers of the *Archiv für Sozialwissenschaft und Sozialpolitik* in 1905.[1] The *Problemstellung* of *The Protestant Ethic* was directly relevant to the Jewish question in Germany, but Weber never addressed this aspect of his thesis directly, despite what must have seemed at the time some obvious occasions to do so. Others had not hesitated in the past to bring out connections between the Jews and the rise of capitalism.

---

1. Weber revised *The Protestant Ethic* considerably in 1920 to make it suitable for incorporation in his series of monographs on world religions and to respond to critics of its thesis. These revisions include additions, deletions, and changes to the text and the footnotes, which already in 1905 rivaled the text in length. (Cf. a footnote opening part 2 of the monograph, which has often been put at 1920 but actually appeared in the 1905 version: "If in the following I have condemned the reader *as well as myself* to the penitence of a malignant growth of footnotes, it has been done in order to give especially the non-theological reader an opportunity to check up the validity of this sketch by the suggestion of related lines of thought" [Weber, *The Protestant Ethic,* 219–20n.5; "Die protestantische Ethik," 6n].) Marianne Weber's statement (*Biography,* 336) that, except for new footnotes, the revised edition is "otherwise unchanged" is erroneous, but has been accepted by many students of Weber's work. In the following I have used Parsons's translation of the 1920 version wherever possible, but have compared this in every instance to the original *Archiv* essay and the revised German edition. Citations to the 1905 *Archiv* text indicate that the relevant passage was changed in 1920. The context usually makes clear whether I am citing a passage in its 1905 or 1920 version. Any ambiguity is addressed in the accompanying note. In many cases it has been necessary to make minor corrections in Parsons's translation, and these are noted in the text where they occur. Parsons often omitted emphases and quotation marks in Weber's text, and these are restored without comment in all quotations below.

There were at least two distinct *Problemstellungen* Weber addressed (corresponding roughly with the first two chapters of *The Protestant Ethic,* respectively). Weber first made reference to discussions about the historical relationship between religion and modern "rationalism," a term that usually meant the spirit of modern science and of the other secular disciplines. A second *Problemstellung* was the Marxist question of the origin of an impersonal or "rational" organization of labor, organized for exploitation by capitalists. Sombart, for example, had already made the connection between capitalism and a rational spirit of duty in a number of publications. Approaches to each of these *Problemstellungen* were ultimately tied to alternative visions of modernity, and Weber was trying in good part to bring this fact out, in order to clarify his own image of modernity.

I

The efforts of liberal Protestant scholarship to construct a rationalist and modernist dogmatic foundation for Christianity were led at this time by the school of Albrecht Ritschl.[2] Ritschl developed a typological scheme that became the liberal point of departure for the historical analysis of the relation between religion and the modern spirit. In his three-volume *History of Pietism* (1880–86), Ritschl compared "world-denying" monasticism and pietism, which departed from the true spirit of Christianity, which is "world-affirming" and "active in the world," as well as committed to "universal social unity," a principle the Catholic church contradicted by its movements toward monasticism, sectarianism, mysticism (a Hellenistic accretion), and individualism. True Christianity is the spiritual power of Christian faith in the world, rediscovered by Luther. The Reformed churches also depart from the Christian spirit in their "ascetic strictness," which tended to lead them into a church form that subjected all things to canons of sanctity. The Lutheran churches adhere to the apostolic doctrines—the hard distinctions between law and religion, discipline and grace, state and church—and ignore church form, which they consider to be on the religiously "indifferent" side of these contrasts. Anabaptist and Calvinist religions became "world-deniers" by virtue of their attack on the creaturely, but they neglect the attack on sin in society. This outcome is also promoted by their separatism. This classification of religions culminated in the view (as expressed by W. R. Ward) that "very remarkably, Anabaptism, Calvinism,

---

2. Cf. Troeltsch, *Absoluteness of Christianity,* 80–83.

Pietism, and enlightenment turned out to be derived from the bad features of medieval Catholicism, and it was Lutheranism that offered a model for an age of liberalism and science."[3]

Weber's Protestant ethic thesis criticizes this classification, but within its interpretive circle of ideas. Weber assumes that religion has had some historical responsibility for the origins of the "rationalism" of modern life:

> A glance at the occupational statistics of any country of mixed religious composition brings to light, with relatively few anomalies and exceptions, a situation which has in recent years provoked discussion in the Catholic press and literature, and in Catholic congresses in Germany, namely, the fact that business leaders and owners of capital, as well as the higher grades of skilled labor, and even more the higher technically and commercially trained personnel of modern enterprises, are overwhelmingly Protestant.[4]

Weber introduces "the Catholic press" in order to establish a *prima facie* case that there is some sort of "inner relationship between certain expressions of the old Protestant spirit and modern capitalistic culture."[5] He cites Georg von Hertling, an academic and politician, for the view that Protestantism and secularism are connected. Von Hertling had tied the spirit of *Wissenschaft* (secular science) in the German universities to secularization. Von Hertling could then argue that German higher education harbored "so many enemies of their [the Catholics'] Christian faith."[6] Another contributor to the debate, writing in the Catholic journal *Academia* in 1899, described the overrepresentation of Jews in the university as due to "the peculiar character of Judaism," as well as to the Jews' "natural desire to keep their offspring in the higher classes, . . . the strong ambition to enter the professions that bring renown through academic education, and a personal strength of will, restlessness, and energy in pursuit of any goal."[7] This discussion,

---

3. W. R. Ward, "Max Weber and the Lutherans," 207.

4. Weber, "Die protestantische Ethik," 1–2; cf. *The Protestant Ethic*, 35.

5. Weber, *The Protestant Ethic*, 45.

6. Weber, "Die protestantische Ethik," 1n.2; cf. Jarausch, *Students, Society, and Politics*, 96–99; quotation from ibid., 99.

7. Fleigen, "Der Anteil der deutschen Katholiken an academischen Studium," cited in Jarausch, *Students, Society, and Politics*, 99. Jarausch cites other *Academia* articles during the last years of the 1890s with titles on the theme "Das Prinzip des Katholicismus und Wissenschaft," arguing for the compatibility between faith and secular studies. Weber cited von Hertling's synthetic *Das Prinzip des Katholicismus und die Wissenschaft*.

with which Weber opens his essay, had originally singled out the Jewish question for attention. Ritschl's work, however, provided a background for attributing unregulated rationalism in modern life to medieval Catholic Christianity. That Weber singles out the Catholic point of view suggests that he is in part adopting the secular animus of *Kulturprotestantismus,* which was at the time seeking to keep the issues of the *Kulturkampf* alive.[8]

The fact that Jews were disproportionately represented in higher education was widely commented on in Weber's day. During the *Antisemitis-musstreit* in the 1880s, statistical peculiarities of the Jewish population were said to reflect the persistence of Jewish solidarity, and this was taken by conservatives to support the view that the Jews were so far unfit for social integration into Germany.[9] A debate on the disproportion of Jews in higher education was initiated in the Prussian Diet in 1890 by Adolf Stoecker, who cited statistics from *Gymnasia* in Berlin, Breslau, Upper Silesia, and Frankfurt.[10] In his response, Heinrich Rickert, Sr., censured Stoecker's "inflammatory speech," appealed to "Christian charity and tolerance," and concluded with a sympathetic evaluation of the Jewish spirit: "Gentlemen, you will not succeed in separating the Jewish spirit, in so far as it is German, from the national spirit." The Minister of Culture, von Gossler, countered Rickert, denying that Stoecker's speech contained "all those outrages censured by the previous speaker," and expanded on the statistical analysis. Von Gossler pointed out that, whereas the population of Prussia is 64.5 percent Protestant, 34 percent Catholic, and 1.29 percent Jewish, the universities have 9.58 percent Jews; 82 percent of all Jews live in cities, compared to 40 percent of the Protestants and 31 percent of the Catholics. To the laughter of the assembly he said in passing that compiling such statistics has "not infringed on the rights of any Jew as yet!" Von Gossler concluded that "One gains the impression that the Gentile creeds supply the large masses of workers, homesteaders, and farm laborers, while a large part of our Jewish fellow citizens do not care to settle in the country but prefer to live in cities. That is the reason for the disproportionate increase

8. Gianfranco Poggi has come to the same conclusion in *Calvinism and the Capitalist Spirit: Max Weber's Protestant Ethic,* 7.

9. Meyer, "Great Debate on Antisemitism," 163.

10. These and other pertinent contemporary statistics are reproduced in Pulzer, *Rise of Political Anti-Semitism,* 12. Pulzer's first chapter is a generally accurate reflection of what was known of Jewish demography at the time. More up-to-date figures are in the statistical appendix to Mendes-Flohr and Reinharz, *The Jew in the Modern World.*

of the Jewish element in our high schools and universities." In an attempt to clarify the status of Stoecker's remarks, von Gossler claimed that Stoecker had not intended to force the administration to adopt any particular measures; "he [only] wanted to point to a phenomenon which exists in our public life" and one which, moreover, "is one of the thorniest [problems] confronting the administration of education, . . . regardless of tolerance."[11]

In 1899, in a public address before the Leipzig branch of the Association to Combat Antisemitism, Rickert called attention to the fact that Jews were demographically concentrated in Protestant areas in Germany. This, he argued, demonstrated the progressive character of German culture, which he identified with *Kulturprotestantismus,* validating its claim to be "the crucial ideological and political protagonist of the national renaissance of our time. . . . It is the basis of the new society that is now being brought into existence." With this Rickert was expressing the same idea that Theodor Mommsen had during the *Antisemitismusstreit,* when he claimed that the Christianity of the German majority no longer posed an obstacle to Jewish assimilation, as it may have in the past, because in the era of the modern nation-state Christianity has shed any sectarian character.[12] Rickert and other concerned majority liberals assumed that the Jewish question would be resolved by the rapid assimilation of the Jews.

Weber may not have shared Rickert's optimism about the speed and the nature of Jewish assimilation, but it was a goal he too hoped for. But despite the glaring disproportion of Jewish attendance at institutions of higher learning, he does not comment on it at all. This is all the more surprising, as the discussion in *The Protestant Ethic* continues by introducing statistics showing an underrepresentation of Catholics and an overrepresentation of Protestants in higher education, noting in passing that Jewish income and participation in higher learning far outstripped that of the other two groups in proportion to their numbers.[13] Weber's reticence about the Jewish question is, however, partly due to the nature of his thesis. By setting up the question of whether Catholics or Protestants have had a hand in the origins of a rationalistic modern spirit, he is preparing the ground for an investigation of types of Christian "rationalism," which he will embark on in great depth in the second part of his essay.

---

11. Speeches reprinted in Massing, *Rehearsal for Destruction,* 288–94.

12. Cf. above, pages 51–52 and 102–4.

13. Weber, "Die protestantische Ethik," 2n.2 and the table at 4n.1; cf. *The Protestant Ethic,* 188–89.

Weber proceeds with a preliminary comparison of Catholicism and Protestantism:

> On superficial analysis and on the basis of certain current impressions, one might be tempted to express the difference by saying that the greater 'otherworldliness' of Catholicism, the ascetic character of its highest ideals, must have brought up its adherents to a greater indifference toward the good things of this world. Such an explanation fits the popular tendency in the judgment of both religions. On the Protestant side it is used as a basis of criticism of those (real or imagined) ascetic ideals of the Catholic way of life, while the Catholics answer with the accusation that "materialism" results from the secularization of all ideals through Protestantism.[14]

The Catholic charge against Protestantism is also often generalized to apply to the ideas of the Enlightenment, or a positive valuation of "the good things of this world" as such.[15] However, contemporary reports from the seventeenth and eighteenth centuries are brought in by Weber to show that intense piety and "an extraordinary capitalistic business sense" were at that time observed to be linked among French Huguenots, Dutch Calvinists, English and American Quakers, the Mennonites in both Holland and East Prussia, and German Pietists. This was not merely a pious mask for an underlying commitment to progress, after the Enlightenment. To the contrary, "the old Protestant spirit" was "directly hostile" to an "alleged more or less materialistic or at least anti-ascetic joy of living."[16]

The Catholics' charges are, therefore, simplistic and confused. However, Weber suggests, they are directed at a valid historical object; there is indeed a connection of some kind between a Protestant religious outlook and the "spirit of capitalism." This whole discussion is purposely inconclusive and is meant, as Weber says in closing the chapter, to justify a fresh inquiry into "the peculiar characteristics of and the differences between those great worlds of religious thought which have existed historically in the various branches of Christianity."[17]

Weber does, however, have specific theses of his own on the role of the Jews, which he touches on in passing in two places in this chapter and in

---

14. Weber, *The Protestant Ethic*, 40.
15. Ibid., 44f.
16. Ibid., 45.
17. Ibid., 45, bottom.

a number of lengthy footnotes in the final chapter of the monograph.[18] In these places Weber discounts the possibility that Jews played any significant role in the rise of the modern capitalist spirit. Of two different reasons he gives for this conclusion, the one elaborated in the first part of the essay has to do with the marginal social position of the Jews. Whatever special role in the economy Jews have had, Weber argues, is due to their minority position and to the fact that opportunities for normal occupational advancement have often been closed to them. Nowhere in the first version of *The Protestant Ethic* does Weber suggest that this affected the *religion* of the Jews (in contrast to his later pariah-people thesis), and the remarks he does make are reasonable and balanced.

One passage in the early part notes "the immense influence of exile in the breakdown of traditional relationships," to which is attached a long note discussing migrant workers as an illustration of this rule. In passing Weber says, "In ancient times the similar significance of the Babylonian exile for the Jews is very striking."[19] In another passage Weber elaborates on the universal tendency of minorities to engage disproportionately in economic activity. He makes this point, however, to show that Catholic minorities retain their traditionalism, while Protestants remain conspicuously active in the economy even when they are in the majority.

National or religious minorities which are in a position of subordination to a group of rulers are likely, through their voluntary or involuntary exclusion from positions of political influence, to be driven with particular force into economic activity. Their ablest members seek to satisfy the desire for recognition of their abilities in this field, since there is no opportunity in the service of the State. This is true today of the Poles in Russia and Eastern Prussia, who have without question been undergoing a more rapid economic advance than in Galicia, where they have been in the ascendant. It has in earlier times been true of the Huguenots in France under Louis XIV, the Nonconformists and Quakers in England, and, last but not least, the Jew for two thousand years. But the Catholics in Germany have shown no striking evidence of such a result [on account] of their position. In the past they have, unlike the Protestants, undergone no particularly

---

18. More remarks on the Jews are added to the text and notes in the 1920 version of the monograph, and many of the original passages are changed as well. These changes will be considered below, in chapter 8.

19. Ibid., 43 and 191n.20.

prominent *economic* development in the times when they were persecuted or only tolerated, either in Holland or England. Thus the basis for these differences must in the main be sought in the inner peculiarities of the confessions, *not* in their external historical-political situations.[20]

This final conclusion, however, that the explanation of contemporary evidence for socioreligious stratification must lie in the respective religious creeds, *rather than* the influence of the environment and historical circumstances, seems rather abrupt. It indicates that Weber's purpose is to dispose of the minority question as having any possible bearing on his thesis. The burden of his thesis, it should be recalled, is to *isolate* religious causes for the modern "spirit."

The other reason for discounting the possibility that the Jews had a hand in the rise of the capitalistic spirit is more elaborate. Talmudic Judaism is extremely formalistic and legalistic in its approach to general moral questions, according to Weber, something that has many parallels in, even direct historical connections to, Puritanism. In fact, it is Puritanism's reception of just these elements from the Old Testament that accounts in large part for the ability of the Puritans to disregard traditional Christian scruples against acquisitive behavior in the marketplace and exceptional achievement in mundane vocations generally. Weber remarks at length on the correctness of contemporary characterizations of Puritanism as "English Hebraism." The truth of this characterization lies in the Puritans' selective approach to the Bible as a source of authority, which was directed at the "Old Testament morality" and thereby "was able to give a powerful impetus to that spirit of self-righteous and sober legality which was so characteristic of this form of Protestantism." There is a direct analogy here "not only to . . . Palestinian Judaism at the time of the writing of the Scriptures, but [to] Judaism as it became under the influence of many centuries of formalistic, legalistic, and Talmudic education."[21] This became important in Puritanism in con-

---

20. Weber, "Die protestantische Ethik," 5–6. In 1920 the remark about the Poles was changed to past tense, and a passage was inserted toward the end about Protestants as majorities and minorities. I have followed Parsons's translation except for the last sentence ("der Grund des verschiedenen Verhaltens muss also der Hauptsache nach doch in der inneren Eigenart, *nicht* in der ausseren historisch-politischen Lage der Konfessionen gesucht werden"). Cf. Weber, *The Protestant Ethic*, 39–40.

21. Weber, "Die protestantische Ethik," 90–91; cf. *The Protestant Ethic*, 165. Weber revised this passage in 1920 to read, simply, "not . . ." at the beginning of this passage, instead of "not only . . ." (". . . nur nicht . . ."), which changes the sense of the passage considerably. See below, page 260.

junction with the idea that one who has received God's grace must, in order to be certain of the gift, prove that he is saved by virtue of the character of his works in the world. This doctrine of proof led the Puritan to treat the Christian duty to love one's enemy in a formalistic way, as a means to demonstrate one's salvation status. This formalistic attitude to the moral law compares favorably with Jewish morality; the formalism of the doctrine of proof "is a subtle intensification and refinement of the ancient Jewish 'eye for an eye,' and is a specimen of Christian charity!"[22]

It might thus seem that Judaism is just as "rationalistic," in the special sense Weber wants to isolate, as Puritanism is. But additional remarks on just this question, the reception of the Old Testament in Puritan thinking, are given to make the point that there are important mitigating factors in Judaism that prevent this development. Briefly, the point is that Judaism's ethical formalism was never directed outward, to the world at large. Thus: "the Puritan conception of 'lawfulness' as *proof* evidently provided a much stronger motive to positive *action* than the Jewish unquestioned fulfillment of all commandments."[23] The same formalism that the Puritans were so receptive to leads in Judaism to the opposite effect, a valorization of the status quo, or "traditionalism." For example, Luther's traditionalism, which sets him apart from the Calvinists and other Puritan branches of Protestantism, is traced to the influence of the Old Testament.

> The authority of the Bible, from which Luther thought he had derived his idea of the calling, on the whole favored a traditionalistic interpretation [of worldly conduct]. The Old Testament, in particular, though a tendency to excel in inner-worldly morality existed only in isolated ascetic suggestions, contained a similar religious idea [of the calling] entirely in this traditionalistic sense. Everyone should abide by his living and let the godless run after gain. That is the sense of all the statements which bear directly on worldly activities. Not until the Talmud is a partially, but not even then fundamentally, different attitude to be found.[24]

---

22. Weber, "Die protestantische Ethik," 13n.; cf. *The Protestant Ethic*, 223n.25. Also ibid., 271n.58, where Ritschl is cited on "Old Testament 'lawfulness' " (most of this lengthy note was added in 1920; but see note 23, below).

23. Weber, "Die protestantische Ethik," 13n.; Weber, *The Protestant Ethic*, 223n.25. The remainder of the paragraph that follows in the latter was added in 1920. Note that Weber is originally somewhat tentative in his remarks. The same is true of some of the related remarks to be considered immediately below.

24. Weber, "Die protestantische Ethik," 45; cf. *The Protestant Ethic*, 83.

Therefore there are elements of both "rationalism" and its opposite, "traditionalism," in the Hebrew heritage the Puritans drew on. This, finally, is the crucial point: the selective reception of the Old Testament by the Puritans simply led to quite different effects than those the Old Testament has within Judaism. "Old Testament rationalism" is evident in

> the influence of the God-fearing but perfectly unemotional wisdom of the Hebrews, which is expressed in the books most read by the Puritans, the Proverbs and the Psalms. . . . But this Old Testament rationalism was as such essentially of a small bourgeois, traditionalistic type, and was mixed not only with the powerful pathos of the prophets, but also with elements which encouraged the development of a peculiarly emotional type of religion even in the Middle Ages [among the Jews].[25] It was thus in the last analysis the peculiar, fundamentally ascetic, character of Calvinism itself which made it select and assimilate those elements of Old Testament religion which suited it best.[26]

The authentic "Old Testament religion," i.e., Judaism, in both its ancient and medieval forms, is quietistic and traditionalistic, and could not have engendered an inner-worldly ascetic ethic.

> The Oriental quietism, which appears in several of the finest verses of the Psalms and in the Proverbs, was interpreted away [by the Puritans], just as Baxter did with the traditionalistic tinge of the passage in the 1st Epistle to the Corinthians, so important for the idea of the calling. But all the more emphasis was placed on those parts of the Old Testament which praise *formal legality* as a sign of conduct pleasing to God.[27]

II

The idea of a "spirit of capitalism" and of its connection to the honorable calling of the modern capitalist and industrial worker, in contrast to the

---

25. As the accompanying note makes clear (reference in note 26, below).

26. Weber, *The Protestant Ethic*, 123; cf. 238n.97.

27. Ibid., 164–65. Weber also mentions once, in passing, the Puritans' revival of the idea of the chosen people, but declines to undertake a comprehensive analysis of the sociological effects of the reception of the Old Testament: "To analyze the effects on the character of peoples of the penetration of life with Old Testament norms—a tempting task which, however, has not yet satisfactorily been done even for Judaism—would be impossible within the limits of this sketch" (ibid., 166).

way in which capitalists and industrial workers were viewed in other cultures, was first introduced into German social science by Sombart, with his book *Modern Capitalism* in 1902.[28] Sombart accepted the productive superiority of industrial capitalism, against the agrarian conservatives in Germany, but he denied that capitalism had any ultimate value. Sombart came under the influence of the nineteenth-century English and German anthropologists of *Hausgemeinschaften,* as did Ferdinand Tönnies, whose early distinction between *Gemeinschaft* (premodern "community") and *Gesellschaft* (impersonal social ties, lacking "community") was originally designed to condemn modern society. Like Tönnies, Sombart considered capitalism to be the pinnacle of *gesellschaftlich* existence, and he hoped for a renewal of *Gemeinschaft.* This, by itself, did not make his social outlook different from the agrarians. His difference with the agrarians lay in his vision of a regenerated *Volksgemeinschaft* in modern times on the basis of socialism, specifically through the trade unions, which he characterized as "the last link in a long chain of *gemeinschaftlich* structures" in his 1896 lectures on "Socialism and the Social Movement in the Nineteenth Century."[29] The romantic ideal of Sombart's socialism led him to shift the Marxist focus on substructure to superstructure, from material life to ideas and attitudes. He did this by distinguishing two different "spirits" of the economy (*Wirtschaftsgesinnungen*), leading to an "economy of needs" and an "economy of unlimited acquisition," respectively. Sombart extended this type of analysis in a 1903 work, *The German National Economy in the Nineteenth Century,* by arguing that certain national groups, such as the Huguenots and the Jews, are prone to "rationalism." But more than these groups, the spirit of modern Germany (*Deutschtum*), as expressed especially in the German sense of *Pflict* (or duty) and *Ehrlichkeit* (or honesty), has caused "factory discipline" and acquisitive "rationality" to dominate our times. In this the Germans stand in marked contrast to the Latin peoples, among whom capitalism has not taken hold. In short, *Deutschtum* caused capitalism.[30]

As we saw in chapter 3, Gustav Schmoller had criticized Sombart's socialism sympathetically at the 1899 meeting of the *Verein für Sozialpolitik.*

---

28. Fischoff, "Max Weber's Sociology of Religion, with Special Reference to Ancient Judaism," chapter 4, 34–35; Mitzmann, *Sociology and Estrangement,* chapters 16 and 17, 186–206.

29. Ibid., 176–77; Mendes-Flohr, "Sombart's *The Jews,*" 159. In an 1897 paper on "Ideals of *Sozialpolitik*" Sombart said that *Gemeinschaften* today were national communities in a mutual struggle for existence.

30. See Mitzmann, *Sociology and Estrangement,* part 3; Mendes-Flohr, "Sombart's *The Jews,*" 92; Weber, *The Protestant Ethic,* 51 and 258n.189.

Later, in a 1903 review of Sombart's *Modern Capitalism,* Schmoller charged that Sombart's derivation of capitalism from a capitalist spirit represents a regression from Marx's own concept of capitalism, which Sombart had identified with in the preface to the book. Marx was to be commended, Schmoller said, insofar as he separated off "all psychological, ethical, and institutional causes; he knows only mechanical-technical economic processes" as capitalism. Sombart is to be faulted not only for his psychological determinism, but even more so for calling the result of the psychological causes he isolated a "capitalist" spirit, "as if it were a consequence of capital per se, and not of the psychic factors that he [Sombart] himself depicts as the direct cause."If Sombart "wants to understand today's economy," then he ought to study "the manner in which the individualist drive for acquisition developed between 1500 and 1900 and cut itself loose from most earlier moral and social restraints."[31]

Weber's discussion of Sombart's thesis in *The Protestant Ethic* appears to be addressed in part to Schmoller's reading of Sombart's thesis. On the one hand, Weber wants to argue against the suggestion that capitalism arose simply by the lifting off of restraints from the acquisitive instinct. This is the type of "rationalism" with which capitalism is associated now, but it was not so in the past. On the other hand, he wants to save Sombart's thesis, that there is an influential "spirit" of capitalism. Thus he gives Sombart high marks for having described vividly aspects of this spirit. But then Weber faults Sombart for being too inconsistent in the development of his thesis. An important part of the problem, according to Weber, is Sombart's understanding of "rationalism" as a lack of restraint, as selfishness, greed, and immorality, or in Sombart's own terminology, as necessarily tied to "calculating" motives. Against this, the thesis of *The Protestant Ethic* is designed to make a sharp distinction between "calculating" *behavior* on the one hand, and *motives* for such behavior on the other hand, motives which may or may not be "rationalistic." For example, a profit-making enterprise obviously requires the calculation of gains and losses from investments, even the calculation of a probability of risk of gain or loss. But among profit-making enterprises, even today a large bank, which depends on a calculably low rate of default on the loans it issues, is run according to a very conservative attitude, compared to a modern retail enterprise, which may take relatively large risks in purchasing new lines of products on the basis of a

---

31. Schmoller's review is discussed and quoted in Mitzmann, *Sociology and Estrangement,* 192n., and Roth's introduction to Weber, *Economy and Society,* lxxvi.

calculation of the as yet unforeseen turns of market demand. Weber called the first approach to gain "traditionalistic," the second "rationalistic," thereby isolating the motives for gain as the crucial variable.[32]

Conceptually, Weber arrived at this position by subjecting Sombart's analysis to a kind of internal criticism. Weber agrees with Sombart's general view that modern capitalistic society is particularly "rationalistic." Part of what Weber wants to say is that what Sombart "really" means by "the spirit of capitalism" is not "calculability" pure and simple, but rather a type of behavior that is self-consciously justified by means of an "ethic." In this effort, however, Weber adopts a standpoint much like Sombart's. The "spirit of capitalism" is a *Gesinnung,* or individual commitment, after Sombart.[33] "Rationalism," then, ought to be understood to be not the behavior itself, but instead a type of motivation, ultimately the "ethic" (if there is one) that makes the behavior understandable.

> This is the basis of our difference from Sombart in stating the problem. Its very considerable practical significance will become clear later. In anticipation, however, let it be remarked that Sombart has by no means neglected this ethical aspect of the capitalistic entrepreneur. But in his view of the problem it appears as a result of capitalism, whereas for our purposes we must assume the opposite as an hypothesis.[34]

This is a fundamental difference in a major social scientific theory on the origins of aspects of modern civilization and the nature of social change. But it should not obscure the equally fundamental unity of view of Weber and Sombart on the theoretical starting points for their respective theses on the spirit of capitalism.

Weber's strategy is to hang the "rationalist ethic" in his sense on English and American Protestantism, to clearly distinguish the German spirit from this ethic, and to trivialize the situational rationalism that arises from marginal social status, social climbing, and tolerated greed—all things Sombart makes a great deal out of in his 1902 and 1903 books. These points are included in a summary of the thesis in the last chapter, where Weber takes up his difference with Sombart again:

> The emphasis on the ascetic importance of a fixed calling provided an ethical justification of *the modern era of specialized man (das moderne*

---

32. See Weber, *The Protestant Ethic,* 65–66.
33. Cf. ibid., 56.
34. Ibid., 193n.6.

Fachmenschentum). In a similar way the providential interpretation of profit-making justified the activities of the *business* man. The superior indulgence of the *seigneur* and the parvenu ostentation of the *nouveau riche* are equally detestable to asceticism. But, on the other hand, it [a fixed calling] has the highest ethical appreciation of the sober, middle-class, self-made man.[35]

Puritanism leads to a "rationalism" that (as with Sombart) must be contrasted to the "spontaneity" of "natural" life.[36] Only, for Weber, this is all to the credit of the Germans; they benefit from "the spontaneous vitality of impulsive action and naive emotion" in Lutheranism,[37] their "spirit" is quite contrary to worldly asceticism.[38] For both Sombart and Weber, England and America stand on the side of "rationalism" and "calculation," France and the Latin peoples stand on the side of "spontaneity" and a naive enjoyment of life.[39] Puritan rationalism destroys this natural spontaneity, but it is (*contra* Sombart) not simply unleashed, as it were, by political freedom and the lifting of restraints off a supposedly ever-present readiness to take a calculating attitude toward all things. Calculating rationalism is not an independent factor, as both Sombart and Schmoller assume. This is demonstrated by the fact that the imposition on "the Latin peoples" of both the spirit of capitalism and political freedom has not led them to renounce their preference for "spontaneity." It has had this result, however, in England.

For England the situation was probably that: (1) Puritanism enabled its adherents to create free institutions and still become a world power; and (2) it transformed that calculating spirit (what Sombart calls *Rechenhaftigkeit*), which is in truth essential to capitalism, from a mere means to economy into a principle of general conduct.[40]

---

35. Ibid., 163. Parsons translates "das moderne Fachmenschentum" as "the modern division of labor."

36. See ibid., 181, top, where "an age of full and beautiful humanity" is illustrated with "the flower of the Athenian culture of antiquity" and contrasted with modern times.

37. Ibid., 126.

38. At ibid., 127–28, Weber speaks of "the antipathy of every spontaneous child of nature to everything ascetic."

39. In 1920 Weber added a more nuanced statement on "national character" (ibid., 173–74).

40. Ibid., 261n.10. Sombart is again cited at ibid. n.14: Watchfulness over the productivity of one's time, leading to the striking of clocks on the quarter-hour,

This is an example of an expressed disagreement with Sombart, but in the context of a tacit and underlying agreement. Notwithstanding his disagreement with Sombart over both the psychological and historical origins of modern "rationalism," Weber transposes uncritically the concept of "calculability" originating in Sombart's work into his own work, seeking to refine it further, but not to fundamentally question its validity. The fundamental meaning of the term derives from the contrast between interpersonal relations in the past and present, as developed by Tönnies's *Gemeinschaft* and *Gesellschaft*, Simmel's "substantive value" and "money value," Sombart, and other German social theorists.[41] The explicit difference—which Weber hammers away at throughout *The Protestant Ethic*—is that "the spirit of capitalism" is not something that is always waiting in the wings, ready to be released from the weak and various restraints that bind it down. It is, rather, an ethic, with definite causes peculiar to it alone, and found in the idiosyncratic development of Christian asceticism under the influence of the Puritan branches of Protestantism. Moreover, this ethic did not originate with the German spirit. "The *formalism* of the Puritan ethic is in turn the natural consequence of its relation to the *law*," and in this is quite distinct from "German *Ehrlichkeit*."[42]

Sombart is, however, correct in his evaluation of modern economic life as rationalistic, insofar as this means the lifting of restraints on the economy as a whole "from its dependence upon the natural organic limitations of the human individual."[43] This is a reference to the *gemeinschaftlich* subthesis of Weber's exposition, worked out later in his work on "psychophysics," that impersonal laws govern individual labor capacities today. Weber is quite willing to call this, with Sombart, a form of "rationalism." But for purposes of explaining the historical origins of this situation, this manner of speaking will not suffice. "It might thus seem," Weber goes on to say, "that the development of the spirit of capitalism is best understood as part

---

for example, is characteristic of "modern vocational man," as "also Sombart in his *Kapitalismus*." But Weber points out, against Sombart, that rational time sense applied to labor in particular began with the medieval monks, thus with Christian asceticism.

41. For explicit acknowledgement of the connection between Weber's own standpoint and Sombart's and Simmel's, see ibid., 193n.6. Compare also Tönnies's early paper, "Historicism and Rationalism," cited in Mitzmann, *Sociology and Estrangement*.

42. Weber, *The Protestant Ethic*, 258n.189.

43. Ibid., 75.

of the development of rationalism as a whole, and could be deduced from the fundamental position of rationalism on the basic problems of life." The modern economic spirit would then appear to be a result of the Enlightenment, its utilitarianism, and its secularizing aims. But "the worldly rational philosophy of the eighteenth century did not find favor alone or even principally in the countries of highest capitalistic development." "Voltairianism," its most virulent form, is "even today the common property of broad upper, and what is practically more important, middle-class groups in the Roman Catholic countries," where capitalism was not so favored.[44]

Part of the burden of the remainder of Weber's essay is to deny the possibility that either social utilitarianism, which he equates with a philosophy for unleashing "eudaemonism," or Roman Catholic rigoristic rationalism caused modern "capitalistic culture." In the course of developing his concept of Protestant inner-worldly asceticism Weber makes frequent comparisons, first, between the ascetic type of "worldly rationalism" and liberal political thought, and second, between "worldly rationalism" and the "otherworldliness" of Catholic piety or the "ethical accounting" attitude promoted by Catholic rationalism.[45] But by the end of the first installment of his essay, Weber's readers could not overlook the implication that "Jewish rationalism" was absolved of its widely assumed historic responsibility for modern capitalism and secularism. The negative debunking of this aspect of the Jewish question was perhaps made conspicuous by Weber's thesis, that the real responsibility for modern "rationalism" ought to be attributed to the role of Protestantism in history.

Sombart's harshness toward the spirit of modern Germany was later to soften and eventually to turn to positive identification. However, it is difficult to avoid seeing in his exposition of the spirit of capitalism at this time a condemnation of the idealistic faith of German society, especially insofar as it is conditioned by German Lutheranism. This came close to an attack on *Kulturprotestantismus*, developed into a modernist philosophy of civic faith by the Inner Mission, the Evangelical-Social Congress, and the wider

---

44. Weber, "Die protestantische Ethik," 34–35; cf. *The Protestant Ethic*, 76–77.

45. See, e.g., Weber, *The Protestant Ethic*, 70, 76–78, 125f., 242n.110 ("the humanistic *indifference* of the Enlightenment") in 1905; in 1920 Weber added two sentences on p. 81, ending with "the liberal utilitarian compromise with the world at which the Jesuits arrived," and a very long note containing a discussion of the Renaissance humanists' "mercantilist social utilitarianism" (pp. 196–98n.12).

Christian-Social movement. Despite Weber's sympathetic approach to Sombart's work, and despite his own principled secular outlook, Weber's deep identification with the conscience of German Protestantism, in its contemporary secular idealist form, must have caused Weber to be repelled by Sombart's thesis. *The Protestant Ethic* can be read in part as an attempt to defend what Sombart called the modern German spirit by absolving it of responsibility for the "rationalism" of modern culture. Nevertheless, Weber accepted the basic construction of the object of analysis Sombart had, he thought, brilliantly isolated, the "spirit of capitalism."

7

Sombart's Sociology of the Jews

In *The Jews and Economic Life* (1911), Sombart adopted Weber's strategy for relating religion to patterns of practical action and applied it to the Jews, arguing that the Jews are religiously motivated to practice "rationalism" regularly. This led Weber to rethink the difference between Puritanism and Judaism, which he had already considered in passing, in the first version of *The Protestant Ethic*, in 1905. The result was less an intellectual confrontation than it was a sympathetic interchange on the question of the historical origins of "the spirit of capitalism" between Sombart and Weber, even though, in the end, there remains disagreement over their respective theses addressing this question. In this interchange, Weber accepted the bulk of what Sombart said about Judaism, including the concept of "Jewish rationalism" (as a type of mind-set, attitude, or motivation), and some but by no means all of what Sombart said about the definition of "the spirit of capitalism." But Weber subjected these topics, as he found them in Sombart, to a clarifying conceptual analysis, as it were. The revised conceptual framework Weber arrived at became the matrix for arranging historical facts in order to address his unique problematic, universal history.

Unlike Sombart, Weber never completed a sustained study of medieval Judaism, as perhaps he had intended. However, his general agreement with Sombart's analysis, which is centered on the medieval and early modern periods, is so close as to lead to the conclusion that Sombart was one of Weber's main sources for evidence on medieval and modern Jewry. Weber's conceptual framework also took over many of Sombart's evaluative presuppositions. These presuppositions are shared by Weber and Sombart despite the particular differences that remain in their respective accounts of the origins of capitalism. In order to identify these presuppositions, as well as many of Sombart's empirical claims Weber took over for his own purposes, it is necessary to survey at length the arguments presented in Sombart's comprehensive exposition in *The Jews,* and then to show how, both explicitly and implicitly, these arguments were for Sombart linked to the Jewish question and to other social issues he thought were related.

The Jews, Sombart says, is a direct response to Weber's Protestant ethic thesis, which is cited as showing that religion can affect economic life.

> In fact, Max Weber's researches are responsible for this book. For anyone who followed them could not but ask himself whether all that Weber ascribes to Puritanism might not with equal justice be referred to Judaism, and probably in greater degree; nay, it might well be suggested that that which is called Puritanism is in reality Judaism. . . . [Weber's study] was the impetus that sent me to consider the importance of the Jew, especially as I felt that the dominating ideas of Puritanism which were so powerful in capitalism were more perfectly developed in Judaism, and were also of course of much earlier date.[1]

As we will see, Sombart thought these were obvious implications of the Weber thesis in light of the vexing Jewish question in German society.

Sombart begins by pointing out that the centers of capitalist growth moved away from Spain, Italy, and certain German cities at precisely the historical moment that the Jews were expelled from those places, in the late fifteenth and sixteenth centuries. The places where Jews fled to, Hamburg, Frankfurt, some French cities, Leghorn in Italy, and especially Antwerp, Amsterdam, and London, were also the places where capitalist growth began at the time.[2] Jews have specialized in trade in luxuries and exportable goods, supporting the view that the main characteristics of "Jew-commerce" have been international trade, especially colonial expansion, and their influence on modern capitalism is tied to this.[3] Not only does the United States owe its very existence to the Jews, for Jews brought gold into the country via the trade with South America when England had threatened to otherwise draw off all American wealth, but "what we call Americanism

---

1. Sombart, *The Jews and Modern Capitalism,* 191–92, 248. Part 1 of the book, "The Contribution of the Jews to Modern Economic Life," deals with European economic history, while part 2, "The Aptitude of the Jews for Modern Capitalism," deals with the religion and history of the Jews. Part 3, which is largely confined to "The Race Problem," is not considered here.

2. Ibid., 11–22. Contemporary accounts from these places are piled up, all indicating that Jews were imported or protected for reasons of state.

3. Ibid., 22–27.

is nothing else, if we may say so, than the Jewish spirit distilled."[4] This is on account of "the early and universal admixture of Jewish elements among the first settlers."

> We may picture the process of colonizing somewhat after this fashion. A band of determined men and women—let us say twenty families— went forth into the wilds to begin their life anew. Nineteen were equipped with plough and scythe, ready to clear the forests and till the soil in order to earn their livelihood as husbandmen. The twentieth family opened a store to provide their companions with such necessaries of life as could not be obtained from the soil, often no doubt hawking them at the very doors. Soon this twentieth family made it its business to arrange for the distribution of the products which the other nineteen won from the soil. It was they, too, who were most likely in possession of ready cash, and in case of need could therefore be useful to the others by lending them money. Very often the store had a kind of agricultural loan-bank as its adjunct, perhaps also an office for the buying and selling of land. So through the activity of the twentieth family the farmer in North America was from the first kept in touch with the money and credit system of the Old World. Here the whole process of production and exchange was from its inception along modern lines. Town methods made their way at once into even the most distant villages. Accordingly, it may be said that American economic life was from its very start impregnated with capitalism. And who was responsible for this? The twentieth family in each village. Need we add that this twentieth family was always a Jewish one, which joined a party of settlers or soon sought them out in their homesteads?[5]

In Europe the Jews' influence was no less important. They helped found modern states by providing supplies to armies and by financing courts and governments from the sixteenth to the eighteenth centuries. They even helped cause the decline of Court Jews by their role in the rise of public

---

4. Ibid., 44, top. Columbus was probably a Jew, since his mother's side may have been of Jewish descent, and "the oldest portraits show him to have had a Jewish face"; and the navigation science as well as the financing of his voyages was provided by Jews; "and the first European to set foot on American soil was a Jew—Louis de Torres" (ibid., 30–32).

5. Ibid., 44.

credit systems.[6] Some passages in the Talmud concerning use of credit instruments and compensation in money in case of burglary show that Jewish law, unlike Roman, Germanic, Christian law, is "friendly toward exchange." This attitude led historically to the establishment of the stock exchange in modern times.[7]

Sombart repeatedly apologizes for the shortcomings in the evidence, especially the lack of quantitative indicators of the degree of participation of Jews in the fields he discusses. His use of a count of industrial directors is typical: "The method is unsatisfactory—naturally so. How is it possible to say with certainty who is a Jew and who is not? How many people are aware, for example, that Hagen of Cologne, who holds more directorships than any other man in Germany, was originally called Levy?"[8] The incon-

---

6. Ibid., 49–60.

7. Ibid., 73–74, 81–83. Sombart relies on contemporary opinions for the historical role of Jews in bill brokerage, the stock exchange, speculation, etc. The claim that the Jews both originated these instruments and played the predominant part in developing the associated economic institutions, as well as the in the development of colonial trade and state formation, is reviewed and refuted in Hertzberg, *The French Enlightenment and the Jews,* chapter 5, 78–137. Many of the facts Sombart cites placing individual Jews or Jewish families in particular firms or enterprises are accurate, but in no field were Jews dominant; cf. Baron et al., *Economic History of the Jews,* especially the sections on ships and sailing, sugar trade and industry, tobacco trade and industries, slave trade.

8. Sombart, *The Jews and Modern Capitalism,* 112. Sombart was severely criticized for using this method repeatedly. Julius Guttman, in a review in the *Archiv für Sozialwissenschaft und Sozialpolitik* in 1913, pointed to this shortcoming: "In so important a country as France, the Jews remained for a long time of very subordinate importance as financiers. The only great Jewish financier discovered by Sombart as far down as the eighteenth century is Samuel Bernard. Bernard, according to the evidence of his baptismal certificate, which has been long available, was a Christian by birth, and the only circumstance that could be adduced in favor of his Jewish descent would be the fact that his father and grandfather had already lived in France as painters." Karl Kautsky followed this up in *Rasse und Judentum* (1914; trans. as *Are the Jews a Race?*) by exposing Sombart's use of the "well-known" Governor-General of the Dutch East India Company, who "bore the name of Cohn (Coen). And we can easily convince ourselves that he was not the only Jewish governor of the Dutch East Indian possessions, if we glance through a set of portraits of these officials." Kautsky responded: "Those who . . . 'know' more of Coen than his name, are of course aware that Coen had nothing to do with Cohn, and that he was as little a Jew as the other governors whose portraits have been examined by our conscientious professor" (Guttman and Sombart quoted, ibid., 122–23).

clusiveness of numbers is thus made to conceal a purported overrepresentation of Jews.

The "medieval spirit" of trade was based on fixed prices, employment, wages, and productive processes, and this social stability was the presupposition of the theory of the just price. Underselling, advertising, and otherwise seeking out customers was considered unethical and unchristian. The many contemporary complaints against the Jews shows that they never felt constrained by these considerations. There were unethical Christian businessmen, but "the whole body of Jews" followed a different system of business ethics: "Hence Jews were never conscious of doing wrong, of being guilty of commercial immorality; their policy was in accordance with a system, which for them was the proper one. They were in the right; it was the other [traditional or Christian] outlook that was wrong and stupid."[9] A crude content analysis of the *Memoirs of Glückel of Hameln* (one of Sombart's favorite Jewish sources) shows 609 occasions in 313 pages where "the authoress speak[s] of money, riches, gain, and so forth," and otherwise indicates the primacy of money values in her scheme of things.[10] Sombart concludes from this that there is a contrast between the outlook of "tradition, the subsistence ideal, the overpowering influence of status," as against "the Jewish outlook [which] was the 'modern' outlook."[11] Similarly, Sombart's main proof of the Jews' role in the origin of securities is that economic organization and economic relationships, including the history of credit instruments, traditionally were stubbornly personal, while from the earliest times the Jews always sought out an impersonal arrangement in these fields.[12]

The second part of Sombart's *The Jews* is devoted to explaining "why the Jews played just the part they did in the economic life of the last two or three centuries." Sombart announces that he will adhere to an objective method, in order to overcome the vagueness "usually met with in connection with the Jewish problem." Objective and subjective factors must be distinguished, he explains, and care in proof as well as in formulation is required, so as to convince "the assimilationist Jew no less than the Nationalist, him who pins his faith to the influence of race [as well as] the

9. Sombart, *The Jews and Modern Capitalism,* 129.

10. Ibid., 131–32. Also 313–15 for the same in the Talmud, 307–9 for money-lending supported in the Bible and Talmud and in the Oxford Papyrus on the Egyptian diaspora in the fourth through fifth centuries B.C.

11. Ibid., 152–53.

12. Ibid., 62ff.

warmest supporter of the doctrine of the environment; . . . the anti-Semite [and] his opponent."[13]

Sombart first formulates his idea of modern capitalism by summarizing his 1909 article in the *Archiv für Sozialwissenschaft und Sozialpolitik,* on "The Capitalist Enterpriser."[14] In this presentation Sombart seems to have incorporated Weber's discussion of various types of capitalism without, however, changing his own standpoint. If anything, the latter is sharpened. Capitalism, "economic rationalism," and the exploitation of wage labor are all treated as equivalent. A capitalist enterpriser combines "enterprising," which Sombart defines as activism in pursuit of a goal, and "trading," which is quickness to make use of any opportunity to turn a profit, especially by "advertising" or convincing. Thus the backdoor hawker, "the Jewish old clo' man," and "the activities of a Nathan Rothschild, who negotiated with the representatives of the Prussian government for a loan of a million," are all "capitalist enterprisers." Use of suggestion to attract customers "of their own free will" is crucial, rather than use of force. Thus the Genoese merchant princes, who had to live in fortified towers, or the early East India settlers who subordinated the natives with brute firepower are not traders in Sombart's sense.[15]

When Sombart turns to what he calls "objective circumstances in the Jewish aptitude" for modern capitalism, he tends to stress the attitudinal characteristics rather than the causes. Because Jews had a legal status as aliens they were always "newcomers," and so "must concentrate their thoughts to obtain a foothold, and all their economic activities will be dictated by this desire. . . . What is all this but the substitution of economic rationalism for time-honored Tradition?"[16] They were not only compelled by their environment to be strangers, but they also became strangers

> because of their almost caste-like separation from the peoples in whose midst they dwelt. . . . And whereas the "others" dealt with a stranger, say, once in ten times or even in a hundred, it was just the reverse

13. Ibid., 157–59.

14. *"Der Kapitalische Undernehmer."* Sombart's translator gives "undertaker" for *der Unternehmer,* but I have everywhere replaced this with "enterpriser," which seems to make more sense in the economic context. A more usual translation, "entrepreneur," has not been used because it does not easily lend itself to a verb form.

15. Sombart, *The Jews and Modern Capitalism,* 160–68, quoted from 167 and 168.

16. Ibid., 176.

with the Jews, whose intercourse with strangers was nine out of 10 or 99 out of 100 times. What was the consequence? The Jew had recourse to the "ethics for strangers" (if I may use this term without being misunderstood) far more frequently than the non-Jew; for the one it was the rule, whilst for the other it was only the exception. Jewish business methods thus came to be based on it.[17]

Legal restrictions on Jewish activity only served to direct their energies into industry and commerce, and also caused them to be indifferent to the political powers of the day, furthering the international scope of their activity:

> The most gifted minds from other social groups devoted themselves to the service of the state; among the Jews, insofar as they did not spend themselves in the Beth Hamidrash [the Communal House of Study], such spirits were forced into business. . . . through their inferior civil position, [the Jews] were enabled to facilitate the growth of the indifference of capitalism to all interests but those of gain. Again, therefore, they promoted and strengthened the capitalistic spirit.[18]

Finally, although Sombart notes the poverty of the Jewish masses (this distinguished socialist statements on the Jewish question at the time), he stresses the effects of Jewish wealth (which he says was characteristic of European exiles from Spain) through money-lending:

> money-lending contains the root idea of capitalism. . . . In money-lending all conceptions of quality vanish and only the quantitative aspect matters. . . . In money-lending there is no thought of producing only for one's needs. . . . In money-lending the possibility is for the first time illustrated that you can earn without sweating; that you may get others to work for you without recourse to force.[19]

Most of these arguments are designed to refute Weber's claims, in *The Protestant Ethic,* that the Jews could not have had a hand in the development of modern capitalism, because their religion promotes "traditionalism," the opposite of "rationalism." Sombart is attempting to show, *contra* Weber, that "rationalism" is the leading characteristic of the Jews.

---

17. Ibid., 176–77.
18. Ibid., 182–83.
19. Ibid., 189.

From "objective circumstances" Sombart, in the longest chapter in *The Jews,* turns to "subjective" causes, that is, to Jewish religion.[20] The selectivity of Sombart's use of evidence is obvious in the earlier chapters of his book, but in this chapter Sombart's selectivity takes on a special character that calls for a brief consideration before we continue with his arguments.

Sombart rejects the polemical anti-Jewish works of Pfefferkorn, Eisenmenger, Röhling, and Dr. Justus "and the rest of that fraternity," which he says are not "scientific," and announces that he will apply a "subjective" interpretation to the sources of Jewish religion instead.[21] As his "sources" he lists the Bible, the Talmud, and some of the medieval compilations of *halachah.*[22] But Sombart's most important method is to rely on what he considers the writings of unchanging Jewish orthodoxy to discover the subjective meaning to Jews of their religion. He says "if you want to study orthodox Judaism you must go to Eastern Europe, where it is still without disintegrating elements—you must go there personally or read the books about it. In Western Europe the orthodox Jews are a small minority."[23] "Hence Reformed Judaism [*sic*] is of no concern to us, and books trimmed to suit modern ideas, such as the great majority of the latest expositions of the 'Ethics of Judaism,' are absolutely useless for our purpose."[24]

But an examination of Sombart's references, which are near-voluminous, shows that he in fact relies almost exclusively on German-Jewish statements of orthodoxy from his own time. His sources are primarily three: L. Stern's *The Rules of the Torah, Which Israel Has Observed in Its Dispersion: A Primer for School and Family* (4th ed., 1904); S. R. Hirsch, the ideologist of modern neo-orthodoxy, *Trials to Israel's Duties in the Dispersion* (4th ed., 1909); and S. Mandl's *The Essence of Judaism* (1904). These are popular inspirational and (in the case of the last one) polemical works designed to effect

---

20. The religious factor "occupies a position midway between the objective and the subjective factors of Jewish development. For, insofar as any religion is the expression of some particular spiritual outlook, it has a 'subjective' aspect; insofar as the individual is born into it, it has an objective aspect" (ibid., 191).

21. Sombart says anything can be proved by reference to the Talmud. "There is nothing surprising in this when it is remembered that to a great extent the Talmud is nothing else than a collection of controversies of the different Rabbinical scholars" (ibid., 203).

22. This and the following should amend recent charges against Sombart, that he simply relied on Eisenmenger and Röhling, in Mendes-Flohr, "Sombart's *The Jews,*" 99n.96, and Oelsner, "Jews in Economic History," 195–97.

23. Sombart, *The Jews and Modern Capitalism,* 197.

24. Ibid., 205.

a religious revival among late nineteenth- and early twentieth-century German Jews, the majority of whom were religiously apathetic. They all take the standpoint of modern religious conservatism, that is, the neo-orthodox movement led by Hirsch, which takes the *halachic* compilation, *Schulchan Aruch,* and Moses Isserles's sixteenth-century modifications of it for German and East European Jewry as authoritative, laying great stress on the individual *mitzvot* or commandments. This movement was no more than three generations old at the time of Sombart's writing, but he took its opinions, which served as an ideology of revival, as his main source.[25] Accordingly, Jewish orthodoxy is defined by Sombart as "strict observation of the precepts" of Judaism, and Stern is cited for the view that, of the 613 *mitzvot,* "All these are binding to all eternity" except the agricultural and political commandments, leaving 126 positive and 243 negative commandments.[26] Mandl and Hirsch are cited for the view that "the principles of Judaism know no change." Sombart concludes from this that the "formalism" of Judaism, which teaches that "righteousness" is no more than "living in strict accordance with the Law" was established with "Pharisaic Rabbinism" and has retained this form unchanged "for two thousand years. . . . Strict orthodoxy still holds fast to this formalism." Hirsch's book is then quoted at length to support the claim that in Judaism holiness and legalism are one and the same:

> Saintly or holy in the Torah sense is he who is able to fulfill the revealed will of God without any struggle and with the same joy as carrying out his own will. This holiness, this complete fusion of the will of man with the divine will, is a lofty goal attainable in its entirety by a few only.[27] Hence the law of holiness refers in the first instance to the striving towards this goal. The striving all can do; it demands a constant self-watchfulness and self-education, an endless struggle against what is low and vulgar, what is sensual and bestial. And obedience to the behests of the Torah is the surest ladder on which to climb to higher and higher degrees of holiness."[28]

25. For the general social, historical, and intellectual background, see Liberles, *Religious Conflict in Social Context.*

26. Sombart, *The Jews and Modern Capitalism,* 195, 205.

27. This is Hirsch's justification for religious separatism for the orthodox within the German Jewish community, i.e., that God requires only that a "saving remnant" of strictly observant Jews be maintained until the end of days, to fulfill the terms of God's messianic promise. This represents an absolute break with the consciousness of premodern Jewish identity.

28. Quoted in ibid., 224.

This suggests to Sombart a certain "psychological process which led to the shaping of Judaism" apart from anything explicitly suggested in religious ethics. "At first God's behests were those that mattered, regardless of their contents. But slowly the contents must needs make themselves manifest to the observer, and a clearly defined ideal of life evolved itself from the word of God. To follow this ideal, to be righteous, to be holy was the heart's desire of each believer."[29]

Sombart's reading of *traditional* Judaism is not merely prejudiced by his use of late nineteenth-century German Jewish neo-orthodox sources, but ironically enough, he has completely misread the intention back of even these sources. S. R. Hirsch and other Jewish intellectuals and community leaders, within and outside neo-orthodoxy—including, for example, Hermann Cohen, but also Moritz Lazarus, the Reform leader we had occasion to consider briefly in an earlier chapter, and whom Sombart even uses as one of his sources[30]—took the *halachic* element in Judaism to be completely consistent with the principles of German humanistic idealism (*Bildungsindividualismus*) as expressed in Kant's ethical philosophy, a belief that goes back at least to Moses Mendelssohn, at the beginning of the nineteenth century.[31] Notwithstanding denominational disputes, nineteenth-century German Judaism encouraged the individual to achieve (in Hirsch's words) "free recourse to the law which all beings submit to out of necessity."[32] The Reform rabbi, Issac Breuer, in *The New Kuzari,* said, "If we want to find out how pure humanity finds its necessary consummation in Judaism all we have to do is study Kant."[33] The development of this theme led at length to the efforts of Leo Baeck and others to define "the essence of Judaism" in polemical responses to Adolph Harnack's 1900 lectures on "the essence of Christianity" and Ernst Troeltsch's 1901 lectures on "the absoluteness of Christianity."[34] At the same time, and in contrast to liberal

---

29. Ibid., 224–25. Sombart also draws on "extracts from Talmudic literature" in S. Schaffer, *The Relation of Law to Morality According to Talmudic Moral and Legal Teachings* (1889). The title is suggestive of both Sombart's and Weber's approach to the "sources."

30. Sombart uses Lazarus's *Ethics of Judaism,* vol. 1 (1898), vol. 2 (1901); English trans. (1904).

31. Cf. Meyer, *Origins of the Modern Jew,* chapter 2, especially 39, 43.

32. Schwartz's paper in Leo Baeck Institute, ed., *Perspectives of German-Jewish History,* 48–52; Hirsch quoted at 51.

33. Quoted in ibid., 49.

34. Tal, *Christians and Jews,* 204ff.; Tal, "Liberal Protestantism," 34–41. See also chapter 8, pages 240–41.

German Jews, Protestant liberal German intellectuals, including Weber and Sombart, were taking a highly critical view of Kantian ethics. They stressed the overly "legalistic" aspect of Kantian ethics, and Weber went so far as to tie this to Kant's Pietist background.[35] Sombart's interpretation of Jewish "formalism," then, involved not only a misreading of historical evidence, pure and simple, but a fundamental failure to understand (or a denial of?) the intended *rapprochement* being made by Jewish intellectuals, religious liberals and conservatives alike, to the majority liberal community.

By "rationalism" Sombart means here the type of ascetic attitude toward everyday life that Weber identified with the Protestant ethic. Sombart has only focused on a different religion than did Weber. Counsel to read only books that relate to Torah, or are useful from that point of view; to avoid amusement reading, emotional enthusiasm, pity (rather than benevolence), sensuality, idle talk; to consider eating a hallowed act for "getting of strength for His service," and to consider the food itself a sacrifice, rather than a means of satisfying the feeling of hunger; a concern to avoid "contact with impurity," especially the opportunity to experience sexual desire[36]—all these maxims are taken from Stern, Hirsch, Lazarus, and Mandl. They are said to be characteristic of a preoccupation with "self-control and circumspection, a love of order and of work, moderation and abstemiousness, chastity and sobriety," virtues essential to Judaism "from Ezra's day to this."[37] The thrust of all these quotations is to advise the "pious" (i.e., observant) Jew to participate fully in this world with a measure of emotional reserve that calls for constant diligence. But all this was at the time part of modern neo-orthodoxy's campaign to combine full assimilation with complete "fidelity" to the *halachah*. Never in premodern times was any such heroic effort required to achieve and maintain *halachic* fidelity. There may be some truth in Sombart's reading of the "ethic" of Judaism, but it was a rec-

---

35. See Weber, *The Protestant Ethic*, 165 and the note there.

36. According to Sombart, the strength of Jewish family life (evidence for which is given with modern statistics comparing the number of illegitimate births to the rate in the general population in Prussia, Würtemberg, Hesse, Bavaria, Russia, among Greek Orthodox, Catholics, Protestants, and Jews) together with Talmudic advice is said to channel the energies of "restrained sexual desires" into "the chase for profits," after Freud (*The Jews and Modern Capitalism,* 234–37).

37. Ibid., 227–33. Modern orthodox authors are quoted over a dozen times in this discussion; around these quotes are grouped selected biblical passages confirming the "spirit" of the quotations, two medieval Jewish sources are cited, and a few secondary accounts of "Jewish ethics," all negative, are also cited in support of the universality of this "spirit" of the Jewish attitude to everyday life.

ommended ethic for nineteenth- and early twentieth-century assimilated German Jews, adopted by the very few who were receptive to Jewish religionists of either a conservative or a liberal bent, and perhaps especially the Orthodox minority sect among the German Jewish community. The advice these religionists offered to Jews on the basis of religious tradition was the same kind of advice that modernist German Christian religious leaders used to revive their own religious communities.

As we have seen, a subthesis of Weber's 1905 *The Protestant Ethic* held that Judaism had the effect of promoting an ethic of traditionalism among the Jews, not rationalism. However, in 1911 Sombart took a page directly from Weber's argument, that the temptations of wealth only drove the Puritan all the more to acquire wealth, as a test of his possession of God's grace, in order to develop his own thesis that the Jews are more rationalistic. In analogy to Weber's argument, Sombart quotes S. R. Hirsch:

> A true Israelite avoids covetousness. He looks upon all his possessions only as a means of doing what is pleasing in the sight of God. For is not the entire purpose of his life to use all his possessions, all enjoyment as the means to this end? Indeed it is a duty . . . to obtain possessions and to increase one's enjoyments, not as an end in themselves but as a means to do God's will on earth.[38]

Religious justifications (Sombart calls them principles of "Jewish moral theology") for gain are piled up: the "selling" of honors in the worship service; the idea of rewards and punishments, which is said to be modeled on a contract between God and each individual Jew, resulting in an "account" of "the balance of commands performed against commands neglected"; the absence of any denunciation of wealth in the Bible or Talmud.[39] For the last point Sombart offers many passages from Bible and Talmud, and "old Amschel Rothschild" (made notorious in Germany because of his staunch support for orthodoxy in Frankfurt) is made to refute a rabbi who piles up counterexamples from the Bible. This imaginary dispute is modeled after a real one, where Sombart reports that his views, given in a public lecture, were "severely criticized on all sides" by reference to such counterexamples. Now Sombart takes the opportunity of outdoing his opponents in such a reference war; notwithstanding his earlier cautions about

---

38. Ibid., 212.
39. Ibid., 213–22.

this method, now he says, "In such cases numbers [i.e., of passages] surely count."[40]

The worldliness of Jewish religion is shown by reference to the disdain for idolatry and for all sensuous forms of worship.[41] From the Talmudic maxim that Torah was given to man as a moral "antidote" to the "evil inclination," Sombart supposes that Judaism led the believer to rationalize rather than to renounce human nature, in contrast to the "other worldly asceticism" of Buddhism or primitive Christianity.[42] This, finally, leads Sombart to propose locating the rise of Jewish rationalism historically. In order to do this, he introduces a distinction between "the religion of [ancient] Israel" and "the Jewish religion." The latter is the work of scribes, and thus the product of intellectualism rather than of authentic piety:

> [Jewish religion] came into being on a deliberate plan, by clever deductions, and diplomatic policy which was based on the cry "Its religion must be preserved for the people." . . . In all its reasoning it appeals to us as a creation of the intellect, a thing of thought and purpose projected onto the world of organisms, mechanically and artfully wrought, destined to destroy and to conquer Nature's realm and to reign itself in her stead. Just so does Capitalism appear on the scene; like the Jewish religion, an alien element in the midst of the natural, created world; like it, too, something schemed and planned in the midst of teeming life. This sheaf of salient features is bound together in one word: Rationalism.[43]

> It is well known that the religion of the Christians stood in the way of their economic activities. It is equally well known that the Jews were never faced with this hindrance. The more pious a Jew was and the more acquainted with his religious literature, the more he was spurred by the teachings of that literature to extend his economic activities.[44]

---

40. Ibid., 216.

41. Ibid., 207–9.

42. "Christianity makes its devotee into a monk, Judaism into a rationalist; the first ends in asceticism outside the world, the second in asceticism within it (taking asceticism to mean the subjugation of what is natural in man)" (ibid., 224–26). This language is unmistakably taken from Weber. Weber himself finds it congenial, as we will see, even though its theoretical significance will be changed.

43. Ibid., 206.

44. Ibid., 222.

The inward holiness that may have existed in early days [i.e., prior to the establishment of "Jewish religion" under the influence of Pharisaic scribes] soon vanished before formalism and legalism. . . . It is generally known, too, that this legalism was a device of the Rabbis to protect Jews against the influences first, of Hellenism, then of Christianity, and finally, when the Second Temple was destroyed, to maintain by its means the national consciousness.[45]

Since the Babylonian exile, "The Jews created the ghetto, which from the non-Jewish point of view was a concession and a privilege and not the result of enmity." Ezra's demand for the divorce of all non-Israelite spouses upon leading a party back to Jerusalem from Babylonia, the continued relations between the Babylonian community and the Palestinian, and later among Hellenic diaspora communities, diaspora support for the Palestinian rebellion in 130 A.D., testimony from antiquity of Jewish hate for outsiders, retention of their separate language throughout the Middle Ages, even in lands where they were not persecuted—all this was the result of the Jews' religion, and had the effect of making Jews consider their non-Jewish neighbors as strangers.[46] An entire collection of *Responsa,* published in *Schmollers Forschungen (Jahrbuch)* (vol. 152) (as well as some apologetic writings by Jewish scholars on the stranger) are cited to show that Deuteronomy (23:20–21) was understood invidiously. Moritz Lazarus's humanistic advice "about the duty of Israel toward non-Jews does his heart all credit, but it is hardly in accord with historical truth."[47] Sombart notes that other, presumably "orthodox," "modern Rabbis" find the rule about interest in Deuteronomy "inconvenient (one cannot understand why)." Their attempts to explain that it applies to heathens or idol-worshipers, but not to all non-Jews Sombart rejects: "the pious Jew who has committed the 198th commandment[48] [to memory] is not likely to draw the fine distinction urged by the learned Rabbis. Sufficient for him that the man to whom he lent money was no Jew, no 'brother,' no neighbor, but a Gentile."[49] Apart from the interest question, the stranger was, however, always accorded less rigorous moral consideration in *halachah,* or religious

---

45. Ibid., 223.
46. Ibid., 238–42.
47. Ibid., 393nn.493, 494.
48. Presumably on interest-taking from non-Jews, but (Sombart neglects to note) after Maimonides' exceptional interpretation as a positive commandment.
49. Ibid., 243. For the same point in Weber, see chapter 8, page 232.

law, according to Sombart.[50] Heinrich Graetz is quoted at length, "surely no prejudiced witness," for the lack of honesty "of the Talmudically trained mind of the Polish Jew."[51] "The higgling of the market"[52] and free competition is said to be the nature of Jewish commercial relations, in contrast to Christian concepts of commerce and enterprise.[53]

These arguments go beyond the attempt to demonstrate that *the Jews* are "rationalistic." They are meant to show that *Judaism* leads to "rationalism." In this way Sombart arrives at an alternative thesis that nevertheless parallels closely Max Weber's, on the relation of religion and rationalism. Sombart's thesis, like Weber's Protestant ethic thesis, is proposed as a means of explaining phenomena—the supposed rationalism of the Jews—that are largely taken for granted. Sombart's presentation is therefore largely circular, and not really dependent on the "facts" he cites. Most of his evidence is inferred from contemporary accounts from the early modern period, attesting to contemporaries' perception of a conspicuous Jewish influence in commerce and banking. There is no independent evidence concerning the degree of Jewish participation in these occupations, however.

Sombart concludes this part of his book with a final tally of "Jewish characteristics." He presents this in the form of a "problem": among other peoples, dispersion leads to assimilation and disappearance, but among the Jews it strengthens their bonds. The disadvantages of semicitizenship were varied, but the activities of the Jews were both strengthened in and channeled into commercial pursuits everywhere despite this. This suggests there are *sui generis* Jewish characteristics. Counterarguments are disposed of: assimilation does not remove special characteristics among the Jews, it only adds to them, according to Sombart; although they lack political, cultural, or linguistic community, the Jews do possess other characteristics of a "nation" or a "people"; differences within the Jewish group do not disprove commonalities that still unite all the subgroups.[54] What are the special characteristics then?

---

50. Ibid., 244. Actually, the opposite was often the case in the Middle Ages, the reasoning being that in public the Jew ought to represent the name of God.

51. Ibid., 246.

52. The phrase is taken from the *Schuchan Aruch, Chosen Mishpat,* sec. 227, and *Mishnah Baba Mezia,* 49b, cited ibid., 247.

53. From *Baba Mezia,* 60a, b; ibid., 247–48.

54. Sombart, *The Jews and Modern Capitalism,* 252–57. "Think of the many groups to which an Englishman may belong. He may be a Catholic or a Protestant, a farmer or a professor, a northerner or a southerner and Heaven knows what else besides. But he remains an Englishman all the same. So with the Jew" (ibid., 256–27).

The characteristics apply to Jewry since the Spanish exile, and to their descendants regardless of their faith.[55] Sombart claims to "say nothing that other people have not said already, Jews whether pious or non-conforming," anti-Semites and philosemites, Heine or Goethe, Marx or H. S. Chamberlain, etc.[56] The characteristics that Sombart finally enumerates are these: (1) Intellectuality: "The Jew certainly sees remarkably clearly, but he does not see much. He does not think of his environment as something alive, and that is why he has lost the true conception of life, of its oneness, of its being an organism, a natural growth. . . . many Jews do not see themselves."[57] (2) Egocentric "practical rationalism," or a "teleological outlook," which results from intellectuality: "The Jew never loses himself in the outer world. . . . He brings everything into relation with his ego."[58] Sombart uses the example of a Russian-Jewish student who came to study Marx with him in Breslau, but never even took a walk: "He will walk through the world without seeing it."[59] Similarly, the literature of Georg Hirschfeld, Arthur Schnitzler, and Georg Hermann: "The great charm of their work lies in this world-aloofness." Their belief "that all things must have an aim" (Sombart cites the Yiddish, *tachlis*) "rob[s] the poetry of Jewish writers of *naivete,* freshness and directness, because Jewish poets are unable to enjoy the phenomena of this world."[60] (3) Mobility, of a "moral or physical" kind: This applies perhaps not to "many Spanish Jews, especially in the Orient, who strike you as being dignified, thoughtful, and self-restrained," but definitely to "their German brethren." "But mobility of mind—quick perception and mental versatility—all Jews possess."[61] (4) Industriousness: Goethe is quoted: "No Jew, not even the most insignificant, but is busy towards the achievement of some worldly, temporary or momentary aim." (5) Adaptability: Advice from the sages is piled up, e.g.,

---

55. Ibid., 255.

56. Ibid., 258.

57. Ibid., 263–64. Also: intellectuality "makes it easy to go from one extreme to the other. That is why you find among Jews fanatical orthodoxy and unenlightened [n.b.] doubt side by side; both spring from the same source," even though he had just said that the Jew "is the born representative of a 'liberal' view of life in which there are . . . only citizens with rights and duties."

58. Ibid., 265.

59. Ibid., 262.

60. Ibid., 267.

61. Ibid., 268.

"when the fox is in authority bow down before him. . . . Bend before the wave and it passes over you; oppose it, and it will sweep you away."[62]

A quote from the contemporary Prayer Book comes next: "May my soul be as dust to every one." Similarly, advice to pretend to accept the faith of the majority, or as Sombart puts it, to "simulate death," was (according to him) a preferred means of defense.[63] Adaptability in this sense is rooted in intellectuality, or as Sombart now prefers to say, in conclusion, "rationalism." "Because of his rationalism he is able to look at everything from without. . . . Any convictions he may have do not spring from his inmost soul; they are formulated by his intellect." Lasalle, for example, could have "played the part of a Prussian Junker as brilliantly as that of a social agitator."[64] This is why, in the United States, you cannot tell a Jew of the second or third generation from a non-Jew. It is why the Jews have an "undoubted talent for journalism, for the Bar, for the stage," and finally, for capitalism.[65] His intellectuality is a talent for abstraction, or for "the substitution of all qualitative differences by merely quantitative ones (value in exchange)." Uniformity tends to cosmopolitanism, "so we have the kindred trio of Capitalism, Liberalism, and Judaism."[66]

Apart from the clear difficulties of finding rational connections between the evidence used and the claims made for it throughout Sombart's whole exposition, special note should be taken of the fact that Sombart is talking about "special characteristics" he finds among contemporary, modern Jews, regardless of their orthodoxy, even though these characteristics are generalized as far back as the time of Ezra; and that nearly all of the evidence for the portrait of Jewish character he presents is also contemporary, and is treated as if it applies to all Jews for the past two or three millennia.

As is already evident, Sombart in a number of places links his analyses of the history and sociology of the Jews to then-current discussions of the Jewish question in Germany. He also mentions once presenting some of these arguments in lecture form where he received sharp criticism from some Jewish listeners.[67] In fact, Sombart was engaged in a lecture tour

---

62. In its original context these pieces of advice had to do with responding to anti-Jewish violence and expulsion.

63. Ibid., 270, 272. For the actual Jewish background for these ideas, see chapter 8, note 59, where this same prayer is used by Weber in an identical way.

64. Ibid., 271–72.

65. Ibid., 273. For Weber's evaluation of American Jewish assimilation, see below, pages 259 and 274.

66. Ibid., 274–75.

67. Cf. above, page 218.

throughout Germany at the time in which he popularized these arguments in order to propose a "solution" of the Jewish question. Sombart's lectures were subsequently published in 1912 as "The Future of the Jews." The extension of his sociology to *die Judenfrage* helped cause Zionism to assume a prominent place in the controversy over modernity in Germany.[68] By "solving" *die Judenfrage,* Sombart meant remedying the plight of the *Ostjuden,* stressing their poverty, lack of civilization, and the fact that many countries were closing their borders to them. Sombart concluded that the Zionist solution to the Jewish question was valid. He soon turned to assimilated Jewry, however. Here, too, he argued that assimilation was not possible, because Germans were now and would always be unwilling to accept Jews. "Daily contacts produced inevitable friction, since Jews and Germans comprised separate and distinct races." Assimilation led only to "Judaizing (*Verjudung*) of such large areas of our public and intellectual life." Jews should be granted civic equality, but they "should have the intelligence and tact not to make full use of this equality." Specifically, they should avoid public office, and the officer corps in particular, for which they were ill-suited by nature.[69]

Zionists reviewed Sombart's lectures favorably, for their propaganda value, eventually adopting Sombart's position as their own.[70] The liberal Jewish establishment, however, had already branded Sombart as a crude anti-Semite, and now advised Jews to avoid his lectures for this reason.[71] In March 1912 an essay of nearly identical tone as Sombart's lectures was published by a Jew, Moritz Goldstein, in *Der Kunstwart,* a nationalist journal for literature and the arts. Goldstein called attention to the contrast between Jewish aspirations to cultural leadership in Germany (he pointed to Max Reinhardt in theatre, Hugo von Hofmansthal in poetry, and Max Liebermann among painters), and the obstacle to realizing these aspirations represented by the attitude of non-Jewish Germans, who persist in treating Jews as aliens. Goldstein's solution to this dilemma was to purge assimilation-minded Jews from all positions of leadership so as to better clear the way for "an open struggle against an equal adversary," the anti-Semites. Ultimately the final solution of the German-Jewish dilemma could come only with emigration to Palestine, he said, and clarifying the conflict between

---

68. Reinharz, *Fatherland or Promised Land?,* 191–202 and following has discussed the impact of these lectures. The following is based on his discussion.

69. Quotes from "The Future of the Jews," in ibid., 191–92; cf. also 163.

70. Ibid., 194ff.

71. Ibid., 191, 193.

Jews and Germans would further reasonable consideration of this solution.[72] The affinity between Sombart's and Goldstein's assumptions about the Jewish question in Germany extended the controversy over Sombart's lectures. This brought together liberal and orthodox Jews on one side, who defined the Jews primarily as a religious community, and anti-Semites and Zionists on the other side, who saw the Jews as an unassimilable social group regardless of their religious affiliation.[73]

Similar issues came up when Sombart organized a symposium on "Jewish Converts" (*Judentaufen*) in 1912. At the symposium, Sombart pointed out that the Jewish population in Germany was no more than one percent now, and under these conditions full assimilation could be hoped for in the future, while amicable relationships would prevail in the meantime. Hermann Bahr and Heinz Ewers, participants in the symposium, drew out the conclusion that Sombart had been making implicitly: if the immigration from the East did not stop, assimilation of the Jews in Germany would become impossible, because the *Ostjuden* were stubborn in their will to retain a separate ethnic identity. If they became the dominant element among Germany's Jews, then the latter would become resistant to that "spiritual transformation which would ultimately effect their blood." The cultured Jews (*Bildungsjuden*) of the West were one thing, but the eastern immigration threatened to halt or even reverse the trend toward assimilation, creating a full-blown national minority within the state. This would be intolerable. M. Erzberger, speaking (he said) on behalf of the assimilated and wealthy German Jewish community, said that Zionism was considered, for this reason, a legitimate response to the "eastern" Jewish problem. By contrast, three other Jewish contributors to the symposium, Ludwig Geiger, L. Gurlitt, and Fritz Mauthner, condemned Zionism as a violation of the German cultural heritage of German Jews. But Mauthner conceded that it may be appropriate for the eastern Jews, because it was closer to their "medieval" mentality. All sides agreed that border closing was called for. Sombart had similarly warned German Jews at the *Judentaufen* symposium, "in their own interests," to discourage *Ostjuden* from migrating into Germany.[74]

Finally, the significance of *The Jews and Economic Life* in the context of Sombart's own work can be noted: From his position in 1903, with *German Economy,* where *Deutschtum* was argued to have had a hand in the origins

---

72. Ibid., 195–97.
73. Ibid., 199.
74. Ascheim, *Brothers and Strangers,* 48–50. Cf. above, pages 114–16.

of modern capitalism, Sombart shifted the historical responsibility fully onto the shoulders of *Judentum*. He did this as a result of his reading and modification of Max Weber's thesis in *The Protestant Ethic*.[75] In the course of this development, Sombart became racist: by 1911 he wants total assimilation through miscegenation, as if blood were the basis for Jewish distinctiveness; and Jewish distinctiveness, because it is necessarily invidious and so inconsistent with community, cannot be tolerated as a permanent feature of society.

However, there remains an inconsistency within Sombart's thesis on the Jews that is important because Weber would exploit it in the development of his own, alternative thesis on the Jews. Sombart often shifts back and forth between the technical meaning of "rationalism" as an ascetic outlook, which he derived from Weber, and "rationalism" as "calculability," which he had also used in his earlier work to mean the routine, amoral utilitarianism of fully developed capitalism. For Weber, calculative rationalism is a concept that accurately describes economic relations in the twentieth century, but is not relevant for an understanding of the historical spirit of capitalism, which he argues was religiously conditioned by Protestantism. Once established, twentieth-century capitalism no longer needs a religious calling. This well-known closing claim of *The Protestant Ethic* was "proven" by Weber in his studies of the "psychophysics of industrial work," which he did for the *Verein für Sozialpolitik* and Naumann's and Göhre's *Nationalsozial Vereinigung* in the 1890s and after 1905. In these studies Weber concluded that, under contemporary conditions, Protestant asceticism could still be found in German Pietist communities, but its effects are "residues of the past," no longer a force for progress, but an obstacle to further rationalization of the labor force.[76] Weber went on to claim that, under current conditions, the cost effectiveness of actions and the "hierarchic authority structure" of modern industry determine "the occupational destiny" of the worker, not any values that he might hold.[77] This indicates that

75. Compare Mendes-Flohr, "Sombart's *The Jews*," 101–2. For a comprehensive survey of Sombart's intellectual development, see Klausner's lengthy introduction to *The Jews and Modern Capitalism*.

76. "The Psychophysics of Industrial Work," quoted in Oberschall, *Empirical Research,* 121; emphasis added. Important clues to Weber's prescientific understanding of "religion" can be found in Marianne Weber's stories about the Oerlinghausen branch of the family, to which both Max and Marianne were related. They ran the textile mill on which Weber's later studies of "psychophysics" were based.

77. Ibid., 121–22; cf. also Marianne Weber, *Biography,* 330–31, 367.

Weber never disagreed with analyses of contemporary capitalism and "capitalist culture" like Sombart's which stressed, often pejoratively, the weakening of moral scruples, secularization, and widespread materialism that supposedly underpin capitalism—all things commonly associated with the idea of "rationalism."

The reason for Weber's stress on the importance of this distinction between amoral calculability and calculability considered as a virtue may have to do with his desire to avoid the anti-Semitic conclusions that Sombart associated with his thesis in such a conspicuous way. For Weber will continue to maintain that the Jews' role in modern capitalism is marginal at best. But although Weber draws somewhat different conclusions than Sombart does about the Jews' place in social development, his portrait of the Jews is no less negative than Sombart's. In Weber's thesis, the distinction between "calculability" and "religious rationalism" leads to the claim that Jewish ascetic or "ethical" rationalism is confined to internal social relations within the Jewish community and to religious ritual. This draws on Sombart's reading of modern Jewish works of religious inspiration. However, Weber also makes use of Sombart's concept of rationalism as amoral "calculability," just as he did, in a limited way, in *The Protestant Ethic*. In Weber's pariah-people thesis, this kind of rationalism describes the Jew's attitude toward the Gentile.

8

Weber's Pariah-People Thesis in
His Sociology

Around 1911–13, when he wrote the section on the sociology of religion
for *Economy and Society*, Weber significantly revised his earlier portrait of
"Jewish traditionalism" in order to accommodate a complicated analysis of
the "pariah" character of Judaism. Weber developed this analysis as a
revision of Sombart's thesis on the Jews. As he did in *The Protestant Ethic*,
Weber accepted all but a few of the putative facts Sombart had used as
evidence for his own thesis, and most of the intermediate conclusions Sombart had drawn from these facts.[1] Beyond this, however, Weber integrated
the problem of Judaism into his own emerging system of universal history.
Weber needed to develop his portrait of Judaism and the Jews in medieval
and modern times because his universal history required the comparison of
religions and their links to types of "rationalism." Compared to *The Protestant Ethic,* where Judaism is said to be marked by traditionalism, after
Sombart's book Weber holds that *religious* rationalism applies to relations
among fellow Jews, and to observance of Jewish religious law, but not to
relations with non-Jews. This is identical to Sombart's portrait of Jews and
Judaism. Weber also accepts Sombart's proposition, that for relations to
non-Jews, *calculative* rationalism governs Jewish behavior. Both of these
claims, that Jews are marked by religious rationalism and by an unscru-
pulous attitude toward outsiders, are central to the Weber thesis. These

---

1. Cf. Roth's introduction to Weber, *Economy and Society,* lxxii-lxxiii; in the
foreword to *Modern Capitalism* Sombart indicated that one of his main goals had
been to marshal as many facts as possible to support his postulate, that the "spirit"
of an economic system was the ultimate cause of its organizational structure: "facts,
facts, facts—this admonition rang in my ears all the time I was writing the book."
Roth comments: "Weber did not consider the postulate feasible, but he was
interested in Sombart's facts and decided to approach them through systematic
comparative study."

two claims are brought together in the Weber thesis by the further claim that both types of rationalism, each in its respective sphere, are rooted in the distinctive development of Judaism since ancient times. In other words, when he developed his sociology of religion Weber focused explicitly on Sombart's "Jewish rationalism" and constructed a special theory to explain its existence: the theory of pariah peoples.

The appearance of Sombart's *The Jews and Economic Life* in 1911 seems to have given Weber an opportunity to apply his philosophical-epistemological rationales for keeping value-conceptual analysis separate from causal analysis. These rationales had guided his work on the Protestant ethic and now provided a standpoint from which to criticize Sombart's theses on the historical role of the Jews. Polemic discussions of modern "rationalism" as a *social problem,* such as took place in the Catholic press, in the *Verein für Sozialpolitik,* in Sombart's works and in connection with Sombart's speeches on the Jewish question, and more generally among the educated public, who associated utilitarianism and Enlightenment philosophies with "rationalism," informed Weber's sociology. One of the basic purposes of his sociology, in fact, was to address the philosophical foundations of such polemics in order to arrive at a consistent, clarified interpretation of what social problems are. This view of concept formation encouraged Weber to identify a "standpoint" from which to criticize Sombart's theses on the historical role of the Jews. This in turn provided an occasion for Weber to develop his general sociology; he did not think the significance of his anticritique of Sombart was confined to the question of "the Jews and capitalism." Nevertheless, many of the more expansive parts of his sociology have their roots in Weber's attempt to ground the stereotypical image of "Jewish rationalism" employed by Sombart.

Sombart's *Problemstellung,* the relation between religion and rationalism in the origins of modern society and culture, was one that Weber shared. Weber felt, however, that the way in which Sombart had approached this *Problemstellung* ought to be broken down into two separate problems: (1) could an attitude or "spirit" of inner-worldly asceticism (Protestantism's contribution to history) have emerged from tendencies internal to Jewish history? and (2) did the Jews create the major *organizational* forms of modern economic life or any part of them? In other words, how might the Jews and Judaism have affected modern rationalism and modern capitalism? Weber reduced the second problem to a definition of the individuality of modern capitalism. The type of capitalism that is found everywhere in history, Weber suggested, involves simple rational accounting of ongoing debits and receipts with a view to a net profit. In contrast to this, Weber underscored two unique features of modern capitalism: its rationalization of productive plants rather than commerce and trade per se, and its disciplined organization of labor.[2] From this point of view, the types of economic organization Sombart had tied the Jews to are all premodern. Once again, Weber affirmed Sombart's facts, but argued they were in need of conceptual clarification:

> In the polemic against Sombart's book [*The Jews and Economic Life*], one fact should not have been seriously questioned, namely that Judaism played a conspicuous role in the evolution of the modern capitalist system. However, this thesis of Sombart's book needs to be made more precise. What were the *distinctive* economic achievements of Judaism in the Middle Ages and in modern times? We can easily list: moneylending, from pawnbroking to the financing of great states; certain types of commodity business, particularly retailing, peddling, and produce trade of a distinctively rural type; certain branches of wholesale business; and trading securities, above all the brokerage of stocks. To this list of Jewish economic achievements should be added: money-changing; money-forwarding or check-cashing, which normally accompanies money-changing; the financing of state agencies, wars, and the establishment of colonial enterprises; tax-farming; . . . banking; credit; and the floating of bond issues. But of all these businesses only a few, though some very important ones, display the forms, both legal and economic, characteristic of Occidental capitalism (as contrasted to the capitalism of ancient times, the Middle Ages, and the earlier period in Eastern Asia). The distinctively modern legal forms include securities and capitalist associations, but these are not of specifically Jewish provenance. The Jews introduced some of these forms into the Occident, but the forms themselves have perhaps a common Oriental (probably Babylonian) origin, and their influence on the Occident was mediated through Hellenistic and Byzantine sources. . . . [For example] the Exchange, as a "market of tradesmen," was created not by Jews but by Christian merchants. . . . medieval legal forms of finance, which were quite un-Jewish in certain respects, were later adapted to economic needs of modern states and other modern recipients of credit.[3]

---

2. Weber, *The Protestant Ethic*, 21.
3. Weber, *Economy and Society*, 612–13; Weber, *General Economic History*, 360.

"Jewish" forms of capitalism are all examples of "pariah capitalism," they are not modern. In other words, in the area of economic organization, the Jews have not shown any creativity; consistent with their pariah character, the Jews were "involved in those legal and entrepreneurial forms evolved by the Middle Ages but not by them." But the crucial proof against the modernity of Jewish capitalism is that domestic industry and the factory system are "strikingly—though not completely—missing from the extensive list of Jewish economic activities."

> How does one explain the fact that no pious Jew thought of establishing an industry employing pious Jewish workers of the ghetto (as so many pious Puritan entrepreneurs had done with devout Christian workers and artisans) at a time when numerous proletarians were present in the ghettos. . . . Again, how does one explain the fact that no modern and distinctively industrial bourgeoisie of any significance emerged among the Jews to employ the Jewish workers available for home industry, despite the presence of numerous impecunious artisan groups at almost the threshold of the modern era?[4]

In contrast to pietist businessmen, even in modern times, the Jews "evinced the ancient and medieval business temper which had been and remained typical of all genuine traders," namely, "the will and the wit to employ mercilessly every chance of profit."[5] This comparison provides the rationale for the extensive analysis of the Jews and Judaism in the long section on "The Sociology of Religion" in *Economy and Society,* where there is hardly a page that lacks a reference to this, as well as to Christianity, among all the other examples from world religions employed. The outlines of the portrait of Judaism and the people who bear this religion is strikingly similar to Sombart's portrait:

> The ultimate theoretical reasons for this fact, that the distinctive elements of modern capitalism originated and developed quite apart from the Jews, are to be found in the peculiar character of the Jews as a pariah people and in the idiosyncrasy of their religion. . . . Also of fundamental importance was the subjective ethical situation of the Jews. As a pariah people, they retained the double standard of morals which is characteristic of primordial economic practice in all communities: what is prohibited in relation to one's brothers is permitted

---

4. Weber, *Economy and Society,* 613–14.
5. Ibid., 614.

in relation to strangers. . . . Although the rabbis made concessions in these matters [to general morality], as Sombart correctly points out, even in regard to business transactions with fellow Jews, this amounted merely to concessions to laxity, whereby those who took advantage of them remained behind the highest standards of Jewish business ethics. . . . That this should have remained the Jewish economic ethic was a foregone conclusion, for even in Antiquity the stranger confronted the Jew almost always as an enemy. All the well-known admonitions of the rabbis enjoining fairness especially toward Gentiles could not change the fact that the religious law prohibited taking usury from fellow Jews but permitted it in transactions with non-Jews. Nor could the rabbinical counsels alter the fact, which again Sombart has rightly stressed, that a lesser degree of exemplary legality was required by the law in dealing with a stranger, i.e., an enemy, than in dealing with another Jew, in such a matter as taking advantage of an error made by the other party. In fine, no proof is required to establish that the pariah condition of the Jews, which we have seen resulted from the promises of Yahweh, and the resulting incessant humiliation of the Jews by Gentiles necessarily led to the Jewish people's retaining a different economic morality for its relations with strangers than with fellow Jews.[6]

The new elements in this portrait of the Jews and Judaism, compared to Sombart's portrait, are few; only the historical significance of the portrait is changed. That is, one side of Sombart's *Problemstellung* is refuted and dismissed, the role of the Jews in the economic organization of modern capitalism. But Sombart's portrait of the calculative attitude of Jews toward Gentiles, sanctioned by Judaism, is affirmed and developed even further by Weber.

The other question, regarding the extent to which Jews promoted a rationalistic *social* ethic, a culture of rationalism, was not so easily answered. The type of practical "rationalism" that finds expression in modern societies is, for Weber, most fully realized in the ascetic ethic of Puritanism. For him, then, the comparative study of "Jewish rationalism" takes its point of departure from the Protestant case. If religion has any relationship to the historical development of modernity, it has to promote activism in the

---

6. Ibid., 614–15. For the original point about the impotence of "the rabbis' idealism," cf. chapter 7, page 220.

world rather than a contemplative escape from the world.[7] An elaborate typology of religious rationalism in particular civilizations follows, the purpose of which is to exclude the possibility that Protestant activism could have arisen in any other religious context. In other words, Weber treats the Jews in history partly in light of the question, why was it the case that modern activism prevailed only among Protestants? He provided a number of related answers to this question:[8]

1. The concept of a transcendental God led to (a) the prohibition of idolatry and consequently to a general disrespect for attempts to achieve mystical possession of the deity; pantheism, an obstacle to activism, was "always regarded [in Europe] as heterodox." It also led to (b) a view of salvation not as union with, but as "ethical justification before God"; that is, salvation had to be proved through some sort of activity in the world. Finally the transcendence of God led to (c) a view of the world as created by God, and this view became an obstacle to an absolute rejection and flight from the world, which was the rule for Oriental religiosity.

2. The idea of the world as imperfect, in Judaism and Christianity, led intellectual inquiry into the cosmos, which occurred in all world religions, away from God, so that piety was borne by laymen and was anticontemplative. In India, by contrast, contemplation of karmic causality was the means to the highest form of piety, leading to illumination and mystical union.

3. Piety tended to become regulated juridically in the West, on the model of God's dominion over the world; this in turn led the pious into the world rather than into contemplation, which is the result of a piety with pantheistic motives.

4. Roman and Jewish rejections of Greek ecstasy-religion combined in Christian monasticism to form an emphasis on labor, in contrast to the more rigorous Hindu and Buddhist monastic disciplines, which aimed at the creation of an extraordinary but nevertheless temporary psychological state.

---

7. See ibid., 551–52: "In the Occident . . . apart from a few representatives of a distinctive quietism found only in modern times, even religions of an explicitly mystical type regularly became transformed into an active pursuit of virtue, which was naturally ascetical in the main." As will become apparent below, Weber was here referring to Christianity and Judaism alike.

8. The following summarizes ibid., 552–56; also 610 for point 4. However, these points guide all of Weber's sociology of religion, including the monographs on the world religions.

5. When monasticism became bureaucratized in India and China, this only heightened the magical character of discipline. The bureaucratization of the Roman Church, however, increasingly systematized otherworldly asceticism in the cloister, "into a methodology of active, rational conduct of life." This set the stage for ascetic Protestantism's integration of "an ethic of vocation in the world with the assurance of religious salvation."

The significance of Judaism in this context is twofold. In the first place, it made concrete historical contributions to, or even was directly responsible for, religious and ethical monotheism, which underlies numbers 1, 2, and 4, as early as ancient times. This has distinguished the direction of Western civilization from that in the East, for Judaism represents a historic breakthrough against the predominance of magic in religion, and this became a resource for all the Western religions, especially Protestantism.[9]

In the second place, Judaism is an object of interest *sui generis*. In general, Weber's sociology of religion, and his sociology as a whole, is developed by constructing comparisons of comparable cases, guided by an interest in possible analogies to the developments he judges to have preceded and led to the rise of modern society. These developments are multidimensional, occurring at the levels of political, economic, scientific-intellectual, even aesthetic and religious social processes. However, Weber's comparison of Jewish and Christian rationalism does not fit this pattern. Whenever he employs Judaism or the Jews for purposes of comparison, he is rarely involved in the discovery of analogies to comparable processes that are tied to the rise of modern culture and society. This follows from what has already been said, for the world-historical significance of Judaism is limited to the creation of monotheism, and monotheism had its main effects from then on, from the standpoint of modern European history, through the development of Christianity. Judaism, therefore, is a fossil from a "universal-historical" point of view.

Far from making Judaism uninteresting, the view that Judaism is a fossil justifies Weber's continuing interest in Judaism. More importantly, this view integrates his conclusions on Judaica into his general system of sociology, which elaborates his theory of the development of modernity. For the Jews have not disappeared from history. Despite the judgment of

---

9. Weber, *The Protestant Ethic*, 165; Weber, *Economy and Society*, 622; Weber, *General Economic History*, 360–61. The most sustained presentation of this thesis is in the first section of "The Sociology of Religion," in *Economy and Society*, 399ff. This particular text is examined in depth in the next section, below.

history on the social importance of their religion and culture, and in the face of extraordinary hardships imposed by exile, the Jews have proved to be a tenacious people. Their tenacity, Weber thinks, has to do with the relationship between other features of their religion besides its monotheism, and the social situation of exile itself. For the Jews, religion and social situation stand in a unique relationship, a relationship that ought to be an object of interest from a "universal-historical" point of view. Most of Weber's attention to the Jews and Judaism in his sociology is designed to explain the origin and persistence of these unique features. Thus, in regard to the sociology of religious rationalism, most religions of salvation, Weber observed, teach their adherents to look down on profit-making and to regard as ethically primary the social duty to contribute aid to the poor and unfortunate. Only Puritanism and Judaism are exceptions to the rule that "An anticapitalistic ethos and welfare orientation is, in effect, a common characteristic of all religions that promise salvation."[10] In another place Weber includes Judaism with early Christianity and ascetic Protestantism as the only three religions that foster a practical ethic of inner-worldly rationalism.[11] Jewry has practiced a "rationalism" similar in kind, according to Weber, to Protestant asceticism.

Once developed Weber had no difficulty incorporating his pariah-people theory into his essays on Protestantism. The version of *The Protestant Ethic* he completed in 1920 elaborated on the difference between the ethic of ancient Judaism and that "of Judaism as it became under the influence of many centuries of formalistic, legalistic, and Talmudic education." He now stressed ancient Judaism's lack of an activistic ethic, in order to argue that it is "far removed from the special characteristics of Puritanism."

> It [ancient Judaism] was however, just as far—and this ought not to be overlooked—from the economic ethics of medieval *and modern* Judaism, in the traits which determined the positions of both [Puritanism and Judaism] in the development of the capitalistic ethos. The Jews stood on the side of the politically and speculatively oriented adventurous capitalism; their ethos was, in a word, that of pariah-capitalism. But Puritanism carried the ethos of the rational organization of capital and labor. It took over from the Jewish ethic only what was adapted to this purpose.[12]

---

10. Weber, *Economy and Society*, 1198.
11. Ibid., 610; Weber, *The Protestant Ethic*, 197.
12. Weber, *The Protestant Ethic*, 165–66, emphases added. For Weber's *Prob-*

The ethic of pariah-capitalism created by medieval and modern Judaism is quite different than the religious ethic of ancient Judaism. However, the ethos of pariah-capitalism is rooted in "rational" religious ideas which originated in ancient times, according to Weber.

But if Judaism possesses a spirit analogous to that of modern rationalism, why did it not foster this spirit prior to and independently of Protestantism? Indeed, why are we, with Sombart, not justified in deriving the spirit of modernity from the "Jewish spirit"?[13] Weber's answer is to be found in the complicated development of his larger sociological theories. Within the context of these theories, the *Problemstellung* of Weber's sociology of Judaism and the Jews is thus twofold. Weber wants to find the ancient-Jewish

---

lemstellung, cf. also *Economy and Society,* 612: "What were the distinctive economic achievements of Judaism in the Middle Ages and in modern times?" For analyses of Weber's *Geschichtsbild* of the Jews primarily on the basis of Weber's *Ancient Judaism* (1952) (which is treated only peripherally in this chapter), see Fischoff's massive dissertation, *Max Weber's Sociology of Religion;* Hahn, *The Old Testament in Modern Research,* 157–73; Liebeschütz, "Weber's Historical Interpretation," and *Das Judentum im deutschen Geschichtsbild,* 330–35.

13. Max Scheler had done just this, in his 1912 study of *ressentiment,* expanded during the war as "Das Ressentiment im Aufbau der Moralen" for his *Gesammelte Abhandlungen und Aufsätze* (1915; trans. as *Ressentiment.*) Scheler formulated his own thesis after Sombart, but in terms that are closer to the pariah-people thesis Weber would develop: "the feelings and ideas of those elements the old 'community' had cast aside (its pariahs) have determined the general image of man and his associations" (ibid., 166). Throughout this study Scheler made generous use of both Weber's Protestant ethic thesis and Sombart's thesis on the Jews, considering them perfectly consistent. The following note on the modern "spirit" is characteristic: "The specifically modern urge to work (the unbridled urge for acquisition, unlimited by need, is nothing but its consequence) is by no means due to a way of thinking and feeling which *affirms* life and the world, as it existed for example during the Italian Renaissance. It grew primarily on the soil of somber Calvinism, which is hostile to pleasure. Calvinism sets a transcendent and therefore unattainable goal for work ('workers in the honor of God'). At the same time, work here serves as a narcotic for the believers, enabling them to support the doubt and uncertainty whether they are 'called' or 'elect.' Max Weber and Ernst Troeltsch have shown this very well in their studies on the Calvinist origin of modern capitalism. Cf. my two essays on the bourgeois in *Vom Umsturz der Werte* and my book *Die Ursachen des Deutschenhaßes.* In Sombart's opinion, the 'Jewish spirit' is one of the chief causes of the development of the capitalist social structure. It is quite in agreement with my thesis that this spirit, which has had a lien on *ressentiment* for a long time, plays a major role in this process" (ibid., 193–94n.27). Scheler's Protestant ethic thesis would have had the same effect on Weber as Sombart's, to make him clarify his terms.

origins of features he considers to be characteristic of early Christianity and Protestant asceticism on the one hand. On the other hand, he is interested in the origins and development of "the pariah ethic" and the "religious rationalism" of later Judaism.

II

In the opening part of "The Sociology of Religion" Weber's exposition of the functional and religious basis for the pariahdom of the Jews comes as the conclusion of an elaborate theory of the origin and evolution of religion itself.[14] In this wider presentation, the case of the Jews is portrayed as one of the most extreme examples of the stultification of pure religion. The whole presentation represents a masterful synthesis of the contemporary consensus among German Protestant theologians and historians of religion and antiquity. Sombart's claims about the ancient religious origins of "Jewish rationalism" followed this same literature and, while Weber was probably more intimately acquainted with this literature than Sombart, Weber uses it to construct a portrait of ancient Judaism that is essentially identical to Sombart's.

The dating of the rise of "rationalism" in prechristian antiquity, in order to show that it is an essential feature of Judaism, was a variation on a common argument in the academic study of Judaism among Protestant historians and biblical scholars around the turn of the century. Uriel Tal has brought to light a common set of conclusions shared by prominent historians, philologists, and theologians fixing the deterioration of Judaism in the time of Ezra and Nehemiah, upon the return of a remnant of the Babylonian captives to Jerusalem (late sixth century B.C.).[15] After the conquest of Palestine by the Assyrians in the eighth century B.C., according to this view, "successive wars, political crises, and economic hardships . . . increased the power of the privileged classes and the priesthood, but . . . impoverished the population and depleted the social and spiritual resources of the country." The prophetic denunciations of domestic life by Jeremiah are taken as evidence of this decline, which led at length to Pharisaism, a "sterile legalism that extinguished all hope of deliverance and made the dissolution of faith certain." Adolph Harnack summed up this development

---

14. See Weber, *Economy and Society,* 399–500.

15. The following is based on Tal, *Christians and Jews,* 191–219, from whom I shall quote liberally.

in his 1900 lectures on "the essence of Christianity" as a pattern of suffering: "For 200 years one blow followed another, beginning with the dreadful days of Antiochus Epiphanus, and the people have still found no rest." Accordingly, the period after the Assyrian conquest was termed generically the postexilic period, indicating the deep and permanent psychological wounds these events were supposed to have had on the Jewish people and religion. According to Tal, "This historical interpretation of pre-Christian Judaism was directed against modern Judaism and supported by the indefatigable researches of biblical scholars who were highly esteemed by both Christians and Jews."[16] Apart from a few apologetic criticisms of the substantive evaluations built into these researches, however, most Jewish intellectuals showed little interest in biblical criticism.[17]

Julius Wellhausen, in *Pharisees and Sadducees* (1874) and later in *Israelite and Jewish History* (1895), "drew a sharp contrast between the formalized sterile worship of postexilic Judaism and the natural religion of the early Israelites for whom religion was the very breath of life." Others also argued that, notwithstanding the high morality embodied in prophetic criticism, the codification of laws and prescriptions in the Bible offered the conscience a relief not possible under the impact of the personal prophetic message recovered by John the Baptist and Jesus. Important works by Friedrich Loofs (1906), C. H. Cornhill (1900), and Eduard Meyer (before and after the turn of the century) also "contributed to this historical construction on the highest scientific and intellectual level and with due circumspection in making value judgments." Meyer argued that because of the postexilic deterioration of Israelite culture, intellectual achievements of the Hellenistic period (including for example, the philosophy of Philo) originate in Hellenistic culture. On the basis of such authorities biblical scholars were "able to prove that the national and ethnic isolation within Judaism began with the return to Zion, as testified by the ordinances of Ezra and Nehemiah in

---

16. Ibid., 194.

17. Ibid., 198n.57. Moritz Güdemann, in *Jüdische Apologetik*, pointed out that Wellhausen and Meyer were justifying the "modern" theological concept that "Judaism is only the withered branch of the religion of the Old Testament whose sap and vitality, by virtue of the New Dispensation, have passed to the side of Christianity" (quoted in Tal, *Christians and Jews*, 192). Also, an 1893 proclamation of seventy-three non-orthodox rabbis repeated an apology that by then had become well established, that the Talmud is binding only insofar as it is consistent with modern rational criticism, and that, as oral law, the Talmud never attained the authority of the written law (see ibid., 75n).

such matters as the relation to the Samaritans, the expulsion of foreign wives, or the cessation of prophecy." Some went on to see in the decline of true religion, by which they meant a religion of love and ethical idealism, a providential retribution against impenitent Jews and a preparation of the social environment for the advent of a Redeemer. The theologian Hermann Gunkel, however, put an environmentalist construction on these developments. In his "The Old Testament in Light of Modern Research" (1905) he suggested that the postexilic rigidification of national life is a natural result of conquest and exile, as happened also to the Patriarchate of Constantinople. Such a historical judgment, he went on to say, need not therefore be seen as a disparagement of Judaism. Eduard Meyer's *Israelites and Their Neighboring Tribes* (1906) refined the critical division of the Bible into narrative layers, said to be written primarily by the "Elhoist" and the "Jahwist" and interwoven from the point of view of the later "Jahwistic historical view," which is dominated by the "Judaistic" tendency. Meyer dated the stages of redaction of the biblical texts by evaluating the degree of authentic prophetic spirit as against the later priestly influences, which "silence prophecy" with "the ritual law and its barren forms [and these] drove out genuine religious and ethical feeling." The "Davidic Psalms" (i.e., 3–46) were isolated as belonging to the era of Ezra and Nehemiah, and Psalms 47–71 as dating two centuries later. But in order to continue to attribute authentic religious value to some of the Psalms, which were still considered indirect sources for Christianity, it was necessary to assign to these earlier, "pre-exilic" dates. Thus the messianic prophecies in Isaiah, and "Deutero-Isaiah" (40–46) were said to originate as far back as the eighth century, while other "layers" of Isaiah were dated as late as the fourth or third centuries. Both Wellhausen and Meyer, despite different methodologies, as well as the liberal Protestant theologians, concurred on this.

This remarkable concurrence across a number of academic and religious fields was part of a general movement of the liberal majority intellectuals in Germany, some active, others only sympathetic, to effect a revival among the general population of idealistic national feeling in order to inject a unifying force into society.[18] The majority liberal view of religious history was an extension of the classical Christian dogma of the transfer of God's favor from Judaism to Christianity with the coming of the Messiah, although this was only one element in a wider context. Alongside their struggle

18. Ibid., 220.

against the persistence of Jewish identity in the Imperial period, the liberal intellectuals were equally concerned to combat the sacramental and ritual traditions of conservative Lutheranism and Catholicism, which they looked upon as magical and irrational in contrast to purely humanistic religious feeling, which was alone appropriate to modern conditions. They felt that to find the roots of authentic religiosity, one must pay attention "not only to the chronological transition from Judaism to Christianity, but [to] the spiritual transition from a consistent monotheistic to a syncretic or even pagan faith" as well. These distinctions led them to identify with Jewish Christianity, to emphasize that Jesus' message was originally addressed to "the lost sheep of the house of Israel" (Matthew 10:6), that John the Baptist revived true prophecy, and that the first three Gospels alone were contemporary to the primitive community of Jewish-Christians, while the fourth Gospel of John, because composed after the second century, was discredited as a source for spiritual Christianity. The desiccated religion of ancient Judaism and the spiritual roots of Jewish Christianity co-existed, however tenuously. Thus the liberal theologian Adolph Deissman claimed in 1905 that "Between the Old Testament and the New Testament there is no gap that cannot be bridged. Those who wish to sever the gospels from the Old Testament and from Judaism cut down the vine at its roots." And this was consistent with Loofs's demand of the religious conservatives, the following year: "The leavened Catholic dough deserves to be swept away . . . the gospels in essence ask of man nothing beyond faith . . . and to be possessed by Jesus the Messiah."[19] On this view, authentic religion, as opposed to outward religious observance or mere belief in religious dogmas, was embodied in the Sermon on the Mount and the Deuteronomic antic- ipations of the Christian golden rule. Apostolic succession, the Trinity, the anthropological interpretation of the Word become flesh, and all the church traditions introduced after the primitive community of apostles were evi- dence of decay and rigidification.

The religion of feeling was considered to be the essence of Christianity. But the same idea was identified with the essence of Judaism, according to liberal Jewish spokesmen, such as Heinrich Graetz, Ludwig and Martin Philippson, Abraham Geiger, and Leo Baeck.[20] Each side claimed pure

---

19. Deissman and Loofs quoted in ibid., 202–3. For the Protestant intellectual bias of these and other personalities in the German "history of religions" school, cf. Hahn, *The Old Testament,* chapters 3 and 4; also papers by Ward and Graf in *Max Weber and His Contemporaries.*

20. Tal, *Christians and Jews,* 214ff.

monotheism for itself. Wellhausen and Meyer, along with Harnack, Troeltsch, and many others on the majority side, used the theory that Jesus had extracted the ethical teachings of the prophets and even the ethical inspiration of the Law from the sterile particularistic Judaism of his day to this effect. Jewish scholars, publicists and teachers claimed that Jesus had said nothing that could not also be found in Hillel and the Pharisees before him. Both sides agreed that Jesus' teachings were rooted in Jewish sources, but they disagreed about the significance of this. Jewish critics put their greatest stress on the apostle Paul's absolute rejection of law, not just the Torah and the commandments. They charged that Paul's position denies man's moral autonomy. Jesus' own criticism of Pharisaic Judaism, they said, was an internal one and did not go as far as Paul, for Jesus was himself a Pharisee. One of the most pointed attacks was made against Adolph Hausrath, who had made Paul's distinction between spirit and flesh central.[21] Hausrath and many other liberal Protestants took this to be a central justification for the need to identify with what they took to be the religion of Jesus. In response, the liberal rabbi Joseph Eschelbacher asserted that "Paul totally denies that it is in the power of human nature to observe the law by its own strength, that is, to fulfill the ethical precepts. Sin dwells within man, in his flesh, and this is the law of his [fellow] members," according to Hausrath.[22] At the same time, Eschelbacher, and liberal Jews generally, interpreted *halachic* law as binding only so far as it was rational. Nevertheless they saw in their rejection of the Christian criticism of law a basic motive for Jewish self-identity, justifying their selective identification with the *halachic* strain within Judaism.[23]

The liberal Protestant bias in the "history of religions" school's idea of religion underlies Weber's discussion of "The Sociology of Religion" in *Economy and Society*. The central theme of Weber's discussion, which is set within the broadest panorama of world history, and within the theoretical context of Weber's "universal historical" preoccupation with the origins of modernity, is the formalization of religion in Israel. Religion is suppressed by priestly authorities until it is revived around the time of Jesus, leading to the formation of the original Christian community. But it, too, decays

---

21. Based on a reading of Epistle to the Galatians 5:17. In his sociology of religion, Weber would make the parallel categories, "religion" and "world," universal descriptive concepts for portraying the fundamental promises upon which all real religions base their appeal.

22. Quoted in ibid., 218.

23. See above, note 17.

under the burden of a priesthood, which promulgates a formalized casuistry of dogmatic tenets under the authority of the Catholic church. True religion, it is implied, has to do with individuals' ability to develop a consistent and personal attitude toward mundane phenomena. They can do this only by conceiving the mundane aspects of life from the point of view of a transcendental image of the world as a unified cosmos. Only prophecy, not a priesthood, can provide the individual with the intellectual tools and the psychological encouragement to adopt such a unified attitude toward the world as such.

The section begins by discussing the lack of transcendental reference in primitive and magical forms of religion before the development of religious universalism, which comes with the rise of monotheism. That is, premonotheistic religions are practically oriented to achievement of immediate goals. In contrast, the Yahweh cult represents the early development of "a first approach to universal monotheism, namely monolatry, as a result of a concrete historical event—the formation of a confederacy." But just as important as this was the ancient Israelites' experience of "international politics." This experience helped stimulate the wider, more "universal" significance that they attributed to Yahweh, in contrast to "the local god of the city of Jerusalem" that came before. This was not a unique development in the history of religions, for elsewhere comparable international social and political experiences, created by the rise of the great ancient empires, "favored the rise of both universalism and monotheism."[24] Weber's view of the beginnings of monotheism thus posits a particular set of experiences that forces one to look beyond one's local community.[25]

The oldest Israelite prophecy, at the time of Elijah, arose in the context of the rise of empire and international commerce.[26] The oldest Hebrew legislation, the Mosaic laws in Deuteronomy, "presuppose a money economy and hence sharp conflicts of interest . . . within the confederacy."[27] The classical prophets were interested in foreign politics rather than social reform; their interest in religious (i.e., legal and ritual) fidelity was "a means to an end," namely, the appeasement of God's wrath, which they saw working

24. Weber, *Economy and Society*, 418–19.
25. Cf. ibid., 448: ". . . the personal, transcendental and ethical god is a Near Eastern concept. It corresponds so closely to that of an all-powerful mundane king with his rational bureaucratic regime that a causal connection can scarcely be denied."
26. Ibid., 441.
27. Ibid., 443.

itself out in what were, from the point of view of the confederacy, international calamities. This is perfectly consistent with the "universalism" of the prophetic message, which means only that the world is conceived of as a whole and that God's action takes place on the plane of world history.[28] Another dimension of "universal religion" in Weber's conception has to do with demands made on the individual, as a condition of salvation. A psychological tension is set up between the individual's religious conception of the cosmos, and the imperfections of mundane existence thrown into relief by this conception. In short, monotheism creates an existential conflict between "religion" and "world."[29]

Weber next turns to the development of a religiously aware community, or congregation (*Gemeinde*). Successful prophecy wins "disciples" or "followers" who "routinize" the religious message and thereby form a "congregation of laymen." But the religious congregation may also be organized by a priesthood. The formation of lay congregations around a priesthood

> was associated primarily with the rise of the great world empires of the Near East, especially Persia. Political associations were annihilated and the population disarmed; their priesthoods, however, were assigned certain political powers and were rendered secure in their positions. This was done because the religious congregation was regarded [by Imperial authorities] as a valuable instrument for pacifying the conquered.

All this follows Eduard Meyer's exposition of the history of ancient Israel, including the conclusion:

> Thus, by virtue of decrees promulgated by the Persian kings from Cyrus to Artaxerxes, Judaism evolved into a religious community under royal protection, with a theocratic center in Jerusalem. A Persian victory would have brought similar chances and opportunities [for long-term survival of the religious community] to the Delphic Apollo and to the priestly families servicing other gods, and possibly also to the Orphic prophets.[30]

---

28. Ibid, 446, 450–51.

29. This formulation, which is worked out in its first form here, is more fully elaborated in the introductory essay to the *Religionssoziologie* series, translated as "The Social Psychology of the World Religions," in *From Max Weber*, 267–301.

30. Weber, *Economy and Society*, 454–55. Cf. chapter 4, pages 163–64, where this example is used to illustrate the logic of universal history.

But this did not happen, and the formation of an active lay congregation, which created demands on the priesthood that its pastoral needs be met, arose uniquely at the time in Israel. Elsewhere religious authorities headed a "mere administrative unit" for taxation and legal jurisdiction, where the laity were religiously passive. However, prophetic religion did not die out; it continued to challenge the priesthood, and a tension arose between prophet and priest centered on their mutual struggle for the religious allegiance of the congregation. The prophets enjoined the laity to reject the priesthood, which they considered to be a form of magic: "The god of the Israelite prophets desired not burnt offerings, but obedience to his commandments."[31] In other words, in contrast to the services offered to the laity by priests, "the technicians of the routine cults," prophets demanded of the individual layman that he adopt "a distinctively religious and meaningful relation to the eternal" as the sole condition for salvation.[32]

A struggle against the prophets ensued in which the priests codified doctrine and the older prophetic messages and took up the task of infusing into the laity its view of "what must and must not be regarded as sacred," in the "simple interest" of "securing its own position against possible attack."

> Prophets systematized religion with a view to unifying the relationship of man to the world, by reference to an ultimate and integrated value position. On the other hand, priests systematized the content of prophecy or of the sacred traditions by supplying them with a casuistical, rationalistic framework of analysis, and by adapting them to the customs of life and thought of their own stratum and of the laity whom they controlled.[33]

"The Jewish retention[34] of circumcision and of the Sabbath taboo" was a product of priestly interests, "intended, as is repeatedly indicated by the Old Testament, to effect separation from other nations, and it indeed produced such an effect to an extraordinary degree."[35] Weber concludes that

---

31. Ibid., 457.

32. Ibid.

33. Ibid., 460.

34. This use of language suggests that there was some sort of sustained attack on these ritual prescriptions by the prophets.

35. Ibid., 462. Similarly, a sharp separation of Christianity from Judaism was the result of the choice of Sunday for the Sabbath by Christians, "although this choice might possibly be accounted for by the Christian reception of the soteriol-

dogma became practically and theoretically important in religion when "priests, congregational teachers, and even the community itself [rather than the individual] became bearers of the religion. This holds for the later Zoroastrians, Jews, and Christians."[36] In Christianity this priestly interest in orthodoxy, "to protect the unity of the community," led at length to "the infallible doctrinal office of the bishop."[37]

The concept of pastoral care is elaborated next, designed in part to support Weber's point, first introduced in *The Protestant Ethic,* that religion can, under certain circumstances, be the most powerful motivating force for individual behavior. "Pastoral care in all its forms is the priest's real instrument of power, particularly over the workaday world." The most effective cases "have been the counselling rabbis of Judaism, the father confessors of Catholicism, the pietistic pastors of souls in Protestantism, the directors of souls in Counter-Reformation Catholicism," and some other examples from eastern religions.[38] Apart from organized pastoral care, however, the subjective pastoral dilemmas of the individual affect "the conduct of life most powerfully when religion has achieved an ethical character. In fact, the power of ethical religion over the masses parallels the development of pastoral care," but this power becomes manifest only within what Weber calls "the rationalism of lay circles [which] is another social force with which the priesthood must take issue."[39]

"Ethical religion" and "religious rationalism" are in fact the same things in Weber's terminology. He now introduces this terminology systematically, although we must jump ahead, to the closing section of "The Sociology of Religion," where the uniqueness of Jesus' religious message is analyzed, to get the real sense of what he means by this equation. In the later section, Jesus' deprecation of wealth is said to be based on "the primordial ethic of mutual help which is characteristic of neighborhood associations of poorer

---

ogical mythos of mystagogic Near Eastern salvation doctrines of solar religion," leading to the choice of the "the day of the sun god." Muhammed's choice of the Friday Sabbath was "probably" designed to separate from the Jews, but he had no comparable animus against the Christians, as his prohibition of wine, which is required in the Christian Communion, might suggest: "his absolute prohibition of wine had too many analogies with comparable ancient and contemporary phenomena."

36. Ibid., 462.
37. Ibid., 463.
38. Ibid., 465. Specifically *not* cited are the various Puritan churches and sects. These, in Weber's construction, put the burden of pastoral care on the individual.
39. Ibid., 465, 467.

people," and Jesus' teachings are said to be connected to the fact that he was a humble artisan and came from a small town, the typical locus of the neighborly ethics he professes. This kind of ethical orientation is, then, associated with such social backgrounds generally. Jesus' ethic is unique, however:

> The chief difference is that in Jesus' message acts of mutual help have been systematized into a *Gesinnungsethik* involving a fraternalistic sentiment of love. The injunction of mutual help was also construed universalistically, extended to everyone. The "neighbor" is the one nearest at hand. . . . Nascent Christianity maintained continuity with the older Jewish prophecies even after the fateful conversion of Paul had resulted in breaking away from the pariah religion.[40]

Now, apart from the connection to ancient Judaism suggested in the last sentence, which I will turn to momentarily, this passage on Jesus' ethic makes a distinction between the "rationalism," or *gesinnungsethisch* character of the religious message, and its "universalism," which has to do with the breadth of the social circle within which "ethical rationalism" is considered binding. This is important to keep in mind as we continue with the presentation of religious evolution in the earlier part of "The Sociology of Religion."

Religious rationalism, in Weber's sense, is an urban form of piety. Lutheranism, "in rather strongly marked contrast to Calvinism, and also to most of the Protestant sects," glorified the peasant, for example. Similarly, "In modern Lutheranism (for this was not the position of Luther himself) the dominant interest is in the struggle *against* intellectualist rationalism and against political liberalism." This is "very largely a reaction against the development of modern rationalism, of which the cities were regarded as the carriers." "What is more, [throughout the Middle Ages] the specific qualities of Christianity as an ethical religion of salvation and as personal piety found their real nurture in the urban environment; and it is there that they created new movements time and again, in contrast to the ritualistic, magical, or formalistic re-interpretation favored by the dominant feudal powers."[41] Judaism, too, is an urban religion, but this has negative connotations in contrast to the urban nature of Christian piety. The agricultural values of "prepmphetic times" became no more than "the expres-

---

40. Ibid., 632–33.
41. Ibid., 471–72.

sion of opposition to urban development" after the exile. "The actual religion had rather a different appearance. . . ." The *haverim* (fellow-Jews) in
the countryside were considered "godless," because "it was virtually impossible for a peasant to live a pious life according to Jewish ritual law. . . .
The practical consequences of postexilic theology, and even more so of the
Talmudic theology, made it extremely difficult for a Jew to practice agriculture."[42] Even modern-day Jews have difficulty combining piety with
agriculture: the Zionist colonies have the same problem as the ancient
Israelite peasantry, for "the eastern European rabbis, in contrast to the more
doctrinaire leaders of German Jewish orthodoxy, have had to construe a
special dispensation" of the sabbatical year for these colonists.[43]

These statements are extremely obscure, for they seem to date "Talmudic" Judaism as far back as the eighth century B.C., but at the same
time they suggest that the Israelite peasants' inability to regularly participate
in the Temple cult in Jerusalem made him a second-class member of the
religious community. The obscurity is lifted somewhat, however, when we
realize that Weber is identifying as "Talmudic" the Deuteronomic laws
pertaining to Temple worship in earliest times, after the consensus of biblical
scholarship in his day. The significant features of Jewish religion, in short,
are portrayed as having undergone no essential change from the earliest
historical times up to today—despite the fact that Weber is well aware of
the myriad concrete changes in the actual compilations, up to the Mishnah
(second-third centuries A.D.) and the Schulchan Aruch (sixteenth century)
as well as the numerous heterodox religious movements that have occurred
up to modern times in Judaism.[44]

This discussion leads Weber to consider the possible bases for different
types of piety in the different social strata in society. Aristocrats and bureaucrats are said to be irreligious in general, because they lack any religious
needs.[45] Many examples are then given to show that, in general, the economically rational strata are always skeptical or indifferent to religion. That

---

42. Ibid., 471. These statements reflect an utter ignorance of the history of the
Jews.

43. Ibid., 470–71. This also illustrates the point made above, that Weber's
comparative method takes a different direction from the general pattern of his
method when it comes to the Jews. Here comparison is made to show the absence
of change and the seeming permanence of fundamental "sociological" features.

44. See the survey of Jewish *halachic* codes in the section "Sociology of Law,"
ibid., 823–28.

45. Ibid., 472–77.

is why there are very few cases of "bourgeois religiosity," especially in the sense of "an ethical or salvation religion," and if such cases exist, an explanation of their exceptional character is called for. This speaks to a line of reasoning introduced by Sombart on the Jews, where much is made of the seeming ubiquity of the Jewish trader. Weber says that such cases of "bourgeois religiosity" do exist, however, and they are the following: Judaism ("the ethical rational religion of the Jewish community was already in Antiquity largely a religion of traders or financiers"), ascetic and sectarian Protestantism, and "Russian schismatic, heretical and rational pietistic sects, especially the Shtundists and Skoptsy." A new generalization is offered that will comprehend these cases:

> the inclination to join an ethical, rational, congregational religion becomes more strongly marked the further away one gets from those strata which have been the carriers of the type of capitalism which is primarily political in orientation . . . [and] the closer one gets to those strata which have been the carriers of the modern rational enterprise, i.e., strata with middle-class economic characteristics in the sense to be expounded later.[46]

This takes in all the exceptional cases with respect to the first generalization except, however, one: the Jews. That is, the question arises, since the Jews are "characteristically" traders and financiers, why are they both "bourgeois" socioeconomically and "rational" religiously? The answer leads to Weber's theory of the fundamental uniqueness of the Jews and their religion.

"From the time of its inception, ancient Christianity was characteristically a religion of artisans. Its saviour was an artisan, and his missionaries were wandering journeymen."[47] Despite the diverse religious currents popular at various times among craftsmen in Christian Europe, there is "a definite tendency towards congregational religion, towards religion of salvation, and finally towards rational ethical religion." This is not the result of economic causes, but rather of "the relative recession in the importance of blood groupings, particularly of the clan, within the [medieval] occidental city." Occupational organizations and voluntary religious associations provide a substitute for blood groupings for the urban dweller in the Occident. In other parts of the world various "factors hindered the city from developing

---

46. Ibid., 477–80; the last quote from 479–80.
47. Ibid., 481. For this and the following, see also Weber, in Runciman, *Selections in Translation,* 174–91, "The Soteriology of the Underprivileged."

in the direction of a community." All nonprivileged classes, in fact, are receptive to an "ethic of compensation." But peasants are "dependen[t] on magic for influencing the irrational forces of nature," and this acts as an obstacle to their adopting the more rational attitude, that they are deserving of just compensation.[48] The lowest social strata, slaves, wage laborers, and the modern proletariat, are so dependent "on purely social factors," that they cannot feel subject to "natural or meteorological processes" or to anything that might be regarded as subject to the influence of magic or providence, "as Sombart has already demonstrated in fine fashion."[49] An established salvation religion, in order to accommodate "the needs of the masses," regularly becomes "mere wizardry." The "characteristic" case is "the emergence of a personal, divine or human savior as the bearer of salvation, with the additional consequence that the religious relationship to this personage becomes the precondition of salvation." Veneration of a *guru* among the Buddhists, of Vishnu among Hindus, of the Christ child among Christians, and other ancient and eastern examples are given. In contrast to these "magical" deifications of a god in human form, the characteristics of "ethical religion" stand out all the more sharply:

> the notion of an impersonal and ethical cosmic order that transcends the deity and the ideal of an exemplary type of salvation are intellectualistic conceptions which are definitely alien to the masses and possible only for a laity that has been educated along ethically rational lines. The same holds true for the development of a concept of an absolutely transcendent god. With the exception of Judaism and Protestantism, all religions and religious ethics have had to reintroduce cults of saints, heroes or functional gods in order to accommodate themselves to the needs of the masses.[50]

These developmental tendencies bring up the question of the general functions of religions for the various social strata.

Weber works Nietzsche's theory of the functions of religion into his own exposition, absolving Christianity of Nietzsche's charge of serving the interests of *ressentiment,* and bringing the full burden of the Nietzschean

---

48. Weber, *Economy and Society,* 481–84.

49. I.e., in Sombart's *The Proletariat* (1906) and *Socialism* (1908) (ibid., 484–86).

50. Ibid., 488.

theory to bear on Judaism.[51] Religion compensates bad fortune by guaranteeing to the pious person a function, mission, or vocation of worth that will be realized in the future.[52] The hope for just compensation is often "a fairly calculating attitude, . . . next to magic (indeed, not unconnected with it), the most widely diffused form of mass religion all over the world."[53] This, however, does not produce a form of religious rationalism; this attitude is no more than utilitarian. The purest form of a *religious* ethic of compensation for the disprivileged, growing out of *ressentiment,* is found in Judaism.

In contrast to the Hindu pariah, who by his aspiration to be reincarnated into a superior caste sought to fit into the established gradation of social ranks of his experience, "the Jew anticipated his own personal salvation through a revolution of the existing social stratification to the advantage of his pariah people."[54] The underlying difference is the lack of *ressentiment* in the former case, its valorization in the latter. In Judaism fidelity to a code of morality is a means to an end; it "serves as a device for compensating a conscious *or unconscious* desire for vengeance. . . . The virtues enjoined by God are practiced for the sake of the hoped for compensation."[55] This situation allows and even directs Jewry to become a pariah people in a surrounding free from castes. For example, in contrast to the Muslim proselytes from among the oriental Christians, who were motivated by enhanced privilege, and despite forced conversions, the Jew always continued to see shame in leaving his coreligionists. Since, as Weber expressed in *The Protestant Ethic,* both Puritan asceticism and the Talmud lead to a "formalistic righteousness," governed by the belief that "it is better and will be more richly rewarded by God if one does a good deed for duty's sake than one which is not commanded by the law," religious and ritual obligations cease to possess independent moral value in these religions.[56] In Judaism, however,

---

51. See Taubes's paper, summarized in Stammer, *Max Weber and Sociology Today,* 187–92, for a discussion of Weber's use of Nietzsche in this context. This should also be put in the context of Weber's adamant rejection of Nietzsche's philosophy of the "transvaluation of values" (See Marianne Weber, *Biography,* 319, 372, 463, 584).

52. Religion also legitimates good fortune; this function of religion is found in "the priestly chronicles of Israel," in contrast to the "popular religion" of ancient Israel.

53. Weber, *Economy and Society,* 490–92.

54. Ibid., 497.

55. Ibid., 495; emphasis added.

56. Cf. Weber, *The Protestant Ethic,* 270.

these obligations are reduced even further to being "practiced for the sake of the hoped for compensation." Daily attention to one's fulfillment of the religious law thus become exercises in retribution. "The Jews' theodicy of disprivilege was greeted by the pitiless mockery of the godless heathen, but for the Jews the theodicy had the consequence of transforming religious criticism of the godless heathen into ever-watchful concern over their own fidelity to the law."[57] Jewish "moralism" acts back on the hope for vengeance, creating a sort of "rational traditionalism," because Jews believe that *halachic* fidelity will ensure their future triumph over the world ("so rock-hard was the collective belief in recompense within the religion of Judaism").

The hope of vengeance which, for pious Jews, was inextricably bound up with the moralism of the Law, since it pervades almost all exilic and post-exilic religious writings, must have been nourished, consciously or unconsciously, for two and a half millennia in almost every divine service of this people with their fixed commitment to the two principles of their religiously hallowed separation from the rest of the world and the this-worldly promises of their God. This hope naturally diminished, in the religious consciousness of intellectuals, as the period of waiting for the Messiah grew longer, and was increasingly replaced by the value of an inward awareness of God as such, or by a bland, emotionally appealing confidence in God's goodness as such, combined with a readiness to be at peace with all the world. This happened especially during periods when the social situation of the communities, condemned as they were to total political impotence, was fairly tolerable. During periods like those of the persecutions at the time of the Crusades, however, there were fresh outbursts of passionate feeling, either in the form of cries to God for vengeance, as vehement as they were fruitless, or in the form of a prayer that the worshiper's own soul might "become as dust" before the enemies who were cursing the Jews, but that he might restrain himself in the face of evil words and deeds and be satisfied simply with wordless fulfillment of God's commandments and keeping his heart open to God.[58]

Evidence of a deep ambivalence about the Jews and their religion can be found in these passages. On the one hand, Weber tries to acknowledge

---

57. Weber, *Economy and Society*, 497.

58. Weber, in Runciman, *Selections in Translation*, 187–88; cf. Weber, *Economy and Society*, 496. Compare Sombart, *The Jews and Modern Capitalism*, 270–72, as quoted above, page 223. For criticisms see the next note.

the influence of a hostile social environment on the way Jews received their own tradition (although one should be suspicious that he singles out intellectuals as the only group affected by environmental pressures). On the other hand, however, the kind of secret hate Nietzsche described as *ressentiment* (for example, in the essay in *Geneology of Morals,* "On Ascetic Ideals," where asceticism is shown to be a consequence of *ressentiment*) is combined with many of Sombart's arguments about "Jewish rationalism" and is made into a permanent, underlying, and determining feature of Jewish consciousness. Fundamental misinterpretations of Jewish religious history—such as Weber's use of Sombart's claims about the prayer *elohai netzor*[59]—as well,

---

59. This is important inasmuch as Weber makes crucial claims about the psychological effects of social-ethical suggestions made in the daily service. See the revised translation of the 1890 ed. of Singer's Prayerbook (London: Bloch, 1962), 6; in the Silverman prayerbook (1946), used by American Conservative congregations, 101. These are the opening lines of the lamentation that closes the (silent) *Amidah* prayer during the morning service. The authority for the prayer dates from the fifth century in the Talmud (Berakhot 17a). The full petition reads as follows: "My God, before I was formed I was unworthy, and now that I have been formed it is as though I had not been formed; I am dust. . . . I am before Thee as a vessel full of shame and confusion. May it be Thy will, O Lord my God, that I sin no more, and the sins I have committed before Thee purge away by Thy great compassion, but not by suffering and evil diseases" (Urbach, *The Sages: Their Concepts and Beliefs,* 614). This specifically denies that suffering is a means of purging sins (ibid., 448), counselling modesty instead, quite the opposite of resentment. From this prayer was derived the precept (also in Berakhot 17a) that "A man should always be subtle in the fear of Heaven," that "he should be on the friendliest of terms with his brethren and relatives, and, indeed, with all men, even with the Gentile in the street, so that he may be beloved in Heaven and well-liked upon earth, and be acceptable to his fellow man" (ibid., 418). The daily service was a point of friction in German history: Salo Baron notes that toward the end of the service, at the conclusion of the first sentence of the *Alenu* (". . . he hath not assigned unto us a portion as unto them [the nations of other lands], nor a destiny as unto all their multitude"), a "derogatory expectoration" was customary (see the Singer Prayerbook, 79). The passage of the *Alenu,* "for they bow down to vanity and emptiness and pray to a god who saveth not" (omitted in the Singer Prayerbook) came under attack continuously after 1370, until in 1703 the Prussian government prohibited its recitation and the customary spitting (Baron, *A Social and Religious History of the Jews,* VII, 251n.17). Also, the image of a politically impotent Jewish community has been cultivated for different reasons by both the Jewish and Christian traditions, and by modern apologists on both sides, but is not historical (Amos Funkenstein, "The Passivity of Diaspora Jewry: Myth and Reality," Jewish Studies Lectureship, University of Pittsburgh; March 12, 1987; Cf. Biale, *Power and Powerlessness in Jewish History*).

perhaps, as an equally fundamental misreading of human psychology, both taken directly from the anti-Jewish stereotypes of *die Judenfrage,* are taken over uncritically into Weber's sociology, where they have similarly invidious significance.

The effects of "Jewish rationalism" could not have spread throughout society because of the peculiar dualism of Jewish social ethics. The kind of mind-set with which Puritanism approaches the field of worldly action is in Judaism confined to ritual and to relations with coreligionists and does not find an adequate outlet in wider pursuits. Puritans approached the economy in particular as a stage upon which piety could be demonstrated, while for Jews it was part of the world of strangers and thus open to moral laxity, not subject to moral principle. For Jews, the field of active moral circumspection is confined to the internal world of the ghetto; but here, too, strict self-control is limited to fulfillment of traditional, detailed precepts of piety. This narrowed the field in which an attitude of "rationalism" could find expression. Jewish rationalism was never directed toward the "rationalization" of social institutions, economic or otherwise; its consequences for the modern world were wholly indirect.[60]

Jewish rationalism, however, like Christian rationalism, is based on the emergence of "religious" or "ethical rationalism" in the ancient Jewish prophets. The world historical role of the prophets lay in their sytematizing the religious world-concept into a *Gesinnungsethik,* and so creating monotheism. "Prophetic religion," heir to the "popular religion" of ancient Israel, in contrast to postexilic Israelite religion, is the first occurrence of religious rationalism. Ascetic Protestantism was not so inhibited as Judaism in applying rationalism to all areas of life. In fact, it is precisely the value it put on an integrated and systematic internalization of rational motives, in principle leaving no field of endeavor exempt from rationalization, that accounts for ascetic Protestantism's role as a revolutionary force in world history. Religious rationalism failed, however, to become institutionalized in a universalistic direction in Judaism, because of the influence of the priesthood, of whom the Pharisees are the heirs in the time of Jesus.[61] Jesus

---

60. Weber, *Economy and Society,* 618.

61. Cf. the last sentence of Weber, *Ancient Judaism,* on the reasons why Jewish converts were not forthcoming after the apostolic era: "And there is the strength of the firmly structured social communities, the family, and the congregation, which the apostate lost without the prospect of finding equally valuable and certain affiliation with the Christian congregations. All of this makes the Jewish community remain in its self-chosen situation as a pariah people as long and as far as the unbroken spirit of the Jewish law, and that is to say, the spirit of the Pharisees, and the rabbis of late antiquity, continued and continues to live on."

revived the prophetic elements of Judaism, and from that point on the paths of Judaism and Christianity diverged. This divergence was made complete by Paul, who, by eating at a common table with the Gentiles, abrogated conclusively the "slave law" of the Jews:

> The dynamic power behind the incomparable missionary labors of Paul was his offer to the Jews of a tremendous release, the release provided by the consciousness of having escaped the fate of pariah status. A Jew could henceforth be a Greek among Greeks as well as a Jew among Jews, and could achieve this within the paradox of faith rather than through an enlightened hostility to religion. This was the passionate feeling of liberation brought by Paul. The Jew could actually free himself from the ancient promises of God, by placing his faith in the new savior who had believed himself abandoned upon the cross by that very God.[62]

Among the historical consequences of this event "was the intense hatred of this one man Paul by the Jews of the Diaspora, sufficiently authenticated as fact."[63]

For Weber, the most striking feature of Judaism, apart from its rationalism, is its dualistic social ethic and the way this is related to the pariah status of the Jews. Despite any possible rabbinical concessions to economic necessity, the new type of conscience represented by the Protestant ethic could never have developed from Jewish rationalism. For the Jew could combine the most pious attachment to his religion and his community with higgling in the marketplace, tax farming, and other "dealings with non-Jews which the Puritans rejected violently as showing the cupidity of the trader."[64] Sombart's concept of the calculating spirit, one type of "rationalism," is the rule for the Jewish treatment of Gentiles, while Jewish *religious* "rationalism" is confined to the formalistic prescriptions of *halachah,* and to the maintenance of community solidarity among the Jews:

> With this people, and in this clear-cut fashion only among them and under other very particular conditions, the suffering of a people's

---

62. Ibid; cf. also Weber, *Economy and Society,* 616–17, 630–34, 622; Weber, *Religion of India,* 37.

63. Weber, *Economy and Society,* 623. This claim is based on a misdating of some Talmudic passages (giving them excessive antiquity), not all of them unambiguous, that could be explicitly anti-Christian.

64. Ibid., 617; cf. the entire section entitled by the editors of the English translation "Jewish Rationalism *versus* Protestant Asceticism" (pp. 615–23).

Community, rather than the suffering of an individual, became the object of hope for religious salvation. The rule [in other religions of salvation] was that the savior bore an individual and universal character at the same time that he was ready to guarantee salvation for the *individual* and to every individual who would turn to him.[65]

A pariah ethic, no matter how rational, is justified internally by the combination of strict duty in fulfilling the insider's religious ethics, as a condition for future redemption, and the ethical indifference or even animosity toward the outside world, especially in regard to economic life. Under these conditions, only traditionalism can arise as the outward style of life within the community; behavior toward those outside the community is relatively free of ethical regulation. Thus, "the economic behavior of the Jews simply moved in the direction of least resistance which was permitted them by [their own] legalistic ethical norms."[66]

This, finally, retains the integrity of the original thesis of *The Protestant Ethic,* which had only in passing considered the Jews, in order to establish a conceptual distance between their role in the rise of capitalism and that of the Puritans. The more elaborate theory of the Jews as pariah people, developed in response to Sombart after 1911, has the same purpose. But it should be apparent that Weber's criticisms of Sombart's treatment of the Jews take the form of a sort of mopping-up exercise, disclaiming for example the Jews' role in creating certain financial instruments, but not denying that Jews made wide use of these instruments. So also Weber took issue with Sombart's subthesis, that the Jews are a nomadic people, a thesis that was supposed to sustain the claim that they remain socially aloof from non-Jewish society by their nature. Weber countered this with a subthesis of his own, that the Jews are a "mountain-people" (a claim made at the time, for example, by Karl Kautsky).[67] This was designed to show that Jews were unfit for agriculture and to explain their predominance in urban areas, by reference to their religion. However the import of these two subtheses is really the same, namely, to suggest that Jews always retain a social distance from their environment, that they are "rationalistic" in the amoral sense.

More important than these internal textual connections, Weber's concept of "Jewish rationalism" is consistent with practical proposals to promote

---

65. "Social Psychology of the World Religions," 273; emphases in original.
66. Weber, *Economy and Society,* 617.
67. See Massing, *Rehearsal for Destruction,* 163–64 for Kautsky.

means for the dissolution of the Jewish population. Weber would not have accepted Sombart's enthusiasm for forced miscegenation as the appropriate means, but a gradualist policy of some sort, leading ultimately to the end of the Jewish group, seems to be a logical conclusion of even a liberal reading of the concept of "Jewish rationalism." It was, in fact, a conclusion commonly made by non-Jewish progressives among Weber's peers.

III

In 1920 Weber revised *The Protestant Ethic,* incorporating the changes he had formulated in response to Sombart on the sociology of the Jews. A brief listing of these changes supports the outline of his view of the history of ancient Israel and the religious basis of Jewish pariahdom established above. It also shows how he accommodated the earlier, restrained thesis of 1905 on Jewish "traditionalism" to his newer thesis that the Jews are a pariah people.

In 1905 Weber said that the formalism of the Puritan duty to obey the rule of brotherly love "is a subtle intensification and refinement of the ancient Jewish 'eye for an eye.' " In 1920 this is changed to: "It is the same transfer of vengeance that is found in parts of the Old Testament written after the exile; a subtle intensification and refinement of the spirit of revenge compared to the older 'eye for an eye.' "[68] In 1905 Weber asserts that the "renaissance of the Old Testament" among the Puritans played a part in "making ugliness more of a 'possible' object for art." In 1920 is added, this "in the last analysis go[es] back to Deutero-Isaiah (ch. 53) and the Twenty-second Psalm."[69] Similarly he added to the text in 1920 the claim that the servant of God reference in Isaiah and the Twenty-second Psalm led to "a deadening of enterprise in worldly activity" among the Jews.[70] These points are designed to support the hypothesis, developed in more general terms, but at greater length in *Economy and Society,* that the sources for the religious valorization of social disprivilege, the psychological basis for pariahdom, can be located in parts of the ancient Hebrew scriptures.[71]

---

68. Weber, *The Protestant Ethic,* 223n.25; compare Weber, "Die protestantische Ethik," 13n.

69. Weber, *The Protestant Ethic,* 273n.66.

70. Ibid., 131, bottom and the note there, at 244n.115.

71. Marianne Weber noted in her preface to the first German edition of *Religionssoziologie* that Weber was actively planning a study of Psalms and of Job, to follow up the monograph. These passages, and some others considered below,

To the passages cited above (in chapter 6), on the Old Testament influence on Luther's traditionalism, Weber added a caveat to the effect that
these traditionalistic elements are not found "in the genuine prophets."
This is similar to a claim made in the 1905 version, that the nontraditionalist
"radical repudiation of the world" of "the apostolic era" led to "indifference" rather than outright conservatism.[72] Nevertheless, the significance of
Hebraic biblicism is changed subtly in 1920 to support the pariah-people
thesis. Weber continues to see Protestantism as having used biblicism to
justify inner-worldly activism. He also allows (in response to Sombart) that
postexilic Judaism retains this same biblicism, but he claims this is confined
to the Jew's obedience to the "ritual" law. This makes the Jews out as
inner-worldly activists (as "rationalistic") in a restricted sense, in the sense
of a strict observance of the religious code, but not in those aspects of
everyday life that are supposedly treated with laxity by the religious code.
Following the arguments of *Economy and Society,* Jewish-Gentile relations
are prominent among those fields of behavior open to lax formal religious
interpretation and, because religious law does contain clear but less than
concrete principles in this area, dualistic principles, Jewish-Gentile relations
becomes a sort of free zone, morally speaking.

In the first version of *The Protestant Ethic,* Judaism's traditionalism and
quietism are stressed in order to contrast it with the "inner-worldly activism"
of Anglo-American Protestantism. The biblical book of Job is said to be
an exception to the general spirit of Judaism, which explains why it became
important to the Puritans. But given the sharp contrast of the "spirits" of
the two religions, it ought to be understandable why the Old Testament's
"praise of formal legality" could be turned into Puritanism's "spirit of self-
righteous and sober legality."

The Puritans repudiated the Apocrypha as not inspired, consistently
with their sharp distinction between things divine and things of the
flesh. But among the canonical books that of Job had all the more

---

indicate the direction that this study would have taken. Cf. also Weber, *Economy
and Society,* 495, where it is claimed that some Psalms "express in the most blatant
form the moralistic satisfaction and self-justification of a pariah people's need for
revenge," and further, that these Psalms color the content of Jewish monotheism.
Weber does not say which Psalms he had in mind, but they are probably Psalms
42–72, especially, 56:8. I thank Professor Bernard Goldstein for this suggestion.
More remarks on the vengeance-motif in medieval Jewish thought are made in
the appendix on Jacob Katz's pariah-people thesis.

72. Weber, *The Protestant Ethic,* 83–84.

influence. On the one hand it contained a grand conception of the absolute sovereign majesty of God, beyond all human comprehension, which was closely related to that of Calvinism. With that, on the other hand, it combined the certainty which, though incidental for Calvin, came to be of great importance for Puritanism, that God would bless His own in this life (and precisely in Job: here alone!)[73] and also in the material sense. The Oriental quietism, which appears in several of the finest verses of the Psalms and in the Proverbs, was interpreted away, just as [Richard] Baxter did with the traditionalistic tinge of the passage in the 1st Epistle to the Corinthians, so important for the idea of the calling.

But all the more emphasis was placed on those parts of the Old Testament which praise *formal legality* as a sign of conduct pleasing to God. They held the theory that the Mosaic Law had only lost its validity through Christ in so far as it contained ceremonial or purely historical precepts applying only to the Jewish people, but that otherwise it had always been valid as an expression of the natural law, and must hence be retained. This made it possible, on the one hand, to eliminate elements which could not be reconciled with modern life. But still, through its numerous related features, Old Testament morality was able to give a powerful impetus to that spirit of self-righteous and sober legality which was so characteristic of the worldly asceticism of this form of Protestantism.[74]

Despite Weber's aim (in 1905) to distinguish between Judaism and Puritanism, and so to eliminate Judaism from suspicion that it bears any historical responsibility for the spirit of capitalism, it is not hard to see why Sombart might have taken precisely this argument of Weber's as support for his formula, "Puritanism *is* Judaism."[75] He was, perhaps, explicitly drawn to this insight by Weber's remarks immediately following the passage quoted above:

Thus when authors, as was the case with several contemporaries as well as later writers [n.b.], characterize the basic ethical tendency of Puritanism, especially in England, as English Hebraism, they are,

---

73. This parenthetical phrase, "(und gerade—in Buch Hiob: nur!—,)" was inserted in 1920. It only adds more stress to the point already made in the original version of the passage, otherwise unchanged from 1905.

74. Ibid., 164–65.

75. Sombart, *The Jews and Modern Capitalism*, 249.

correctly understood, not wrong. We may think not only of Palestinian Judaism at the time of the writing of the Scriptures, but of Judaism as it became under the influence of many centuries of formalistic, legalistic, and Talmudic education. The general tendency of the older Judaism toward a naïve acceptance of life as such was far removed from the special characteristics of Puritanism.[76]

This suggests a qualitative difference between the spirit of "older" Judaism and of later, Talmudic Judaism. From this Sombart was encouraged to develop his sharp distinction between "Israelite" and "Jewish" religion, and then, in this revised form, to propose his equation of Puritanism and Judaism. In so doing, of course, he was forced to deny Weber's 1905 argument that Judaism could not be held responsible for *modern* "rationalism," on account of its "traditionalism." In the passage, Weber tries to make this point by claiming that the Protestant appropriation of the book of Job had nothing in common with the "Oriental quietism" into which it was originally integrated. But, as a note originally appended to the passage above suggests, Weber's first thesis on the Jews and Judaism was perhaps not as unequivocal as this:

The enormous influence which, for instance, the second commandment ("thou shalt not make unto thee a graven image") has had on the development of the Jewish character, its rationality and abhorrence of sensuous culture, cannot be analyzed here. However, it may perhaps be noted as characteristic that one of the leaders of the Educational Alliance in the United States, an organization which carries on the Americanization of Jewish immigrants on a grand scale and with astonishing success, told me that one of the first purposes aimed at in all forms of artistic and social education work was "emancipation from the second commandment." To the Israelite's prohibition of any anthropomorphic representation of God (s.v.v.!) corresponds in Puritanism the somewhat different but in effect similar prohibition of the idolatry of the flesh. To be sure, numerous characteristics connected on principle to Puritan morality are also related to Talmudic Judaism. For instance, it is stated in the Talmud (in Wuensche, *Babyl. Talmud,* II, 34) that it is better and will be more richly rewarded by God if one does a good deed for duty's sake than one which is not commanded

---

76. Weber, *The Protestant Ethic,* 165, corrected according to Weber, "Die protestantische Ethik" (1905).

by the law. In other words, loveless fulfillment of duty stands higher ethically than sentimental philanthropy. The Puritan ethic would accept that in all essentials. . . . But nevertheless the Talmudic ethic is deeply saturated with Oriental traditionalism. "R. Tanchum said to ben Chanilai, 'Never alter a custom' " (Gemara to Mishnah, VII, i, 86b, no. 93 in Wuensch: it is a question of the cost of day laborers). The only exception to this is relations to strangers.—Moreover, the Puritan conception of "lawfulness" as *proof* [of one's possession of grace] evidently provided a much stronger motive to positive *action* than the Jewish unquestioned fulfillment of all commandments. . . . On Old Testament "lawfulness" compare for example Ritschl, *die christliche Lehre von der Rechfertigung und Versöhnung*, II, 265.[77]

Sombart could easily have found support for his distinction between "the religion of ancient Israel" and "Judaism" from this clarifying note of Weber's.

In 1920 Weber significantly revised both the main passage above and the note to it, mainly by addition, in order to prevent Sombart's interpretation. Now, after the (unchanged) remark about "English Hebraism," it reads:

It is necessary, however, not to think of Palestinian Judaism . . . but of Judaism as it became under the influence of many centuries of formalistic, legalistic, and Talmudic education. Even then one must be very careful in drawing parallels. The general tendency of older Judaism toward a naive acceptance of life as such was far removed from the special characteristics of Puritanism. It was, however, just as far—and this ought not to be overlooked—from the economic ethics of medieval and modern Judaism.[78]

"Not only" Palestinian Judaism, as well as medieval and modern Judaism, has become in 1920, "*not* . . . Palestinian Judaism," but *rather* Talmudic Judaism. In the revised note, the "connection on principle" between Puritan morality and Talmudic Judaism has become: "As far as Talmudic Judaism is concerned, some fundamental traits of Puritan morality are certainly related to it." The passages from Wuensch's edition of the Talmud follow unchanged. Then comes a concession (to Sombart?) that an ethic of success

---

77. Weber, *The Protestant Ethic*, 90–91n. (unchanged from 1905).
78. Ibid., 165–66.

is found in Judaism, but its *effects* are mitigated, as compared with Puritanism, by "the double ethic" of Judaism:

> Acts toward a stranger were allowed which were forbidden toward a brother. For that reason alone it was impossible for success in this field of what was not commanded but only allowed to be a sign of religious worth and a motive to methodical conduct in the way in which it was for the Puritan. On this whole problem, which Sombart, in his book *Das Juden und das Wirtschaftsleben,* has often dealt with incorrectly, see the essays referred to above [i.e., in Weber's Collected Essays in *Religionssoziologie*]. The Jewish ethics, however strange that may at first sound, remained very strongly traditionalistic.[79]

The note ends with a (new) notice that the English Puritans took the Jews to be supporters of an unethical type of capitalism, associated with "war, government contracts, State monopolies, speculative promotions, and the construction of financial projects of princes." This is made to support the (new) conclusion in the text (above), "That Jewish capitalism was speculative pariah-capitalism, while the Puritan [type] was bourgeois organization of labor."[80]

One cannot help but see Weber's simultaneous attempts to save the original, strategic thesis that Judaism is traditionalism, to incorporate the new thesis that Judaism is a religion of and for social pariahs, and to distance himself from Sombart, as overly strained. The changes made to the above passages seem to reflect a direct influence of Sombart on Weber, on the question of the role of Judaism on "the Jewish ethic." Weber wants to accept in all essentials what Sombart has said on this. He does not want to concede, however, that the Jews have had a decisive hand in the origins of capitalism. To forestall this conclusion, Weber is led to expand on the significance of "the double ethic" in Judaism. This becomes the key to saving his original Protestant ethic thesis while at the same time letting in all that Sombart has said (and he was not alone, nor was he the first) about the characteristics of "Jewish rationalism."[81] With this side of Sombart's

---

79. Ibid., 270–71 n.58.

80. The same point is reiterated at ibid., 180, top (added in 1920): "Here also lay the difference of the Puritan economic ethic from the Jewish." Things were not put so sharply in 1905.

81. For example, a new concept added to the 1920 edition, "disenchantment of the world" (*Entzauberung der Welt*), in two places (ibid., 105, 117, top) uses "the Jews" as a prominent case, the earliest authors of a religion designed to

thesis Weber never disagrees. On the contrary, as he did with Sombart's original treatment of the history of "calculability," Weber here again directs his effort and learning to further refining Sombart's historical portrait of the Jews and Judaism. Actually, the changes in the first and second versions of these passages are not that great; they are in the form of an elaboration rather than a change in the basic point. For even in the 1905 footnote Weber emphasized the "rationality of the Jewish character" as it developed up to the time of immigration to America and, with regard to "Oriental traditionalism," claimed that "the only exception to this is relations to strangers." Sombart chose to emphasize these aspects of Weber's analysis, forcing Weber to elaborate on these later. In important respects Weber's pariah-people theory is a revision of Sombart's thesis on the Jews, which he finds to be consistent with his own conceptualization in part only.

Many other parallels between Sombart's and Weber's portraits of the Jews and Judaism could be listed. Despite Weber's efforts to highlight what he presented as crucial differences in their respective theses on the Jews and Judaism, their respective treatments of Judaism and the Jews diverged only where Sombart's and Weber's theoretical and practical interests diverged. Neither Weber nor Sombart is really studying or describing "Judaism," neither is engaged primarily in correcting errors or tendentiousnss in the literature they used. Rather, each was *constructing* "Judaism," and in related ways insofar as they were members and products of the same society, culture, class, and milieu. Weber's liberal nationalism and Sombart's *gemeinschaftlich* socialism were both rooted in the expectation that modern society would be unified by means of a common national culture. Both portraits of the Jews serve to "prove" that Judaism and Jewish identity must become more and more effaced as modern society develops. The Jews' continued existence as a social community, whether based on religious affiliation or common ethnic identification, cannot be tolerated indefinitely on the basis of such views.

---

function without magic. Sombart would not criticize this claim; indeed, he introduced it first. Weber's revision of Sombart's thesis does not alter this. Weber came to see "Jewish rationalism" as rooted in a religious idea of vocation, as in Puritanism: in the chapter on Luther, Weber added passages in 1920 to a long note on the derivation of the meaning of *"Beruf"* claiming that references to Jesus Sirach in the Talmud show that the crucial verses Luther translated with *"Beruf"* were *originally* based on a very similar concept in Hebrew, the *hoch,* which "really did mean something similar to our calling, namely one's fate or assigned task" (ibid., 207n.3, bottom, and 208).

IV

The theoretical significance of Weber's portrait of the Jews and Judaism is not confined to his sociology of religion. The concept of pariah people had for Weber direct relevance for the sociological conceptualization of fundamental processes of group formation. Weber seems to have believed that the case of the Jews represented the ideal type of the formalization or rationalization of the primordial consciousness of group-boundedness from the rest of the social world, permanently perpetuated by virtue of the religious sanctification of pariahdom he thought he had discovered in Judaism. To trace the full ramifications of this assumption throughout the development of Weber's sociology would be a formidable task, for the group formation of the Jews represents the opposite of the development he constructed—"fraternization"—in the monograph-length chapter on "Non-legitimate Domination" in *Economy and Society,* which treats the development of ancient and medieval cities as the potential source for modern models of national citizenship.[82] The broad theory he pursues here and in many other places is that on the one side there stands the possibility of group closure, which in its furthest development leads to the formation of the "ethnic group" and is, in its most extreme form, represented by the Jews, an ethnic group that has developed religious justifications for its social closure, making social closure a condition of salvation. This final development, as Weber's sociology of religion suggests, is very rare, because there are so few cases of "salvation" religions in the technical sense that Weber has laid down there. In fact, the only case that has ever existed of a religious sanctification of group closure, if we follow Weber's presentation, is the case of the Jews. On the other side, the Athenian democratic city and the medieval free cities break down all kinds of local or narrow solidarities, and at length give rise to the modern concept of political citizenship. The concept of citizenship is based on the free association of individuals forming a political community.

A full examination of this line of thought and the numerous theoretical consequences within Weber's sociology that result will not be undertaken here. It must suffice for now merely to survey the main points in this line of thought, as they are developed by Weber in some discussions of his formal definitions of ethnicity, the nation, and status-group formation. In

---

82. Cf. Weber, *Economy and Society,* part 2, chapter 16, 1212ff. ("The City") and chapter 15, 1158ff. ("Hierocracy").

Economy and Society there is a chapter on "Ethnic Groups"[83] that includes a critique of racial definitions of the concept and ultimately a critique of the concept of ethnicity itself, associating it with notions of mass culture, which are rejected. Weber claims that the actual usage behind the concept more closely resembles the concept of the nation. Subsequent definition of the nation involves comparison of the cases of Poles, Slavs, Alsatians, and Baltic Germans (those Germans under the Imperial Russian administration) respectively, each to Germans.

Next comes comparison, respectively, of the small western European states, of language groups, of groups identified by loyalty to common customs or to a tradition, religion, or to "political memories," either coterminous with or existing as special groups within a nation-state in the modern sense—each of these are compared to the Imperial German Reich. But ultimately the definition arrived at makes "nation" depend upon an aspiration to political power and "greatness." Thus Switzerland is not a nation. The ideal type for "nation" is the contemporary German Reich, in contrast to "the Germans 150 years ago, when they were essentially a language group [only] without pretensions to national power."

Another chapter in *Economy and Society* is related to this, on "The Nation."[84] Here much of the same ground is covered as in the chapter on ethnic groups, but now the nation is defined as a *subgroup* within the citizenry of a nation-state. In other words, the focus of this chapter is on the "national" minority. In passing Weber considers "whether the Jews may be called a 'nation.'" "Most of the time, the answer will be negative." He then points out that various Jewish parties differ on this question, as do the various "peoples of their environment."[85]

These discussions are connected to Weber's famous sociological distinction between "class" and "status," and the lengthy analyses associated with the distinction in various parts of his work, especially throughout *Economy and Society,* and in the book on Indian religions. The latter, in turn, points directly to his treatment of Judaism and the Jews. For it is in his analysis of the Indian caste culture that Weber first introduced at length the related notions of "guest people" and "pariah people." Weber apparently worked out the class-status distinction with the problem of social inclusion and

---

83. Ibid., part 2, chapter 5, 385–98.
84. Ibid., part 2, chapter 9, section 5, 921–26. Compare Mommsen, *German Politics,* 238–39.
85. Weber, *Economy and Society,* 923.

exclusion in mind and this, he felt, required a consideration of the place of the Jews in history and society.

In *The Religion of India* the concept of "status" is defined succinctly to refer specifically to the social recognition of caste identity as its most extreme or characteristic example.[86] The purpose of the definition is to set up a contrast to "class," which is prestige or social honor recognized socially by virtue of a person's property ownership and wealth, in short esteem for one's economic situation. Against this, caste is social rank recognized mainly by differences in and peculiarities of life-style or manners and customs, and it is said to stand apart from class on this account.

Weber offers the hypothesis that the Indian outcastes originated from groups or tribes that became economically dependent on a conquering host. The hypothesis subsequently becomes a basis for his conceptualization. Collective economic dependence alone, however, classifies a group as a "guest people," and Weber offers the analogy of the gypsies in Europe, "a typical ancient Indian guest people which, in contrast to others, has wandered outside of India." If, on the other hand, they also segregate themselves from their social environment ritually, a condition most clearly indicated by the prohibition of intermarriage[87] and of the freedom to eat in common with outsiders, the guest people can also be termed a pariah people. He again offers the example of the gypsies but now adds, "in another manner, the Jews of the Middle Ages."[88]

All these ideas are further developed in *Economy and Society,* in the chapter on "Status Groups and Classes"[89] and in a section on "The Distribution of Power Within the Political Community: Class, Status, Party."[90] The latter was written sometime between 1910 and 1914, the former later, between 1918 and 1920.[91] In the later version, Weber depicts the caste as a segregated ethnic group, and an "ethnic group" was defined earlier as a group whose solidarity rests on a belief in a common "racial" or hereditary

---

86. Weber, *Religion of India,* 39.
87. For suggestions concerning the vexing problem, as perceived by non-Jewish Germans at the time of Weber's writing, of simultaneous claims to societal integration and reluctance to intermarry on the part of German Jews, see Tal, *Christians and Jews,* 49, 59n, 66, 94, 116, 267, 278, 295.
88. Weber, *Religion of India,* 11–13. See also Schmueli, "The Pariah People," 172–74.
89. Weber, *Economy and Society,* part 1, chapter 4, 302–7.
90. Ibid., part 2, chapter 9, section 6, 926–39.
91. Cf. Roth's introduction to ibid., lxv and c.

("blood") origin. He then goes on to outline the conceptual relationships that exist among castes, status groups, and pariah peoples: status groups cultivate their honor in opposition to others and so are normally absolutely isolated socially; a caste structure brings status groups with mutual disdain together by introducing a common system of super- and subordination, i.e., this turns a horizontal differentiation of groups into a vertical one, usually by assigning functional qualities to the life-style of each group; finally, a pariah people continues to cultivate its honor, like a status group and a caste, but now projects its basis into a future end of days. In other words, a pariah group invariably develops the ideology of a "chosen people."[92] This ideology was also discussed in the sections on ethnic groups and the nation, where it is said to be a general tendency of all ethnic and national groups.

These discussions of the "chosen people" myth exhibit an indecisiveness and even confusion in conceptualization. Weber appears to be elaborating what he took to be the really "significant" elements of the image of the Jews as social pariahs, in areas of his sociology that seem on their face not to be directly related to this topic. This suggests that he generalized aspects of the pariah image in the process of providing theoretical underpinning for various substantive areas in formal sociology. In other words, the theoretical implications of the pariah-people thesis go well beyond the sociology of religion, where such implications might be expected. They have to do with Weber's basic understanding of nation, ethnic group, status group, group formation, and the integration of groups in society (*Vergesellschaftung*). A pariah people and a nation are really homologous phenomena in Weber's thought. The former is the most extreme example of a national minority, and of group closure. The nation differs from a national minority only in size. All the same aspects of social closure and mythology that characterize a pariah people (beliefs in the "chosen people" and in "racial" destiny) are part of Weber's definition of the nation.[93]

---

92. Compare Schmueli, "The Pariah People," 174–76.

93. The homology between the concepts of pariah people and nation suggests that Weber sees something of his own national aspirations in the Jews. Perhaps he perceived a parallel between his own view of Germany's place in the world and the Jews' place in Germany and other modern societies. This is the implication of a statement he made in 1919, arguing that the German nation's status as a "pariah people" became particularly naked on account of the defeat on the battlefield (see Mommsen, *German Politics*, 321–22).

9

Conclusions

Two major conclusions emerge from a study of Max Weber's construction of a sociology of the Jews and Judaism. The first is that this part of Weber's sociology is not isolated from his broader interests in history and society. Although he was reluctant to embark on such a project, once he took up the sociology of the Jews he brought to bear on it ideas about the nature of society and intergroup relations that he had already given sustained thought to in the 1890s, in his analysis of what he called the "denationalization" of rural eastern Germany, and in his analysis of German industrialization. A model of society was adopted and refined by him in the process of confronting contemporary German social problems in this period, a model that resonated positively with those who looked to the academic class for moral leadership in the Second Reich. By the turn of the century Weber had emerged from a period of mental breakdown and scholarly paralysis with a renewed commitment to the systematic study of historical and modern societies from the standpoint of this model of society. His primary interests were in the origins of this type of society and the manner in which this society was now developing. These were not unrelated questions, since an understanding of the critical historical breakthroughs and obstacles to the development of this type of society could, he thought, lead to a deeper understanding of what was required in the present to promote this development. This was the inspiration behind the program of comparative historical scholarship he embarked on after the turn of the century, which he called universal history. In a special series of methodological essays he blocked out the philosophical foundations for a theoretical approach to history and society that would be informed by this inspiration. In these essays he justified at great length a method of forming concepts for systematic sociological research that would reflect an internally consistent standpoint which, he argued, was ultimately rooted in the cultural values of the investigator and his age. These methodological rationales were intimately connected with the actual sociological method he initiated with his famous essay on *The Protestant Ethic*. Although the Protestant ethic thesis had become a special topic within the vast body of sociological work he had completed by 1920, there was perhaps no aspect of his entire *corpus* that was not somehow formally related to that original work in both method and substance. As his methodological essays show, Weber conceived this unity to be grounded in a substratum of cultural values, and this, finally, is what integrates each part of his sociological work into the whole. In other words, the systematic nature of Weber's sociology is not primarily formal, but rather ideological or cultural.

The question remains as to what the cultural values are that inspire Weber's sociology and integrate the parts within the whole. This is the area addressed by the second conclusion. Given an interest in the specific values that guide Weber's sociology, a number of different conclusions of this kind are possible, depending on what parts of Weber's work one concentrates on. I have chosen a limited task in this area and can claim only limited conclusions as a result.

I have already made ample remarks, in chapters 1, 5, and 8, above, indicating the seriousness of the empirical shortcomings of Weber's treatment of the history and sociology of the Jews.[1] However, the shortcomings of Weber's scholarship in this special field cannot be explained by the limitation of the sources available to him, nor by lack of scholarly expertise or lack of desire to achieve a sympathetic understanding of different religious standpoints on his part. For an explanation we must turn to the contemporary social and intellectual climate of opinion and the place of Weber's thought within it. When we do this we uncover hitherto unappreciated aspects of Weber's work.

My second conclusion, then, opens up a large field of inquiry into which few have ventured. The usual interest in Weber's work focuses on an internal explication of concepts. But this approach leaves the underlying assumptions of those concepts implicit. The "internal" announcement in the methodological essays, which Weber continued throughout his career to consider valid, that the critique of concepts in the social sciences is fundamentally a clarification of the cultural values of the scholarly community, runs counter to the assumptions of this approach. Yet that position is no more than an invitation to speculate on the underlying values of Weber's sociology. This

---

1. See also the appendix.

must be done by reconstructing the contexts, both social and intellectual, within which Weber worked, and which gave his concepts their original meaning. This has been my focus in the preceding chapters, for the specific texts of Weber's I have chosen to examine. I now want, in a tentative way, to work back from the meaning of Weber's concepts of group and society to specific opinions these imply on the Jewish question, and so to a more direct characterization of Weber's social values than has been possible so far.

II

At the end of often tortuous elaborations of concepts Weber arrived at conclusions that appear to justify one "solution" to the Jewish question that was favored among many German liberals and conservatives among a variety of "solutions" that were discussed at the time (including those who felt the question was not legitimate in the first place). Many of those who were among the most modern and progressive within the Gentile majority, not just conservative reactionaries or stubborn traditionalists, expressed an intolerant impatience with the Jews, whom they expected should return the gift of emancipation by assimilating to the general social and cultural type within the nation. Thus emancipation was usually seen by even the most progressive Gentiles as a means to the end of normalizing minority-majority relations under the new conditions of open and "civil" societies. Emancipation, the granting of equal civil rights, was given to the Jews as a conditional gift, it was a strategy of social engineering, designed to "solve" the Jewish question. What was expected in return was that Jews would cease to organize their attentions around an ancient subculture and social group and turn toward the center along with all other citizens. Equality was equalitarianism, freedom was the freedom to leave behind local group allegiances and join the national group. Freedom and equality were homogenizing principles; they were not necessarily the friends of tolerance.

The place Weber accords to the Jews and Judaism in his system also seems designed to show that, since their condition as pariahs is caused by certain ethical commitments rooted in their religion, the Jewish question is to be resolved by the elimination of the religiously conditioned identity of the Jews. Both Weber's and Sombart's sociology of the Jews, which we have seen are closely tied and very similar, support the view that a Jewish presence in society is antithetical to the full development of a unified German cultural life. Both anti-Semites and philosemites shared this view. The difference was that anti-Semites wanted to *exclude* Jews from German society, and they actively lobbied for legislation that would have this effect in various institutions, particularly those that were administered by the state, which included posts in higher education, politics, the military, as well as the government and civil service generally. Philosemites, in contrast, wanted to *accept* Jews *conditionally* into German society, because they thought "assimilation" would end the conflict between Jewish and German forces, a conflict generally recognized as a "social problem." But assimilation for non-Jewish liberals in Wilhelmian Germany meant the end of Jewish character traits.

Many of the traits that liberals saw in the Jews are incorporated in the image of a pariah people, a concept that in Max Weber's work represents a *Geschichtsbild* which his sociology of the Jews and Judaism is designed to explain. This image in the end includes the feature of "traditionalism," which Weber emphasized originally in the first version of the Protestant ethic thesis; traditionalism was important mainly in connection with the arguments about the preconditions of modern capitalism. But these arguments have been reduced to excurses in Weber's final work. What remains is a historical-theoretical scaffolding implicitly supporting a particular "solution" to *die Judenfrage* in Germany, one that requires, out of sympathetic concern, that Jews abandon their religious beliefs, at least those with putatively direct or indirect social implications.

Weber understood this to entail the dissolution of the Jewish tradition itself, or the abandonment of efforts to assert the universal validity and vitality of the tradition.[2] In a number of arresting places in his letters, addresses, or his sociology, Weber brings the central principles of his pariah-people thesis to bear on the Jewish question. Because the underlying reference of his sociology of the Jews, as with his sociology generally, is the field of present-day social problems, these occasional references to "the Jewish question" have special significance. One example is a letter to E. J. Lesser in 1913, where Weber takes up the question of the viability of modern Zionism and the hope for Jewish normalization. I reprint the letter here in full:

---

2. To this compare the quite different conclusion of Liebeschütz, "Weber's Historical Interpretation," 58, that "His [Weber's] subject remains the understanding of Jewish society in the time when the modern organization of economic life was formed [i.e., sixteenth-eighteenth centuries]; . . . Weber has not left his readers in doubt that emancipation [in the nineteenth-twentieth centuries] had changed this situation."

Judaism and especially Zionism has as its inner premise a *highly concrete* "promise." Will a profitable colony, an autonomous small state, hospitals, and good schools ever act as a "fulfillment" of those grandiose promises, or will they to a much greater extent be a critique of them? And even a university? For its *meaning*—which would certainly be a heterogeneous one in relation to the economic purpose of the settlement—would be that the Jews' feeling of *dignity* could be restored by the existence and the intellectual possession of this ancient holy place in this form—just as once the Jewish Diaspora was sustained by the realm of the Maccabees after its war of independence against the world empire of the Seleucids; as the Germans all over the world were sustained by the German Empire; and Islam was sustained by the existence of the caliphate. But Germany is, or at least seems to be, a *powerful* empire and the realm of the caliph still occupies an extensive territory. But what can the Jewish state at best be today? And what about a university that would offer only the same things as the others?[3] It would certainly not be a matter of indifference, but it still could not be compared to the old *temple*.

What, then, is the chief lack? *It is the temple and the high priest.* If *these* existed in Jerusalem, everything else would be of secondary importance. It is true that a devout Catholic also demands a pontifical *state,* though it be of the smallest dimension. But even without one, and even more without one, his feeling of dignity is enhanced by the fact that the politically powerless Pope of Rome, as the purely spiritual ruler of a people of 200 million, is infinitely *more* than the "king" of Italy, and that everyone feels this. A hierarch of 12 million in the world (who mean what the Jews simply are not and do not mean!)— that, of course, *would* be something of really great significance for the Jews' feeling of dignity, and it does not matter whether they are believers or not. But where is Zadok's stock?[4] Where are there the Orthodox who would submit to such a hierarch, who would be *permitted*—by the law!—to allow him even one-tenth of the importance which the Pope has in every diocese and parish, far more by virtue of the *disciplina morum* [discipline of manners] and the universal

3. Probably referring to the Institute of Technology in Haifa (the Technion), for which a German-language preparatory high school was founded in 1911. Cf. Reinharz, *Fatherland or Promised Land?,* 218.

4. I.e., the Sadducees, who claimed descent from the family of Zaddok, the high priest.

bishopric than by virtue of his relatively very insignificant infallibility? Where is it possible to do anything like that *today?* It seems to me that the real problems of Zionism are bound up with the fact that *this* is where the values *would* lie that really concern the Jewish national feeling of dignity but are closely connected with religious conditions.[5]

This letter reveals the fundamentally fantastic nature of Weber's perception of the Jewish question. There is almost no statement in this letter that accords with the facts of Jewish life and aspiration as they were known at the time. The only conceptual possibility Weber considers that, we now know, had a good chance of actually being realized—the elevation of Jewish dignity by a Zionist "empire"—Weber himself dismissed out of hand. (Weber thinks the identity of ethnic Germans outside the Fatherland is sustained by the prestige of the German Empire.) The fantastic nature of Weber's diagnosis of Zionism is, however, less interesting than the self-confidence he feels in applying his sociological concepts, derived from his scholarly analysis of the pariah situation of the Jews, to the struggles of those Jews who were his contemporaries and fellow countrymen.

Weber's contrast between the Jewish and the Catholic community shows that he does not believe that Jewish solidarity exists. This is his principle reason for skepticism regarding the prospects of Zionism. But Jewish solidarity would, from his perspective, have to be based on religious authority. The existence of a system of authoritative pastoral care makes it possible for Catholics to sustain their solidarity without a national center, in terms of which they would be a diaspora. Because the Jews lack a comparable pastoral system and, therefore, a comparable basis for religious authority, not even a Zionist secular restoration could sustain their dignity. Only the temple and the high priest could give *Judaism* the religious authority it now so obviously lacks, and which would be one possible source for Jewish solidarity. The authority of Judaism over the Jews is conceived by Weber on the analogy of the political authority of an empire, which he thought fit the Catholic case as well.

The most important conviction of Weber's that comes through in this letter is that, invariably, "the Jewish national feeling of dignity," for it to exist, must be "closely connected with religious conditions." Weber makes no distinction between the social significance of traditional, "Talmudic" Judaism, and that of modern Zionism, which existed at the time in a bewildering variety none of whose versions, however, were religious in the

---

5. Marianne Weber, *Biography,* 469–70.

traditional sense. His efforts to point out the "shortcomings" of Zionism are all rhetorical examples showing how far what is possible for Zionism falls short of religious ideals. But there was simply no one at the time among Zionist activists who was holding out a restoration of the Temple as an ideal. And yet this did not lessen the "meaning" of Zionism for its proponents. It does, however, *for Weber*. Weber is plainly reading into current Jewish history the quasi-religious presuppositions—really *cultural* presuppositions—of his sociology of the Jews. This must be counted as one of the "outstanding examples of the failure of sociological predictions," as Schmueli has put it.[6]

Weber's analysis of Zionism is of a piece with his well-known allusion to the situation of modern Jewry in closing "Science as a Vocation." After stating his view that the only truly noble attitudes to life are, on the one hand, "intellectual integrity," which eschews "prophecy" and accepts "the disenchantment of the world" as the "fate of our times," or, on the other hand, "an intellectual sacrifice in favor of an unconditional religious devotion," Weber goes on to state what judgment must be made of the latter from the former point of view, that of *Wissenschaft*. "The many who today tarry for new prophets and saviors" are in the same situation as the Jews, whom the watchman's song in Isaiah advised to "inquire" about the meaning of exile. "The people to whom this was said has inquired and tarried for more than two millennia, and we are shaken when we realize its fate. From this we want to draw the lesson that nothing is gained by yearning and tarrying alone, and we shall act differently. We shall set to work and meet the 'demands of the day.'"[7] This statement presupposes the liberal nationalist view that the final fate of the Jews is radical assimilation and ultimately the dissolution of their religion as a force for particularism or, in Weber's version of this view, the end of the Jews' pariah status. This assumption about "the fate of the Jews" provides the standpoint from which Weber criticized E. J. Lesser's Zionism too.

Another implicit assumption of the liberal nationalist approach to the Jewish question, that the social consequences of the Jewish religious tradition include antipathy to Christians, and so Jews will continue to remain aloof from society as long as they retain some attachment to that tradition,

6. Schmueli, "The Pariah People," 211–13, considers Weber's thoughts on Zionism.

7. "Science as a Vocation," 155–56. Weber derived this image of the Jews' "tarrying endurance" from his (questionable) reading of the so-called "suffering servant" passages in Isaiah. Cf. below, appendix, note 5.

however reformed, is also made in Weber's analyses above and, indeed, is made far more explicit in his sociology of the Jews than most liberals were willing to make it. I have already examined this assumption in Weber's treatment of the historical pariah status of the Jews at length. But the few places in his sociology where he takes up the question of modern Jewry make this especially apparent. The "rationalism" of the Jews' attachment to ritual prescriptions, according to Weber, did not lessen for Zionists setting up colonies in Palestine. In a passage in *Economy and Society* I included in the analysis in the last chapter, Weber says a special rabbinic suspension of the requirement in the Holy Land of a sabbatical year was needed before such colonies could be established.[8] More revealing is his attempt to explain the success of Jewish assimilation in America, England, Holland, and perhaps other "Puritan nations" in contrast to Germany, in another place in *Economy and Society,* by reference to a supposed affinity between Judaism and Puritanism:

> The Jews who were actually welcomed by Puritan nations, especially the Americans, were not pious orthodox Jews but rather Reformed [*sic*] Jews who had abandoned orthodoxy, Jews such as those of the present time who have been trained in the Educational Alliance, and finally baptized Jews. These groups of Jews were at first welcomed without any ado whatsoever and are even now welcomed fairly readily, so that they have been absorbed to the point of the absolute loss of any trace of difference. This situation in Puritan countries contrasts with the situation in Germany, where the Jews remain—even after long generations—"assimilated Jews." These phenomena clearly manifest the actual kinship of Puritanism to Judaism.[9]

The penultimate sentence, where Weber uses the quotation marks around German "assimilated Jews," indicates that he (and many of his contemporaries) do not believe these Jews are really assimilated, as are American Jews.

---

8. See above, page 247.

9. Weber, *Economy and Society,* 623, in connection with his remarks on how the apostle Paul supposedly released the Jews who would follow him from the pariah situation, with a more universal social ethic. This was apparently an important point for Weber, for Marianne Weber provides a substantial report of Max's contact with the superintendent of the Educational Alliance in New York in 1904, and he made the same point in 1905 in *The Protestant Ethic;* cf. *Biography,* 302–4, where some rather insensitive comments on Jews from Max Weber's letters also occur, and above, page 259, for the passage in *The Protestant Ethic.*

One might reasonably wonder at this point how Weber could be so oblivious to Jewish realities. One reason is that perhaps all, certainly most of the Jews he knew were extreme assimilants themselves. That is, the Jews who entered Weber's circle had abandoned all attachments to the Jewish group. For example, Heinrich Braun was a baptized Jew; Georg Simmel was brought up in a family where both parents converted from Judaism; Georg Jellinek was an assimilant.[10] This was simply a result of the fact that those who asserted their attachment to the Jewish group in any form were systematically excluded from faculty positions in Germany. Jewish students, too, were predominantly social climbers, and they generally experienced the *civitas academiae* as alien to them (Georg Lukacs, Martin Buber, Leo Baeck, and Franz Rosenzweig are only among the most well known examples).[11] For example, they voted in only meager numbers compared to other groups of students in the momentous faculty elections in the 1880s, which pitted nationalist anti-Semites against individualist liberals.[12] The Frei Wissenschaft Vereinigung, with which the Sozialwissenschaftliche Studentenvereinigung that Weber helped advised was associated, was abused as "Jewish" by Christian students in the 1890s, but it was considered by the assertive members of the Verein Jüdischer Studenten to be "an association of characterless assimilants and deserters from Jewry."[13] However, these social experiences would not have given rise to the intellectual form Weber gave them without his adherence to the social outlook of the liberal nationalists.

III

Among progressive liberal academic activists, "social policy" was designed to achieve the social unification of the German nation, specifically to break down intermediate social groups and promote the re-formation of the population along the lines of economic class. Weber looked favorably upon the "class struggle" of modern society for this reason. Class struggle was a phenomenon that would not be superceded by any "higher" socialist stage of society. It was a dynamic stage of society itself of permanent value, superceding the feudal stage and resolving all premodern antagonisms of "status" oriented (*ständisch*) strata into modern "classes."

---

10. Cf. Schorsch, *Jewish Reactions to German Anti-Semitism*, 97, 165, 191–95.

11. According to Jarausch (*Students, Society, and Politics*, 100) Jewish students' degree of assimilation was tantamount to "complete amalgamation by conversion."

12. Kampe, "Jews and Antisemites," 64–65.

13. Ibid., 86; cf. above, pages 58–61.

It was shown in chapter 3 that Weber's preference for a class analysis of modern society determined in important respects his practical policy proposals for excluding Poles from eastern Germany and resettling the east with "German" peasants. This analysis, despite its differences over practical proposals, brought Weber very close to the Marxist analysis of society. His intellectual sympathy for the socialist outlook was, perhaps, what motivated him to solicit the participation of Eduard Bernstein, the leader of revisionist socialism, in the pages of the *Archiv für Sozialwissenschaft und Sozialpolitik,* and it undoubtedly played a role in the development of Weber's close intellectual interaction with Sombart.[14] Bernstein's revisionism combines ethical missionizing to the proletariat and statism (both principles he shared with the Lassalleans, who insisted on universal, secret, and equal suffrage as a means of power for the proletariat) with the German nationalists' rejection of classical liberalism's notion of the economically weak state, and with a rejection of Marx's theory of the inevitability of international socialism powered by an immiserated proletariat.[15] Bernstein himself built a bridge to the neo-Kantian intellectuals in the course of developing his revisionist alternative to orthodox Marxism. His study of the English civil war came out in 1895 as "Socialism and Democracy in the Great English Revolution," and was reviewed in the *Historische Zeitschrift* by Georg Jellinek, who gave it high marks.[16] This review probably piqued Weber's interest, leading to his inquiries with Bernstein and perhaps stimulating his own thesis on the religious roots of the modern spirit. The controversy over Bernstein's views within the Social Democratic Party led him to set down his ideas more systematically in *Die Voraussetzungen des Sozialismus und die Aufgaben der Sozialdemokratie* (1899; trans. *Evolutionary Socialism,* 1909), a book that became the bible of Revisionism and allowed him to return from England in 1901, where he had been in exile since the beginning of the antisocialist law. In that year Bernstein gave a paper in Berlin, "How Is Scientific Socialism Possible?" extending the neo-Kantian elements already in *Voraussetzungen.* He rejected Marxist determinism by making a sharp distinc-

---

14. See Mommsen, *German Politics,* 112–13 for comments on Weber's relation to Bernstein and the Social Democrats.

15. Gay, *The Dilemma of Democratic Socialism: Eduard Bernstein's Challenge to Marx,* 79–83. Although Bernstein (a Jew) was early infatuated with Eugen Dühring's socialism, he was shocked by Dühring's anti-Semitism, which Bernstein experienced when visiting him in the late 1870s, when the anti-Semitic movement was just heating up (cf. ibid., 83–92).

16. Ibid., 49–54.

tion between *Wissenschaft* and various -isms or ethics. Socialism, he said, is a system of ethics and so cannot lay claim to scientific truth; it must nevertheless take "unbiased" (*tendenzlos, tendenzfrei*) knowledge into account. He proposed a "critical socialism" rather than a scientific one and said that its philosophical source could be found in the "back to Kant" movement.[17]

In the 1890s, after the lapse of the antisocialist law, the Social Democrats began to work within the state under Bernstein's leadership, renouncing overtly revolutionary aspirations. Against Rosa Luxemburg's denouncing of the Revisionists as "parliamentary opportunists," Bernstein claimed that the Social Democrats had become a "democratic Socialist reform party."[18] This transformation, largely in response to the realization that the largest number of Social Democratic voters were not party members but were in the trade unions, which were antirevolutionary, was closely analyzed by Weber's student Robert Michels in the *Archiv* in 1906. Michels praised Bernstein's accomplishment: "The social composition of the party has remained overwhelmingly proletarian."[19] This made the party, as Weber had demanded in his critique of Naumann, a "class party," in contrast to its revolutionary-intellectual cast in the early 1890s. This development, in turn, made the reformist intellectuals of Weber's generation quite receptive to "Bernstein's rewriting of Marxism without dialectics, his demonstration that the middle class was not disappearing, [and] his attempts to combine the Marxist theory of value with the new marginal utility approach" of Menger, in contrast to Schmoller and the older *Kathedersozialisten,* in *Voraussetzungen.*[20]

It is unlikely that Weber was responding, with his sociology of the Jews, to Marx's own essays of 1844, "On the Jewish question." Most of the

---

17. Ibid., 66, 145–50. Later in 1924 Bernstein described his point of view in these terms: "My way of thinking would make me a member of the school of Positivist philosophy and sociology. And I would like to have my lecture ["How Is Scientific Socialism Possible?"] taken as proof of this attitude of mine" (ibid., 153–54n.71). In 1924 this would have identified Bernstein with those dealing with the dilemma of historicism and realism, in addition to Weber, for example Troeltsch, von Wiese, and Mannheim.

18. Ibid., 101.

19. Bernstein himself was obliged to respond to claims by R. Blank in the *Archiv* a year earlier, that the proportion of bourgeois supporters of the party was growing, by stressing the party's domination by "the point if view of the workers" and the principle that they are "the leading class" (ibid., 106–9).

20. Ibid., 127; cf. 119–30.

copies of the *Deutsche-Französische Jahrbucher,* which was published in Paris and in which Marx's essays were published, were confiscated by the Prussian authorities at the border, effectively blocking knowledge about Marx's essays in Prussia, and there was little comment on them at that time.[21] Marx's essays were next printed in pamphlet form, in extracts in 1881 by Eduard Bernstein, at the time of the *Antisemitismusstreit,* featuring many of their sharpest formulations against "the Jewish spirit."[22] It is even less likely that Weber would have understood the original philosophical context of Marx's essays, which were part of an internal debate within left-Hegelianism in the 1840s, and were specifically designed to try out Feuerbach's "transformative method" on Hegelian philosophy. Weber would have found the language of "species being" and the "essence" of man strange, language Marx abandoned shortly after he wrote the essays and which he criticized pointedly in *Kapital* and in other of his writings that were available to Weber from the 1890s on.[23] The full texts of Marx's 1844 essays were not available until Franz Mehring published them in 1902 in a *Nachlass* collection of Marx and Engels's writings. Mehring introduced Marx's essays with a hostile account of early nineteenth-century Jewry that concluded: "These few pages [i.e., Marx's essays] obviate the mountain of literature that has since appeared on the Jewish question."[24] By then, however, Weber's own commitment to the class-analytic standpoint and to national-cultural unity as the basis for the social constitution of modern society, developed in the 1890s, had been fully formed.

However, it is very likely that Weber was influenced by the contemporary Marx*ist* analysis of the Jewish question and anti-Semitism that was current around the turn of the century. Weber's sympathetic reception of Sombart's work in general is one indication that the socialist approach to the Jewish question was not far from his mind. However, Sombart's position had important differences with the accepted socialist position on the Jewish question, some central, some symptomatic of the central differences:

21. Carlebach, *Karl Marx and the Radical Critique of Judaism,* 187–88.

22. Wistrich, *Socialism and the Jews,* 47–48.

23. Cf. Carlebach, *Marx and the Radical Critique of Judaism,* part 2, 92–184, especially 174–82; Massing, *Rehearsal for Destruction,* 157–59.

24. Carlebach, *Marx and the Radical Critique of Judaism,* 268–69. Mehring's introduction also praised Treitschke's "objective" criticism of Jewish traits. This was probably more directly influential for Sombart's views. Cf. also Massing, *Rehearsal for Destruction,* 158.

1. Sombart made the Jews central in the rise of capitalism; socialists generally considered the role of the Jews in the economy to be a sideshow, masking the deeper structures of class exploitation.

2. Sombart emphasized the nomadic ideal as one of the sociological foundations for Jewish rationalism; Karl Kautsky, by contrast, rooted the stereotype of Jewish rationalism in the supposition that the Jews were a "mountain-people," a view Weber took over against Sombart.[25]

3. Sombart was pessimistic about the prospects for Jewish assimilation in Germany, and this brought him close to Zionism as a possible "solution" to the Jewish question; socialists rejected Zionism because they looked forward to the "dissolution" of the Jewish group and their incorporation into the class struggle against social exploitation. This made the socialists positively disposed toward the ideal of assimilation.

4. Sombart was not reluctant to express himself in a manner that appeared openly anti-Semitic to many; socialists were generally self-consciously committed to social equality, practically as well as theoretically, notwithstanding their tactical use of the traditional stereotypical imagery of Jewish economic roles. Socialists stood out from the general climate of "polite" anti-Semitism in Wilhelmian Germany by the great pride they took in having a conspicuous number of Jews among the ranks of their members and leaders. They saw in this confirmation of the appeal they sought to cultivate among the oppressed.[26]

On all these issues Weber rejected Sombart's views and took a position consistent with the revisionist socialists. He seems to have considered Sombart's attitude toward the Jewish question to be inconsistent with the class-analytic standpoint. However, Weber accepted much of Sombart's portrait of the Jews as a community which, so far as it was governed by religion, necessarily behaved in an invidious manner with respect to its social environment, free from normal moral restraints in its pursuit of commerce. Ironically, his numerous disagreements with Sombart on matters of detail seemed to confirm in Weber's mind the validity of the general object around

---

25. See Massing, *Rehearsal for Destruction*, 163–64.

26. See Bernstein's account of "Jews and German Social Democracy" (Yiddish, 1921), translated in ibid., 322–30, and Massing's own account, 201–204, especially the revealing story of the reception of Paul Singer, a Jewish merchant and later Social Democratic deputy, who gave a speech at a worker's meeting in the 1880s (pp. 203f).

which their dispute centered.[27] "Jewish rationalism," which Sombart came to focus on after a number of changes in his basic standpoint toward the historical analysis of capitalism, was a phenomenon that both he and Weber considered to be self-evidently *sui generis*.

Weber's own views can be better understood in light of the socialist analysis of the question of peasant emancipation, an issue on which Weber had a clear position. Peasant emancipation became a concern of the Social Democrats after 1890, and they conceived peasants to be among the "perishing intermediary groups" in modern society.[28] Their attention was directed to the peasants at this time because of the rise of racial, "rabble-rousing" anti-Semitism, which was directed to the rural districts and appeared to be in competition with socialism for the allegiance of rural workers. They thought that anti-Semitism could unite the backward strata of German society, such as the rural masses, into a progressive national force which would subsequently turn to the socialist movement, once it realized what its true interests were. Both orthodox Marxists, such as August Bebel and Karl Kautsky, who were committed to an international worker's struggle, and revisionist Marxists, such as Heinrich Braun and Eduard Bernstein, who favored state-socialism and a national forum for the class struggle, agreed on this analysis.[29] The two sides differed, however, on how the peasants, once "awakened" to their exploitation by the anti-Semites, were to turn to Social Democracy. This tied the agrarian question and the response to anti-Semitism together in a necessary way for German socialists. The revisionists came out for some sort of state protection for peasants' property, just as Max Weber did in his Freiburg address, but this violated orthodox Marxist principles, which prescribed promotion of a maximum class polarization in order to usher in the inevitable class war for the final emancipatory revolution. For the orthodox Marxists, this latter solution was the only cure for the ills of capitalist society. Under Kautsky's leadership, the reform program of the revisionists was defeated at the 1896 convention of the Social Democratic Party, even though by then Bebel and Karl Liebknecht, who were radicals, had become involved in formulating the proposed reforms of the revisionists. This meant that the party would adopt a tactical

---

27. This has general parallels: Weber's response to disputes over his work seems always to have led to a reaffirmation of the "standpoint" on which his views were based. This is probably connected to his construal of methodology.

28. The following is based on Massing, *Rehearsal for Destruction,* 178–83.

29. Braun expressed such a view on Social Democracy as early as 1893, in an article in his *Archiv,* quoted at length in ibid., 262–63n.21.

passivity toward the anti-Semitic movement, but this had little to do with the Jews themselves.

The socialist response to anti-Semitism among peasants indirectly brought increased attention to *die Judenfrage* itself. The accepted socialist analysis of the Jewish question looked upon Jewry as a parasitical element in the modern market economy, still following the selfish utilitarianism motivated by Jewish religion. Modern conditions changed their economic function, but the Jews' economic aptitude was an unchanging feature of their character since medieval times. These "Jewish characteristics" were, however, individual, not social. This held out the hope that Jews would assimilate into society by dropping all trace of their historical identity. These ideas were expressed by Karl Kautsky when he said, in response to the Kishinev massacre in 1903 against the anti-Semites, "The unscrupulousness of international Jewish and Christian capital, and its instruments, makes it an accomplice of the Kishinev infamy. Jewish solidarity, the solidarity of the Jews from all classes, has become an empty phrase."[30] Kautsky also accused Zionism of "accepting the anti-Semitic premise that Jews were a *Gastvolk* in the Diaspora," referring specifically to Herzl. This became a common criticism of Zionism, especially by eastern European Jewish socialists writing in German journals.[31] At the turn of the century there was a large population of uprooted and impoverished craftsmen, artisans, and pedlars in the east, as a result of the Tsarist government's policy of forced settlement of millions of Jews into the Pale of Settlement. In 1908, Kautsky wrote an article in *Die Neue Zeit* to undercut the Jewish labor movement (*Bund*) that was fast emerging among this population. He employed the term *caste* to characterize the Jews, trying to show thereby the necessity of eventual Jewish assimilation into the general international socialist movement:

> If one wants to characterize the role played in the Middle Ages and even today by the Jews of Eastern Europe, one can do this much better by describing them as a "caste" than as a nation. It is not among the nations with which we are concerned here, but among the castes of India that we find phenomena which correspond to the status

---

30. Ibid., 146. The same point was made earlier, by the socialist Jacob Stern in a negative review of Herzl's *Der Judenstaat,* in *Neue Zeit* in 1896. The review is translated in ibid., 321.

31. Wistrich, *Socialism and the Jews,* 157–58.

of the Jewish community as it has been constituted since the destruction of Jerusalem and the advent of Christianity.[32]

Kautsky argued that the preservation of this caste structure was only possible by virtue of Russian or Rumanian policy.

Kautsky was criticized by M. B. Ratner in 1911 in the revisionist journal, *Sozialistische Monatshefte,* for reviving the discredited notion of Marx's, that the peoples of the East, including the Slavs, were "historyless." "Until now, nobody came to the grotesque idea of comparing the Jewish people in their millions with an Indian caste."[33] But Kautsky's purposes were really philosemitic, in contrast to Marx himself, who portrayed Jewish characteristics as more ineradicable. Kautsky was the first among modern socialists to establish the Marxist analysis of the necessity for the historical economic role of the Jews to disappear in the face of the development of a modern economy, and his argument is based on quite different principles from Marx's.[34] But the persistence of Jewish separatism, in the labor *Bund* and in Zionism for example, was a problem for this view. Kautsky came to explain it as a "mental ghetto" that persisted in the absence of the real one. In his 1914 *Race and Judaism,* he gave clear expression to this view: "Judaism . . . is one of the last remnants of the feudal Middle Ages, a social ghetto which is still maintained in the consciousness after the real ghetto has disappeared. We have still not completely emerged from the Middle Ages as long as Judaism still exists among us. The sooner it disappears, the better it will be for society as well as for the Jews themselves."[35] Kautsky's view that the Jews are like a caste was designed to deny their peoplehood or national-minority status, from the standpoint of a radical class analysis of society.

The difference between Kautsky and Weber has to with the latter's nationalism which, in this case, perhaps made Weber less ruthless and more of a gradualist in his denial of legitimacy to Jewish identity. For the socialists used class analysis to frame their image of a future society where all classes would be dissolved; the polarization of society into two "pure" classes,

---

32. "Nationalität und Internationalität," quoted in ibid., 144.

33. Quoted in ibid., 145.

34. This was the rationale for the official Marxist claim in Imperial Germany that anti-Semitism is an ephemeral phenomenon in modern times, a position Marxists were forced into after 1882, when the overt anti-Semitism of the competing Stoecker movement, because it was associated with support of the antisocialist laws, became impossible for the labor movement (ibid., 48).

35. Quoted in ibid., 153.

proletarians and capitalists, was a prelude to this end. Progressive or liberal nationalists also used class analysis, but they looked forward to class polarization leading to the formation of one unified group, the nation, within which peaceful class struggle could continue to take place. This became part of the revisionist Marxist standpoint, dominating the Social Democratic Party's line after 1903. Compared to orthodox Marxists, who were internationalist, progressive nationalists in Germany, like Weber, and revisionist Marxists, such as Heinrich Braun, were social-integralist in their outlook. For them the value of class struggle lay in the wider unifying function it performed for the modern nation. But an additional presupposition of valuable class struggle for Weber was always common identification with a shared culture, that is, a "national" culture in the ethnic sense, to the exclusion of subcultures within the nation-state, although he rarely if ever put it so directly as this. Thus Weber upheld the "right to association" of the workers and the employers, respectively, but condemned Catholic associations and Jewish secular ethnic (i.e. nationalist or Zionist) associations.[36]

IV

Still another avenue that helps us uncover the values underlying Weber's sociology of the Jews lies in an examination of what pariah meant "in the usual European sense." Recall that Weber gave notice that his use of the term *pariah* was present-oriented (in *The Religion of India*) in order to clearly distinguish his use of the term from the usual reference to Indian low castes.[37]

The first use of the term in reference to the Jews occurs, although obliquely, in the 1823 play by Michael Beer, *Der Paria*, which ran on the stages of Berlin and many German cities for many months.[38] In Beer's play, the protagonist, Gadhi, is a member of the Indian Pariah caste who rescues a noble Raja's daughter from the duty to submit to the funeral pyre of her dead father. Breaking the rules of caste separation, he marries her and they live quietly and bear a son. "Ignored and hated by his fellow-humans, he fears them more than the bloody beasts of the forest with whom it is easier to strike up a friendship." He and his wife desire only to be able to think and act as individuals, a plea that is expressed in the play in the theistic-

---

36. Mommsen, *German Politics,* 117ff.
37. Weber, *Religion of India,* 13. Cf. above, pages 13ff.
38. See Lothar Kahn, "Michael Beer (1800–1833)," 149–60.

Enlightenment terms of the period. An upper-caste man, ignorant of the marriage, is smitten by the beauty of Gadhi's wife, whom he chances upon while walking in the forest, and the clash exposes their mixed marriage, with fatal consequences. The couple are now duty-bound to die, but the upper-caste man is moved to take in their son. They die happy, therefore, in the knowledge that their son can be the first pariah to live like a human. Two years after its first showing, Heinrich Heine "commented on the vast pity which *Der Paria* was still arousing everywhere."[39] In the same year Goethe had studied the problem of the pariah in his *Trilogy of Passion* and expressed praise for Beer's play the following year.[40]

Closer to Weber's own time, Bernard Lazare was lecturing in France and publishing pamphlets around the turn of this century in which he distinguished the nonemancipated, traditional Jew as the "unconscious pariah" from the modern Jew, whose virtue lay in being a "conscious pariah." This was part of a sustained analysis Lazare was making at the time of the historical causes of anti-Semitism that he argued has its historical roots in Christianity, and in modern times is being promoted by the clerical movement, and by the socialist movement, which he portrayed as sealing the pariahdom of the Jews by excluding them from its ranks. This analysis finally led Lazare to embrace Jewish nationalism, or noncolonialist Zionism.[41] At about the same time, Karl Kautsky made similar comments in the

39. Quotes from ibid., 155–57 (summary of the play) and 156n.22.
40. Raphael, "Max Weber and Ancient Judaism," 55n.42.
41. See "Jewish Nationalism" (1898) and "Nationalism and Jewish Emancipation" (1899), in Lazare, *Job's Dungheap,* especially 65–67 and 99–102; also Wilson, *Bernard-Lazare,* 235 and chapters 10–11 passim. Hannah Arendt's well-known valorization of the concept of the Jewish pariah, although explicitly citing Weber as one of her authorities, has its source in these passages from Lazare. The sharp difference in the way Arendt and Weber use the term, respectively, has been discussed at length by Cahnman, "Pariahs, Strangers, and Court-Jews," 163–65, and has also been noted by Momigliano, "A Note," 313. For Arendt the term is part of a two-sided typology of nineteenth-century European Jews. For her, the "pariah" is an assimilated Jew whose minority identity is sustained by a rebellious and critical identification with the majority culture, while the "parvenu" (according to Arendt) exhibits the fawning assimilation of the Jew who becomes no more than a social climber and completely renounces any basis for minority identification (see Arendt's 1944 paper, "The Jew as Pariah: A Hidden Tradition," excerpted in Arendt, *The Jew as Pariah, and Other Essays*). Weber's usage, if it can be compared with Arendt's at all, takes in both these types and, quite unlike Arendt, ties these traits to religious influences.

German-language newspaper of the Jewish Labor *Bund* in eastern Europe, the *Arbeiterstimme*.

> In India the lowest social stratum despised by all and cast away is called "the pariahs." The common idea is that pariahs can be only found in barbarous Asia, but they exist in civilized Europe too. . . . If the Russian nation is the most enslaved on earth, the Russian proletarians have a worse life than any other proletarians. There are no other proletarians kept in such systematic ignorance; there are no other proletarians deprived to such a degree of all the means of organization—of those means which help them to resist more or less the power and force of capitalism. There are no proletarians upon whom unemployment falls so heavily, because nowhere do peasants so quickly swell the numbers of proletarians. But if the Russian people suffers more than other peoples, if the Russian proletariat are more exploited than others, there exists a group of proletarians, who are still more oppressed, exploited and persecuted than others: these pariahs among pariahs are the Jewish proletarians in Russia.[42]

This was also the time when Theodor Herzl called Baron Hirsch and the Jewish financial elite in Germany pariahs, by which he meant the precarious position they were in vis-à-vis the state authorities: "You have to live on tenterhooks lest anyone deprive you of your rights or property."[43] The term, or at least it's image, was also used in more openly malicious ways by anti-Semites, but this was normally rejected by Jews. For example, Adolph Fischoff, a liberal leader, said of Karl Lueger's anti-Semitic movement: "They wish to reduce us to healots, to humiliate us as pariahs, but we are not the national material out of whom slaves can be made."[44] On the other hand, German-Jewish intellectual Zionists often used the term to refer to *Ostjuden,* in contrast to themselves. Their Zionism was specifically a "solution" to the *Ostjudenfrage,* as in this 1903 statement by the sociologist, Franz Oppenheimer, referring to colonization in Palestine: "Funds will flow in more quickly than human material, and before this generation has departed the last pariah of Europe will have been transformed into a free

---

42. Kautsky, "A Pariah among Proletarians," 1.
43. Quoted in Arendt, *The Jew as Pariah,* 126n.
44. Cit. Wistrich, "Liberalism, *Deutschtum* and Assimilation," 112. Fischoff's principled social pluralism is worth comparing to Weber's cultural nationalism.

citizen of his own homeland."[45] (Oppenheimer himself had no intention of emigrating from Germany.)

All these examples of the use of the term *pariah* differ in an important respect from Weber's usage. The term is used in these cases to call attention to the victimization of Jews by their non-Jewish social environment and often to evoke pity for the Jews on this account. In contrast to this, Weber uses the term to describe a condition determined by the Jews' own attitude to their environment. Weber also uses the term to evoke pity for the Jews, and so he intends to refrain from using the term in any way that could be construed as derogatory.[46] But his usage breaks from the way it was employed "in the usual European sense."[47] What makes Weber's use different, of course, is that it is part of an overall *thesis* on the *causes* of the pariah situation of the Jews. That is, when Weber says that the Jews are pariahs, he means something much more definite and historically elaborate than the usual use of the term, which he has said provides his point of departure.

Weber may have been responding to the criticisms of the Indian analogy leveled at Kautsky when he carefully distinguished between the cases of the Jews and the Indian low castes. For the place where Weber makes this distinction[48] is unusually labored, and gives the appearance of speaking to a previous debate over terminology. This would also fit his general approach to social-problem controversy, namely, the application of a conceptual clarification of the issues. Perhaps the dispute over Kautsky's language played an important role in the genesis of Weber's pariah-people thesis, providing him with a "standpoint" from which to elaborate his critique of Sombart that was consistent with both men's class-analytic presuppositions. This would have been both a "revision" of Kautsky and a radicalization of Sombart, much after the revisionist socialism of the time, which was marked by the concessions it made, from the standpoint of orthodox Marxism, to nationalism.

---

45. From a letter to Herzl pub. in *Die Welt* with the latter's approval, quoted in Bein, "Franz Oppenheimer as Man and Zionist," 81.

46. Cf. Weber, *Religion of India,* 233; "Science as a Vocation," 156 (quoted above). Cf. also Liebeschütz, "Weber's Historical Interpretation," 62–63.

47. There is also the possibility that the cases cited above were designed to promote a judgment with regard to "the Jewish question," viz., that the non-Jewish environment bears the sole responsibility for anti-Semitism, and that Weber was distancing himself from this position as much as an overtly anti-Semitic position.

48. Cf. above, pages 13–14.

V

In closing let me venture a final synthesis of Max Weber's view of the Jewish question in the Germany of his day, as reflected in his sociology of religion, the few explicit places he brings this to bear on the Jewish question (cited herein), and his general outlook on modern society.

Weber seems to have thought that the common belief among many liberal activist Jews that they had a mission within German culture, as well, perhaps, as the neo-orthodox fanaticism among a minority of Jews, was rooted in remnants of the idea of their chosenness which they sought to revive. The fundamental assumption here lies in the sharp separation Weber made between premodern and modern types of society. Certain features of the past were, on this view, being inexorably eroded by modernity. These features included Jewish identity. Modernity, on this view, holds out an alternative to Jewish identity that has, on account of its historical position, a higher value. This justifies the demand that Jewish identity be sacrificed for citizenship. Under the conditions given by the emergence of the modern nation-state, those who persisted in asserting their distinctive religioethnic identity would understandably be suspected of being ungrateful for the new lease on life that was being held out to them. Worse, their stubborn distinctiveness smacked of resentment toward those who, admittedly, had in past times so mistreated them. But all that had changed now, and persisting cultivation of a separate life-style could only be construed as the survival of a dimly perceived religious consciousness. Those who persisted were bringing malice upon themselves. In other words, the pariah status of the Jews is religiously conditioned, from within the Jewish community. Such beliefs also justified complacency about anti-Semitism, which Weber (like many other non-Jewish liberals and conservatives) thought was a *fait accompli*.[49] This view originated in the climate of Weber's student days, with the rise and continuing strength of anti-Semitism among university students, after it had waned among German adults. But this view carries with it a large degree of blaming the victims.

This perspective on the Jewish question is not liberal. This is not necessarily a presentist criticism of Weber, from the standpoint of a later

---

49. For example, a passage in "Science as a Vocation," 134: "If the young scholar asks for my advice with regard to habilitation [qualifying for an academic appointment], the responsibility of encouraging him can hardly be borne. If he is a Jew, of course, one says *lasciate ogni speranza*. But one must ask every other man."

generation; it can be made with reference to the context of his own time as well. Some liberal assimilationists in Weber's generation, on both Jewish and Gentile sides, were still willing to allow denominational significance for Judaism alongside other legitimate faiths into the indefinite future, even though they, too, wanted to dispose of deeper ethnic and national identification among Jews. For them, the Jewish question referred to discriminatory social and legal arrangements, rather than to anything inherent in the Jewish way of life. Marxists often shared this perspective on the Jewish question. Compared to such a view (which was not without practical, political significance at the time), Weber takes a harsher view of the Jewish question. Nevertheless, Weber's denial that the Jews are a nation, together with his view that their pariahdom has made them a perpetual guest-people, in contrast to all other guest-peoples, made Weber immune to anti-Semitic theories of international Jewish solidarity and world-conspiracy.[50] This is consistent with a gradualist view of the process of Jewish assimilation that is easily more tolerant than anti-Semitism was at the time. Yet Weber's readiness to employ and develop common stereotypes of Jews and Jewish thinking in order to address the Jewish question was not unique. He was only attempting to more consciously mold special conceptual categories in a way that would make them consistent with his own cultural commitments.

Many commentators on Weber's political views have observed that it was in large part from the standpoint of his cultural-nationalist commitment that Weber considered limitations to the degree and direction of liberal development to be necessary in Germany.[51] Many of his liberal proposals are means toward the end of national social and cultural unification rather than being of value in and for themselves. An ethic of professional duty, whatever its ideological foundations, and complete acceptance of the modern division of labor and industrial capitalism was, in Weber's conception, the norm for the modern order. Anything to the left or right of this he labelled derisively as utopian cosmopolitanism or reactionary romanticism, respectively. But more important for our purposes, this perspective led Weber to view all kinds of social strata that stood between the state and the individual as outmoded under capitalist conditions and so destined to wither away. Such groups included peasants, Junkers, Catholics, Jews, and (at least before the Russian Revolution) ethnic Slavs in Germany insofar as they

50. *Contra* Rubenstein, "Anticipations of the Holocaust," 170.
51. Cf. Mommsen, *German Politics,* passim; Struve, *Elites against Democracy,* 114–48, passim.

sought to cultivate a distinctive life-style alongside the national life and a particular sense of their own esteem.

The importance of an active "universal" social outlook on the part of the masses was impressed upon Weber at an early age by the older generation of liberal nationalist politicians, religionists, and secular intellectuals and this value became a touchstone of his social outlook throughout his adult life. The value of such an outlook, if held by the masses, lay in its power to socially unite the German nation. Accordingly, Weber's social agenda aimed at invigorating all classes with cultural nationalism, which he thought was such a universal outlook, so countering the growing power of bureaucratic and economic rationalism. He conceived this in terms of a "cultural struggle" to achieve one form of rationalism, a psychological and moral rationalism, against another, the amoral calculative rationalism of the state, the market, and increasingly all modern *Anstalten*. This analysis of modernity was blocked out by Weber first in *The Protestant Ethic,* where the "religious rationalism" of the Puritans is given the role of nation-building by encouraging the psychological characteristics required of a modern free citizenry. For Weber the problem today is that the aspirations of subnational groups of all sorts are governed by calculative rationalism, not the kind of *Gesinnung* upon which the modern nation-state should be based. Indeed, this circumstance lies at the root of all the social problems he thought Germany faced.

This should chasten those neo-Weberians who consider Weber's insistence that social reality is now a mix of class, status, and party conditions for life chances and the cultivation of life-styles to be a valuable expression of methodological pluralism. For Weber's vocabulary, at least in its original intent, conceals a utopian element that parallels Marx's vocabulary, though it is quite different: status and party groupings *ought* to wither away in the course of modern development, leaving only economic class and individual will or independence. These are the only conditions under which an ethically rational social organization is possible. If we probe just a bit further we will find there are, for Weber, cultural preconditions for this utopian development: each individual ought also to possess an ethic that will attach each to the common social organization, the nation. In other words, rational social organization requires an underlying *gemeinschaftlich* solidarity.

The important point to make here is that national identification is inconsistent, on Weber's view, with minority religious identification. This is expressed in Weber's sociology with his elaborate pariah-people thesis of the Jews, which leads invariably to the conclusion that Judaism must not remain intact if modern society is to develop fully. The thesis, however, is perfectly consistent with the acceptance of Jews as individuals, *rather than Jews*. That is, it is consistent with a conditional acceptance of Jews in society. Such a view, that Jews must drop their Judaism if they wish to become full participating members of society, grows directly out of Weber's class analysis of society, not his sociology of the Jews. Rather, his sociology of the Jews appears to be an artifact of his deeper commitment to a radical class outlook coupled to cultural nationalism. It is an important example of a general assumption Weber made throughout his work, that the Kantian "civil personality" requires freedom from secondary social groups to identify with the sociopolitical center.[52]

Weber's radical class outlook led to the same conclusions about German Poles and Catholics, namely, that to achieve full status as citizens, they must be able to act "freely" on the basis of their economic-class interests, and this meant breaking with their historical social identity within the nation-state. This identity, for Poles, Catholics, and Jews, was as much a product of their members' willful identification with a history of their own as it was a product of German majority consciousness. Weber, however, masked this two-sided process of minority identification by thinking of all such groups as *ständisch,* vestiges of the past in a modern society. The same social assumption that a Weberian sociology of "class versus status" makes, that minority identification is antithetical to the ideal of a modern society, is expressed in Weber's sociology of "congregational" "salvation" religions, where the conditions for the rise of an active religious congregation are isolated and the directions toward which the commitments of an active mass population might develop are distinguished. These directions amount to a choice between prophetic or priestly leadership, respectively. This choice parallels the Protestant liberal intellectuals' struggle against church and de-nominational leadership by Protestant, Catholic, and Jewish religious leaders, whether orthodox or liberal, in Weber's day. "Priestly" leadership of a congregation will invariably lead to formalistic allegiance to a set of dogmas, and these dogmas are systematized in order to maintain the power

---

52. Compared to Marx, Weber even uses a similar historical model to construct his version of the modern trend: like Marx's valorization of the free associations of medieval craftsmen, Weber valorizes the free cities of the European Middle Ages, which he thinks introduced the idea of citizenship into western political and cultural history. These medieval "citizens" achieved a workable solidarity on the basis of a free association of those bound together by nothing more than a common *Gesinnung.* Cf. above, page 263.

of religious leaders over the masses. The favored alternative development is for charismatic, "prophetic" leaders to hold out a heroic "ethic" to the masses, and to encourage them, by the prestige of their message and person, to adopt this same "ethic" independently, as their own, on the model of Jesus' *Gesinnungsethik*. German national unification was idealized in such terms by Weber. He thought unification should be based on the consensus of a politically educated public, a consensus he thought could not be achieved without extraordinary leadership from the top. The substance of this consensus lies in the individual's independent acceptance of a common culture whose preservation would be the unquestioned goal of domestic and foreign policy.

It is important to appreciate the manner in which Weber's outlook excludes the minority member. The radical separation of "class" from "status" in his perspective functions to exclude groups that fall outside three classes Weber affirms: capitalists, workers, and the *Gelehrten*. Other classes of persons must be seen, from this point of view, as anachronistic "status" groups. This denies to the members of ethnic and religious groups an equal status alongside the three privileged groups. For, in Weber's perspective, one cannot achieve individuality, and thus full consideration as a citizen, outside these three classes.[53]

It is difficult to avoid seeing the competition among social groups in Germany for the fruits of full inclusion in society as the real, underlying foundation of Weber's outlook. This competition, rather than the absence of a common "ethic," marked the most important social problems of Weber's time. This is most clear for the struggles of the German Poles, and the majority's efforts to preserve their social and economic privileges are explicitly expressed in Weber's own portrait of the "cultural" effects of "economic extrusion" in eastern Germany, which he developed in the 1890s. The challenge to the "cultural" hegemony of the Protestant majority is equally clear in the struggles of German Catholics, who comprised one-

---

53. I find qualified support for my view that Weber's concept of class is theoretically inadequate in the conclusion of Holton and Turner's more sustained analysis ("Has Class Analysis a Future?" 196): "the persistence of the class idiom is explicable more in terms of the metaphorical characteristics of class rhetoric than any clear intellectual persuasiveness. And while a weak [neo-Weberian] *Gesellschaftlich* version of class theory is defensible, this is by itself a rather slender basis upon which to construct an account of social inequalities and their connection with group formation and social change." Holton and Turner nevertheless seek to portray Weber's sociology as a "liberal challenge" to "*Gemeinschaftlich* accounts of class."

third of the population, making them the largest minority in Weber's Germany. The threat posed by German Jews, who never exceeded one or two percent of the population, was mythical. During the period of Weber's career his own class, the *Gebildeten,* had become more closed than ever in its history. Weber took it upon himself to speak out against Catholic universities, and his support for individual Jews in the academy was, in his mind, called for by the transitional stage he hoped German Jewry were passing through, on their way to complete effacement of their historical identity. These Jews were "culturally" acceptable to liberals among the established elite. Deep historical irony (perhaps tragedy as well) attaches to the fact that the mandarin ideology of *Bildung* justified these Jews' upward mobility, in their minds, while it justified majority liberal mandarins in making an extra effort to overlook these same persons' Jewishness.

It should be apparent that Weber's outlook is not consistent with social pluralism, the acceptance of the autonomous development of group life within national societies. But more than this, Weber applied the standard of a universal outlook (in his special sense) not only to the evaluation of current social and political events. This standard is also fundamental to a world-developmental outlook that is directly (but oftentimes less than explicitly) reflected in the outline of universal history he constructed. This outline, densely filled in with allusions and contrasts across the centuries and the continents, has been a leading inspiration in modern social thought. The intellectual authority of this outline has, at least in important part, rested on the assumption that liberal and progressive values inform Weber's "universal historical" perspective. But this assumption is false. The social outlook that informs Weber's work is profoundly myopic; it led Weber to dismiss social pluralism and democratic rationales that justify a sympathetic and positive approach to pluralism, both in his scholarly and in his extrascholarly discourse. Where this outlook was shared by other important or influential thinkers, activists, and politicians, it led to the same results. Furthermore, this outlook had an effect on Weber's methodology. His method of analysis is not empiricist, but rather deeply subjective. Together these inadequacies in the theoretical and formal structure of his thought make it invidious. This may not, by itself, condemn Weber's thought. But it makes it difficult to read Weber as naively as has been done in the past.

This study shows that Weber's theory of religious development, in its general, evolutionary aspects, and his analysis of the social role of religious change in modern times, have very little, if any, factual basis and are rooted in contemporary stereotypes.[54] Weber's work embodies a profoundly ambivalent understanding of religion, an ambivalence shared by many Protestant liberal intellectuals in his day, and this approach to religion is a central node in his thinking about modernity as a whole. The invigoration of a "national" citizenry with a *Gesinnungsethik* is conceived by Weber as a "progressive" *intervention* in modernity. His sociology of religion claims to find this same kind of intervention, in a few exemplary cases, under widely differing historical and social conditions. Therefore the intervention is not itself modern. This suggests that it is from this quasi-religious point of view (itself rooted in a "hunger for wholeness," in Peter Gay's phrase)[55] that the Weberian class-analytic perspective becomes invidious. It remains to determine just what other aspects of his sociology "that we, the inheritors and interpreters of his thought, are likely to find most problematical or suspect."[56]

All this suggests to me that there are analogies between the Heidegger problem and the Weber problem. Richard Wolin's conclusions about Heidegger, for example, also apply to Weber's thought: "His sensibility is clearly not at home in the modern world. His critique of modernity, whatever its relevance, consequently takes on an *exaggerated* character; and it is precisely its 'exaggerations' that must be called into question."[57] What other aspects of modernity besides its pluralism has Weber either slighted or exaggerated? I hope this book has provided an introduction to one way of reading Weber critically, and so beginning to frame such questions less tentatively than I have here.

---

54. I have thought for some time that Robert Merton did a better job of finding the links between Puritanism and the restrained interpersonal styles that dominate "civil society" among Westerners than Weber did. The key to Merton's original analysis was the recognition that a struggle over *public opinion* had to be won by "Puritan values," not a struggle over individual souls. See R. K. Merton, *Science, Technology and Society in Seventeenth Century England* (New York: Howard Fertig, 1970; orig. pub. 1938) and my "Misunderstanding the Merton Thesis: A Boundary Dispute Between History and Sociology," *Isis* 74 (September 1983): 368–87; excerpted in I. Bernard Cohen, ed., *Puritanism and the Rise of Modern Science* (New Brunswick, N.J.: Rutgers University Press, 1990), 233–45.

55. Gay, "The Hunger for Wholeness: Trials of Modernity." At a number of points (for example, p. 80, where Sombart and Tönnies are mentioned), Gay suggests that the intellectual foundations of the popular, more massive "hunger for wholeness" in the Weimar period were laid down by Weber's generation. Gay also treats the Heidegger problem at length (pp. 82–84).

56. Wolin, "Recent Revelations concerning Martin Heidegger and National Socialism."

57. Ibid., 95.

Appendix

The Pariah-People Thesis
of Jacob Katz

There is one important defense of the Weber thesis by a well-known Jewish historian that ought to be considered in light of my review of the literature criticizing Weber's sociology of the Jews, in chapter 1, above. Jacob Katz has, in a number of publications, come out with qualified support for the pariah concept, criticizing Schmueli's attack on Weber, for example, from this point of view:

> The sociological definition of the Jewish community as pariah-people by Max Weber has the same starting point as the more impressionistic namegiving by the anti-Jewish critics. Weber's definition has been much discussed and censured, recently by Ephraim Schmueli. . . . Whatever one thinks of the evaluation of Jewish existence that is involved in Weber's definition, the factual basis of the castelike structure of the Jewish community remains valid.[1]

Katz has consistently employed the term as a descriptive sociological concept in his own research on the social history of the Jews. However, even this conditional defense of the concept ought to be clearly distinguished from the Weber *thesis,* something that is obscured by Katz's use of the term, and especially by his use of Weber as an authority for employing the term *pariah people.*[2] There are at least two important differences between

---

1. Katz, *Out of the Ghetto,* 257n.34.
2. See, for example, Katz, *Prejudice to Destruction,* 320: "The term 'pariah,' suggested by Max Weber for a description of the Jewish status in medieval society, though it does not exactly accord with its original {n.b.} Indian connotation, well characterizes the situation of the Jews. It hints at ritualistically secured socio-economic separation, combined with social degradation. The pariah status implies, or at least explains, *the Jew's image in Gentile eyes,* which assumed in the source of time an increasingly sinister and even diabolical character" (emphasis added).

Weber's and Katz's use of the concept of pariah-people. First, Weber applied the term to Jewish existence as far back as the eighth century B.C. and, unlike Katz, claimed that it was an accurate description of the outlook of modern Jewry as well. Second, Weber stressed the self-willed character of Jewish pariahdom,[3] and explicitly argued that the presence or absence of hostility toward the Jewish community was irrelevant to either the origins of or the persistent effects he claimed resulted from the Jews' own perception of themselves as pariahs.

Most important, however, these differences with regard to Katz's usage make sense only in the context of Weber's thesis, which Katz seems to have distanced himself from, as in the quote above where Katz makes reference to what he considers the invidious starting point for the Weber thesis. To be sure, there are sources for the resentment theodicy that Weber makes central to his thesis. Katz himself cites Rashi, who elaborated on the biblical promise of heavenly judgment in the end of days, applying it to the Christian peoples who, since they "helped forward the affliction" of Israel in Exile, beyond the divinely ordained measure (Zech. 1:15), would be visited with God's retribution in person. However, this interpretation, Katz notes, was one part of a "blurred and inconsistent" vision of the end of days, and Rashi's construction was taken from the context of interfaith disputation, where acrimony would be expected to be high. Moreover, the supposition that such ideas were an expression of Jewish resentment of Christians was drawn out most pointedly by Christian disputants, not Jewish ones.[4]

On the basis of such evidence, there remains the question of how far such ideas affected the day-to-day understanding of their social position on the part of most Jews, or whether in the absence of a context of religious competition such ideas would have arisen at all. On the Jewish side, such ideas were entertained always in light of the need to explain the problem of Exile, but not the problem of generalized suffering as such. This latter problem was never recognized as a specifically religious problem in Judaism,

---

See also Katz, *Exclusiveness and Tolerance: Jewish-Gentile Relations in Medieval and Modern Times,* 55–56; Katz, "The Jewish Diaspora: Minority Position and Majority Aspiration," 68–69.

3. So did Arendt, but she did not attempt to tie this to Judaism, as Max Weber did. For Arendt, the attitude of the pariah could, in principle, be adopted by a member of any minority group, and does not depend on any religious or ideological beliefs. Cf. chapter 9, note 41.

4. Katz, *Exclusiveness and Tolerance,* 17f., 51, 104–13.

and Weber's claims for the universality of the problem of suffering as such for the development of religions is probably rooted in German Pietistic ideas, which draws on the centrality of the individual's inability to fulfill divine commandments. According to German Pietism, which Weber seems to have used as an inspiration for concept-formation in the sociology of religion, in order to achieve salvation the individual needs to experience generalized suffering as a result of failing to achieve fidelity to the moral or religious law. For example, Weber claimed that, *within the Jewish tradition,* this was the significance of the "suffering servant" passages in Isaiah (40–55). According to Weber, these passages justify the value of blameless suffering, on account of social persecution, as a means of religious purification leading to salvation. "The meaning of it all is plainly the glorification of the situation of the pariah people and its tarrying endurance."[5] This confirmed for Weber his dating of the origins of Jewish pariahdom as well, from the time of the first exile.

But there is no evidence, outside Weber's own reading of Isaiah, that these passages were ever read in this way in Judaism, then or afterwards. Moreover, the instinctive religious reaction to the exceptional sufferings of the Exile was not resentment and the expression of a hope of ultimate revenge (as the Weber thesis has it). The first reaction at the popular level was to attribute exceptional sufferings to the sins of the Jewish community, occasionally to the sins of the Jewish people as a whole.

The single revision that Katz would make of Weber's thesis is to consider as central what Katz calls the Jews' historic "mental reservation" regarding the majority's ascription of low status to the Jews.[6] Jewish messianism in particular, he says, shows that Jews always "refus[ed] to be degraded to the eternal role of *pariah* minority."[7] Both Christians and Muslims considered the exile of Jews from their homeland to be an expression of divine disfavor, while the Jews themselves considered it to be a temporary interregnum prior to the restoration of the ancient commonwealth.[8]

Another crucial point, I think, in evaluating the empirical veracity of the Weber thesis, is that the retribution theodicy, whether or not it was

---

5. See the lengthy discussion of these passages in Weber, *Religion of India,* 369–90, quoted here at 375. Cf. also Liebeschütz, "Weber's Historical Interpretation," 56.

6. See Katz, *Exclusiveness and Tolerance,* 50, 62, 63.

7. See ibid., 80–81, for medieval sources; the quotation from Katz is taken from the reference in the next note.

8. Katz, "Jewish Diaspora," 70–72.

marginal for the Jewish understanding of their social cosmos, was confined to an identifiable historical context, Askenazic Jewry from the Carolingian era to the sixteenth century in Europe. From the sixteenth to the eighteenth century, as Katz has shown, two things occurred to alter the exclusiveness of Jewish attitudes toward Christians. These were the development of Judaism into a closed system of thought (which Weber attributes to Judaism for a much earlier date) and a relative slackening of religious competition toward Christianity from the Jewish side, which resulted in indifference toward Christianity, opening the door to religious rationales for positive tolerance which had not occurred before.[9]

These developments were internal to traditional, "Talmudic" Judaism. These developments, along with the relatively brief period in which something like a theodicy of resentment was entertained within Judaism, show that Weber's thesis that a "pariah *ethic*" is intrinsic to Judaism is false. By the nineteenth century Jews, many of whom had not broken mentally with traditional Judaism, even though they may have become apathetic to the demands of religious fidelity, responded not only openly to the Gentile world, but with positive sympathy:

> Whereas in the Middle Ages Jews were wont to put up with their legally fixed *pariah* status—with compensation being deferred until the Messianic era—once the idea of naturalization and emancipation caught on [in the nineteenth century], the discrimination involved in the inferior position—even though their position had immensely improved since Ghetto times—appeared intolerable.[10]

Here Katz is using the phrase "pariah status" in a completely different way than Max Weber used it. It refers for Katz to a status *imposed* on the Jews, with the connotation that there is a corresponding image of the Jew held by Gentiles that serves to justify this status. (This is consistent with Sartre's analysis.) This is not, however, what Weber meant by describing the Jews as a pariah people.

It should be clear that I do not differ with Katz on the historical facts, nor on their interpretation for the most part. Indeed, my own reasons for keeping open the question of the veracity of the pariah-people concept relies heavily on Katz's historical research.[11] My difference with Katz on the

---

9. Katz, *Exclusiveness and Tolerance*, 133–38, 156ff.

10. Katz, "Jewish Diaspora," 74–75.

11. I also depend on Katz in chapters 2 and 3 to characterize the context in which Weber developed the concept.

meaning and justification of the term *pariah* in reference to the Jews is conceptual. It also has to do with Katz's use of Weber as an authority for the use of the term.

In short, Katz cites Weber for his use of the pariah concept, but this is highly misleading, for he would not himself defend the Weber thesis, and in fact his use of the concept is altogether different than Weber's.

Bibliography

Ackerman, Walter. *Out of Our People's Past: Sources of the Study of Jewish History* (New York: The United Synagogue Commission on Jewish Education, 1977).

Aldenhoff, Rita. "Max Weber and the Evangelical-Social Congress," in *Max Weber and His Contemporaries,* ed. Wolfgang J. Mommsen and Jürgen Osterhammel, 193–202 (London: Unwin Hyman, 1987).

Anderson, Margaret Lavinia, and Kenneth Barkin. "The Myth of the Puttkamer Purge and the Reality of the *Kulturkampf:* Some Reflections on the Historiography of Imperial Germany," *Journal of Modern History* 54 (1982): 647–86.

Angress, Werner T. "Prussia's Army and the Jewish Reserve Officer Controversy before World War I," *Yearbook of the Leo Baeck Institute of Jews from Germany* 17 (1972): 19–42; with comments by T. R. Degarf and L. Cecil, 43–60.

Arendt, Hannah. *The Jew as Pariah, and Other Essays* (New York: Grove Press, 1978).

Ascheim, Steven. *Brothers and Strangers: The East European Jew in German and German Jewish Consciousness, 1800–1923* (Madison: University of Wisconsin Press, 1982).

Ascher, Abraham. "Professors as Propagandists: The Politics of the *Kathedersozialisten,*" *Journal of Central European Affairs* 23 (1963): 282–302.

Barkin, Kenneth D. *The Controversy over German Industrialization, 1890–1902* (Chicago: University of Chicago Press, 1970).

Baron, Salo W. *A Social and Economic History of the Jews,* 17 vols. (New York: Columbia University Press, 1952ff.).

Baron, Salo W. et al., eds., *Economic History of the Jews* (New York: Schocken Books, 1975).

Bein, Alex. "Franz Oppenheimer as Man and Zionist," *Herzl Yearbook* 7 (1971): 71–127.

Bergstraesser, Arnold. "Wilhelm Dilthey and Max Weber: An Empirical Approach to Historical Synthesis," *Ethics,* 1946, 92–110.

Biale, David. *Power and Powerlessness in Jewish History* (New York: Schocken Books, 1986).

Bibliography

Bochenski, J. M. *Contemporary European Philosophy* (Berkeley: University of California Press, 1957).

Bodley, John H., *Victims of Progress,* 3d ed. (Mountain View, Calif.: Mayfield Publishing Co., 1990).

Bramsted, Ernest K. *Aristocracy and the Middle Classes in Germany: Social Types in German Literature, 1830–1900,* rev. ed. (Chicago: University of Chicago Press, 1964).

Bruun, Hans H. *Science, Values and Politics in Max Weber's Methodology* (Copenhagen: Munksgaard, 1972).

Cahnman, Werner J. "Pariahs, Strangers and Court-Jews: A Conceptual Clarification," *Sociological Analysis* 34 (1974): 155–66.

Carlebach, Julius. *Karl Marx and the Radical Critique of Judaism* (London: Routledge and Kegan Paul, 1978).

Chickering, Roger. "Dietrich Shaefer and Max Weber," in *Max Weber and His Contemporaries,* ed. Wolfgang J. Mommsen and Jürgen Osterhammel, 334–44 (London: Unwin Hyman, 1987).

———. *We Men Who Feel Most German: A Cultural Study of the Pan-German League, 1886–1914* (Boston: Allen and Unwin, 1984).

Evans, Ellen Lovell. *The German Center Party, 1870–1933: A Study in Political Catholicism* (Carbondale: Southern Illinois University Press, 1981).

Factor, Regis A., and Stephen P. Turner. "The Limits of Reason and Some Limitations of Weber's Morality," *Human Studies* 2 (1979): 301–34.

———. "Weber's Influence in Weimar Germany," *Journal of the History of the Behavioral Sciences* 18 (1982): 147–56.

Fischoff, Ephraim. "Max Weber's Sociology of Religion, with Special Reference to Ancient Judaism" (Ph.D. thesis, New School for Social Research, 1942).

Fleischmann, Eugene. "Max Weber, die Juden, und das Ressentiment," in *Max Webers Studie über das Antike Judentum,* ed. Wolfgang Schlucter (Frankfurt: Suhrkamp, 1981).

Friedrich, Carl J. "Some Observations on Weber's Analysis of Bureaucracy," in *Reader in Bureaucracy,* ed. R. K. Merton et al. (Glencoe, Ill.: The Free Press, 1952).

Frye, Bruce B. "A Letter from Max Weber," *Journal of Modern History* 39, no. 2 (June 1967): 119–25.

Gay, Peter. *The Dilemma of Democratic Socialism: Eduard Bernstein's Challenge to Marx* (New York: Columbia University Press, 1953).

———. "The Hunger for Wholeness: Trials of Modernity," in *Weimar Culture: The Outsider as Insider,* 70–101 (New York: Harper Torchbooks, 1970).

Gerth, Hans. "Max Weber's Political Morality," in *Max Weber's Political Sociology: A Pessimistic Vision of a Rationalized World,* ed. Ronald Glassman, 29–38 (Westport, Conn.: Greenwood Press, 1984); reprint of a lecture given at Hokkaido University, Japan, 1964.

Bibliography

Gilam, Abraham. "A Reconsideration of the Politics of Assimilation," *Journal of Modern History* 50 (March 1978): 103–11.

Graf, Friedrich Wilhelm. "Friendship between Experts: Notes on Weber and Troeltsch," in *Max Weber and His Contemporaries*, ed. Wolfgang J. Mommsen and Jürgen Osterhammel, 215–33 (London: Unwin Hyman, 1987).

Guttman, Julius. "Max Webers Soziologie des antiken Judentums," in *Max Webers Studie über das antike Judentums: Interpretation und Kritik*, ed. Wolfgang Schlucter (Frankfurt: Suhrkamp, 1981); first appeared in 1925 in *Monatsschrift für die Geschichte und Wissenschaft des Judentums* 69.

Hagen, William W. *Germans, Poles, and Jews: The Nationality Conflict in the Prussian East, 1772–1914* (Chicago: University of Chicago Press, 1980).

Hahn, Herbert F. *The Old Testament in Modern Research*, expanded edition (1954; Philadelphia: Fortress Press, 1966).

Hauschildt, Elke. "Polish Migrant Culture in Imperial Germany," *New German Critique* 46 (Winter 1989): 155–71.

Helmreich, Ernst, ed. *A Free Church in a Free State? The Catholic Church in Italy, Germany, France, 1864–1914* (Boston: D. C. Heath, 1962).

Hertzberg, Arthur. *The French Enlightenment and the Jews: The Origins of Modern Antisemitism* (New York: Schocken Books, 1968).

Holborn, Hajo. "German Idealism in the Light of Social History," in *Germany and Europe* (Garden City, N.Y.: Doubleday, 1970).

Holstein, J. A. "Max Weber and Biblical Scholarship," *Hebrew Union College Annual* 46 (1975): 159–79.

Holton, Robert J., and Bryan S. Turner. "Has Class Analysis a Future? Max Weber and the Challenge of Liberalism to *Gemeinschaftlich* Accounts of Class," in *Max Weber on Economy and Society*, 160–96 (London: Routledge, 1989).

Honigscheim, Paul. *On Max Weber* (New York: Free Press, 1968).

Hughes, H. Stuart. *Consciousness and Society: The Reorientation of European Social Thought, 1890–1930* (New York: Vintage Books, 1961).

Jarausch, Konrad H. *Students, Society, and Politics in Imperial Germany: The Rise of Academic Illiberalism* (Princeton: Princeton University Press, 1982).

Jaspers, Karl. "Max Weber as Politician, Scientist, Philosopher," in *Leonardo, Descartes, Max Weber: Three Essays* (London: Routledge and Kegan Paul, 1965).

Käsler, Dirk. "In Search of Respectability: The Controversy over the Destination of Sociology during the Conventions of the German Sociological Society, 1910–1930," *Knowledge and Society: Studies in the Sociology of Culture, Past and Present* 4 (1983): 227–72.

Kahn, Lothar. "Michael Beer (1800–1833)," *Yearbook of the Leo Baeck Institute of Jews from Germany* 12 (1967): 149–60.

Kampe, Norbert. "Jews and Antisemites at Universities in Imperial Germany (II). The Friedrich-Wilhelms-Universitaet of Berlin: A Case Study on the Students' 'Jewish Question,'" *Yearbook of the Leo Baeck Institute of Jews from Germany* 32 (1987): 43–101.

Katz, Jacob. *Exclusiveness and Tolerance: Jewish-Gentile Relations in Medieval and Modern Times* (New York: Schocken Books, 1962).

———. *Out of the Ghetto: The Social Background of Jewish Emancipation, 1770–1870* (Cambridge: Harvard University Press, 1973).

———. *From Prejudice to Destruction: Anti-Semitism, 1700–1933* (Cambridge: Harvard University Press, 1980).

———. "The Jewish Diaspora: Minority Position and Majority Aspiration," *The Jerusalem Quarterly* 25 (Fall 1982): 68–78.

Kautsky, Karl. "A Pariah among Proletarians," *Justice* (Journal of the English Social Democratic Federation), Feb. 22, 1902, 1; reprinted from *Arbeiterstimme,* Dec. 1901.

———. *Are the Jews a Race?* (New York: International Publishers, 1926).

Kilker, Ernest. "Weber on Socialism, Bureaucracy, and Freedom," *State, Culture, and Society* 1, no. 1 (Fall 1984): 76–95.

———. "Max Weber and Plebiscitarian Democracy: A Critique of the Mommsen Thesis," *International Journal of Politics, Culture and Society* 2, no. 4 (Summer 1989): 429–65.

Lamberti, Marjorie. *Jewish Activism in Imperial Germany: The Struggle for Civil Equality* (New Haven: Yale University Press, 1978).

———. "Liberals, Socialists and the Defence against Antisemitism in the Wilhelminian Period," *Yearbook of the Leo Baeck Institute of Jews from Germany* 25 (1980): 147–62.

Lazare, Bernard. *Job's Dungheap* (New York: Schocken Books, 1948).

Leo Baeck Institute of Jews from Germany. *Perspectives of German-Jewish History in the Nineteenth and Twentieth Centuries* (Jerusalem: Academic Press, 1971).

Liberles, Robert. *Religious Conflict in Social Context: The Resurgence of Orthodox Judaism in Frankfurt am Main, 1838–1877* (Westport, Conn.: Greenwood Press, 1985).

Liebeschütz, Hans. "Treitschke and Mommsen on Jewry and Judaism," *Yearbook of the Leo Baeck Institute of Jews from Germany* 7 (1962): 153–82.

———. "Max Weber's Historical Interpretation of Judaism," *Yearbook of the Leo Baeck Institute of Jews from Germany* 19 (1964): 41–68.

———. *Das Judentum im deutschen Geschichtsbild von Hegel bis Max Weber* (Tübingen: Mohr, 1967).

Löwith, Karl. *Max Weber and Karl Marx* (1932; London: Allen and Unwin, 1982).

Massing, Paul. *Rehearsal for Destruction: A Study of Political Anti-Semitism in Imperial Germany* (New York: Harper and Row, 1949).

Masur, Gerhard. *Prophets of Yesterday: Studies in European Culture, 1890–1914* (London: Weidenfeld and Nicolson, 1963).

Mendes-Flohr, Paul R. "Werner Sombart's *The Jews and Modern Capitalism*—An Analysis of Its Ideological Premises," *Yearbook of the Leo Baeck Institute of Jews From Germany* 21 (1976): 87–108.

Mendes-Flohr, Paul R., and Jehuda Reinharz, eds. *The Jew in the Modern World: A Documentary History* (New York: Oxford University Press, 1980).

Meyer, Michael A. "Great Debate on Antisemitism—Jewish Reaction to New Hostility in Germany, 1879–1881," *Yearbook of the Leo Baeck Institute of Jews from Germany* 11 (1966): 137–70.

———. *The Origins of the Modern Jew: Jewish Identity and European Culture in Germany, 1749–1824* (Detroit: Wayne State University Press, 1967).

Mitzmann, Arthur. *The Iron Cage: An Historical Interpretation of Max Weber* (New York: Alfred A. Knopf, 1970).

———. *Sociology and Estrangement: Three Sociologists in Germany [Tönnies, Sombart, and Michels]* (New York: Alfred A. Knopf, 1973).

Momigliano, Arnaldo. "A Note on Max Weber's Definition of Judaism as a Pariah-Religion," *History and Theory* 19 (1980): 313–18.

Mommsen, Wolfgang J. *The Age of Bureaucracy: Perspectives on the Political Sociology of Max Weber* (New York: Harper and Row, 1974).

———. "Max Weber as a Critic of Marxism," *Canadian Journal of Sociology* 2 (1977): 373–98.

———. *Max Weber and German Politics (1890–1920)* (Chicago: University of Chicago Press, 1985).

———. "Personal Conduct and Societal Change: Towards a Reconstruction of Max Weber's Concept of History," in *Max Weber, Rationality and Modernity*, ed. Scott Lash and Sam Whimster (London: Allen and Unwin, 1987).

Mommsen, Wolfgang, and Jürgen Osterhammel, eds. *Max Weber and His Contemporaries* (London: Unwin Hyman, 1987).

Mosse, George L. *German Jews beyond Judaism* (Bloomington: Indiana University Press, 1985).

Mosse, Werner E. "The Conflict of Liberalism and Nationalism and Its Effect on German Jewry," *Yearbook of the Leo Baeck Institute of Jews from Germany* 15 (1970): 125–39.

Mosse, Werner E., Arnold Paucker, and Reinhard Ruerup, eds. *Revolution and Evolution: 1848 in German-Jewish History* (Tübingen: Mohr, 1981).

Oberschall, Anthony. *Empirical Social Research in Germany, 1848–1914* (The Hague: Mouton, 1965).

O'Boyle, Lenore. "Liberal Political Leadership in Germany, 1867–1884," *Journal of Modern History* 28 (1956): 338–52.

Oelsner, Toni. "The Place of the Jews in Economic History as Viewed by German Scholars," *Yearbook of the Leo Baeck Institute of Jews from Germany* 7 (1962): 183–214.

Poggi, Gianfranco. *Calvinism and the Capitalist Spirit: Max Weber's Protestant Ethic* (Amherst: University of Massachusetts Press, 1983).

Portis, Edward Bryan. *Max Weber and Political Commitment: Science, Politics, and Personality* (Philadelphia: Temple University Press, 1986).

Pulzer, Peter. "Why Was There a Jewish Question in Imperial Germany?" *Yearbook of the Leo Baeck Institute of Jews from Germany* 25 (1980): 133–46.
———. *The Rise of Political Anti-Semitism in Germany and Austria,* rev. ed. (Cambridge: Cambridge University Press, 1988).
Rabil, Albert, Jr. "Pluralism (1690–1960) and the Meaning of the 1960s," Eighth Annual Memorial Lecture of the Society for Values in Higher Education, delivered at the Sixty-sixth Fellows' Meeting, Colorado College, August 14, 1989; published separately by *Soundings: An Interdisciplinary Journal,* 1990.
Raphael, Freddy. "Max Weber and Ancient Judaism," *Yearbook of the Leo Baeck Institute of Jews from Germany* 18 (1973): 41–62.
Reinharz, Jehuda. *Fatherland or Promised Land: The Dilemma of the German Jew, 1893–1914* (Ann Arbor: University of Michigan Press, 1975).
Ringer, Fritz K. *The Decline of the German Mandarins: The German Academic Community, 1890–1933* (Cambridge: Harvard University Press, 1969).
———. "The German Academic Community," in *The Organization of Knowledge in Modern America, 1860–1920,* ed. Alexandra Oleson and John Voss (Baltimore: Johns Hopkins University Press, 1979).
———. *Education and Society in Modern Europe* (Bloomington: Indiana University Press, 1979).
———. "Differences and Cross-National Similarities among Mandarins," *Comparative Studies in Society and History* 28, no. 1 (Jan. 1986): 145–64, with a reply by Sven-Eric Liedman, 165–68.
———. "The German Mandarins Reconsidered," mimeo, n.d.
Rosenthal, Harry Kenneth. *German and Pole: National Conflict and Modern Myth* (Gainesville: University Presses of Florida, 1976).
Roth, Guenther. Review essay, *Contemporary Sociology* 13, no. 4 (July 1984): 403–6.
———. "Marx and Weber on the U.S.—Today," in *A Marx-Weber Dialogue,* ed. Robert J. Antonio and Ronald L. Glassman, 215–33 (Lawrence: University Press of Kansas, 1985).
———. "Marianne Weber and Her Circle," *Society* (Jan.-Feb. 1990): 63–69.
Rubenstein, Richard L. "Anticipations of the Holocaust in the Political Sociology of Max Weber," in *Western Society after the Holocaust,* ed. Lyman H. Letgers (Boulder, Colo.: Westview Press, 1983), with responses by Gordon Zahn and Guenther Roth, 184–90, and a rejoinder by Rubenstein, 190–96.
Ruerup, Reinhard. "Jewish Emancipation and Bourgeois Society," *Yearbook of the Leo Baeck Institute of Jews from Germany* 14 (1969): 67–91.
Runciman, W. G., ed. *Weber: Selections in Translation* (Cambridge: Cambridge University Press, 1978).
Sartre, Jean-Paul. *Anti-Semite and Jew (Reflexions sur la Question Juive)* (Paris: Paul Morihen, 1946; New York: Schocken Books, 1948); an essay written in October 1944.

Scaff, Lawrence A. *Fleeing the Iron Cage: Culture, Politics, and Modernity in the Thought of Max Weber* (Berkeley: University of California Press, 1989).

Scheler, Max. *Ressentiment* (New York: Schocken Books, 1972).

Schiper, Itzhak. "Max Weber on the Sociological Basis of the Jewish Religion," *Jewish Journal of Sociology* 1 (1959 [1924]): 250–60.

Schlucter, Wolfgang. *The Rise of Western Rationalism: Max Weber's Developmental History* (Berkeley: University of California Press, 1981).

———, ed. *Max Webers Studie über das antike Judentum. Interpretation und Kritik* (Frankfurt: Suhrkamp, 1981).

Schlucter, Wolfgang, and Guenther Roth. *Max Weber's Vision of History: Ethics and Method* (Berkeley: University of California Press, 1984).

Schmueli, Ephraim. "The Pariah-People and Its 'Charismatic Leadership': A Reevaluation of Weber's 'Ancient Judaism,'" *Proceedings of the American Academy of Jewish Research* 36 (1968): 167–247.

Schnädelbach, Herbert. *Philosophy in Germany, 1931–1933* (Cambridge: Cambridge University Press, 1984).

Schön, Manfred. "Gustav Schmoller and Max Weber," in *Max Weber and His Contemporaries,* ed. Wolfgang J. Mommsen and Jürgen Osterhammel, 59–70 (London: Unwin Hyman, 1987).

Schorsch, Ismar. *Jewish Reactions to German Anti-Semitism, 1870–1914* (New York: Columbia University Press, 1972).

Schwartzchild, Steven S. "The Democratic Socialism of Hermann Cohen," *Hebrew Union College Annual* 27 (1956): 417–38.

Schroeter, Gerd. "Weber and Weimar: A Response to Factor and Turner," *Journal of the History of the Behavioral Sciences* 18 (1982): 157–62.

Sharlin, Allan N. "Retrospective: Max Weber," *Journal of Modern History* 29 (1977): 110–15.

Sheehan, James J. *German Liberalism in the Nineteenth Century* (Chicago: University of Chicago Press, 1978).

Shils, Edward, ed. *Max Weber on Universities: The Power of the State and the Academic Calling in Imperial Germany* (Chicago: University of Chicago Press, 1976); reprint of *Minerva* 11, no. 4 (1973).

Sombart, Werner. *The Jews and Modern Capitalism,* intro. Samuel Z. Klausner (New Brunswick, N.J.: Transaction Books, 1982).

Sorkin, David. "Wilhelm von Humboldt: The Theory and Practice of Self-Formation *Bildung*), 1791–1810," *Journal of the History of Ideas* 44, no. 1 (Jan. 1983): 55–73.

———. *The Transformation of German Jewry, 1780–1840* (New York: Oxford University Press, 1987).

Stammer, Otto, ed. *Max Weber and Sociology Today* (New York: Harper and Row, 1971).

Stern, Fritz. "The Burden of Success: Reflections on German Jewry," in *Art, Politics, and Will: Essays in Honor of Lionel Trilling* (New York: Basic Books, 1977).

————. *Gold and Iron: Bismark, Bleichröder, and the Building of the German Empire* (New York: Random House, 1977).

Struve, Walter. *Elites against Democracy: Leadership Ideals in Bourgeois Political in Germany, 1890–1933* (Princeton: Princeton University Press, 1973).

Suchy, Barbara. "The Verein zur Abwehr des Antisemitismus, II," *Yearbook of the Leo Baeck Institute of Jews from Germany* 30 (1985).

Sutton, F. X. "The Social and Economic Philosophy of Werner Sombart: The Sociology of Capitalism," in *An Introduction to the History of Sociology*, ed. Harry Elmer Barnes (Chicago: University of Chicago Press, 1948).

Tal, Uriel. "Liberal Protestantism and the Status of the Jews in the 'Second Reich,' 1870–1914," *Jewish Social Studies* 26, no. 1 (Jan. 1964): 23–41.

————. *Christians and Jews in Germany: Religion, Politics and Ideology in the Second Reich, 1870–1914* (Ithaca: Cornell University Press, 1975).

————. "German-Jewish Social Thought in the Mid-Nineteenth Century," in *Revolution and Evolution: 1848 in German-Jewish History*, ed. Werner E. Mosse, Arnold Paucker, and Reinhard Ruerup, 299–328 (Tübingen: Mohr, 1981).

Tenbruck, Friedrich H. "Max Weber and Eduard Meyer," in *Max Weber and His Contemporaries*, ed. Wolfgang J. Mommsen and Jürgen Osterhammel, 234–67 (London: Unwin Hyman, 1987).

Theiner, Peter. "Friedrich Naumann and Max Weber: Aspects of a Political Partnership," in *Max Weber and His Contemporaries*, ed. Wolfgang J. Mommsen and Jürgen Osterhammel, 299–310 (London: Unwin Hyman, 1987).

Tims, Richard Wonser. *Germanizing Prussian Poland: The H-K-T Society and the Struggle for the Eastern Marches in the German Empire, 1894–1919* (New York: Oxford University Press, 1941).

Toury, Jacob. "The Jewish Question—A Semantic Approach," *Yearbook of the Leo Baeck Institute of Jews from Germany* 11 (1966): 85–106.

Troeltsch, Ernst. "The Idea of Natural Law and Humanity in World Politics," appendix 1 to Otto Gierke, *Natural Law and the Theory of Society, 1500 to 1800*, trans. Ernest Barker, 201–22 (Cambridge: Cambridge University Press, 1934).

————. *The Absoluteness of Christianity and the History of Religions* (Richmond, Va.: John Knox Press, 1971).

Tucker, Robert C., ed. *The Marx-Engels Reader*, 2d ed. (New York: W. W. Norton, 1978).

Turner, Stephen, and Regis Factor. *Max Weber and the Dispute over Reason and Value: A Study in Philosophy, Ethics, and Politics* (London: Routledge and Kegan Paul, 1984).

Urbach, E. E. *The Sages: Their Concepts and Beliefs* (Jerusalem: Magnes Press, 1975).

Ward, W. R. "Max Weber and the Lutherans," in *Max Weber and His Contemporaries*, ed. Wolfgang J. Mommsen and Jürgen Osterhammel, 203–14 (London: Unwin Hyman, 1987).

Bibliography

Warren, Mark. "Max Weber's Liberalism for a Nietzschean World," *American Political Science Review* 82, no. 1 (March 1988): 31–50.

Weber, Marianne. *Max Weber: A Biography* (New York: John Wiley and Sons, 1975).

Weber, Max. "Die protestantische Ethik und der 'Geist' des Kapitalismus," *Archiv für Sozialwissenschaft und Sozialpolitik*, n.s., 20 and 21 (1905): 1–54, 1–110.

———. *General Economic History* (New York: Greenberg, 1927).

———. *The Protestant Ethic and the Spirit of Capitalism* (New York: Scribner's, 1930).

———. "Religious Rejections of the World and Their Directions," in *From Max Weber: Essays in Sociology*, ed. Hans Gerth and C. W. Mills, 323–59 (New York: Oxford University Press, 1946).

———. "The Social Psychology of the World Religions," in *From Max Weber: Essays in Sociology*, ed. Hans Gerth and C. W. Mills, 267–301 (New York: Oxford University Press, 1946).

———. "The Protestant Sects and the Spirit of Capitalism," in *From Max Weber: Essays in Sociology*, ed. Hans Gerth and C. W. Mills, 302–22 (New York: Oxford University Press, 1946).

———. "Science as a Vocation," in *From Max Weber: Essays in Sociology*, ed. Hans Gerth and C. W. Mills, 129–56 (New York: Oxford University Press, 1946).

———. "Objectivity in Social Science and Social Policy," in *The Methodology of the Social Sciences*, ed. Edward Shils, 50–112 (New York: Free Press, 1949).

———. "Critical Studies in the Logic of the Cultural Sciences," in *The Methodology of the Social Sciences*, ed. Edward Shils, 113–88 (New York: Free Press, 1949).

———. *Ancient Judaism* (New York: Free Press, 1952).

———. *The Religion of India: The Sociology of Hinduism and Buddhism* (New York: Free Press, 1958).

———. *Economy and Society: An Outline of Interpretive Sociology* (New York: Bedminster Press, 1968).

———. *Gesammelte Aufsätze zur Wissenschaftslehre*, 3d ed. (Tübingen: Mohr, 1968).

———. *Gesammelte Aufsätze zur Religionssoziologie*, 6th ed., 3 vols. (Tübingen: Mohr-Siebeck, 1972).

———. "Max Weber on Race and Society," *Social Research* 38, no. 1 (Spring 1971): 30–41.

———. "Max Weber, Dr. Alfred Ploetz, and W. E. B. Du Bois," *Sociological Analysis* 34, no. 4 (Winter 1973): 308–12.

———. *Roscher and Knies: Logical Problems of Historical Economics*, trans. Guy Oakes (New York: Free Press, 1975).

———. "Developmental Tendencies in the Situation of East Elbian Rural Laborers," *Economy and Society* 8, no. 2 (May 1979): 177–205.

———. "The National State and Economic Policy (Freiburg Address [1894])," *Economy and Society* 9, no. 4 (Nov. 1980): 428–49.

Bibliography

Willey, Thomas E. *Back to Kant: The Revival of Kantianism in German Social and Historical Thought, 1860–1914* (Detroit: Wayne State University Press, 1978).

Wilson, Nelly. *Bernard-Lazare: Antisemitism and the Problem of Jewish Identity in Late Nineteenth Century France* (Cambridge: Cambridge University Press, 1978).

Winckelmann, Johannes, ed. *Die Protestantisch Ethik I* (Munich: Siebenstern, 1975).

———, ed. *Die Protestantisch Ethik II* (Munich: Siebenstern, 1975).

Wistrich, Robert S. *Socialism and the Jews: The Dilemmas of Assimilation in Germany and Austria-Hungary* (Rutherford: Fairleigh Dickinson University Press, 1982).

———. "Liberalism, *Deutschtum* and Assimilation," *Jerusalem Quarterly* 42 (Spring 1987): 100–118.

Wolin, Richard. "Recent Revelations concerning Martin Heidegger and National Socialism," *Theory, Culture, and Society: Explorations in Critical Social Science* 7, no. 1 (Feb. 1990): 73–96.

Index

Index

A Note on the Author

GARY A. ABRAHAM is an associate professor of sociology at St. Bonaventure University and the author of articles about Max Weber in *Theory and Society* and *International Journal of Politics, Culture, and Society*. Abraham won the Social Science History Association's first President's Book Award in 1988.